SOMETHING ABOUT THE AUTHOR®

Something about
the Author *was named
an "Outstanding
Reference Source,"
the highest honor given
by the American
Library Association
Reference and Adult
Services Division.*

ISSN 0276-816X

SOMETHING ABOUT THE AUTHOR®

**Facts and Pictures about Authors
and Illustrators of Books for Young People**

volume 129

GALE®

THOMSON
™
GALE

Detroit • New York • San Diego • San Francisco • Cleveland • New Haven, Conn. • Waterville, Maine • London • Munich

THOMSON

GALE

Something about the Author, Volume 129

Project Editor
Scot Peacock

Editorial
Karen V. Abbott, Katy Balcer, Frank Castronova, Sara Constantakis, Anna Marie Dahn, Alana Joli Foster, Madeline Harris, Arlene M. Johnson, Michelle Kazensky, Julie Keppen, Jennifer Kilian, Joshua Kondek, Lisa Kumar, Marie Lazzari, Thomas McMahon, Jenai Mynatt, Judith L. Pyko, Mary Ruby, Anita Sundaresan, Maikue Vang, Denay L. Wilding, Thomas Wiloch

Research
Michelle Campbell, Nicodemus Ford, Sarah Genik, Barbara McNeil, Tamara C. Nott, Gary J. Oudersluys, Tracie A. Richardson, Cheryl L. Warnock

Permissions
Debra Freitas, Lori Hines

Imaging and Multimedia
Dean Dauphinais, Robert Duncan, Leitha Etheridge-Sims, Mary K. Grimes, Lezlie Light, Michael Logusz, Dan Newell, David G. Oblender, Christine O'Bryan, Kelly A. Quin, Luke Rademacher

Composition and Electronic Capture
Gary Leach

Manufacturing
Stacy L. Melson

LIBRARY OF CONGRESS CATALOG CARD NUMBER 72-27107

ISBN 0-7876-4717-9
ISSN 0276-816X

Printed in the United States of America
10 9 8 7 6 5 4 3 2 1

Contents

Authors in Forthcoming Volumes

Below are some of the authors and illustrators that will be featured in upcoming volumes of *SATA*. These include new entries on the swiftly rising stars of the field, as well as completely revised and updated entries (indicated with *) on some of the most notable and best-loved creators of books for children.

Brent Ashabranner: Ashabranner writes informative books for children about the social issues facing a variety of cultures in the United States and other countries. The author has been praised for his knowledge of the customs and lifestyles of many groups of people. He received the Christopher Award for *Into a Strange Land: Unaccompanied Refugee Youth in America.* In 2002 Ashabranner published *The Washington Monument: A Beacon for America.*

Peter S. Beagle: Considered a master fantasist as well as a distinguished writer of nonfiction, Beagle is celebrated for his originality, inventiveness, skill with plot and characterization, and rich, evocative literary style. In addition to novels, he has written short stories, poetry, essays, and screenplays for film and television and has edited and contributed to anthologies. He is perhaps best known as the author of *The Last Unicorn,* a fantasy that describes the quest of the title character to discover the last of her species.

Susan Stevens Crummel: Crummel has written several picture books for children that critics have deemed humorous and clever manipulations of classic nursery rhyme characters and scenarios. Her 2001 work *And the Dish Ran Away with the Spoon* was a Notable Book selection by the American Library Association.

Etienne Delessert: Award-winning Swiss children's writer, illustrator, publisher, and filmmaker Delessert has been credited by many critics as one of the fathers of the modern picture book for children. He has written and illustrated such well-respected books as *How the Mouse Was Hit on the Head by a Stone and So Discovered the World* and created the popular character Yok-Yok, who has been featured in both picture books and animated films.

Paul Geraghty: South African-born author and illustrator Geraghty has penned a number of picture books, each illustrated with his colorful artwork. Beginning his work as a picture book creator with *Over the Steamy Swamp,* Geraghty has gone on to create a number of entrancing picture-book offerings, among them *Monty's Journey, Solo,* and *Tortuga,* for which he received the Prix de Cherbourg/Octeville in 2001.

Steven Kellogg: Author and illustrator Kellogg is perhaps best known for his children's picture books about Pinkerton the Great Dane, his series of "color" mysteries for younger readers, and his adaptations of American legends, such as those about Paul Bunyan, Pecos Bill, Johnny Appleseed and Mike Fink. In 2001 Kellogg published *A Penguin Pup for Pinkerton,* another in his popular series about the lovable pooch.

Marie G. Lee: In her young adult novels *Finding My Voice, If It Hadn't Been for Yoon Jun, Saying Goodbye,* and *Necessary Roughness,* Lee explores issues of ethnocentrism, racism, as well as more ordinary teenage concerns. Lee, an Asian American, writes out of her own deeply felt experiences growing up in America's heartland, the only Korean in her small hometown.

Asenath Odaga: Odaga, a Kenyan author, depicts everyday activities in children's lives, both at home and at school. She believes it is important for her readers to learn about their national identity, and much of her fiction draws on the oral tradition of her community. In some cases, as in *Thu Tinda: Stories from Kenya,* she modernizes folk stories. For her young adult audience, Odaga creates fiction that addresses social concerns and values conflicts in urban settings.

Posy Simmonds: A English author and illustrator for children and adults as well as a cartoonist and graphic novelist, Simmonds is celebrated for her originality, creativity, intelligence, artistic talent, and incisive social commentary. Her works for children include *Lulu and the Flying Babies* and its sequel, *The Chocolate Wedding.*

Nadine Bernard Westcott: Westcott is a popular author and illustrator whose artwork has graced the pages of books by such authors as Barbara Maitland, Florence Parry Heide, Teri Sloat, and singer/songwriter Raffi. Westcott has also published a number of self-illustrated picture books that bring to life traditional folk songs and tales, including *I Know an Old Lady Who Swallowed a Fly* and *I've Been Working on the Railroad.*

Lisbeth Zwerger: Born in Vienna, Austria, Zwerger is recognized internationally as one of the finest illustrators of children's literature. Providing the drawings for such classic narratives as O. Henry's *The Gift of the Magi* and Charles Dickens's *A Christmas Carol,* Zwerger is a recipient of the prestigious Hans Christian Andersen Award.

Introduction

Something about the Author (*SATA*) is an ongoing reference series that examines the lives and works of authors and illustrators of books for children. *SATA* includes not only well-known writers and artists but also less prominent individuals whose works are just coming to be recognized. This series is often the only readily available information source on emerging authors and illustrators. You'll find *SATA* informative and entertaining, whether you are a student, a librarian, an English teacher, a parent, or simply an adult who enjoys children's literature.

What's Inside SATA

SATA provides detailed information about authors and illustrators who span the full time range of children's literature, from early figures like John Newbery and L. Frank Baum to contemporary figures like Judy Blume and Richard Peck. Authors in the series represent primarily English-speaking countries, particularly the United States, Canada, and the United Kingdom. Also included, however, are authors from around the world whose works are available in English translation. The writings represented in *SATA* include those created intentionally for children and young adults as well as those written for a general audience and known to interest younger readers. These writings cover the entire spectrum of children's literature, including picture books, humor, folk and fairy tales, animal stories, mystery and adventure, science fiction and fantasy, historical fiction, poetry and nonsense verse, drama, biography, and nonfiction.

Obituaries are also included in *SATA* and are intended not only as death notices but also as concise overviews of people's lives and work. Additionally, each edition features newly revised and updated entries for a selection of *SATA* listees who remain of interest to today's readers and who have been active enough to require extensive revisions of their earlier biographies.

New Autobiography Feature

Beginning with Volume 103, *SATA* features two or more specially commissioned autobiographical essays in each volume. These unique essays, averaging about ten thousand words in length and illustrated with an abundance of personal photos, present an entertaining and informative first-person perspective on the lives and careers of prominent authors and illustrators profiled in *SATA*.

Two Convenient Indexes

In response to suggestions from librarians, *SATA* indexes no longer appear in every volume but are included in alternate (odd-numbered) volumes of the series, beginning with Volume 57.

SATA continues to include two indexes that cumulate with each alternate volume: the Illustrations Index, arranged by the name of the illustrator, gives the number of the volume and page where the illustrator's work appears in the current volume as well as all preceding volumes in the series; the Author Index gives the number of the volume in which a person's biographical sketch, autobiographical essay, or obituary appears in the current volume as well as all preceding volumes in the series.

These indexes also include references to authors and illustrators who appear in Gale's *Yesterday's Authors of Books for Children, Children's Literature Review,* and *Something about the Author Autobiography Series.*

Easy-to-Use Entry Format

Whether you're already familiar with the *SATA* series or just getting acquainted, you will want to be aware of the kind of information that an entry provides. In every *SATA* entry the editors attempt to give as complete a picture of the person's life and work as possible. A typical entry in *SATA* includes the following clearly labeled information sections:

- *PERSONAL:* date and place of birth and death, parents' names and occupations, name of spouse, date of marriage, names of children, educational institutions attended, degrees received, religious and political affiliations, hobbies and other interests.

- *ADDRESSES:* complete home, office, electronic mail, and agent addresses, whenever available.

- *CAREER:* name of employer, position, and dates for each career post; art exhibitions; military service; memberships and offices held in professional and civic organizations.

- *AWARDS, HONORS:* literary and professional awards received.

- *WRITINGS:* title-by-title chronological bibliography of books written and/or illustrated, listed by genre when known; lists of other notable publications, such as plays, screenplays, and periodical contributions.

- *ADAPTATIONS:* a list of films, television programs, plays, CD-ROMs, recordings, and other media presentations that have been adapted from the author's work.

- *WORK IN PROGRESS:* description of projects in progress.

- *SIDELIGHTS:* a biographical portrait of the author or illustrator's development, either directly from the biographee—and often written specifically for the *SATA* entry—or gathered from diaries, letters, interviews, or other published sources.

- *BIOGRAPHICAL AND CRITICAL SOURCES:* cites sources quoted in "Sidelights" along with references for further reading.

- *EXTENSIVE ILLUSTRATIONS:* photographs, movie stills, book illustrations, and other interesting visual materials supplement the text.

How a SATA Entry Is Compiled

A *SATA* entry progresses through a series of steps. If the biographee is living, the *SATA* editors try to secure information directly from him or her through a questionnaire. From the information that the biographee supplies, the editors prepare an entry, filling in any essential missing details with research and/or telephone interviews. If possible, the author or illustrator is sent a copy of the entry to check for accuracy and completeness.

If the biographee is deceased or cannot be reached by questionnaire, the *SATA* editors examine a wide variety of published sources to gather information for an entry. Biographical and bibliographic sources are consulted, as are book reviews, feature articles, published interviews, and material sometimes obtained from the biographee's family, publishers, agent, or other associates.

Entries that have not been verified by the biographees or their representatives are marked with an asterisk (*).

Contact the Editor

We encourage our readers to examine the entire *SATA* series. Please write and tell us if we can make *SATA* even more helpful to you. Give your comments and suggestions to the editor:

BY MAIL: Editor, *Something about the Author,* The Gale Group, 27500 Drake Rd., Farmington Hills, MI 48331-3535.

BY TELEPHONE: (800) 877-GALE

BY FAX: (248) 699-8054

Something about the Author Product Advisory Board

The editors of *Something about the Author* are dedicated to maintaining a high standard of excellence by publishing comprehensive, accurate, and highly readable entries on a wide array of writers for children and young adults. In addition to the quality of the content, the editors take pride in the graphic design of the series, which is intended to be orderly yet inviting, allowing readers to utilize the pages of *SATA* easily and with efficiency. Despite the longevity of the *SATA* print series, and the success of its format, we are mindful that the vitality of a literary reference product is dependent on its ability to serve its users over time. As literature, and attitudes about literature, constantly evolve, so do the reference needs of students, teachers, scholars, journalists, researchers, and book club members. To be certain that we continue to keep pace with the expectations of our customers, the editors of *SATA* listen carefully to their comments regarding the value, utility, and quality of the series. Librarians, who have firsthand knowledge of the needs of library users, are a valuable resource for us. The*Something about the Author* Product Advisory Board, made up of school, public, and academic librarians, is a forum to promote focused feedback about *SATA* on a regular basis. The five-member advisory board includes the following individuals, whom the editors wish to thank for sharing their expertise:

- **Eva M. Davis,** Teen Services Librarian, Plymouth District Library, Plymouth, Michigan

- **Joan B. Eisenberg,** Lower School Librarian, Milton Academy, Milton, Massachusetts

- **Francisca Goldsmith,** Teen Services Librarian, Berkeley Public Library, Berkeley, California

- **Monica F. Irlbacher,** Young Adult Librarian, Middletown Thrall Library, Middletown, New York

- **Caryn Sipos,** Librarian—Young Adult Services, King County Library System, Washington

Acknowledgments

Grateful acknowledgment is made to the following publishers, authors, and artists whose works appear in this volume.

ALVAREZ, JULIA. Alvarez, Julia, photograph by Sara Eichner. Reproduced by permission of William Eichner.

ANDREWS, TAMRA. Andrews, Tamra, photograph. Reproduced by permission.

ANTHONY, PIERS. All photographs reproduced by permission of the author.

APPELT, KATHI. Dyer, Jane, illustrator. From an illustration in *Oh My Baby, Little One*, by Kathi Appelt. Harcourt Brace & Company 2000. Illustrations © 2000 by Jane Dyer. Reproduced by permission of Harcourt, Inc. and Curtis Brown, Ltd.

BASKIN, NORA RALEIGH. Baskin, Nora Raleigh, photograph. Reproduced by permission.

BAYLEY, NICOLA. Bayley, Nicola, illustrator. From an illustration in *All for the Newborn Baby,* by Phyllis Root. Candlewick Press, 2000. Illustrations © 2000 by Nicola Bayley. Text © 2000 by Phyllis Root. Reproduced by permission of the publisher Candlewick Press, Inc., Cambridge, MA./ Bayley, Nicola, illustrator. From an illustration in *Katje, the Windmill Cat*, by Gretchen Woelfle. Candlewick Press, 2001. Illustrations © 2001 by Nicola Bayley. Text © 2001 Gretchen Woelfle. Reproduced by permission of the publisher Candlewick Press, Inc., Cambridge, MA./ Bayley, Nicola, illustrator. From an illustration in *The Mousehole Cat*, by Antonia Barber. Walker Books, Ltd., 1990. Illustrations © 1990 by Nicola Bayley. Text © 1990 by Antonia Barber. Reproduced by permission of the publisher Candlewick Press, Inc., Cambridge, MA, on behalf of Walker Books Ltd., London.

BOGAN, PAULETTE. Bogan, Paulette, and her two dogs, kissing a cartoon dog, photograph. Reproduced by permission.

BOLOGNESE, DON(ALD ALAN). Illustration by Don Bolognese from *Rescue in Space*, by Elaine Raphael. Published by Cartwheel Books, a division of Scholastic Inc. Illustrations copyright © 2000 by Don Bolognese. Reprinted by permission./ Illustration by Don Bolognese from *Buddy: The First Seeing Eye Dog*, by Eva Moore. Illustration copyright © 1996 by Don Bolognese. Reprinted by permission by Scholastic Inc.

BROWN, KEN (JAMES). Brown, Ken, illustrator. From an illustration in *What's the Time, Grandma Wolf?* by Ken Brown. Peachtree, 2001. Illustrations © 2001 by Ken Brown. Reproduced by permission.

BYMAN, JEREMY. Byman, Jeremy, photograph. Reproduced by permission of Jeri Rowe.

CALHOUN, DIA. Blondon, Herve, illustrator. From a jacket of *Firegold*, by Dia Calhoun. Winslow Press, 1999. Illustrations copyright © 1999 by Herve Blondon. Reproduced by permission./ Spirin, Gennady, illustrator. From a cover of *Aria of the Sea,* by Dia Calhoun. Winslow Press, 2000. Reproduced by permission.

CAMERON, ANN. Cameron, Ann, photograph by Bill Cherry. Reproduced by permission./ Marten, Ruth, illustrator. From a jacket of *The Secret Life of Amanda K. Woods*, by Ann Cameron. Frances Foster Books, 1998. Copyright © 1998 by Ann Cameron. Jacket copyright © 1998 by Ruth Marten. Reproduced by permission Farrar, Straus and Giroux, LLC.

COOKE, TRISH. Oxenbury, Helen, illustrator. From an illustration in *So Much*, by Trish Cooke. Candlewick Press, 1994. Illustrations © 1994 by Helen Oxenbury. Text © 1994 Trish Cooke. Reproduced by permission of the publisher Candlewick Press, Inc., Cambridge, MA.

CUMMINGS, PRISCILLA. Cummings, Priscilla, photograph. Reproduced by permission.

DALY, MAUREEN. Cover of *Seventeenth Summer*, by Maureen Daly. Archway Paperback, NY, 1985. Reproduced by permission of Simon & Schuster Children's Publishing Division./ Dennis, Wesley, illustrator. From an illustration in *The Small War of Sergeant Donkey*, by Maureen Daly. Bethlehem Books, 2000. Reproduced by permission

ELISH, DAN. Photograph from *The Transcontinental Railroad: Triumph of a Dream*, by Dan Elish. Millbrook Press, 1993. Photograph courtesy of the Oakland Museum of California. Reproduced by permission.

ELLIS, DEBORAH. Milelli, Pascal, illustrator. From a jacket of *The Breadwinner*, by Deborah Ellis. Groundwood Books, 2001. Reproduced by permission

UHLIG, SUSAN. Uhlig, Susan, photograph. Reproduced by permission.

URE, JEAN. Ure, Jean, photograph. Reproduced by permission of Jean Ure./ Cover of *Daffy Down Donkey*, by Jean Ure. Barron's, 1999. Reproduced by permission of Barron's Educational Series, Inc. Hauppauge, NY 11788./ Cover of *Foxglove*, by Jean Ure. Barron's, 1999. Reproduced by permission of Barron's Educational Series, Inc. Hauppauge, NY 11788.

USCHAN, MICHAEL V. Uschan, Michael V., photograph. Reproduced by permission.

WADDELL, MARTIN. All photographs reproduced by permission of the author.

SOMETHING ABOUT THE AUTHOR

AFFABEE, Eric
See STINE, R(obert) L(awrence)

*   *   *

ALVAREZ, Julia 1950-

Personal

Born March 27, 1950, in New York, NY; daughter of a physician; married Bill Eichner (a physician and farmer), June 3, 1989. *Education:* Attended Connecticut College, 1967-69; Middlebury College, B.A. (summa cum laude), 1971; Syracuse University, M.A., 1975; attended Bread Loaf School of English, 1979-80.

Addresses

Agent—Susan Bergholz Literary Services, 17 West 10th St., No. 5, New York, NY 10011-8769.

Career

Novelist and poet. Poet-in-the-schools in Kentucky, Delaware, and North Carolina, 1975-78; Phillips Andover Academy, Andover, MA, instructor in English, 1979-81; University of Vermont, Burlington, VT, visiting assistant professor of creative writing, 1981-83; George Washington University, Washington, DC, Jenny McKean Moore Visiting Writer, 1984-85; University of Illinois—Urbana, assistant professor of English, 1986-88; Middlebury College, Middlebury, VT, associate professor of English, 1988-1998, writer-in-residence, 1998—; writer. Operator of cooperative coffee plantation in Dominican Republic. *Member:* PEN American Center (member, national members council, 1997-99), Sigma Tau Delta (honor member).

Julia Alvarez

Awards, Honors

Benjamin T. Marshall Poetry Prize, Connecticut College, 1968 and 1969; prize from Academy of American Poetry, 1974; creative writing fellowship, Syracuse University, 1974-75; Kenan grant, Phillips Andover Academy, 1980; poetry award, La Reina Press, 1982; exhibition grant, Vermont Arts Council, 1984-85; Robert Frost Poetry fellowship, Bread Loaf Writers' Conference, 1986; Third Woman Press Award, first prize in narrative, 1986; award for younger writers, General Electric Foundation, 1986; National Endowment for the Arts grant, 1987-88; syndicated fiction prize, PEN, for "Snow"; grant from Ingram Merrill Foundation, 1990; Josephine Miles Award, PEN Oakland, 1991, and notable book designation, American Library Association (ALA), 1992, both for *How the García Girls Lost Their Accents;* ALA Notable Book designation, and National Book Critics Circle award finalist, both 1994, both for *In the Time of the Butterflies;* Jessica Nobel-Maxwell Poetry Prize, 1995; honorary D.H.L., John Jay College of the City University of New York, 1996; Alumni Achievement Award, Middlebury College, 1996; Literature Leadership Award, Dominico-American Society of Queens, 1998; named Woman of the Year, *Latina Magazine,* 2000.

Writings

NOVELS

How the García Girls Lost Their Accents, Algonquin Books of Chapel Hill (Chapel Hill, NC), 1991.
In the Time of the Butterflies, Algonquin Books of Chapel Hill (Chapel Hill, NC), 1994.
Yo! (sequel to *How the García Girls Lost Their Accents*), Algonquin Books of Chapel Hill (Chapel Hill, NC), 1996.
In the Name of Salomé, Algonquin Books of Chapel Hill (Chapel Hill, NC), 2000.
How Tía Lola Came to Visit Stay (young adult), Knopf (New York, NY), 2001.

POETRY

(Editor) *Old Age Ain't for Sissies,* Crane Creek Press, 1979.
The Housekeeping Book (also see below), illustrated by Carol MacDonald and Rene Schall, [Burlington, VT], 1984.
Homecoming (includes poems from *The Housekeeping Book*), Grove Press (New York, NY), 1984, revised edition, Dutton (New York, NY), 1995.
The Other Side/El otro lado, Dutton (New York, NY), 1995.
Seven Trees, Katran Press (Syracuse, NY), 1999.

OTHER

My English, Algonquin Books of Chapel Hill (Chapel Hill, NC), 1990.
Something to Declare (essays), Algonquin Books of Chapel Hill (Chapel Hill, NC), 1998.
The Secret Footprints (picture book), illustrated by Fabian Negrin, Knopf (New York, NY), 2000.
A Cafecito Story, Chelsea Green (White River Junction, VT), 2001.

Before We Were Free (young adult), Knopf (New York, NY), 2002.

Contributor to anthologies, including *The One You Call Sister: New Women's Fiction,* edited by Paula Martinac, Cleis Press (Pittsburgh, PA), 1989; *The Best American Poetry 1991,* edited by David Lehman, Scribner's (New York, NY), 1991; *Poems for a Small Planet: Contemporary American Nature Poetry,* edited by Robert Pack and Jay Parini, Middlebury College Press (Middlebury, VT), 1993; *Mondo Barbie,* edited by Lucinda Ebersole and Richard Peabody, St. Martin's Press (New York, NY), 1993; *Growing up Female: Short Stories by Women Writers from the American Mosaic,* edited by Susan Cahill, Penguin (New York, NY), 1993; *A Formal Feeling Comes: Poems in Form by Contemporary Women,* edited by Annie Finch, Story Line Press, 1994; *New Writing from the Caribbean,* Macmillan (New York, NY), 1994; and *Expansive Poetry: Essays on the New Narrative and the New Formalism,* edited by R. S. Gwynn, Story Line Press, 1999.

Contributor of fiction to periodicals, including *Caribbean Writer, Commonwoman, Greensboro Review, High Plains Literary Review, Green Mountain Review, New Mexico Humanities Review, Story,* and *Syracuse Magazine.* Contributor of poetry to periodicals, including *Barataria Review, Burlington Review, Caribbean Writer, Florilegia, George Washington Review, Green Mountain Review, Helicon Nine, Jar, Kentucky Poetry Review, Kenyon Review, Latinos in the U.S. Review, Poetry, Poetry Miscellany, Wind,* and *Womanspirit.*

Contributor of translations to *Barataria Review, Bitter Oleander, Pan American Review, Pulse: The Lamar Review,* and *Tower.* Editor of *Special Reports/Ecology,* 1971.

Alvarez's work has been translated into Spanish.

Adaptations

In the Time of the Butterflies was adapted as a television movie starring Salma Hayek for Showtime, 2001.

Sidelights

Novelist and poet Julia Alvarez is an author who straddles two cultures. Raised in the Dominican Republic, she left that country at age ten in 1960 to avoid her father's imprisonment due to his involvement in a plot to overthrow dictator Rafael Trujillo. Although her home and career have been based primarily in New England, Alvarez has continued to visit the Dominican Republic. Its people and culture figure strongly in her writing for both children and adults. Her writing is often semi-autobiographical—she claims as her motto "El papel lo aguante todo," ("Paper holds everything")—and she focuses on the issues confronting immigrant women like herself.

Although Alvarez was born in New York City, she spent the next ten years in the Dominican Republic, living in an extended family where several generations of extended family lived in close proximity to one another in homes surrounded by gardens, amid fragrant tropical flowers and sheltered by tall, wide-leafed tropical foliage. In 1960, after her physician father was discovered to have been involved in a plot to overthrow dictator Rafael Trujillo, Julia and her family abandoned their comfortable lifestyle and fled to New York City, where Alvarez's father eventually found a job as a physician. In their new country, young Alvarez had to master a second language and adjust to a new culture and a new urban way of life. "I think of myself at ten years old, newly arrived in this country, feeling out of place, feeling that I would never belong in this world of United States of Americans who were so different from me," she once recalled. "Back home in the Dominican Republic, I had been an active, lively child, a bad student full of fun with plentiful friends. In New York City I was suddenly thrown back on myself. I looked around the schoolyard at unfriendly faces. A few of the boys called me a name. I didn't know what it meant, but I knew it couldn't be anything good from the ugly looks on their faces."

Although life in the United States proved isolating to the young Alvarez, it also had some positive aspects. The wealth of books available for the taking at a nearby public library quickly made her an avid reader; libraries had been a rarity in the Dominican Republic. "And then, magic happened in my life. I didn't even recognize it as magic until years later: it looked like schoolwork, a writing assignment. An English teacher asked us to write little stories about ourselves. I began to put into words some of what my life had been like in the Dominican Republic. Stories about my gang of cousins and the smell of mangoes and the iridescent, vibrating green of hummingbirds. Since it was my own little world I was making with words, I could put what I wanted in it. I could make things up. If I needed more yellow in that mango, I could put it in. Set amapola blooming in January. Make the sun shine on a cloudy day. If I needed to make a cousin taller, I could make her grow two inches with an adjective so she could reach that ripe yellow mango on the tree. The boys in the schoolyard with ugly looks on their faces were not allowed into this world. I could save what I didn't want to lose—memories and smells and sounds, things too precious to put anywhere else."

Alvarez found that her time spent writing created a "place where I felt I belonged and could make sense of myself, my life, all that was happening to me. I realized that I had lost the island we had come from, but with the words and encouragement of my teacher, I had discovered an even better world: the one words can create in a story or poem. 'Language is the only homeland,' the exiled Polish poet, Czeslow Milosz, has said. And that was where I landed when we left the Dominican Republic, not in the United States but in the English language."

After graduating from high school in 1967, Alvarez spent two years at Connecticut College before the experience of winning that school's poetry prize made her focus on creative writing. Transferring to Middlebury College, she earned her B.A. in 1971, and followed it up with an M.A. in creative writing from Syracuse University in 1975. A job at Middlebury College drew her to Vermont in 1988, and she has continued to make her home in that state. Between college graduation and her arrival at Middlebury, Vermont, Alvarez considered herself a "migrant writer," traveling from one adjunct instructor position to another. As she recalled in an article in *Library Journal,* "In those thirteen years, I had over fifteen addresses. As a writing instructor, I was not paid very well nor given stipends to hire movers, so everything I owned had to fit in my little Volkswagen. This included, of course, my books, which took up a large percentage of the space. When I hit the critical mass of not having any space left in the tiny trunk or backseat, I had the difficult task of deciding what to leave behind." Alvarez viewed this continued process "an excellent test of what books are worth your bother as a reader."

Alvarez's first book-length work of fiction, *How the García Girls Lost Their Accents,* was published in 1991. Divided into three sections, the book is composed of fifteen interrelated stories which focus on the four sisters—Sandi, Yolanda, Carla, and Fifi—as they are forced to leave their family in the Dominican Republic and go into exile in the United States. When readers first meet the García sisters, they are all grown up, but the second section of the book shows their evolution from immigrants into true '60s American girls, coping with typical teen pressures involving boys, schoolwork, and fitting in. The last group of stories travel back in time to the years 1956-1960, and recount the girls' childhood in the Caribbean. Donna Rifkind, writing in the *New York Times Book Review,* praised Alvarez for "beautifully captur[ing] the threshold experiences of the new immigrant, where the past is not yet a memory and the future remains an anxious dream." Stephen Henighan in the *Globe and Mail* characterized *How the García Girls Lost Their Accents* as a "humane, gracefully written novel."

Yo! continues the story of the four García sisters. "Yo," Spanish for "I," is also the nickname of Yolanda García who, like Alvarez herself, has grown up to become a writer. Each chapter in *Yo!* is told by a different narrator, all of whom know Yolanda and see her in a different light. A *Publishers Weekly* reviewer hailed *Yo!* as a "splendid sequel" to *How the García Girls Lost Their Accents,* and observed that "Alvarez's command of Latino voices has always been impeccable, but here she is equally adept at conveying the personalities of a geographically diverse group of Americans."

The 2001 young adult novel *How Tía Lola Came to Visit Stay* was inspired by Alvarez's fond memories of the many aunts and uncles she left behind in the Dominican Republic when she and her family were forced to flee. In the novel, a boy named Miguel and his younger sister Juanita experience a change in their home after their Aunt Lola comes for a visit that becomes permanent.

Although Miguel's home in Vermont is far chillier than Lola's native Caribbean, changes in the children's family prompt the well-meaning but sometimes overly affectionate aunt to make New England her new home, warming everyone around her with her generosity, Carribean traditions, and sense of fun.

Alvarez has also captured the imagination of younger readers with her first picture book, *The Secret Footprints,* which is based on a legend from the Taino tribes. Enhanced by the vividly colored illustrations of Fabian Negrin, Alvarez's story takes readers to the Dominican Republic and the tale of a hidden tribe of nocturnal creatures called ciguapas who live in small, secluded underwater caves located along the coast. When a young and curious ciguapa named Guapa leaves her secret cave to explore the lands away from the coast, she is taken in by a forest family who thinks she has severely twisted both her ankles—ciguapas have feet that naturally face to their back, unlike land-dwellers, so tracking them by following their footprints leads their pursuers in the wrong direction. While they race off to fetch the doctor, Guapa leaves the house and returns to her ocean home. Praising the book in *Booklist,* Connie Fletcher commented that "Children will be ensnared by the danger the creatures face and cheered by the story's resolution." Alvarez's "language flows ... effortlessly," according to *School Library Journal* reviewer Barbara Scotto, "setting a mood of ease" for young readers.

Alvarez's novels *In the Time of the Butterflies* and *In the Name of Salomé* focus on adults attempting to live under a repressive political regime. *In the Time of the Butterflies* fictionally recounts the tragic true story of the four Mirabal sisters, three of whom were imprisoned and ultimately killed after denouncing Trujillo's dictatorship during the 1960s. *In the Name of Salomé* is based on the life of nineteenth-century Dominican poet and political activist Salomé Ureña de Henriquez and her daughter, Camila, the latter who grows up to be a college professor at Vassar and returns to the Caribbean to put her mother's papers in order after Salomé's early death. Veronica Scrol noted in *Booklist* that in *In the Name of Salomé,* "Alvarez uses the experience of the mother and daughter to ask the deeper question: Who are we as a people?" In her *Christian Science Monitor* review of the novel, contributor Kendra Nordin maintained that Alvarez creates the experience "of sitting at the feet of an old woman recounting her long life in jumbled order, but with emphasis on important moments, passionate impressions, wisdom learned and shared."

In addition to novels and books for young children, Alvarez has written the essay collection *Something to Declare,* about her observations on life, and is the author of a number of highly acclaimed volumes of poetry. Her 1995 collection, *Homecoming,* contains a section titled "Housekeeping" that focuses on the mundane housekeeping tasks that provide the poet with continuity. An autobiographical poem and a separate collection of over forty sonnets rounds out the work, which *Library Journal* contributor Christine Stenstrom called a "vivid and engaging collection." *The Other Side/El otro lado* contains a long poem about living in an artist's colony near a poor Dominican fishing village.

Biographical and Critical Sources

BOOKS

Authors and Artists for Young Adults, Volume 25, Gale (Detroit, MI), 1998.
Contemporary Literary Criticism, Volume 93, Gale (Detroit, MI), 1996.
Dictionary of Hispanic Biography, Gale (Detroit, MI), 1996.

PERIODICALS

American Book Review, August-September, 1992, Elizabeth Starcevic, "Talking about Language," p. 15.
Americas, January-February, 2001, Ben Jacques, "Julia Alvarez: Real Flights of Imagination," pp. 22-30.
Belles Lettres, spring, 1995, Janet Jones Hampton, "The Time of the Tyrants," pp. 6-7.
Bloomsbury Review, March, 1992, Catherine Wiley, interview with Alvarez, pp. 9-10.
Booklist, March 15, 1992, p. 1361; August, 1998, Donna Seaman, review of *Something to Declare,* p. 1952; March 15, 2000, Veronica Scrol, review of *In the Name of Salomé,* p. 1292; August, 2000, Connie Fletcher, review of *The Secret Footprints,* p. 2143, and Isabel Schon, reviews of *In the Time of the Butterflies* and *Yo!,* p. 2154; February 15, 2001, Hazel Rochman, review of *How Tía Lola Came to Visit Stay,* p. 1138.
Boston Globe, June 28, 2000, Vanessa E. Jones, "Writing Her Book of High Grace."
Callaloo, summer, 2000, p. 839.
Christian Science Monitor, October 17, 1994, Katherine A. Powers, review of *In the Time of the Butterflies,* p. 13; July 6, 2000, Kendra Nordin, "Recalling the Dreams of a Caribbean Past."
Commonweal, April 10, 1992, Ilans Stavans, "Daughters of Invention," pp. 23-25.
Faces, February, 1999, Stephanie Prescott, "Julia Alvarez: Dominican American Storyteller," p. 30.
Globe and Mail (Toronto, Canada), August 31, 1991, Stephen Henighan, review of *How the García Girls Lost Their Accents,* p. C6.
Hispanic, June, 1991, p. 55.
Hungry Mind Review, winter, 1994, Dwight Garner, "A Winter's Revolution," p. 23.
Kirkus Review, March 15, 1991, p. 336.
Knight-Ridder/Tribune News Service, June 7, 2000, Margaria Fichtner, review of *In the Name of Salomé,* p. K6045; August 9, 2000, Mary Ann Horne, review of *In the Name of Salomé,* p. K3161.
Library Journal, August, 1994, p. 123; April 15, 1995, Rochelle Ratner, review of *The Other Side/El otro lado,* p. 80; April 1, 1996, Christine Stenstrom, review of *Homecoming,* p. 84; August, 1998, Nancy Shires, review of *Something to Declare,* p. 88; May 1, 2000, Eleanor J. Bader, review of *In the Name of Salomé,* p. 151; September 1, 2000, Julia Alvarez, "Noah's Ark Choices," p. 168.
Los Angeles Times, January 20, 1997, p. E3; March 23, 1997, Maria Elena Fernandez, "Two Sides of an American Identity," p. E1.

Los Angeles Times Book Review, February 26, 1995, p. 8.

MELUS, spring, 1998, Julie Barak, "Turning and Turning in the Widening Gyre": A Second Coming into Language in Julia Alvarez's *How the García Girls Lost Their Accents,* p. 159.

Nation, December 30, 1991, pp. 863-864; November 7, 1994, pp. 552-556.

New England Review & Breadloaf Quarterly, winter, 1986, Fred Muratori, review of *Homecoming,* pp. 231-232.

Newsweek, April 20, 1992, p. 78; October 17, 1994, Susan Miller, "Family Spats, Urgent Prayers," p. 77.

New York Times Book Review, October 6, 1991, Donna Rifkind, "Speaking American," p. 14; December 18, 1994, Roberto González Echevarría, "Sisters in Death," p. 28; July 16, 1995, Philip Gambone, review of *The Other Side/El otro lado,* p. 20; February 9, 1997, Abby Frucht, "That García Girl!," p. 19; September 20, 1998, Christina Cho, review of *Something to Declare;* July 16, 2000, Suzanne Ruta, "Daughters of Revolution," p. 24.

New York Times Magazine, March 23, 1997, Molly O'Neill, "The Farm Team," pp. 67-68.

Nuestro, November, 1984, p. 34; March, 1985, p. 52; January-February, 1986, p. 32.

People, January 20, 1997, Clare McHugh, review of *Yo!,* p. 33; September 21, 1998, Laura Jamison, review of *Something to Declare,* p. 49.

Poetry, August, 1996, p. 285.

Progressive, July, 1995, p. 39.

Publishers Weekly, March 18, 1996, p. 67; October 14, 1996, review of *Yo!,* p. 62; December 16, 1996, Jonathan Bing, "Julia Alvarez: Books That Cross Borders," pp. 38-39; May 15, 2000, review of *In the Name of Salomé,* p. 86; August 14, 2000, review of *The Secret Footprints,* p. 354; February 26, 2001, review of *How Tía Lola Came to Visit Stay,* p. 87.

School Library Journal, September, 1991, p. 292; September, 2000, Barbara Scotto, review of *The Secret Footprints,* p. 213.

Sojourners, May, 2001, Jim Wallis, review of *In the Name of Salomé,* p. 53.

Tribune Books (Chicago, IL), January 26, 1997, section 14, p. 2.

USA Today Magazine, March, 1999, Steven G. Kellman, review of *Something to Declare,* p. 80.

Washington Post Book Review, January 19, 1997, p. 9.

Women's Review of Books, July, 1991, Cecilia Rodríguez Milanés, "No Place like Home," p. 39; May, 1995, pp. 6-7; September 21, 1998, Laura Jamison, review of *Something to Declare,* p. 49.

World & I, December, 2000, Linda Simon, "Poetry and Patria: In Her Fourth Novel, Alvarez Explores Personal and Political Exigencies in the Lives of Two Passionate Women," pp. 232-236.

World Literature Today, summer, 1992, Bruce Novoa, review of *How the García Girls Lost Their Accents,* p. 516; autumn, 1995, p. 789; autumn, 1997, Cynthia Tompkins, review of *Yo!,* winter, 2001, Fernando Valerio-Holguín, review of *In the Name of Salomé,* p. 113.

OTHER

Creative Loafing Online, http://web.cin.com/ (July 26, 2001), Amy Rogers, "Magical History."

Frontera Magazine, http://www.fronteramag.com/issue5/ (July 26, 2001), Marny Requa, "The Politics of Fiction."

*   *   *

ANDREWS, Tamra 1959-

Personal

Born March 31, 1959, in Pittsburgh, PA; daughter of Chalmer T. (a civil engineer) and Isobel (a homemaker; maiden name, Namy) Price; married Carlton Andrews (an imaging scientist), September 6, 1980; children: Cristen Rene, Carolyn Michelle. *Education:* Attended Trinity University (San Antonio, TX), 1977-1979; University of Texas—Austin, B.A. (English), 1980, M.L.I.S., 1987.

Addresses

Office—St. Edwards University, 3001 South Congress, Austin, TX 78704-6489. *E-mail*—tamraa@admin.stedwards.edu.

Career

University of Texas—Austin, librarian, 1987-90; Austin Community College, Austin, TX, reference librarian, 1992-96; Southwest Texas State University, Austin, TX, reference librarian, 2000-2001; St. Edwards University,

Tamra Andrews

Austin, TX, reference librarian, 2000—. *Member:* Society of Children's Book Writers and Illustrators, Writers League of Texas.

Writings

Legends of the Earth, Sea, and Sky, ABC-CLIO (Santa Barbara, CA), 1998, also published as *Dictionary of Nature Myths: Legends of the Earth, Sea, and Sky* Oxford University Press (New York, NY), 2000.
Nectar and Ambrosia: An Encyclopedia of Food in World Mythology, ABC-CLIO (Santa Barbara, CA), 2000.

Columnist for *Austin Health and Fitness,* 1992-93, and *Star Date,* 1994-95. Contributor of articles to periodicals, including *Boys' Life, U.S. Kids,* and *California Astrologer.* Writer of scripts on astronomy for *Star Date,* a radio program on National Public Radio. Contributor to reference books.

Sidelights

Tamra Andrews's work as a professional librarian led her to discover an interest in writing nonfiction works. While an astronomy librarian at the University of Texas, she became interested in historical astronomy and sky legends. During her three-year stint there, she began to write freelance radio scripts and articles for *Star Date,* a syndicated program on National Public Radio, which was produced by the McDonald Observatory at the university. After about eight years of writing about astronomical myths and legends, Andrews earned a spot as a columnist. "I pitched an idea to the editor of *Star Date* magazine for a regular column, and began writing 'Star Lore,' a column full of captivating stories ancient people told to make sense of the world around them. I delved into mythology with a passion," Andrews told *SATA.*

Eventually Andrews sold the idea of a book on legends and natural phenomena to reference book publisher ABC-CLIO. Writing *Legends of the Earth, Sea, and Sky* proved to be both satisfying and a learning process for it contains 350 entries on deities, legends, myths, and practices of various cultures dealing with non-living phenomena, such as wind, stars, fire, and the seasons. "Writing *Legends of the Earth, Sea, and Sky* was undoubtedly the most enlightening experience I've had as a writer," she told *SATA.* "The task seemed overwhelming at first, writing an encyclopedia from scratch, organizing mass quantities of information, and presenting it in a way that would attract young readers. I knew that to capture the magic of ancient myths, I'd have to write in a lively, conversational tone, and that involved doing something rather unconventional for a reference book." Although *Library Journal* reviewer Katherine K. Koenig complained about the conversational style, according to a *Booklist* critic, *Legends of the Earth, Sea, and Sky* "makes fascinating reading." Proof positive for the book's accessibility was its publication in paperback by Oxford University Press. "To me this meant that I had succeeded in creating a reference book that appealed

to a general audience, one that people could enjoy browsing through just for fun."

Andrews's next book was an encyclopedia of food myths surrounding various plants, game animals, beverages, spices, and other staples. In each entry she highlighted the role it played in the mythology of such cultures as Asian, Native American, European, African, and those of ancient Greece and Rome. "Writing reference books for young adults is a monumental task, and writing *Nectar and Ambrosia* seemed even more daunting than writing *Legends of the Earth, Sea, and Sky,*" Andrews added. "The information I needed to put together to create an encyclopedia of food myths came from a wide array of disciplines. This book, I knew, would challenge me to be even more organized and even more disciplined about my research." Yet Andrews was not daunted because she had learned valuable research and organization skills and developed her own voice writing the previous book. "By this time, I felt comfortable with my research skills and with my writing style, and I knew the organization process that worked with the last book. I also knew that writing a book composed of separate entries was much easier for me than writing one long continuous narrative." According to a *Booklist* reviewer, Andrews used "flowing, absorbing prose" to tell her tales and has succeeded in creating a work suitable for the general reader.

Biographical and Critical Sources

PERIODICALS

Booklist, March 1, 1999, review of *Legends of the Earth, Sea, and Sky,* p. 1251; May 15, 2000, Dona Helmer, review of *Legends of the Earth, Sea, and Sky,* p. 1774; February 1, 2001, review of *Nectar and Ambrosia: An Encyclopedia of Food in World Mythology,* p. 1076; July, 2001, Barbara Bibel, review of *Nectar and Ambrosia,* p. 2034.
Choice, April, 2001, M. A. Kascus, review of *Legends of the Earth, Sea, and Sky,* p. 1434.
Library Journal, January, 1999, Katherine K. Koenig, review of *Legends of the Earth, Sea, and Sky,* p. 84; February 1, 2001, John Charles, review of *Nectar and Ambrosia,* p. 80.
School Library Journal, May, 1999, Mary H. Cole, review of *Legends of the Earth, Sea, and Sky,* p. 148.
Sky & Telescope, November, 1999, "Stories in the Sky," p. 179.*

*   *   *

ANNIE-JO
See SUHR, Joanne

ANTHONY, Piers 1934-
(Robert Piers, a joint pseudonym)

Personal

Full name Piers Anthony Dillingham Jacob; born August 6, 1934, in Oxford, England; came to United States, 1940, naturalized U.S. citizen, 1958; son of Alfred Bennis and Norma (Sherlock) Jacob; married Carol Marble, June 23, 1956; children: Penelope Carolyn, Cheryl. *Education:* Goddard College, B.A., 1956; University of South Florida, teaching certificate, 1964. *Politics:* Independent. *Religion:* "No preference." *Avocational interests:* Tree farming, archery.

Addresses

Office—c/o Tor Books, 175 Fifth Ave., New York, NY 10010.

Career

Novelist. Electronic Communications, Inc., St. Petersburg, FL, technical writer, 1959-62; freelance writer, 1962-63, 1966—; Admiral Farragut Academy, St. Petersburg, FL, teacher of English, 1965-66. *Military service:* U.S. Army, 1957-59. *Member:* Authors Guild, Authors League of America, National Writers Union.

Awards, Honors

Nebula Award nomination, Science Fiction Writers of America, 1966, for short story "The Message"; Nebula Award nomination, 1967, and Hugo Award nomination, World Science Fiction Convention, 1968, both for *Chthon;* science fiction award, Pyramid Books/*Magazine of Fantasy and Science Fiction*/Kent Productions, 1967, and Hugo Award nominations, 1969, both for *Sos the Rope;* Hugo Award nomination, 1969, for novella *Getting through University,* and 1970, for *Macroscope;* Nebula Award nominations, 1970, for short story "The Bridge," and, 1972, for novelette *In the Barn;* British Fantasy Award, 1977, and Hugo Award nomination, 1978, both for *A Spell for Chameleon.*

Writings

SCIENCE FICTION

Chthon, Ballantine, 1967.
(With Robert E. Margroff) *The Ring,* Ace Books, 1968.
Macroscope, Avon, 1969.
(With Margroff) *The E.S.P. Worm,* Paperback Library, 1970.
Prostho Plus, Berkley, 1973.
Race against Time, Hawthorne, 1973.
Rings of Ice, Avon, 1974.
Triple Detente, DAW Books, 1974.
Phthor (sequel to *Chthon*), Berkley Publishing, 1975.
(With Robert Coulson) *But What of Earth?,* Laser (Toronto, Ontario, Canada), 1976, corrected edition, Tor Books, 1989.
(With Frances T. Hall) *The Pretender,* Borgo Press, 1979.

Mute, Avon, 1981.
Ghost, Tor Books, 1986.
Shade of the Tree, Tor Books, 1986.
(Editor with Barry Malzberg, Martin Greenberg, and Charles G. Waugh) *Uncollected Stars* (short stories), Avon, 1986.
Total Recall, Morrow, 1989.
Balook, illustrated by Patrick Woodroffe, Underwood-Miller, 1990.
Hard Sell, Tafford, 1990.
(With Roberto Fuentes) *Dead Morn,* Tafford, 1990.
MerCycle, illustrated by Ron Lindahn, Tafford, 1991.
(With Philip Jose Farmer) *Caterpillar's Question,* Ace Books, 1992.
Killobyte, Putnam, 1993.
The Willing Spirit, Tor Books, 1996.
Volk Internet 1996, Xlibris, 1997.
(With Clifford Pickover) *Spider Legs,* Tor, 1998.
(With J. R. Goolsby and Alan Riggs) *Quest for the Fallen Star,* Tor, 1998.
(With Julie Brady) *Dream a Little Dream,* Tor, 1999.
(With Jo An Taeusch) *The Secret of Spring,* Tor, 2000.
(With Ron Leming) *The Gutbucket Quest,* Tor, 2000.
Realty Check Pulpless, Xlibris, 2000.

"OMNIVORE" SERIES; SCIENCE-FICTION NOVELS

Omnivore, Ballantine, 1968.
Orn, Avon, 1971.
Ox, Avon, 1976.

"BATTLE CIRCLE" SERIES; SCIENCE-FICTION NOVELS

Sos the Rope, Pyramid, 1968.
Var the Stick, Faber, 1972.
Neq the Sword, Corgi, 1975.
Battle Circle (omnibus volume; contains *Sos the Rope, Var the Stick,* and *Neq the Sword*), Avon, 1978.

"CLUSTER" SERIES; SCIENCE-FICTION NOVELS

Cluster, Avon, 1977, published as *Vicinity Cluster,* Panther (London, England), 1979.
Chaining the Lady, Avon, 1978.
Kirlian Quest, Avon, 1978.
Thousandstar, Avon, 1980.
Viscous Circle, Avon, 1982.

"TAROT"; SCIENCE-FICTION TRILOGY

God of Tarot, Jove, 1979.
Vision of Tarot, Berkley Publishing, 1980.
Faith of Tarot, Berkley Publishing, 1980.
Tarot (contains *God of Tarot, Vision of Tarot,* and *Faith of Tarot*), Ace Books, 1988.

"BIO OF A SPACE TYRANT" SERIES; SCIENCE FICTION NOVELS

Refugee, Avon, 1983.
Mercenary, Avon, 1984.
Politician, Avon, 1985.
Executive, Avon, 1985.
Statesman, Avon, 1986.

FANTASY

Hasan, Borgo Press, 1977.

(With Robert Kornwise) *Through the Ice,* illustrated by D. Horne, Underwood-Miller, 1989.

(With Mercedes Lackey) *If I Pay Thee Not in Gold,* Baen, 1993.

"MAGIC OF XANTH" SERIES; FANTASY NOVELS

A Spell for Chameleon, Del Rey, 1977.
The Source of Magic, Del Rey, 1979.
Castle Roogna, Del Rey, 1979.
The Magic of Xanth (omnibus volume; contains *A Spell for Chameleon, The Source of Magic,* and *Castle Roogna*), Doubleday, 1981, published as *Piers Anthony: Three Complete Xanth Novels,* Wings Books, 1994.
Centaur Aisle, Del Rey, 1982.
Ogre, Ogre, Del Rey, 1982.
Night Mare, Del Rey, 1983.
Dragon on a Pedestal, Del Rey, 1983.
Crewel Lye: A Caustic Yarn, Del Rey, 1985.
Golem in the Gears, Del Rey, 1986.
Vale of the Vole, Avon, 1987.
Heaven Cent, Avon, 1988.
Man from Mundania, Avon, 1989.
(With Jody Lynn Nye) *Piers Anthony's Visual Guide to Xanth,* illustrated by Todd Cameron Hamilton and James Clouse, Avon, 1989.
Isle of View, Morrow, 1990.
Question Quest, Morrow, 1991.
The Color of Her Panties, Avon, 1992.
Demons Don't Dream, Tor Books, 1993.
Harpy Thyme, Tor Books, 1994.
Geis of the Gargoyle, Tor Books, 1995.
Roc and a Hard Place, Tor Books, 1995.
Yon Ill Wind, Tor Books, 1996.
Faun and Games, Tor Books, 1997.
Zombie Lover, Tor Books, 1998.
Xone of Contention, Tor Books, 1999.
The Dastard, Tor Books, 2000.
Swell Foop, Tor Books, 2001.
Up in a Heaval, Tor Books, 2001.

"INCARNATIONS OF IMMORTALITY" SERIES; FANTASY NOVELS

On a Pale Horse, Del Rey, 1983.
Bearing an Hourglass, Del Rey, 1984.
With a Tangled Skein, Del Rey, 1985.
Wielding a Red Sword, Del Rey, 1986.
Being a Green Mother, Del Rey, 1987.
For Love of Evil, Morrow, 1988.
And Eternity, Morrow, 1990.

"DRAGON'S GOLD" SERIES; FANTASY NOVELS

(With Robert E. Margroff) *Dragon's Gold,* Tor Books, 1987.
(With Robert E. Margroff) *Serpent's Silver,* Tor Books, 1988.
(With Robert E. Margroff) *Chimaera's Copper,* Tor Books, 1990.
(With Robert E. Margroff) *Orc's Opal,* Tor Books, 1990.
(With Robert E. Margroff) *Mouvar's Magic,* Tor Books, 1992.
(With Robert E. Margroff) *Three Complete Novels* (contains *Dragon's Gold, Serpent's Silver,* and *Chimaera's Copper*), Wings Books, 1993.

"APPRENTICE ADEPT" SERIES; SCIENCE-FICTION/FANTASY NOVELS

Split Infinity, Del Rey, 1980.
Blue Adept, Del Rey, 1981.
Juxtaposition, Del Rey, 1982.
Double Exposure (omnibus volume; contains *Split Infinity, Blue Adept,* and *Juxtaposition*), Doubleday, 1982.
Out of Phaze, Ace Books, 1987.
Robot Adept, Ace Books, 1988.
Unicorn Point, Ace Books, 1989.
Phaze Doubt, Ace Books, 1990.

"MODE" SERIES; SCIENCE FICTION/FANTASY NOVELS

Virtual Mode, Putnam, 1991.
Fractal Mode, Putnam, 1992.
Chaos Mode, Putnam, 1993.
DoOon Mode, Tor Books, 2001.

"JASON STRIKER" SERIES; MARTIAL ARTS NOVELS

(With Roberto Fuentes) *Kiai!,* Berkley Publishing, 1974.
(With Roberto Fuentes) *Mistress of Death,* Berkley Publishing, 1974.
(With Roberto Fuentes) *The Bamboo Bloodbath,* Berkley Publishing, 1974.
(With Roberto Fuentes) *Ninja's Revenge,* Berkley Publishing, 1975.
(With Roberto Fuentes) *Amazon Slaughter,* Berkley Publishing, 1976.

"GEODYSSEY" SERIES; HISTORICAL SCIENCE FICTION

Isle of Woman, Tor Books, 1993.
Shame of Man, Tor Books, 1994.
Hope of Earth, Tor Books, 1997.
Muse of Art, Tor Books, 1999.

Also author of *Climate of Change,* in progress.

OTHER

Steppe (science fiction/history), Millington, 1976, Tor Books, 1985.
Anthonology (short stories), Tor Books, 1985.
Bio of an Ogre: The Autobiography of Piers Anthony to Age Fifty, Ace Books, 1988.
Pornucopia (erotic fantasy), Tafford, 1989.
Firefly (novel), Morrow, 1990, Avon, 1992.
Tatham Mound (historical fiction), Morrow, 1991.
Alien Plot (short stories), Tor Books, 1992.
Letters to Jenny (nonfiction), Tor Books, 1993.
(Editor with Richard Gilliam) *Tales from the Great Turtle,* Tor Books, 1994.
How Precious Was That While (memoir), Tor Books, 2001.

Contributor to *Science against Man,* edited by Anthony Cheetham, Avon, 1970; *Nova One: An Anthology of Original Science Fiction,* edited by Harry Harrison, Delacorte Press, 1970; *Again, Dangerous Visions,* edited by Harlan Ellison, Doubleday, 1972; *Generation,* edited by David Gerrold, Dell, 1972; and *The Berkley Showcase,* edited by Victoria Schochet and John Silbersack, Berkley Publishing, 1981. Also contributor, with Robert E. Margroff under joint pseudonym Robert Piers, of a short story to *Adam Bedside Reader.* Contributor of short stories to periodicals, including *Analog, Fantastic,*

Worlds of If, Worlds of Tomorrow, Amazing, Magazine of Fantasy and Science Fiction, SF Age, Vegetarian Times, Twilight Zone, Books and Bookmen, Writer, Gauntlet, Chic, Far Point, Starburst, Vertex, and *Pandora.*

Adaptations

Macroscope, A Spell for Chameleon, The Source of Magic, Castle Roogna, Through the Ice, Virtual Mode, and *Fractal Mode* have been adapted to audio cassette.

Sidelights

Within a childhood affected by illness and isolation, prolific science fiction and fantasy author Piers Anthony escaped by immersing himself in books. "From the time I was 13, I had been hooked on science fiction," Anthony recalled in an interview with the *Science Fiction Radio Show* (*SFRS*) published in *The Sound of Wonder.* "It's what I did for entertainment. It was a whole different world, multiple worlds, each one of them better than the one I knew. And so when I thought about writing [science fiction], I thought I could be original because I had read everything in the field." He began to write at age twenty, deciding in college to make writing his career. As an adult, Anthony's escape became his livelihood. His many popular series—including the ongoing "Magic of Xanth" novels—and his various novels and collections add up to more than one hundred books since 1967. "I am an SF writer today," he told Cliff Biggers in a *Science Fiction* interview, "because without SF and writing I would be nothing at all today."

Among the traumatic events of Anthony's youth were his family's moves to Spain when he was five and to the United States the next year, the loss of his cousin to cancer at fifteen, and his parents' divorce at eighteen. As members of the Quaker faith, his parents were involved with the British Friends Service Committee during the Spanish Civil War, and Anthony spent the first years of his life in England under the care of his grandparents and a nanny. When he and his sister joined his parents after the war, they "seemed like acquaintances rather than close kin," the author recounted in his *Something about the Author Autobiography Series* (*SAAS*) entry. The family soon moved to the United States, where Anthony found it difficult to fit in. He often had to deal with bullies at school, and this compounded the alienation he suffered because of his parents' divorce. "The dominant emotion of my later childhood was fear," he recalled in his essay. "Fear of bigger kids at school, of a monster in the forest, and fear of the corpse. Fear, really, of life. I hated being alone, but others neither understood nor cared, so I was alone a lot. That is, often physically, and almost always emotionally. Today when I get a letter from a reader who feels almost utterly alone, I understand, because I remember."

In addition, the young Anthony had difficulty at school. "Everyone in my immediate family was academically gifted except me," he continued in *SAAS*. "I was the dunce who made up for it all, pulling the average down." It wasn't until he was an adult that he discovered his academic problems had been due to some type of learning disability; "in my day things like learning disabilities or dyslexia didn't exist, just stupid or careless children." Nevertheless, encouraged by his parents, who read and told stories to him, Anthony became a regular reader. "I think that nightly reading, and the daytime storytelling when we worked together outside, was the most important influence on my eventual choice of career. I knew that books contained fascinating adventures, and those stories took me away from my dreary real life."

After eight years of submitting stories to magazines, Anthony sold his first piece, "Possible to Rue," to *Fantastic* in 1962. In the next several years, he worked variously as a freelance writer and English teacher, but finally decided to devote all of his time to writing. *Chthon,* Anthony's first novel, was published in 1967, received numerous award nominations, and caught the attention of both critics and readers in the science fiction genre. The next year brought a prize from a contest jointly sponsored by Pyramid Books, Kent Productions, and the *Magazine of Fantasy and Science Fiction* for *Sos the Rope,* the first entry in the "Battle Circle" series.

Chthon traces the escape efforts of Aton Five, imprisoned on the planet Chthon and forced to work in its garnet mines. A *Publishers Weekly* reviewer commented on the many elements of the book, including language, myth, suspense, and symbolism, "a bursting package, almost too much for one book, but literate, original and entertaining." Those elements—and Anthony's liberal use of them—would become his trademark. In a detailed analysis of *Chthon* and its sequel, *Phthor,* in his study *Piers Anthony,* Michael R. Collings noted Anthony's liberal references to mythological symbols. Literary references are present as well, exemplified by the resemblance of the prison caverns of Chthon to Dante's depiction of Hell in *The Inferno.* In *Chthon,* "Anthony has created a whole new world, a dream universe which you find yourself living in and, after a while, understanding," Leo Harris declared in *Books and Bookmen.* "Very poetic and tough and allegorical it all is, and it will rapidly have thee in thrall." While *Chthon* focuses on Aton's life, *Phthor* follows Aton's son, Arlo, who symbolizes Thor of Norse mythology. "The mythologies embedded in *Chthon* and *Phthor* go far beyond mere ornamentation or surface symbolism," Collings noted. "They define the thematic content of the novels. Initially, there is a clear demarcation between myth and reality. Yet early in *Chthon* Anthony throws that clear demarcation into question."

Anthony's first trilogy begins with *Sos the Rope,* based on a chapter of his 1956 B.A. thesis novel titled "The Unstilled World." The first installment of the "Battle Circle" books, *Sos the Rope* explores the efforts of a group of radiation survivors led by Sos as they attempt to rebuild their society after the Blast. Yet the resulting Empire soon becomes a destructive force and Sos sets out to destroy it. The novel speaks against the dangers of centralized civilization and overpopulation: millions of shrews, like the Biblical plague of locusts, invade the area and consume every living creature within their reach. Eventually the horde destroys itself with its enormity and its wholesale pillaging. The shrews' rampage and ultimate demise serve as a metaphor for man's overcrowding and abuse of the environment. Humankind, like the shrews, will be decimated when it outgrows the Earth's ability to sustain it. In *Var the Stick* and *Neq the Sword,* the "Battle Circle" story is completed. The books' titles are actually characters' names; the trilogy's warriors are named after their weapons. Collings observed similarities to the epic works of Homer, Virgil, and John Milton in "Battle Circle," which "investigates the viability of three fundamental forms of epic: the Achilean epic of martial prowess; the Odyssean epic of wandering; and the Virgillian/Miltonic epic of self-sacrifice and restoration."

The "Omnivore" trilogy provided a forum for Anthony to further his exploration of the dangers humankind continues to inflict upon itself, and introduced his support of vegetarianism. "Like *Battle Circle, Chthon,* and *Phthor,*" Collings observed, "*Omnivore* deals with control—specifically, with controlling the most dangerous omnivore of all, man." Three interplanetary explorers, the herbivorous Veg, carnivorous Cal, and omnivorous Aquilon, play out Anthony's views. The three journey to the planet Nacre, reporting back to investigator Subble and subsequently revealing to readers their adventures and clues to the secret threatening to destroy Earth. In the sequel, *Orn,* the three explorers venture to the planet Paleo, which resembles the Earth of sixty five million years past, and encounter Orn, a creature whose racial memory endows it with the knowledge of its ancestors and enables it to survive the changes bombarding its planet. In *Ox,* the final volume of the trilogy, Veg, Cal, and Aquilon gradually uncover the existence of a sentient super-computer while exploring alternate worlds. As with other Anthony books, reviewers noted that the "Omnivore" volumes contain substantial discussions of technical and scientific issues. A *Publishers Weekly* reviewer described *Ox* as "a book for readers willing to put a lot of concentration into reading it." The similarly complex *Macroscope,* described by Collings as "one of Anthony's most ambitious and complex novels," seeks to place man in his proper context within the galaxy. The book increased Anthony's reputation but, due to a publisher's error, was not submitted for consideration for the important Nebula Award and lost one crucial source of publicity. Nevertheless, *Macroscope* was a milestone in Anthony's career. In a *Luna Monthly* review, Samuel Mines declared, "*Macroscope* recaptures the tremendous glamour and excitement of science fiction, pounding the reader into submission with the sheer weight of its ideas which seem to pour out in an inexhaustible flood."

Beginning with the "Cluster" series, Anthony began writing "trilogies" that expanded past the usual three books. "Cluster" became a series of five, and the still-active "Magic of Xanth" has been supplemented by the companion book *Piers Anthony's Visual Guide to Xanth.* The "Apprentice Adept" series, with seven entries published between 1980 and 1990, was also originally planned as a trilogy. In the case of the "Xanth" books, Anthony attributed his decision to continue the series to reader response. "We did a third [Xanth novel], and said, 'Let's wrap it up as a trilogy and not do any more,'" Anthony remarked to *SFRS.* "Then the readers started demanding more, and more, and more, and finally both the publisher and the author were convinced. It's hard to say 'No' when the readers are begging for more."

Anthony branched out from science fiction into fantasy writing with *A Spell for Chameleon,* the first of the "Xanth" books, published in 1977. Although one early work, *Hasan,* was fantasy, it was his second fantasy novel, *Chameleon,* that established Anthony in the genre. The switch to fantasy came as a result of Anthony's much-publicized split with his first publisher, Ballantine Books. As the author related to *SFRS,* Ballantine "was sending me statements-of-account that were simply not true. I sent a letter demanding a correct statement and correct payments. Rather than do that, they blacklisted me for six years." Anthony moved to Avon Books; six years later, with a new administration at Ballantine, the author found himself invited back and wanted to give Ballantine another chance. His contract at Avon, however, prohibited him from writing science fiction for another publisher, so he decided to try fantasy. Luckily, Anthony knew and liked the fantasy editor at Ballantine, Lester del Rey; Ballantine's Del Rey imprint went on to publish the first nine "Xanth" novels as well as the early "Apprentice Adept" and "Incarnations of Immortality" entries. Anthony differentiates between his science-fiction and fantasy works in their content as well as their popularity. "For the challenge and sheer joy of getting in and tackling a difficult problem and surmounting it, science fiction is better," Anthony remarked to *SFRS.* "But if I need money, fantasy is better." He later added, "I talk about writing fantasy in the sense of doing it for the money, but I also enjoy it. If I didn't enjoy it, I wouldn't do it for the money."

The "Xanth" series is still continuing, over two decades after its first book. The "Xanth" stories are generally less complex and easier to read than Anthony's earlier works, appealing to younger readers as well as adults. *A Spell for Chameleon,* a 1978 Hugo Award nominee, introduced Bink, who tackles another recurring topic in Anthony's novels: maturity and control. The first "Xanth" installment chronicles Bink's growing-up; later volumes feature his son, Dor. The land of Xanth, which closely resembles the state of Florida, is a place where everyone and everything—even a rock or tree—has a magical talent, except Bink. *Chameleon* follows Bink on his quest to discover his talent or face exile to the boring, powerless land of Mundania. In the process, Bink gains not only knowledge of his talent but emotional maturity as well. Bink sets out on another adventure in *The Source of Magic,* assigned to discover the source of all magic in Xanth. In *Castle Roogna,* Bink's son Dor travels eight hundred years back in time to rescue his nurse's boyfriend. Throughout each book, Bink and Dor encounter innumerable illusions and feats of magic. "Piers Anthony apparently decided to invest his magical land of Xanth with every fantastical conception ever invented," a reviewer for *Isaac Asimov's Science Fiction Magazine* remarked. "It has quests, enchanted castles, riddles, unicorns, griffins, mermaids, giants (not to mention invisible giants), zombies, ghosts, elves, magicians, man-eating trees, enchantresses, and a host of inventions from Anthony's own fertile mind."

"The Magic of Xanth" continued with *Centaur Aisle, Ogre, Ogre,* and *Night Mare,* the next "trilogy" of "Xanth" books. The first of these finds Dor filling in for Xanth's King Trent while he and Queen Iris take a trip to Mundania, a good experience for Dor since he will one day become king. When the king and queen fail to return, Dor sets out on another adventure. Anthony once again explores the process of maturing, as Dor leads a search party through Xanth and into Mundania, and falls in love with Princess Irene. In *Ogre, Ogre,* the half-human, half-ogre Smash must protect the half-human, half-nymph Tandy. A stupid, insensitive creature at the beginning of the tale, Smash gradually acquires more human traits until he finally realizes that he is in love with Tandy.

Later entries in the series added to Anthony's portrait of the fantastic land of Xanth, with storylines including the rescue of the kingdom by a creature responsible for delivering bad dreams (*Night Mare*), the adventures of three-year-old Princess Ivy, lost and wandering in the forest with newfound friends Hugo and the Gap Dragon (*Dragon on a Pedestal*), the diminutive Golem's quest to rescue a lost baby dragon and prove himself worthy of attention (*Golem in the Gears*), Prince Dolph's protest against the Adult Conspiracy that keeps children ignorant of adult matters (*Heaven Cent*), Princess Ivy's trip to Mundania in search of Good Magician Humfrey (*Man from Mundania*), and the search of Gloha, Xanth's only half-harpy/half-goblin, for advice from Magician Trent to further a quest for her true love (*Harpy Thyme*). Richard Mathews applauded the "Xanth" series in *Fantasy Review,* asserting that it "ranks with the best of American and classic fantasy literature."

Anthony's use of puns and other language tricks is a hallmark of the "Xanth" novels. "In Xanth," Collings noted, Anthony "incorporates much of this interest in language in furthering the plot and in establishing the essence of his fantasy universe. In Xanth, language is literal, especially what in Mundania would be called metaphors." As a result, the critic continued, "breadfruit bears loaves of bread; shoetrees bear shoes in varying sizes and styles; nickelpedes are like centipedes, only five times larger and more vicious; and sunflowers are flowers whose blossoms are tiny suns blazing at the top of the stalk—a potent weapon if an enemy looks directly at them." In a *Voice of Youth Advocates* review of *Ogre, Ogre,* Peggy Murray found that Anthony's stories, "full of sophomoric humor and bad puns, have tremendous appeal with YA fantasy readers." In fact, some of the puns in *Harpy Thyme* were sent to Anthony by his readers.

In the *Sarasota Herald Tribune,* Cindy Cannon commented, "I can't think of a better place to meet up with centaurs, merfolk, zombies, ghosts, magically-talented humans and assorted half-breeds of every shape and kind than in one of Piers Anthony's many Xanth novels." She also noted that since the beginning of the series in 1977, the "original characters have seen several generations of their offspring star in their own tales (or tails, if they be centaurs)." And, she notes, "Where else will you hit an imp ass, eat pun-kin pies, see a river bank lien or meet a character named Ann Arky?" Amusingly, Anthony, who lives in Inverness, Florida, has made Xanth the same size and shape as his home state, and place names in Xanth are often wittily twisted versions of Floridian ones.

Cluster, the first novel in the series of the same name, was published in the same year as the first "Xanth" book. Intergalactic travel and adventure are again the subjects in the "Cluster" books, in which Anthony introduces the concept of Kirlian transfer, a type of out-of-body travel that requires much less energy than the outmoded "mattermission." The Kirlian transfer and other innovations are fundamental to the outcomes of the First and Second Wars of Energy, described in the first two volumes, and to the battle of an intergalactic force against the space amoeba in *Kirlian Quest.* "More than anything, the Cluster series is an exercise in enjoyment" for Anthony, Collings remarked. The author relishes the opportunity to create bizarre beings and situations unlike any the reader has experienced. The original "Cluster" trilogy led to *Tarot,* published in three volumes as *God of Tarot, Vision of Tarot,* and *Faith of Tarot.*

From the ending of *Kirlian Quest,* Anthony created *Tarot,* which he had intended for publication as one volume. Anthony emphasized in his interview with *SFRS* that *Tarot* is not a trilogy, but "a quarter-million-word novel." The novel was published not only in three parts, but in two different years. "It bothered me because I feel that this is the major novel of my career," Anthony remarked in the *SFRS* interview published in 1985. "Split into three parts and published in two years—it washed me out totally. I had no chance to make a run for any awards or anything like that. It was simply gone." He resents referrals to the book as a trilogy because they imply that each volume is a full novel, when in fact they are each one-third of a novel. Brother Paul, a character introduced in the "Cluster" trilogy and featured in *But What of Earth?,* is the central figure in *Tarot,* in which Anthony attempts to develop a definition of God. Collings acknowledged that the "brutality, horror, and disgust" present in the book were not unlike those of many other Anthony novels, but combined with religious references proved controversial and offensive to many readers. *Tarot* "is certainly not for the squeamish, nor is it altogether for those who enjoyed the first installment of Tarot civilization in the Cluster novels. Anthony himself admits this," Collings noted.

Anthony returns to pure fantasy in the "Incarnations of Immortality" series, which begins with *On a Pale Horse* and is set in "a world very much like ours, except that magic has been systematized and is as influential as science," a *Publishers Weekly* reviewer commented. The abstract concepts of Time, War, Nature, Fate, and Death are all real people—the Incarnations—and all are involved in the battle of Satan against God. In *Bearing an Hourglass,* a grief-stricken man agrees to take on the role of Chronos, the Incarnation of Time, and soon finds himself locked in a battle with Satan. *Booklist* reviewer Roland Green noted the religious and ethical content of the series that "even people who may disagree with [Anthony's] ideas will recognize as intelligently rendered." Subsequent volumes feature the Incarnations of Fate (*With a Tangled Skein*), War (*Wielding a Red Sword*), Nature (*Being a Green Mother*), Evil (*For Love of Evil*), and finally, Good (*And Eternity*). "This grand finale showcases Anthony's multiple strengths" including his humor, characterizations, and themes, a *Library Journal* reviewer declared.

Virtual Mode is a novel "to which teens relate well," Anthony remarked to *Authors and Artists for Young Adults* (*AAYA*). Published in 1991, *Virtual Mode* introduced the "Mode" series, in which characters traverse the universe through the use of "skew paths" anchored by other people. As the anchors change, the paths and destinies of the travelers are affected and new stories are presented. In *Virtual Mode,* Darius of Hlahtar ventures to Earth to bring the girl he loves, the suicidal Colene, back to his universe. Together Darius and Colene discover that they must build a skew path to complete the journey. *Publishers Weekly* writer Sybil Steinberg described Colene as "a clearly defined character, virtues, flaws and all" who is "brought fully to life in this skillful, enjoyable book."

Similarly, YA readers will enjoy *MerCycle,* Anthony's story about five people recruited to pedal bicycles under the waters of the Gulf of Mexico on a secret mission to save the Earth from collision with a meteor. The novel was originally written in 1971 but then shelved after it was unable to find a publisher. After establishing his reputation as a best-selling author, Anthony returned to the manuscript, revised it extensively, and added it to his oeuvre. The story deals heavily with themes of human nature and survival: the bicyclists experience being "out of phase" and "phased in" to other Earth life, are kept unaware of their mission, and meet up with Chinese mermaids. "The result," wrote a critic in *New York Times Book Review,* "is an engaging tall tale, spun out of the most unpromising raw material."

According to *AAYA*, Anthony noted that, like *Virtual Mode, Tatham Mound* is another of his works most likely to appeal to young adults. The story of fifteen-year-old Throat Shot, a sixteenth-century Florida Indian, *Tatham Mound* is based on an actual Indian burial mound discovered in North Florida and features historically accurate reconstructions of Spanish explorer Hernando de Soto's march across Florida and his battles with the Indian tribes of the area. A *Library Journal* reviewer described *Tatham Mound* as a "heartfelt tribute to a lost culture" and a "labor of both love and talent."

Also based on history, but spanning eight million years, are the works in the "Geodyssey" series—*Isle of Woman* and *Shame of Man. Isle of Woman* is comprised of a series of vignettes that center on the lives of two prehistoric families who are reborn into succeeding centuries up to twenty-first century America. According to Jackie Cassada in a *Library Journal* review, *Isle of Woman* is Anthony's "most ambitious project to date." *Shame of Man* explores evolution one generation at a time, beginning with families of gorillas and chimpanzees on through the Homo Sapiens of 2050 A.D. Called "speculative fiction" by *Voice of Youth Advocates* reviewer Kim Carter, *Shame of Man* encompasses more than twenty-five years of Anthony's research in "history, archaeology, anthropology, and human nature," as well as showcasing some of the author's own theories on these subjects.

In *How Precious Was That While,* a sequel to his earlier autobiography, *Bio of an Ogre,* Anthony noted that the response of his readers means far more to him than any comments made by literary critics. He is devoted to his many readers, and often spends two days a week answering their letters.

Virtual Mode, Tatham Mound, and *Shame of Man* exemplify Anthony's desire to produce works of lasting value along with those written simply for entertainment. While he wants readers to enjoy his work, the author hopes also to provoke contemplation of the serious issues he presents. "I'd like to think I'm on Earth for some purpose other than just to feed my face," Anthony remarked to *SFRS*. "I want to do something and try to leave the universe a better place than it was when I came into it." He commented in the *St. Petersburg Times,* "Today, I am turning back to serious writing with direct comment on sexual abuse in *Firefly* and on history in novels like *Tatham Mound.*"

Biographical and Critical Sources

BOOKS

Authors and Artists for Young Adults, Volume 11, Gale (Detroit, MI), 1993, pp. 9-19.
Collings, Michael R., *Piers Anthony,* Starmont House, 1983.
Contemporary Literary Criticism, Volume 35, Gale (Detroit, MI), 1985, pp. 34-41.
Lane, Daryl, William Vernon, and David Carson, *The Sound of Wonder: Interviews from "The Science Fiction Radio Show,"* Volume 2, Oryx, 1985.
Something about the Author Autobiography Series, Volume 22, Gale (Detroit, MI), 1996.

PERIODICALS

Analog, January, 1989, p. 182; August, 1992, pp. 165-166.
Booklist, July, 1984, p. 1497; October 15, 1999, p. 424; April 15, 2000, p. 1527; October 15, 2000, p. 426; March 1, 2001, p. 1232.
Books and Bookmen, April, 1970, Leo Harris, pp. 26-27.

Fantasy and Science Fiction, August, 1986, pp. 37-40.
Fantasy Review, March, 1984, Richard Mathews, pp. 24-25.
Horn Book, October 6, 1989, p. 84.
Isaac Asimov's Science Fiction Magazine, September, 1979, p. 18.
Kirkus Reviews, August 15, 1993, p. 1034.
Kliatt, November, 1992, p. 13.
Library Journal, December, 1989, p. 176; August, 1991, p. 150; September 15, 1993, p. 108; October 15, 1998, p. 104; January, 1999, p. 166; October 15, 1999, p. 111; May 15, 2000, p. 129; October 15, 2000, p. 108; April 15, 2001, p. 137.
Luna Monthly, September, 1970, Samuel Mines, p. 22.
New York Times Book Review, April 20, 1986, p. 27; September 13, 1992, p. 28.
Publishers Weekly, June 5, 1967, p. 180; July 26, 1976, p. 78; September 2, 1983, p. 72; July 25, 1986, p. 174; August 29, 1986, p. 388; May 29, 1987, p. 73; February 10, 1989, p. 58; August 11, 1989, p. 444; August 25, 1989, p. 58; April 20, 1990, p. 61; May 11, 1990, p. 251; August 10, 1990, p. 431; December 21, 1990, p. 57; January 4, 1991, p. 61; October 18, 1991, p. 55; July 20, 1992, p. 237; November 29, 1993, pp. 57-58; September 5, 1994, p. 96; September 21, 1998, p. 79; December 14, 1998, p. 61; April 26, 1999, p. 61; September 27, 1999, p. 78; March 6, 2000, p. 88; May 1, 2000, p. 55; October 2, 2000, p. 64; March 5, 2001, p. 66; July 23, 2001, p. 59.
Sarasota Herald Tribune, November 26, 2000, p. E4; July 23, 2001, p. 59.
Science Fiction, November, 1977, Cliff Biggers, p. 60.
St. Petersburg Times, July 13, 2001, p. P5.
Voice of Youth Advocates, April, 1983, p. 44; December, 1992, p. 290; August, 1994, p. 152; February, 1995, p. 343.
Writer, August, 1989, pp. 11-13, 35.
Writer's Digest, January, 1991, p. 32.

OTHER

Piers Anthony's Web site, http://www.hipiers.com/ (August 20, 2001).*

* * *

Autobiography Feature

Piers Anthony

My American grandfather was known as the Mushroom King; he had started growing edible mushrooms in his cellar, and built it into a business that made him a millionaire. He didn't have much formal education, but was a savvy businessman; two weeks before the great stock market crash of 1929 he sold the business. I believe that about half of the mushrooms produced in the United States still come from the region around West Chester, Pennsylvania, where he started it, though now it is split between a number of companies. He married, and his wife died of cancer; he remarried, and she also died. He married a third time, Caroline, and she survived him, living to the age of ninety-nine.

My father, Alfred, was the opposite of rich; he was intellectual. His mother, my grandfather's first wife, was in the hospital, and he visited her there. She asked him to go out and read the words at the entry to her ward, and he did. They were in Latin, and he didn't understand them, but he described them to her as well as he could. She thanked him. Next day she was dead. She seemed to have given up the struggle to live. He always felt guilty, because the words he had conveyed to her identified the ward: it was for incurables. He had given his mother the news that destroyed her hope. He went to England to continue his education, where they took it more seriously than they did

in America. He was to graduate from Oxford University, but that isn't my immediate concern. He met a British girl, Joyce, and really liked her. But when summer passed, and a new semester started, she wasn't there. She had caught a fever, maybe typhoid fever, maybe from polluted water when she went camping, and died. He was never to get over that. Again he had been cursed by death. Indeed, I know of only one person who ponders death as much as I do: my father. Later he met another British girl, Norma, who graduated from Oxford with top honors, and she was the one he married. He sent my grandfather a newspaper clipping reporting the marriage: that was the extent of his announcement. Later they both went on to earn Ph.D.'s. The relationship didn't work out, but in the course of their marriage my sister and I were born. I arrived in AwGhost 1934, and Teresa in OctOgre 1935. Bear with me on the oddly spelled months; I was later to make my fortune in funny fantasy, and I renamed the months accordingly. There are oddities about me that I will try to explain here; I'm not normal, and I relate well to other abnormals. For now it is enough to know that everyone in my immediate family was academically gifted except me. I was the dunce who made up for it all, pulling the average down.

I think we children were something of an afterthought, because our parents did not seem to be unduly interested in

Piers Anthony, 1995

us. Instead they went to Spain to do relief work with the British Friends Service Committee, feeding starving children. They were members of the Religious Society of Friends, more popularly known as Quakers, and the Quakers are known for silent meetings for worship, good business practice, integrity, and good works. This was among the latter. In 1936 the Spanish civil war started, a kind of prelude to World War II, wherein Spain's own military fought to take over the country from the civilians. In three years it was successful, but it was hell on the children. So my parents were helping to keep those devastated children alive, by importing food and milk and feeding them on a regular basis. It was worthy work, and I don't fault it, but there was a personal cost.

It was not safe for my sister and me during the Spanish war, so we remained in England, cared for by our British grandparents and a nanny. I loved that nanny, whom I

thought of as my mother. I remember when she took us to the park in London, and there was a bird hopping on the ground. We feared it was injured, so we told the keeper. He picked up the bird and stretched out its wings, to ascertain whether they were broken. He concluded that the bird was all right, and set it down again. I was amazed; it seemed that there was no bird there, just folded wings. I wondered whether it would be possible to make another bird by folding paper cleverly enough. Would it come alive?

I also remember going to the hospital at age four. For years I said I went there to be born, until my mother corrected me: I had been born earlier. She was in a position to know, though she did not acquaint me with the details. So this visit was actually for a tonsillectomy, an operation thought necessary at the time for all children.

In 1939 we joined our parents in Spain, for the war there was then over. This was my first real crisis of identity, because my parents seemed like acquaintances rather than close kin. The nanny was the one I really knew, but she wasn't going. I think of it in retrospect as root pruning: it may be necessary to transplant the young tree, and the tree looks complete, but it isn't. It is hurting where it doesn't show. I had abruptly lost what I valued most, and it was the beginning of a downward spiral that was to leave me depressive even decades later. I never saw the nanny again. I understand she was a Scottish girl, perhaps one of two similar sisters, very good with children. Surely so, for I remember no evil of her; I remember only happiness of a kind I was never to achieve again.

Spain was interesting in new ways. My sister had a nice little Spanish dress. I remember waking alone in my bedroom in Barcelona and seeing moving patterns on the wall. It was the morning sunlight outlining a neighboring palm tree, casting shadows through my window. To me it was like a show; as the wind blew the fronds, the shadows moved back and forth, sometimes almost all the way off the wall. I loved to watch it. Later I got to see a real movie: a cartoon of the three little pigs and the big bad wolf. Absolutely fascinating! Also my first experience with an elevator. Here was this little room we went into, and suddenly it moved, and when the door opened again, everything outside had changed. It was like magic, and for years thereafter I imagined magical rooms that could take me anywhere I wanted to go.

And my first ice cream cone. The funny thing was, the ice cream was square, not round. I think that supplies must have been limited, so that they lacked the tubs and scoops, and had to use packaged ice cream. The man crammed it into a cone, and I ate it and loved it. By the time I reached the bottom of the cone, the ice cream there was melting. But it was a great experience. And we got a pair of sandals made from string; the soles were this mass of coiled string, actually hemp. I don't think they lasted long, because the string tended to unravel, but they were nice.

There was also the old man who told me stories and played a trick on me: he gave me a candy, and ate one himself, then took back the wrappers and balled them and wrapped them in another wrapper so cunningly that it looked just like a real candy. Then my sister arrived, and he gave it to her. I could hardly contain myself, waiting to see her dismay as it turned out to be empty. But she unwrapped one, two, three wrappers—and there was a candy inside. The joke had been on me.

At one point we went to a hotel in a nearby town, Tossa, about forty miles up the Mediterranean coast from Barcelona, on top of a steep hill; we thought no car could get up that hill, but a man in a motorcycle zoomed right up it, amazing us. I remember swimming in the warm Mediterranean sea. Actually I couldn't swim; I was floating on an inflated raft. It banged into another, and I fell off, sinking under the salty water. I was quickly rescued—it was only about two feet deep—but it was a memorable experience. I remember the big cigar-shaped balloons that moved silently over the beach: military blimps, I think.

Another time I was walking with my family when I realized that I had somehow gotten lost; I was with strangers. I didn't know what to do, so I just kept going. They seemed to accept me; the woman even gave me roasted peanuts. Later my mother came to recover me. It must have been a baby-sitting device; my mother had

slipped away unseen so that I wouldn't make a fuss. But that had left me without moorings, uncertain of my fate. I had discovered that my mother could disappear without warning. I never did that to my own children.

Another time my father was playing with us, showing us magic blocks. He was really better at games and stories than my mother was. He put a coin on one, and covered it with a block-shaped shell, then removed the shell—and the coin was gone. Where could it be? We looked all over. It occurred to me that it might be hidden under the block, so I picked it up—and another shell came off, with the coin under it. My father departed in a huff; I had spoiled the trick. I really hadn't meant to.

And I remember Easter: I was given a huge wooden egg. It opened, and inside was a model of a sailing ship and a number of chocolates. Thereafter I loved Easter, though I think none since has been as great. But I also remember my sister and I standing in the garden with tape stuck across our mouths, evidently our punishment for talking out of turn. I don't approve of that sort of punishment, and don't know whether our parents knew of it. Another time we were with a woman doing laundry in the cellar, which was a converted jail cell, and a young man came and locked the gate, shutting us in. The woman screeched at him so violently that he had to return to let us out. He was Jorge, pronounced "Hor-Hee," and was always fun.

It was in Spain that my sister Teresa and I suffered a shock that was to mark us in separate ways for life. I will tell it first as I saw it. I was in a room, alone, when I heard my sister protesting something. So I followed the sound, going to see what was the matter. I saw her on a counter of some sort, with a group of adults clustered around her. She was trying to get away, but couldn't. Then her screams became piercing; they were torturing her. I saw her little feet pounding the counter as she cried to run away, but could not. They were doing something to her face; I think I saw a splash of water. Then, when they had hurt her enough, they let her go, and turned to see me standing there. "He saw!" one said. At that point my terrible memory fades out. It was to remain for fifty years as a disconnected scene I couldn't explain, until at last it clicked into place, like a piece of a puzzle: that was when my sister had her tonsillectomy. The full story I had learned before, but never connected to my horrible vision. When it was time for her operation, my mother inquired of the local medical facilities, and was told they had no safe anesthetic. The war had devastated Spain, and many supplies were low or gone. So they would have to do it without any pain killer. "Not on *my* child!" my mother said. So they agreed: they would find something. She brought the child in to the clinic, telling me to stay in the waiting room, and took Teresa on in. Whereupon the nurses snatched the child away from her, took her to the counter, propped her mouth open, and cut out her tonsils while she screamed. That was the way it was done in Spain at the time.

I don't think my mother knew that I had seen it happen. I never spoke of it. It was my private horror. I knew then that doctors existed to make children hurt. That was confirmed when I was ill in Spain; a doctor came, checked me over, then asked for a spoon. He turned it over and poked it deep into my mouth until I vomited on the bed. Satisfied, he departed; he had made me hurt enough. Later experiences with horrible needles added to it; I remember one needle being stuck slanting under the skin, and a fluid injected so that the skin swelled up in an excruciating blister while I was held down, screaming. Vaccination, they called it. By whatever name, its point was obvious; no doctor could let a child go without hurting it. My parents, strangely, never protested.

Our departure from Spain was another ugly matter. My father liked Spain, and wanted to remain there. I have mixed feelings about that; I liked Spain too, but I am not at all sure I would have had a worthwhile life there. But fate took the decision out of our hands. As I understand it, Adolf Hitler of Nazi Germany was trying to get Generalissimo Franco of Spain to join the Axis, and a meeting between them was scheduled. Security was tight. And there was my father, with a lot of money, near the border. He was there to buy food to feed a trainful of Jews being deported from Germany. So they "disappeared" him: they arrested him and dumped him in prison, uncharged. For three days my mother desperately tried to find out what had happened to him. The Spanish authorities denied knowing anything about it. Meanwhile he was confined with other men in a dungeon cell, whose sanitary facility was a trench. There were female prisoners too, in another cell, only theirs had no trench; periodically they were herded to the male cell to do their business, while the men stood around and watched, seeing whatever they could see. One prisoner was allowed a visitor, who brought a hot drink to him in a thermos; Alfred got them to put a postcard of his into the empty thermos, to be taken out and mailed. My mother received the card, and so learned of what had happened. Armed with that, and with the forceful assistance of a wealthy Quaker of influence who could have cost Spain a lot of needed monetary assistance, she was able to get them to admit that they did after all have a prisoner of that name. But dictatorships don't admit mistakes, so they agreed to let him go only on condition that he depart the country. The relief mission of that area was shut down, and thereafter the children had to survive as well as they could without that food. I like to think that some people are alive today because of what my parents did in Spain. I was later to write a novel, *Volk,* relating to Spain and Germany and World War II, but have not as yet found a publisher for it, because it is controversial.

So it was that we left Spain. I remember traveling from Barcelona to Madrid, the capital city, where we toured the big earthworks around the city: its former defenses. Then we went on to Lisbon, Portugal, to catch the ship to America. I remember stopping high in a mountain pass to go touch the spongy bark of a cork tree, and driving way up on a high hill where there was a kind of amusement park. There were many small stands with toy trains. My mother put in a coin, and the little train buzzed around and around its little mountain on its little tracks. Finally it disappeared into a tunnel and didn't come out: the show was over. In Lisbon we took a taxi, and the cabby unfolded a child seat from the floor or somewhere, a novelty. We also got to ride in paddleboats; foot pedals made the paddles go around, and the boats moved forward. So it was fun. But not without its cautions. I remember seeing my mother naked for the first and only time, there, and being amazed to see that she had hair on her crotch. It had never occurred to me

that adults were different from children. But what appalled my mother was the fact that the hotel room was overrun with roaches.

Even our voyage on the ship to America was unusual. I did not know it at the time, but the former King Edward VIII of England was on that ship with us. He had gotten interested in an American divorcée, and had a difficult choice: the crown or the woman. Romance had won, and he gave up his throne and married her. They happened to be in Portugal at this time. The Nazis thought he was sympathetic to their cause, and hoped to abduct him and talk him into supporting them politically. But they fouled up, and didn't get him, and he boarded the ship, going to Bermuda. That was the *Excalibur,* the same ship and the same voyage we were on, the last trip out before the war shut off such travel. No, I don't believe I ever saw the erstwhile king, but I do remember seeing his car unloaded in Bermuda: it dangled from a crane line dropped into the hold, and was swung out onto the dock. I had my sixth birthday on the ship, where I had a cake made of sawdust because they lacked provisions for a real one; they brought it to us with the candles burning, and then we couldn't eat it. Later my own children were to be jealous: *they* never got a cake made of sawdust. I was given a harmonica, and I loved it, and played it endlessly as I walked around the deck. I still wonder whether the former king of England was gritting his teeth somewhere, wishing that kid would cut out the noise. And I had my first bout with seasickness; I remember my father holding me up so I could vomit over the rail, seeing it fall down into the distant water. There was also a swimming pool set up on the deck; the canvas had a leak in one corner, and I got to play in that jet of water. I think my elder daughter inherited that delight; she was hyperactive, but could play endlessly in flowing water.

The trip took ten days, and we made it safely to New York. I think I remember seeing the Statue of Liberty, without understanding its significance. I was an immigrant, a subject of the Queen; that statue welcomed folk like me. We docked, and my American grandparents—yea, the Mushroom King, and his third wife, Caroline—met us and drove us to Pennsylvania, the Quaker State. My mother was uncertain of her reception by my father's folks, for she was not even American, and might be considered an intruder, but Caroline, similarly new to the family, welcomed her, and that started a friendship that was to last fifty years, until they died just a month apart.

My memories of that time are scattered, but some do stand out. My grandfather Edward's house was at the end of a street in West Chester, Pencil Vania (well, I warned you about my funny fantasy), with a fish pond behind and a rolling meadow leading down to the highway and a golf course beyond it. It was like a slice of heaven. The house was large, and even had a maid's quarters with a separate little winding stairway for her. Fascinating! Grandfather was hard of hearing, so at meals had a hearing aid that looked like a toaster; my father joked about putting bread in it. Grandfather's wife was known as Aunt Caroline, carried across from the way she was known in her own family. Later I liked to refer to her as my wife's step-grandmother-in-law. She was a great person, competent and diplomatic and very much a Quaker, speaking with "thee" in the manner of the elder generation. So, as I became acquainted with my American relatives, I liked them.

We spent a while at Grandfather's cabin in Seaside Park, New Jersey (no parody for that state; I already have a mental picture of a freshly purchased garment). That was on the Atlantic beach, and was sheer delight. There was a boardwalk that extended endlessly north and south. There was the white sand and the constant washing sea. There was a telescope on the front porch that seemed magical. Once I saw a tiny dot on the horizon, but when the telescope focused in it, it became a yacht with girls running around its decks and jumping into the water. I never had a city apartment, but can appreciate the lure of a high rise telescope; who knows what sights one might see. There was an amusement park, with little machines that you looked into, and turned a crank on the side, and they flipped the pages of picture books, making them become animated cartoons. I loved that. Today's more sophisticated animation is far superior, yet I loved those magic moving pictures.

Another time I was ill, and had to be quarantined. Was it German measles? I don't know. I was at a house somewhere else, and only my mother was there with me. I spent the long hours drawing things on a sketch pad. I remember the bread she brought: huge slices that were incredibly delicious with butter. So this illness was a pleasant experience.

We moved to a place called Pendle Hill. It was a kind of Quaker school for adult studies. We had a little apartment squeezed in the rear of one of the buildings. I was given a scooter, and I loved it; I scooted constantly. Years later I learned the penalty: my right leg became an inch longer than the left leg, because I had always pushed with it. That wasn't discovered until a chiropractor looked at me; at a glance he saw my uneven stance, and put me on two scales, one foot to each. I weighed 100 pounds, divided 60-40. I had to wear a corrective shoe to force my stance to change, enabling my legs to grow back to the same length.

It wasn't all fun. A neighbor boy invited me over, but he wasn't necessarily as friendly as he seemed. He had a big dog, which he would encourage a stranger to pet; after a moment the dog would leap up, growling, scaring the child, and the boy would laugh. Another time some of his other friends were there, so he told me to go home. Realizing that I was being dissed, I balked. When he threatened to push me, I threatened to kick him. He stepped in and punched me in the face. Completely defeated, in tears, I fled. I didn't tell, but I remembered. Today when someone tries to push me around, I am apt to find a way to make him regret it. I don't like bullies. When my second daughter was treated exactly the same way, I went immediately to the scene and got it straightened out. Another time, when three boys beat up my two girls, I went and virtually challenged the eldest boy's father; had he not departed quickly, I might have tried to do to him what his boy had done to my girls, and take him down and grind his face in the dirt. As it was, I merely called the police and sent them to the errant household. At any rate, I did make my point; his boy never touched my girls again. When my elder daughter's college

The family at Treasure Island Beach, 1970-71

treated her contemptuously, I wrote a sharp letter to the college president, to similar effect; their unfair action was instantly reversed. I am not small any more, and I saw to it that my children did not suffer as I had. I don't claim to be always nice, but there's always justice in my cases, and I have taken down many bullies, in my fashion, though the arena is no longer physical. Few have cared to tangle with me a second time.

I started school. Somehow what I did was never satisfactory to the teacher. She showed me another student's paper, which was much neater than mine, but I couldn't do it the way the teacher wanted. In fact it took me three years and five schools to make it through first grade, because I couldn't learn to read and write. My sister, in contrast, had no trouble at all. She had the good fortune to catch tuberculosis and spent six months in bed, so our mother taught her to read. She entered first grade with a sixth-grade reading skill. People would come up to me and say "Aren't you thrilled to have a smart sister like her?" Somehow I didn't see it that way; maybe I was too dull to appreciate such a blessing. In my day things like learning disabilities or dyslexia didn't exist, just stupid or careless children. It wasn't until I saw the trouble my daughter had in school that I realized what must have been my problem. Actually it was more complicated than that, and I may still not understand the whole of it, slow learner that I am. Theoretically intelligence doesn't change through life, but tests showed me to be subnormal early, and normal later, and superior later yet, and my success in school and life varied accordingly. So the kid who couldn't read later became an English teacher, and a highly successful writer. How could I have been so dull before, and so smart after, if IQ is fixed?

Well, it's possible. First, I may indeed have had a problem in seeing and learning writing. Eyes do not mature immediately, and some studies have shown that many children suffer measurable ocular damage from the close work demanded in school. That's one reason that so many adults, myself included, need glasses for reading. We protected our dyslexic daughter by having her wear special glasses in first grade, so that her eyes would not be damaged, and as an adult she didn't need glasses. But most children are not that fortunate. I may also have had something like dyslexia, and it took me time to learn to compensate. It was as if I had an analog mind in a digital world. When I did learn to handle it, I started forging ahead, and in adult life few have ever thought me stupid, and some of those who have, have been surprised when they learned more of me. In fact I think it may be that only those who are not as smart as I am ever think me to be dull. I have an analogy I like: suppose a sports car races with a locomotive. At the starting line, the car races ahead. If the finish line is a hundred yards away, there's no contest. But if the finish line is three thousand miles away, the locomotive will win, because once it gets up steam it proceeds at a very high rate of speed without pausing. So I was a loser as a child, but not as an adult; my locomotive had finally gotten up speed, and it left most others behind. There is one more thing: I was always slow. I was slow to learn to walk, and to speak. I am still slow to catch on to new things. I was slow to grow, and slow to reach maturity. I am still slow to eat, and still read slowly. That is not a euphemism for stupid; I just take my time, but I get there in

the end. Like the locomotive. Give me a timed test and I will not be a high scorer, but I can compete on an open-ended basis. School is timed, but life is an open-ended experience.

So school was difficult for me. It didn't help having to learn a new school, with its different grounds, teachers, students, and rules, every time I started to catch on to the way of one. One teacher, instead of encouraging me, chastised me for mispronouncing my a's: "There's an *a* in that word! Grass, not grawss." She was trying to correct my English accent. No wonder I had a problem. The students weren't any better. In winter I had a fast little sled, a Flexible Flyer, and that was fun. But at one of the schools the old students threw all the sleds of the new students into the river. They were there in plain view in the water, but the teachers ignored it. Teachers just didn't seem to have much awareness of justice. Or of education. That was over fifty years ago, but I'm not sure it has changed much.

One of the schools was in New York state, with beautiful grounds. It was a boarding school. I was later to see some of the bright caring reports it sent back to my family. They were fantasy; the reality was something else. My main early entertainment was playing in the adjacent garbage dump, because the good facilities were off-bounds to us. As a first grader, I was the lowest of the low. Older students took me into a room and told me to take off my clothes. I did so, but gradually became suspicious; to be slow is not to be entirely out of it. So I dressed again and managed to break away, escaping to my own dorm. That night we were watching a movie, and suddenly someone was wading into me, hitting me, pummeling me, beating me up. The teachers paid no attention. I fled out of the building, into the surrounding forest, escaping the beating. I hid behind a tree, wary of pursuit. Indeed it seemed incipient, because as I watched the building, I heard frequent yelling and pounding, as of a gang about to break down the door and charge out. I was terrified. It continued for a long time, and finally I realized that they weren't actually coming out. So I sneaked around to the other side, and up the stairs, and into bed, and they never spied me. Why should they? I hadn't even been missed. Later I realized that what I had seen was the outside of the indoor basketball court; the pounding had been the ball and people hitting the wall as they played. If only I had realized that earlier, I would have been spared an evening of terror. So what of the boy who was beating on me? It took me years to put that together: I think he was the one who had been guarding the door during my "initiation"; I had pushed by him and escaped, and that made him mad. Bullies don't like to let anyone escape. So next time he saw me he waded into me. A first grader couldn't stand up to a second or third grader. I lived in fear of him, until finally other students decided that enough was enough. They brought us together and had us shake hands, declaring peace. "But what if he goes after me again?" I asked. "Then *we'll* beat *him* up," they said. That did indeed took care of it; they weren't bluffing. Justice had come, no thanks to the teachers or school administration.

Yet such things seldom happen of their own accord, and I suspect there was more to it. An older boy befriended me. His name was Craig Work, and he was the child of a

The author with wife Carol, daughters Cheryl and Penny, and Canute, "visiting Aunt Caroline's house at Bayside Drive, winter 1970-71"

black father and white mother, and his IQ had been tested at 180. I realize, in considerable retrospect, that he must have had thorough experience in the rough and tumble of life among children. I didn't know of racism then, and didn't care that his skin was brown, but surely there were others who did. He was a great friend, and once he started associating with me, things started turning better. I think he had something to do with it. His mother later reported something he had said to her: "Mom, I'm a peaceful kind of guy, and I don't like to fight. But they *make* you fight." Yes indeed. Craig helped teach me how to fight, and that in itself made a difference. I was no longer such an easy target. In fact it got so that I never lost unless my opponent was substantially larger than I. I wasn't weak, just small. So later, when others tried me out, and found me tougher than expected, they became friends instead of enemies. But at the beginning, at boarding school, I'm sure the considerable shadow of Craig protected me more than somewhat. And of course there were always boys who *were* substantially larger, so I wasn't yet out of the wilderness.

My experience with Craig was to affect my social attitude. No one ever had to tell me that racism wasn't nice; I knew it from the time I first learned of it. My best friend really *had* been black. When I see racism, I have a kind of mental picture of filth and grubs exposed under a rock. I have trouble understanding how such folk can stand their

own company. I don't believe in Hell, but if by some mischance it exists, I think it must be stocked with racists.

But school was only one of the growing problems of my life. I had been toilet trained in England and Spain, but in America I started wetting the bed at night. This continued for several years. I was checked into a hospital, and that was another awful experience: periodically a group of adults would enter my room, and that was always mischief. Sometimes they wanted to poke a finger into my various orifices, including the rectum—the entire medical establishment seemed to be fascinated with that orifice, so that they even had pretty nurses take my temperature that way. Sometimes they brought deadly needles, inflicting pain on me in the manner that doctors always did to children. Once I woke to hear a cluster of nurses just outside my door, whispering avidly. "Just take it and *shove it in!*" one was saying. I was terrified; what were they going to do to me? Was it my turn to be tortured the way my sister had been in Spain? Surely it must be a knife they would use. But nobody said a word to me. I realized that they were planning to do it by surprise; without warning would come that sudden thrust, while I screamed helplessly. All in all, I was never able to truly relax, even in sleep. Since I wet my bed only when soundly asleep, I didn't do it in that hospital. In the end they reported to my parents that there was nothing organically wrong with me; no physical cause for my bed-wetting. They were right, in their fashion, but what they didn't know could fill a volume. I learned later that it was supposed to have been a briefer visit, for observation only, but that there had been a delay in the insurance payment, so they had held me as it were at ransom for several extra days, until they got their payment. I had suffered all that extra time because of a bureaucratic snarl. So what was it with the nurses? I think now that they had merely been exchanging stories in the hall, and it was sheer coincidence that my room was the closest one, so that I could overhear. No surgery had been scheduled for me; that fear had been groundless. If only I had known!

So what was the matter with me? My bed-wetting did not abate. Then I began to suffer twitches. Every few seconds I would fling my head around, or give a hard shake to both my hands. Why did I do it? It was like a cough: you can hold it back only so long before it has to come out. Naturally these actions brought further ridicule down on my head. It was evident that I was a pretty fouled-up child. Oh, I would have loved to he normal, but I wasn't. Yet that, too, was not the major thing.

It started innocently enough, while I was still in that long first grade. This was in New Hampshire, I think. We went to an amusement park that was all inside a big building, another novelty to me. All kinds of things were going on there. There was a huge hollow man-statue with an entrance at the base and exit at the top; I think there was a spiral stairway inside. People were constantly going through it. Every so often the statue would go HO HO HO and wiggle just a little, and the folk inside it would scream. I think that from inside it seemed that the whole thing was falling. My father went on it while we watched, and reported on what he experienced. At one point, beyond the statue, was a room with a table full of nice watches, and a sign saying TAKE ONE. But when he tried to, he found that it was fastened to the table, and electrified; he got a shock. One has to be wary, in a fun house. Later fun houses had jets of air that blew up girls' dresses so that their underwear showed; somehow the girls didn't find that as amusing as the boys did. Then my father took me on a ride through the horror house. This was weird and exciting. Ghostly creatures appeared and launched at the cart, scaring me. Then suddenly a stone wall appeared before us, and we were headed right for it, about to crash—and the cart dropped an inch or so to a lower track, feeling just like a crash. We swung on around the wall, safe after all, and in due course emerged from the darkness. It had been a phenomenal thrill.

But that night I had a terrible dream. It consisted of just four pictures, or brief scenes. In the first, my sister and I were walking along a city street with our mother. That was all; nothing remarkable. In the second, she stopped at a standing structure, like a telephone booth. She entered it, but then the door wouldn't open, and she was caught inside. The third picture was a forest glade, with an altar, and a woman was lying on it. I knew it was my mother. At the edge of the glade stood a man, and beside him was a lion. The fourth scene was just the man, lifting the lion up in his arms, as if hefting it for weight. That was all—but it so terrified me that I woke screaming. My mother was soon there to comfort me, but it was not possible to expunge the awfulness. I don't normally believe in dream interpretation; I think that most of it is fantasy, and that even the experts know almost nothing of the real nature of dreams. Right: I alone know their true nature, and I'll cover that in a moment. But this particular dream, simple as it seems, had formidable meaning, and is the very essence of terror. Here is the interpretation: the first picture is just the introduction, and it was taken from experience. The setting was Spain, and my sister and I did walk along the street with our mother. The second picture refers to the time she made a phone call from a booth, and the door stuck; she did get out, but for a moment I was worried. This connected to something that was preying on my mind, even then: she had said that she might have to have an operation. Little was explained to the children, leaving much to the imagination. Just as when she spoke of seeing a book that had been made into a movie, and I thought that meant that they projected the pages of the book onto the screen for everyone to read, I thought that the operation meant that they would stretch her out on a table and cut into her body with knives. It was horrible to contemplate. The memory of the phone booth was twined with the thought of that operation, as if first they had to catch her so they could do it to her. So, later, when that memory returned in the dream scene, the horror was building, for this time she was indeed caught. The third scene was crafted in part from an experience I had had when walking in the country: I had come across an animal skull. It was the vast, bleached, hollow-eyed bone of a cow, and I understood that death had come to this creature, and this was all that was left of it. That setting, between forest and field, was in my dream, and so it was a place of death. My mother was laid out there for the knife. Her absence from the fourth scene was

The author circa 1980

significant: she must have been eaten by the lion, and now the man, who might have been the anonymous surgeon or perhaps was really my father, was weighing the lion to see how much it had gained. My mother was horribly dead.

So this dream was crafted from several assorted memories, assembled into a horrible whole. But why did it occur? The immediate trigger was the emotion of the horror house ride; it had shaken loose deeper fears. But those fears had been building before then, and they were related to my bed-wetting and compulsive twitches. This is the root of the larger story. For our family was coming apart. My parents were in the process of separating, though they themselves may not have realized it at that point. The marriage had not been ideal from the start; they were two intelligent, liberal, socially conscious Quakers, but their subtle differences doomed their union. As I see it, he was a creature of the country, while she was a creature of the city. He liked the self-sufficiency of the farm and forest; she preferred the civilization of the city. He could work quietly logging or gardening alone; she longed for the thickly clustered conveniences of the populated metropolis. He liked being largely free of the works of mankind; she couldn't stand a house without hot water or internal sanitary facilities. Note how the dream sequences with the woman are in the city, and with the man are in the country. Their ideal life styles were poles apart. There was of course more to it than that, but that was enough; he was headed for the farm and she for the city, and ultimately their marriage sundered, leaving them free to find their ideal habitats. There were quarrels, there were reconciliations, there were negotiations, there were compromises, but the end was inevitable. Later this divergence was to be expressed in my fiction: there was the planet Proton, with cities and pollution, and the magic land of Phaze, with forests and unicorns. Yet they were merely aspects of one realm, the city and the country merging. I liked both, and wanted the two to be joined, but they kept separating.

Meanwhile, it was hell on the children, as divorces usually are. I liken it to standing on a mountain, but then the mountain quakes and collapses, and becomes an island in a heaving sea. I was standing there, and my footing was eroding. It became an iceberg, floating in that treacherous sea, and then the ice split so that one of my feet was on each section. The sections separated, leaving me no way to escape the fate of the icy water. So while I was not physically mistreated, emotionally I was suffering. I spoke of root pruning when I lost the nanny in England; now I was pruned again, having lost the second country—Spain— and the remaining foundation of the unified family. No wonder the stress manifested in various ways, such as bed-wetting and twitching; I had no legitimate way to handle it. They say that stupid folk don't have as many emotional problems as smart folk, being too dull to realize how bad things are. The way I was reacting, I must have been far smarter than I seemed.

So how did I survive? There came a point when I realized that my problems were really not of my own making, but stemmed from the stress between my parents. I declared, in effect, emotional independence. I weaned myself away from the family, emotionally, and began building my own framework. It was a long and difficult job, like a climb from a deep and treacherous pit, but in time I got there. My parents were shocked when I stated

that they were people I knew and liked, but did not love, yet it was the truth. That was the state I had needed to achieve for emotional survival. It wasn't ideal, it wasn't pretty, but it was the only way. I don't regret the decision; I regret the necessity for it. How would it have been if Joyce, my father's early love, had lived, and they had married, and I had been their child? I suspect I would have been far happier as a child—and never have become a writer. So I can't really fault the circumstances that brought me into this realm and made me what I am, however uncomfortable they may have been.

Now on this matter of dreams: I have an insatiable curiosity about the nature of the universe and mankind's place in it, and my profession of writing allows me to explore it all, seeking answers. I have fathomed a number of things to my satisfaction before they were clarified by the scientists, and this is one of them. This discussion will get somewhat intellectual, but I'll try to make it intelligible. It has been said that we waste a third of our lives in sleep. Baloney; nature doesn't work that way. It has been said that we use only ten percent of our brains. Baloney, again. While we are up and about we are constantly receiving impressions. Now consider what happens to them: are they just dumped into a virtual vat in the brain and stored for future use? It may seem that way at first blush, but a little thought shows that this is impractical. If you buy groceries for the next week's meals, do you just dump them pell-mell into the freezer? Chances are you sort them and put them carefully in a number of spots reserved for them, so that you won't find week-old milk squished under the canned beans, or fresh lettuce coated with cocoa powder. So that when you need butter in a hurry, you won't have to unload the whole freezer to find it, and then have to thaw it on the stove. (That reminds me of the story my mother told of the day the refrigeration was too cold: "The ice cream's been in the oven for twenty minutes, and still isn't soft enough to cut." It also reminds me of the time I took a pat of butter and dropped it on my plate, and it clinked.) It takes time to sort things properly, but you learn to do it, because it's better than the alternative. The same is true for anything else; you separate it and sort it and store it for future convenience.

So is it any different with memories? Obviously they are well organized, because all our past experience can quickly be brought to bear on a present event. If we spy a small red roughly spherical object before us, we know almost immediately whether it's the dog's rubber ball or a giant cherry bomb, and treat it accordingly. But when did we do the massive sorting and filing of memories that allowed us to classify it so rapidly? For such work does take time. I was for some years a file clerk, and I learned that there is no paper so lost as one that has been misfiled or mislabeled. If you're using an unfamiliar program, with a deadline for an obnoxious assignment, how do you find an article on cooking squash, if the file isn't organized? Under C for Cooking, or S for Squash, or F for Food, or U for Ugh—who wants it? In fact you have not only to file accurately, you have to cross-reference, so that under COOKING is a note saying SEE SQUASH, along with other notes saying SEE POTATOES, SEE BROCCOLI, SEE BALONEY, and so on. Also under FOOD, and under

At home with horses Sky Blue and Misty, circa 1980

UGH. That way you can quickly find anything when you don't know how the ditsy file clerk classified it. Well, your brain has to do that job too, only it's a lot more complicated than just a list of recipes. Your entire ongoing life experience has to he sorted and classified and filed in memory for instant retrieval. It doesn't just happen; it has to he organized.

When do you do it—in your sleep? Yes, actually. Part of that ninety percent of the brain that ignorant experts think is unused is actually used for that considerable cross-referencing and filing chore. And since you are way too busy in the daytime to do it, the chore must wait for the brain's downtime: at night. Think of a computer that has some really hot features you'd like to play with, but someone else is using it now; what do you do? You schedule a session during its downtime, when no one else is using it. That's what your brain does. When you sleep, precious little is coming in from outside. So it calls up the fresh memories of the day, that have been held in temporary storage, and processes them. It takes one memory, such as that of the personable person of the opposite gender who smiled at you during lunch, and compares it rapidly to your prior lifetime's experience, in the manner of a computer checking for a word beginning with WOW. Whenever there's some sort of match, it looks farther, and when there's a significant match, it considers

the matter and strengthens the neural pathways that actually make memory. But this aspect takes intelligence, because most of the day's impressions are not very important in terms of the rest of your life, and you don't want to clutter your memory with them.

For example, if that person was your sibling, you can dump that memory right there. But if there are matches to a similar smile yesterday by a person you well might want to get lost with in a stranded elevator, this bears further consideration. How would it be, if the two of you are going to the sixth floor, and the power fails, and one of you is a bit scared and the other is a bit protective, and you mesh rather nicely, and then a kiss sort of happens, and then the alarm goes off and it's morning, and all you remember is a rather pleasant dream about an elevator. And so you process everything, and the occasional images that take more serious form as you explore their bypaths are what you call dreams. It's not wasted time at all; it's vital to your well being. Your whole future may be guided in your dreams. But you can't afford to remember most of them, because they are the sorting process, and any dream you remember has to be treated as a memory and run through that classification mill itself. You would rapidly encounter the phenomenon of diminishing returns.

Now you know what dreams are for. Don't bother to tell your science teachers; they're not ready for this yet.

Just be smugly satisfied in your secret understanding of what modern science does not yet know. With luck, you'll dream about that elevator again tonight, and the alarm won't go off so soon.

And so I survived the horror of my devastating dream, though it haunted me every night for three years thereafter. When I closed my eyes I saw that corpse and knew its identity. I tried to make it go away, and in my imagination it would move off-screen, but another would appear, and another, until they were cruising by like the cars of a long train. It may sound funny, but it was killing my sanity. If I seem a bit crazy here, well, now you have half a notion how I got that way. I had an active imagination, and it didn't stop with corpses. By day I saw monsters. They followed me as I walked home from school through the forest alone, and hid behind the trees when I turned to look. They lurked under my bed, ready to grab my ankles if I was careless enough to put them in reach. They were everywhere. I had to have a night-light, for light was the only thing that kept them at bay. Today I put those monsters into my fiction, and I love them. But fantasy monsters don't chase adults, only children. So the dominant emotion of my later childhood was fear. Fear of bigger kids at school, of a monster in the forest, and fear of the corpse. Fear, really, of life. I hated being alone, but others neither understood nor cared, so I was alone a lot. That is, often physically, and almost always emotionally. Today when I get a letter from a reader who feels almost utterly alone, I understand, because I remember.

That wasn't all. One doctor had a simplistic remedy for my bed-wetting: I was to have no liquid after 4 p.m. So to my accumulated discomforts was addled that of thirst. The bed-wetting continued unabated, but I longed for a drink of water. Later in life I had a kidney stone, and I wonder whether it could have started long before, during my years of dehydration.

Meanwhile, I endured, having no alternative. Each morning I would wake soaking in urine, because the rubber sheet that protected the mattress caused the brine to pool around me. I would get up—I remember dancing on the floor in winter, because it was so cold on my feet—go downstairs to the bathroom, which had no toilet but did have a basin of cold water. Once I had to break the ice on the water before I could use it to wash. I would soak the washcloth, grit my teeth, and start washing my chest. After a few strokes my body would warm the cloth, and it would be easier. I would wash my midsection, getting the urine off, then run back shivering upstairs to my room to dress. Sometimes I couldn't resist putting the wet cloth to my mouth and sucking a little of the water out, to abate my thirst, feeling guilty because I wasn't allowed anything to drink until breakfast. Ironically, I now must drink more water than I like, to keep my urine diluted so that I won't have another kidney stone. I developed a real hatred of being cold, having experienced so much of it so unpleasantly; that's one big reason I now live in Florida. Later in the day I would wash out the sheet, a tedious chore with cold water. My parents didn't call it punishment, but it was my penalty for my persistence in wetting the bed: I had to clean up my own mess. I got the message in this and other ways: I was a burden to the family.

My fondest imagination was that one day I would wake up and discover that it had all been a horrible dream, and I was really back in England with the nanny. But it never happened. I pondered my life, and concluded that if I could be given a choice to either live it over exactly as it had been, or never to exist at all, I would prefer the latter. The net balance was negative; though I had never been verbally, physically, or sexually abused, by conventional definition, my existence simply wasn't worth it. My past was unpleasant, and my prospects for the future bleak.

But it wasn't all bad. My parents did care, though they did not understand how the world seemed from my perspective. They encouraged me to paste up gold stars on a chart for every night I remained dry, motivating me to change my behavior. Unfortunately they did not address its true cause, which lay closer to their own behavior than they would have cared to admit, so such things weren't very effective. But there was one thing that did impress me. My father offered two remedies: he could arrange for a sympathetic group to pray for me, or he could take me on a trip to the city to talk with a knowledgeable woman. I never had have much faith in the supernatural, so I chose the trip. It was always a pleasure to get away from the wilderness and into civilization. I think my love of trains, especially the old steam engines, stems from that: a train was the big, powerful, fascinating machine that carried folk to interesting places. That doesn't mean that I hated the country; today I am an environmentalist, and live on my own tree farm. But I also have central heating, TV, radio, a telephone, computer, car, and the other benefits of civilization.

I forget whether the trip was to New York or Philadelphia, but the woman was Mrs. West. She explained to me how you could not see electricity, or hear it, or smell it, but nevertheless it existed, and you knew that when you turned on a light or some appliance. Similarly, she said, you couldn't see or hear God, but he nevertheless existed. Now that's a rationale I can accept, and it may be the reason I became an agnostic rather than an atheist. I remember being told about Santa Claus: a jolly fat man who squeezed down the chimney and brought presents to all the children in the world, in a single night. I didn't buy it. Then I was told about God: a big old white man with a long white beard sitting on a cloud, looking down at mortal folk. I don't buy that either. I make my living from fantasy, but I always knew the difference between fantasy and reality. I am a realist. But I understood the difference between lack of evidence, and proof. If you're driving on a mountainous road, and you want to pass the slow car ahead, and you don't see any oncoming traffic, you don't just assume that none exists. You don't pass on a turn. You wait until you can see ahead on a straight stretch. To do otherwise is dangerous.

So while I have never seen persuasive evidence of the supernatural, and really don't believe in ghosts or flying saucers, and like the great playwright George Bernard Shaw I am wary of a man whose god is in the sky, I don't feel free to declare that there is no God. So I am agnostic, not presuming to define the nature of God. And if you define God as Truth, Justice, Compassion, Beauty, Honor, Decency, and the like, then I did believe. But the bigotry I have seen in so many religions prevents me from joining any of them; I don't think that any great religious leaders, including Jesus Christ, ever intended their followers to practice anything like the Inquisition or the Crusades or jihads, converting others by sword and torture. In fact I think that if Jesus returned to the world today, his tears would flow to see what has been wrought in his name. He was a man of tolerance and peace, and he welcomed even a prostitute to wash his feet. I think that he and I could have a compatible chat, and he would not object to my philosophy any more than I object to his. And I think that the bigots would crucify him again, in the name of religion. So I am agnostic, and satisfied to be so. When I grew up, I married a minister's daughter, and we don't have any quarrels about religion. My background was Quaker, hers Unitarian-Universalist, both "liberal" religions, and I like to think that when good work is quietly being done, there is apt to be either a Quaker or a U-U person involved.

So I appreciated Mrs. West's rationale, without being persuaded of the existence of God. After that she took me to a bookstore and bought me a book. No, not a religious one; it was a storybook with games. On one page a little dog had gotten its leash hopelessly tangled in the furniture: could I untangle it? That was an example of a type of fiendishly challenging puzzle I have encountered also in other settings. To solve it, you have to fashion a loop elsewhere, pass it through a couple of holes, and around the dog; then it can be freed. I, being slow on the uptake, must have struggled with it for months. So it was that wonderful book that was my prize from that trip. Perhaps it contributed to my love of books—I, who had had such trouble even learning to read. Today I earn my living by writing books, and many of them incorporate challenges and puzzles.

But the thing that impressed me most about that trip was the proof it represented that my father really did care. He had taken a lot of trouble to make that trip with me, and I enjoyed all of it. When I had children of my own, I made it a point to take them on similar trips, giving them the experience of airplane flights (today's equivalent of the train), hotels, restaurants, and far places. We also read to them, just as my father had read to my sister and me every night. I think that nightly reading, and the daytime storytelling when we worked together outside, was the most important influence on my eventual choice of career. I knew that books contained fascinating adventures, and those stories took me away from my dreary real life. Today I spend even more of my time away from real life; my very name, Piers Anthony, is a pen name relating to the things I imagine. I have entered the realm of stories, and hope never to leave it. So that trip was fundamentally reassuring in a vital way, and I think it helped lay the foundation for my emotional recovery.

And the truth is that though I would not have cared to live my early life over, today the balance has changed, and I would be satisfied to live my whole life over, rather than never to have existed. Because my physical life improved too, and though progress has never been easy, taken as a whole my life is a good one. Two major things contribute to that well-being: my wife and my career. Those who seek advice for happiness can have mine: find the right spouse and the right career. Unfortunately today's world makes the achievement of such things difficult.

It would be tedious to detail the rest of my schooling, so I'll skip it, and just say that of the ten schools I attended through college, the third best was Westtown School in Pencil Vania, where I boarded four years and graduated with an indifferent record; the second best was The School in Rose Valley, also in Pencil Vania, where I completed grades five through seven in two years, and Goddard College, in Vermont, where I got my degree in creative writing. In fact Goddard was like entering paradise. It was at the time perhaps the most liberal college in America, with fewer than seventy-five students, no tests or grades, informal clothing, and a pervasive egalitarianism. That is, there was no hierarchy of students, no initiations or discrimination, everyone was friendly and helpful, and teachers were called by their first names. That doesn't mean that everything was perfect, and I did have some severe problems there. At one point I was suspended for a week for opposing a regressive faculty policy, and as with other conflicts I have had, I think it is now generally conceded that I had the right of the case. But overall, Goddard set me on course for my future, with my practice in writing, and my wife, and I now support it generously financially, being one of its richest graduates.

Ah, yes, romance. When I was eleven I loved a girl who was twelve. I'm not one to sneer at puppy love or crushes; it was the most intense love I am aware of experiencing, and it lasted for three years despite a complete lack of encouragement on her part. She was slender, had long brown hair, wore glasses, and was a smart and nice person. She taught me to play chess, and today I still work the daily chess puzzles in the newspaper. So in certain respects she defined my interest in the opposite gender. Let's pause, here, for a statement about terms: technically, gender means the grammatical identification of certain classes of words, while sex refers to whether a person or animal is male or female. But because sex also means the activity of procreation, this gets confusing and sometimes embarrassing. There is the story of the woman who filled out a job application form, writing in the box marked SEX "Occasionally." There is the suspicion that the Equal Opportunity Amendment to the Constitution, that would have protected women from discrimination, failed to pass because some people thought it meant sex as in copulation. So I prefer to use the word gender, where there is no confusion, and to hell with the purist grammarians. I never liked the subject of grammar much anyway. At any rate, when I later encountered a smart brown-haired girl with glasses in college, I married her. Now you know why. (My wife says that's an oversimplification. I can't think why. It's been forty years and she still has glasses and brown hair, and handles the family finances and goes online with her computer, something I'm not smart enough to do.) She was a tall girl, standing 5'9" in bare feet, while I had been the shortest person, male or female, in my high school classes. Butt in five years, from ninth grade to the second year of college, I grew almost a foot, so I was a full inch and a half taller than she. I tease her about that: I had to do it, to be ready for her. Men judge women by their figure; women judge men by their height.

After college, life was rough. My wife and I spent most of a year trying to make a living in northern Vermont, and I had trouble getting work because I insisted that I needed fifty dollars a week to support my family, and most jobs didn't pay that much. I finally landed a dollar-an-hour, fifty-hour-week job with American News, delivering magazines and paperback books to stores. Then, at the end of the summer, the boss approached me as I was punching out my time card on Friday. "Don't come in Monday." That was it. It seemed it was a summer job, not the permanent one I had been told. No advance notice, no severance pay, just gone. After that the only job I could get was selling health insurance—and you know, it's rough if you represent the policies honestly and are in an economically depressed region. When driving, I took my eye off the road to verify the address, and at that moment hit a reverse-banked turn and started to go out of control. I hit the brakes—and they locked, and the car sailed off a six-foot bank at forty miles an hour. I remember wondering whether I would recover consciousness after landing. It rolled over, and I found my head in the back seat. The roof had caved in six inches—which was exactly the head clearance our VW Bug had. I was lucky; I came out of it with only a bruised shoulder. That was in the stone age, before seat belts; you bet I've always used one since. My grandmother Caroline sent money to enable us to get the car repaired, and my mother sent what money she could spare to enable us to live. Meanwhile my wife was pregnant, but having trouble. I took her to the hospital, where she lost the baby. Suddenly we had no prospective child, and I was eligible for the draft. Since I wasn't making it economically anyway, I volunteered to go in immediately. At least it would guarantee a paycheck for two years.

I was lucky, again: I was in the army from 1957 to 1959, between Korea and Vietnam. My wife joined me at Ft. Sill, Oklahoma, where I was an instructor in basic math and survey. It was an artillery base, and it takes calculation to survey in the big guns, so that they can fire exactly on target. You have to know where you are, before you know

Anthony in his office, 1995

where you're going. Later they tried to make us all "volunteer" to sign up for savings bonds, at two-and-a-half percent interest, but we needed the money for groceries and rent, so I didn't sign. So they harassed my whole unit, trying to make it put pressure on me to sign, but the others supported me instead, because nobody likes getting pushed around. Remember, once I got free of childhood, I got ornery about being bullied. I even went to the battalion commander with a charge of extortion against the first sergeant. The Lt. Colonel heard me out courteously for an hour and a half, but did not feel the evidence was conclusive. So I didn't get the sergeant canned, but I made him sweat, and I suspect he got a private reprimand. It was one more notch in the minor legend I became in the army. Strangers would come up to shake my hand. But the authorities were not amused. They booted me as instructor and sent me to another unit, as well as depriving me of any promotions. It's the army way. They didn't care as much about quality instruction—I was so effective a teacher that they wouldn't give me leave time to visit home, and in the end they had to pay me extra for over a month of unused leave—as they did about 100 percent bond participation. So, taken as a whole, the army was a waste of time for me, but it did pay my way, and covered my wife's month-long hospitalization and second miscarriage, a medical expense that could have bankrupted us otherwise.

After the army, we moved to Florida. I like to say that I traveled from Vermont to Florida the hard way: via two years in the army. That's how we came in out of the cold. I worked in industry as a technical writer for three years, and later I was an English teacher in high school. But what I really wanted to do was write, and finally we took the plunge: my wife, having suffered her third miscarriage, went to work, and I stayed home and tried to be a writer. The agreement was that if I didn't make it in a year, I would give up my foolish dream and focus on earning a living in Mundania. I had a fifth cousin who did just that; after failing at writing, he became an executive at Sears Roebuck and did well. But I made it: I sold two stories, and in that year earned a total of $160 from writing. Now I'm slow, but finally it penetrated: that wasn't enough income to sustain a family. That's when I actually became a teacher. But I kept writing stories on the side, selling one every six months or so. Finally, in 1966, I retired from teaching, which job I liked no better than the others, and returned again to writing. This time I focused on novels instead of stories, and the larger amounts of money earned from novels enabled me to make a living, barely, though my wife continued to work. So it was lean, but it was writing, and that's what I wanted.

Thereafter, with the help of modern medicine, we were finally able to have two children we could keep. I think of this blessing as being like the monkey's paw. That famous story was about an old couple who had a severed monkey's paw that would grant three wishes, but it granted each wish in such a way that the result was worse than before. So they wished for money—and got it when their son was killed and his insurance came to them. Horrified, they wished for him to return—so the corpse was roused and heading for their door as one of the walking dead, before they wished him gone again and were done with it. I would never have been able to take the risk of staying home and writing, if my wife had not been free to earn the family income instead—and she was free only because all three of our babies had died. Had we had a choice, we would never have let them go. But now I was a successful writer, and we got our two daughters too. Thus we had everything we had wanted: success in writing, and a regular family.

But I was never a regular person, as this autobio surely makes clear. My life as a writer was just as problematical as my life elsewhere. I'm a square peg, and life offers mostly round holes. I think I didn't have the most trouble of any writer in the science fiction fantasy genre, as that dubious honor belongs to Harlan Ellison, but I think I can fairly claim second place. (Harlan himself was somewhat baffled by me, and our relations have been mixed.) A publisher cheated me, so I demanded an accurate statement of account. Instead, I got blacklisted: publishers refused to buy from me. Even a writer's organization, which supposedly existed to help writers against errant publishers, tacitly sided with the publisher, though they were in a position to know that I had the right of the case. Writing is not necessarily a nice business, and justice is not always served. I dumped the writer's organization, called Science Fiction Writers Association, and have been hostile to it ever since, for good reason. The blacklist was rough; I accumulated eight unsold novels. But one publisher didn't honor the blacklist, so I survived. Also, I got a literary agent, the same one who handled Robert Heinlein, then the genre's leading writer. That messed up the blacklisters, because they knew that if they annoyed that agent, they'd never see work by Heinlein. Then something remarkable happened: apparently the errant publisher cheated one too many writers, faced legal retribution (I hadn't had the money to make a real case), and the proprietors had to flee their own company. The new administration hired editors who were friendly to me; they checked the company books and realized what had happened, and invited me to return. I was wary, but tried it, as I really wanted to work with their editor, Lester del Rey. He was in charge of fantasy, so I wrote a fantasy book. That was *A Spell for Chameleon,* the first Xanth novel.

None of us knew it at the time, but fantasy was about to take off for the stratosphere, and the "Xanth" series rode that rocket right on up. This was, as I see it, for two main reasons: Lester del Rey was an apt editor who knew a commercial novel when he saw one; he developed Stephen Donaldson, Terry Brooks, David Eddings, and others, in addition to me, and became arguably the most successful book editor the genre has seen. The other was his wife, Judy-Lynn del Rey, who named Del Rey books. I call her a giant, and I wrote her into Xanth as the lovely but deadly Gorgon, and she even sent in puns for it, like Gorgon-zola cheese, and was duly credited in the Author's Note, like any other young fan. "I *am* a young fan!" she said. But the humor went beyond that, for physically Judy-Lynn was a dwarf, standing something like three-and-a-half feet tall. But she was smart and tough, and she could really promote her books. She was the publisher who first put *Star Wars* into print. So Lester's editing and Judy-Lynn's promotion made a publishing phenomenon like few have seen in our time, and Del Rey Books soon dominated the genre. The fifth Xanth novel, *Ogre, Ogre,* became the first fantasy original paperback (that is, one that never had a hardcover

edition) to make the big national bestseller lists. My income moved from that initial $140 to more than a million dollars a year, and all our financial problems were behind us. The blacklist was gone, destroyed at its source; all the editors who had blacklisted me were out of power, and not eager to advertise what they had done. I wasn't actually responsible for getting them canned, not directly, but I believe that none of them cared to mess with me again. It's that bully syndrome; when the tables turn, the bullies flee.

With success came fan mail, and I do my best to answer it, though about one third of my working time is now taken up by it. Sometimes it seems that half my readers want to become writers themselves; unfortunately, only about one in a hundred will ever sell anything, because the competition is great. A number of the letters are serious, such as those from suicidally depressed teens. I understand depression, because despite my phenomenal commercial success (not critical success; critics claim that I don't write anything worthwhile) I remain mildly depressive. It seems that most writers and artists are depressive; I guess I'm lucky that it's not worse for me. So though I am old and most of them are young, we relate well. A number have credited me with saving their lives, just by responding and understanding. I drew on what they told me to make the character Colene in "The Mode" series: age fourteen, smart, pretty, and secretly slicing her wrists. Many have told me how well they relate to her; they wonder how I could know their inner truths so well. I don't know, really, but I listen well. I also have a novel, *Firefly,* that is apt to freak out school officials, because it deals graphically with sexual abuse, but I have had many letters from women who thank me for bringing this ugly matter out into the open. So readers should beware; not all my work is frivolous fantasy. Some of it is savage.

But no glory lasts forever. Judy-Lynn had a stroke, and died. Problems caused me to leave Del Rey Books though I really didn't want to, and in time my career crested and diminished. Publishers made promises and then reneged, to my cost. It remains a perilous business, and as in life, writing skill is not always rewarded, and justice is not necessarily served. There seems to be a small anonymous cadre of critics whose purpose in life is to spread false stories about me. I tackle these head-on when I encounter them, but it's like dealing with pickpockets: they are hard to catch in the act. It started when I was accused of being an ogre—at conventions I had never attended. It hasn't stopped. I have been called a Satanist, maybe because Satan is a character in a couple of my novels, and a possible child molester, and some even hint that I must be into bestiality because there are mythical half-human creatures in my fiction, like centaurs and mermaids. Some accuse me of unethical behavior, though they can't document it. I presume that other successful folk have similar problems; those who are not successful want to drag down those who are, and are not choosy about their methods. But the great majority of those who write to me are supportive. Still, it's more fun climbing up the mountain of Parnassus—that's what the literary establishment is called—than tumbling down it! Today other fantasy writers are surging ahead, and I wish them well, though I am sorry to be left behind. I still write funny fantasy, and I have answered an average of 150 fan letters a month for a number of years, but my real interest now is in historical fiction. I regard *Tatham Mound,* about the American Indians who encountered the Spanish explorer Hernando de Soto, as the major novel of my career, and the historical "Geodyssey" series as the major work of my career. I am now in my sixties, and know I won't live forever, so I'm doing what I always really wanted to do, and that is to explore the whole human condition, and to help others to understand it. I like to think that those young readers who like funny Xanth will in time graduate to my historical fiction, and find it as satisfying in a different way. I love writing, and when I die I expect to be halfway through a great novel.

APPELT, Kathi 1954-

Personal

Born July 6, 1954, in Fayetteville, NC; daughter of William H. Cowgill and Patricia Walker Childress; married Kenneth L. Appelt (a teacher), January 6, 1979; children: Jacob, Cooper. *Education:* Texas A & M University, B.A., 1979; additional study at University of Iowa, 1980-82. *Politics:* Democrat ("yellow dog"). *Religion:* Unitarian.

Addresses

Home and office-1907 Comal Circle, College Station, TX 77840. *Agent*—Marilyn Marlow, Curtis Brown Ltd., 10 Astor Pl., New York, NY 10003.

Career

Texas A & M University, College Station, TX, instructor in continuing education, 1992; Jacques' Toys and Books, Bryan, TX, children's book buyer, 1992-94, consultant, 1994—. Secretary, Brazos Pre-Natal Clinic, 1985-87; affiliated with La Leche League, 1988-92; board member, Unitarian Fellowship of Brazos Valley, 1992-94; copresident, Parent Teacher Organization, Willow Branch Intermediate School, 1994-95. *Member:* Society of Children's Book Writers and Illustrators (regional advisor for Brazos Valley Chapter, 1992—).

Awards, Honors

C. K. Esten Award, Texas A & M University, 1974, for outstanding student in theatre arts; American Booksellers Association Pick of the Lists citation, and International Reading Association Teacher's Choice Award, both for *Elephants Aloft;* Best Books for Young Adults selection, American Library Association (ALA), and Books for the Teen Age selection, New York Public Library, both for *Just People and Paper—Pen—Poem: A Young Writer's Way to Begin;* Best Books for Young Adults and Quick Pick for Reluctant Readers selections, ALA, both for *Kissing Tennessee, and Other Stories from the Stardust Dance.*

Writings

The Boy Who Loved to Dance, illustrated by Sioux N. Morales, Pecan Tree Press, 1986.

Elephants Aloft, illustrated by Keith Baker, Harcourt (San Diego, CA), 1993.

The Best Kind of Gift, Morrow (New York, NY), 1994.

Bayou Lullaby, illustrated by Neil Waldman, Morrow (New York, NY), 1995.

The Bat Jamboree, illustrated by Melissa Sweet, Morrow (New York, NY), 1996.

The Thunderherd, illustrated by Elizabeth Sayles, Morrow (New York, NY), 1996.

Watermelon Day, illustrated by Dale Gottlieb, Holt (New York, NY), 1996.

A Red Wagon Year, illustrated by Laura McGee Kvasnosky, Harcourt (San Diego, CA), 1996.

Just People and Paper—Pen—Poem: A Young Writer's Way to Begin, photographs by Kenneth Appelt, Absey & Co., 1996.

I See the Moon (poetry), illustrated by Debra Reid Jenkins, Eerdmans (Grand Rapids, MI), 1997.

Cowboy Dreams, illustrated by Barry Root, HarperCollins (New York, NY), 1999.

Bats on Parade, illustrated by Melissa Sweet, Morrow (New York, NY), 1999.

Someone's Come to Our House, illustrated by Nancy Carpenter, Eerdmans (Grand Rapids, MI), 1999.

Swamp Bear, Morrow (New York, NY), 1999.

Hushabye, Baby Blue, illustrated by Dale Gottlieb, Harper-Festival (New York, NY), 2000.

Toddler Two-Step, illustrated by Ward Schumaker, Harper-Festival (New York, NY), 2000.

Bats around the Clock, illustrated by Melissa Sweet, Morrow (New York, NY), 2000.

Kissing Tennessee, and Other Stories from the Stardust Dance, Harcourt (San Diego, CA), 2000.

Oh My Baby, Little One, illustrated by Jane Dyer, Harcourt (San Diego, CA), 2000.

(With Jeanne Cannella Schmitzer) *Down Cut Shin Creek: The Pack-Horse Librarians of Kentucky,* HarperCollins (New York, NY), 2001.

Rain Dance, illustrated by Emilie Chollat, HarperFestival (New York, NY), 2001.

Bubbles, Bubbles, illustrated by Fumi Kosaka, HarperFestival (New York, NY), 2001.

The Alley Cat's Meow, illustrated by Jon Goodell, Harcourt (San Diego, CA), 2001.

Mother bird tells her preschooler all the ways her love remains with him while she is away at work. *(From Kathi Appelt's* Oh My Baby, Little One, *illustrated by Jane Dyer.)*

Incredible Me!, illustrated by G. Brian Karas, HarperCollins (New York, NY), 2002.

Where, Where Is Swamp Bear?, illustrated by Megan Halsey, HarperCollins (New York, NY), 2002.

Red and Ginger, Harcourt (San Diego, CA), 2002.

Bubba and Beau, Best Friends, illustrated by Arthur Howard, Harcourt (San Diego, CA), 2002.

The Best Kind of Gift, illustrated by Paul Brett Johnson, HarperCollins (New York, NY), 2003.

Also guest columnist for the *Bryan College Station Eagle,* 1982—, and *Dallas Times Herald,* 1990-92.

Sidelights

Kathi Appelt is the author of a number of illustrated storybooks for young readers, as well as several works of fiction for older readers. Woven within her fanciful stories Appelt sometimes hides a lesson, as in *Elephants Aloft,* a tale of two young elephants traveling to India that is composed using prepositions, or *Bat Jamboree,* a counting book described by a *Publishers Weekly* contributor as "grinningly batty." Other books, such as *Cowboy Dreams,* the Cajun-inspired *Bayou Lullaby,* and *Oh My Baby, Little One,* present quiet, reassuring rhymes perfect for bedtimes, while picture books such as *Watermelon Day* reflect a young child's love of simple pleasures, such as waiting for the day when a garden-grown watermelon is large enough to eat. Calling it "a tale that celebrates both summertime and the magic of anticipation," *School Library Journal* contributor Lisa S. Murphy praised *Watermelon Day* as "a love song to a simple pleasure," while a *Kirkus Reviews* critic noted that "Appelt has a way with similes" in this story about patience.

Born in 1954, Appelt "can hardly remember a time in my life when I wasn't writing," as she once told *SATA.* "In my childhood home, my mother allowed my two sisters and I—encouraged us really—to draw on the inside walls of our garage. It was funny. You could chart our progress in drawing and writing by moving your eyes up from the baseboards to eye-level. At the bottom were our early scribbles and at the top could be found our attempts at poetry."

A graduate of Texas A & M University in 1979, Appelt was married the same year and she and her husband went on to have two sons. "I attribute my desire to write for children to [them]," she explained. "I'm sure that without them, children's books would have remained a mystery, especially since the only children's books I remember from my childhood were horse books—*Black Beauty, My Friend Flicka,* and everything that was written by Will James and Marguerite Henry." While Appelt published her first book for children in 1986, it was not until the publication of *Elephants Aloft* in 1993 that her prolific writing career got into full-swing. During the next seven years she published eighteen books for young people, among them a nonfiction work about the craft of writing that was illustrated with photographs by her husband, Kenneth Appelt.

Picture book texts are Appelt's most common writing projects, and her books have been praised by many critics. Reviewing her 1996 picture book *A Red Wagon Year, School Library Journal* contributor Kathy Mitchell praised Appelt's "uncomplicated, rhyming text," while in *Booklist,* Julie Corsaro praised the "artful verse" used in this "buoyant take on a mainstay of the preschool curriculum." Noting the "timely theme" and "classic delivery" of Appelt's *Oh My Baby, Little One,* a *Publishers Weekly* reviewer added: "As comforting as morning sun, this sweet ... rhyming poem will reassure both preschoolers and their working parents that separation is only temporary."

Appelt goes a little batty with a series of picture books illustrated by Melissa Sweet. In *Bats on Parade,* a group of musically inclined bats march in formations that illustrate multiplication concepts: "Up marched the saxophones,/ all 25—/sopranos and altos,/ they came five by five." Fifty-five stagestruck bats strut their stuff in *Bat Jamboree,* which does the Radio-City Music Hall show one better by culminating in a startling bat pyramid. Calling *Bat Jamboree* a "witty combination of counting book and theatrical experience," *School Library Journal* contributor Lisa S. Murphy noted that the work would likely inspire readers to "cook ... up their own backyard jamborees."

Appelt's 1994 book *Down Cut Shin Creek: The Pack Horse Librarians of Kentucky,* coauthored with Jeanne Cannella Schmitzer, is a nonfiction work for older readers that recounts the history of the Depression-era government-sponsored project that organized a group of women equestrians and trained them to navigate the paths of the Appalachians to deliver books and other reading materials to poor families living in the moun-tains of Kentucky. Calling it an "evocative account that finally gives these librarians their due," Randy Meyer praised the book in his appraisal for *Booklist,* noting its extensive bibliography and archival photographs. Angela J. Reynolds noted favorably the "clear, thorough information" presented by the authors, and added in her *School Library Journal* review that *Down Cut Shin Creek* "paints a complete picture of one [New Deal Works Projects Administration] project."

While Appelt has written articles for newspapers and magazines, children's books have remained her first love. "I feel particularly committed to children," she explained, "and the difficult odds facing them in this country. One of my own personal missions is to change what we call children—that is, I would like to see them called a 'priority' rather than a 'resource.' I don't feel we've done a very good job with our 'resources' and I don't like the connotation that children are something that can be mined or exploited. Rather, they should be something that gets our top attention, something that receives our most intensive care and love."

While like most writers Appelt writes her picture book texts and novels on a computer, poetry is another matter. "Whenever I write poetry, I still yearn for the actual feel of the pencil against the grain of the paper," she admitted. "I like being forced to slow my thoughts down, allowing me to catch the rhythm of the line. I write every day for the most part, and I find that if I miss a day, I become somewhat grouchy. So my family encourages me to get my writing in."

Biographical and Critical Sources

BOOKS

Appelt, Kathi, *Bats on Parade,* Morrow (New York, NY), 1999.

PERIODICALS

Booklist, December 15, 1993, Elizabeth Bush, review of *Elephants Aloft,* p. 762; March 15, 1995, Julie Corsaro, review of *Bayou Lullaby,* p. 1333; May 15, 1996, Kay Weisman, review of *The Thunderherd,* p. 1590; October 1, 1996, Julie Corsaro, review of *A Red Wagon Year,* p. 356; March 15, 1997, Shelley Townsend-Hudson, review of *I See the Moon,* p. 1224; January 1, 1999, Ilene Cooper, review of *Cowboy Dreams,* p. 885; April 1, 1999, Stephanie Zvirin, review of *Bats on Parade,* p. 1419; March 1, 2000, Ilene Cooper, review of *Oh My Baby, Little One,* p. 1249; May 1, 2000, John Peters, review of *Bats around the Clock,* p. 1675; June 1, 2000, Debbie Carton, review of *Kissing Tennessee,* p. 1879; April 1, 2001, John Peters, review of *Rain Dance,* p. 1476; July, 2001, Randy Meyer, review of *Down Cut Shin Creek,* p. 1994; October 1, 2001, Kathy Broderick, review of *Bubbles, Bubbles,* p. 322.

Bulletin of the Center for Children's Books, May, 1997, Deborah Stevenson, review of *I See the Moon,* pp. 311-312.

Horn Book, May, 2001, review of *Down Cut Shin Creek,* p. 345.

Horn Book Guide, spring, 1994, p. 18; spring, 1997, Tanya Auger, review of *A Red Wagon Year,* p. 10, and Sheila M. Geraty, review of *Bat Jamboree,* p. 18.

Kirkus Reviews, March 1, 1996, review of *Watermelon Day,* p. 370; June 1, 1999, review of *Someone's Come to Our House,* p. 880.

New York Times Book Review, August 13, 2000, review of *Oh My Baby, Little One,* p. 16.

Publishers Weekly, February 13, 1995, review of *Bayou Lullaby,* p. 77; June 24, 1996, review of *Bat Jamboree,* p. 58; January 27, 1997, review of *I See the Moon,* p. 97; January 18, 1999, review of *Cowboy Dreams,* p. 338; May 31, 1999, review of *Someone's Come to Our House,* p. 86; February 14, 2000, review of *Oh My Baby, Little One,* p. 196; April 10, 2000, review of *Kissing Tennessee,* p. 100; November 26, 2001, review of *Where, Where Is Swamp Bear?,* p. 60.

School Library Journal, January, 1994, Marianne Saccardi, review of *Elephants Aloft,* pp. 80-81; April, 1995, Judy Constantinides, review of *Bayou Lullaby,* p. 97; June, 1996, Lisa S. Murphy, review of *Watermelon Day,* p. 92; August, 1996, Carol Schene, review of *The Thunderherd,* p. 115; September, 1996, Lisa S. Murphy, review of *Bat Jamboree,* p. 170; December, 1996, Kathy Mitchell, review of *A Red Wagon Year,* p. 84; February, 1999, Steven Engelfried, review of *Cowboy Dreams,* p. 77; June, 1999, Adele Greenlee, review of *Bats on Parade,* p. 85; August, 1999, JoAnn Jonas, review of *Someone's Come to Our House,* p. 124; April, 2000, Martha Topol, review of *Oh My Baby, Little One,* p. 90; June, 2000, Wendy S. Carroll, review of *Bats around the Clock,* p. 100; July, 2000, Tana Elias, review of *Toddler Two-Step,* p. 68; September, 2000, Alison Follos, review of *Kissing Tennessee,* p. 225; May, 2001, Angela J. Reynolds, review of *Down Cut Shin Creek,* p. 161; December, 2001, Janet M. Bair, review of *Bubbles, Bubbles,* p. 88, and Olga R. Kuharets, review of *Rain Dance,* p. 88; January, 2002, Wanda Meyers-Hines, review of *Where, Where Is Swamp Bear?,* p. 89.

OTHER

Kathi Appelt Web Site, http://www.kathiappelt.com (March 3, 2002).*

B

BASKIN, Nora Raleigh 1961-

Personal

Born May 18, 1961, in Brooklyn, NY; daughter of Henry P. (an artist and professor) and Arlene (Mayerson) Raleigh; married Steven M. Baskin (a clinical psychologist), October 11, 1986; children: Sam Raleigh, Ben Raleigh. *Education:* State University of New York—Purchase, B.A. (with honors), 1983. *Religion:* Jewish.

Addresses

Home—87 Birch Hill Rd., Weston, CT 06883. *Agent*—Nancy Galtt, 273 Charlton Ave., South Orange, NJ 07079. *Email*—norabaskin@aol.com.

Career

Writer; teacher of creative writing and Jewish history. *Member:* Society of Children's Book Writers and Illustrators, Connecticut Press Club.

Awards, Honors

"Flying Starts" selection, *Publishers Weekly,* and Top Ten Youth Novel, *Booklist,* 2001, both for *What Every Girl (Except Me) Knows.*

Writings

What Every Girl (Except Me) Knows (young adult novel), Little, Brown (Boston, MA), 2001.

Essays published in *Boston Globe Sunday Magazine* and *Aim* magazine.

Work in Progress

A second novel for young adults, about a twelve-year-old girl struggling to regain trust in the world and trust in herself, for Little, Brown.

Nora Raleigh Baskin

Sidelights

Nora Raleigh Baskin told *SATA:* "Truth—I started writing seriously in 5th grade. I began with poetry. All I remember about my first poem was that it had something to do with reincarnation. It was short but startlingly profound (so I thought). But what I remember most was my teacher's reaction. She loved it. My life was changed. I had discovered the power of words.

"By 6th grade I was writing short stories and keeping journals. I read constantly and my early writing was always influenced by what I was reading. At one point I became interested in Helen Keller and Annie Sullivan. I wrote a short story, in first person, about a blind and deaf girl struggling to express her thoughts. By high school I had attempted my first short novel, weaving my life into the events of World War II. I was a Jewish girl escaping Nazi Germany after my mother's death and searching for my missing father.

"Writing was my way of articulating all the emotions and all the drama I found myself exploring during those years. Even my senior thesis in college was a jumble of feelings and experimental writing based on my life experiences. It was, of course, extremely terrible.

"I think I was trying to make sense of all the confusion and unanswered questions. And I believed I could find some kind of truth if I put it down on paper. I was young, and I believed in words—as my father would say. Now, I'm not so young (not *as* young) but I still believe in words.

"However, it did take me a long time to realize that truth is only the way you remember it. It is all in the interpretation. I realized that *my* truth was *mine* to manipulate. And I began to write real fiction. I was finally able to care more about the story than the fact. I wrote *What Every Girl (Except Me) Knows* with this in mind. Take what you need and what you want and let go of everything else. And the amazing thing was when I did just that, I was free. I was free from the burden of my own history. I was free as a writer to create. To write."

The characters in Baskin's first novel, *What Every Girl (Except Me) Knows,* exemplify the author's belief about truth being a personal matter. Gabby Weiss, the girl in Baskin's title, begins her story with the feeling that she needs someone to teach her what every girl who has a mother knows. Since her own mother died when she was three, Gabby must look elsewhere for information on how to grow up female. Fortunately, Gabby loves her father's girlfriend, Cleo, and at first Cleo ably fills the role of mother for the girl, taking her shopping and celebrating the arrival of Gabby's first period. But when Cleo breaks up with Gabby's taciturn father, Gabby decides to jog her memory of her biological mother by returning to the apartment where the family lived when she was alive. In this way, critics declared, Baskin ably combines a coming-of-age story with a family mystery, in which the nature of Gabby's mother's death is finally revealed. Since no one in the family is allowed to discuss Gabby's mother, each has lived alone with the conviction that they were the cause of it. "What's especially moving here is that everything is true to Gabby's viewpoint," asserted Hazel Rochman in *Booklist.* A reviewer for *Publishers Weekly* praised Baskin's "bittersweet, emotionally complex first novel," focusing on the author's creation of well-rounded and likable male as well as female characters. Renee Steinberg's review in *School Library Journal* similarly praised this "engrossing coming-of-age story peopled with characters about whom it is easy to care."

Biographical and Critical Sources

PERIODICALS

Booklist, June 1, 2001, Hazel Rochman, review of *What Every Girl (Except Me) Knows,* p. 1878.
Publishers Weekly, April 2, 2001, review of *What Every Girl (Except Me) Knows,* p. 65.
School Library Journal, April, 2001, Renee Steinberg, review of *What Every Girl (Except Me) Knows,* p. 138.

OTHER

Nora Raleigh Baskin Web Site, http://www.norabaskin.com (February 22, 2002).

* * *

BAYLEY, Nicola 1949-

Personal

Born August 18, 1949, in Singapore; daughter of Percy Howard (a company director) and Ann Barbara (Crowder) Bayley; married John Hilton (a barrister), December 21, 1979; children: Felix Percy Howard. *Education:* Attended St. Martin's School of Art; Royal College of Art, diploma, 1974.

Addresses

Home—London, England. *Office*—c/o Candlewick Press, Attn: Author Mail, 2067 Massachusetts Ave., Cambridge, MA 02140.

Career

Illustrator of children's books. Work exhibited at St. Martin's School of Art, 1967-71, and Royal College of Art Graduate Exhibition, 1971-74.

Awards, Honors

Kate Greenaway Medal commendation, 1981, Children's Choice Award, Children's Book Council and International Reading Association, 1982, and Bologna Book Fair Prize, 1983, all for *The Patchwork Cat;* Kurt Maschler Award runner-up, Book Trust in London, 1983, for *The Mouldy.*

Writings

SELF-ILLUSTRATED CHILDREN'S BOOKS

(Compiler) *Nicola Bayley's Book of Nursery Rhymes,* Jonathan Cape, 1975, Knopf (London, England), 1977.
(Compiler) *One Old Oxford Ox* (counting book), Atheneum, 1977.
(Compiler) "Copycats" series (includes *Parrot Cat, Polar Bear Cat, Elephant Cat, Spider Cat,* and *Crab Cat*), Knopf (New York, NY), 1984.
(Compiler) *As I Was Going Up and Down and Other Nonsense Rhymes,* Macmillan (New York, NY), 1986.

Mowzer the cat lulls the Great Storm-Cat with singing and purring so Old Tom the fisherman can bring in fresh fish for the starving townspeople of Mousehole. (Illustration from The Mousehole Cat, *written by Antonia Barber and illustrated by Bayley.)*

(Compiler) *Hush-a-Bye Baby and Other Bedtime Rhymes,* Macmillan (New York, NY), 1986.

(Compiler) *Bedtime and Moonshine: Lullabies and Non-sense,* Macmillan (New York, NY), 1987.

(Compiler) *The Necessary Cat: A Celebration of Cats in Picture and Word,* Candlewick Press (Cambridge, MA), 1998.

ILLUSTRATOR

Richard Adams, *The Tyger Voyage,* Knopf (London, England), 1976.

Christopher Logue, adapter, *Puss in Boots* (pop-up book), Jonathan Cape, 1976, Greenwillow (London, England), 1977.

Russell Hoban, *La Corona and the Tin Frog, and Other Tales,* Jonathan Cape, 1978, Merrimack, 1981.

William Mayne, *The Patchwork Cat,* Knopf (London, England), 1981.

Mayne, *The Mouldy,* Knopf (London, England), 1983.

Paul Manning, "Merry-Go-Rhymes" series (includes *Cook, Fisherman, Clown,* and *Boy*), Walker, 1987.

Antonia Barber, *The Mousehole Cat,* Macmillan (New York, NY), 1990.

Jan Mark, *Fun With Mrs. Thumb,* Candlewick Press (Cambridge, MA), 1993.

Phyllis Root, *All for the Newborn Baby,* Candlewick Press (Cambridge, MA), 2000.

Gretchen Woelfle, *Katje, the Windmill Cat,* Candlewick Press (Cambridge, MA), 2001.

Sidelights

Nicola Bayley fills her works for young children with elegantly detailed and lushly colored illustrations. Many of her books contain collections of nursery and nonsense rhymes which are accompanied by delicate, miniature pictures. Bayley's illustrations have also found their way into the works of other authors, and it was one of her drawings that motivated Richard Adams to write *The Tyger Voyage.* Bayley is "a brilliant young English artist whose pictures glow like late-medieval manuscripts," described Alison Lurie in the *New York Times Book Review.* A *Junior Bookshelf* reviewer asserted: "Bayley

Bayley's detailed watercolors portray Mary's lullaby of the world rejoicing at the birth of Jesus. (From Phyllis Root's All for the Newborn Baby.*)*

belongs to one of the oldest traditions in children's books.... Her art is mannered, but very well-mannered, exquisite and in perfect taste."

Bayley was born in Singapore in 1949, but spent her childhood in both China and Hampshire, England. As a student at an English boarding school, she was excused from sports and games because of "growing pains." Instead, she spent most of her afternoons in the art room, receiving encouragement from both her parents and her art teachers. Originally planning to be a fashion designer, Bayley sent out a portfolio of fashion and textile designs to a variety of art schools. Accepted at St. Martin's School of Art in London, she took a number of graphic design courses before concentrating in her final years there on illustration. From St. Martin's, Bayley went to the Royal College of Art, also in London, where she continued her education and further developed her style of illustration.

Upon graduating, Bayley began working for Jonathan Cape, the publisher of her first book, *Nicola Bayley's Book of Nursery Rhymes.* "Enchanting detail, a Victorian style, and luminous colors" fill this collection of twenty-two Mother Goose rhymes, related Ruth M. McConnell in *School Library Journal.* "There is a great variety of fanciful pattern, with each turning of the page a surprise." Bayley's next work for Jonathan Cape came in the form of Richard Adams's *The Tyger Voyage.* The book was a result of Bayley's depiction of the old rhyme, "Three Thick Thumping Tigers Taking Toast for Tea." Her painting so inspired Adams that he wrote his narrative poem around it, and Bayley rendered the rest of the illustrations.

In works that followed, Bayley retells and collects the writings of others, adding her own illustrations. Her retelling of *One Old Oxford Ox* was published in 1977, and consists of "an alliterative counting rhyme tailored to trip the tongue, and the pictures shine from wide creamy borders," commented Karla Kuskin in the *New York Times Book Review.* "These miniature vistas have such melting brightness they might be fashioned of stained glass." In *Hush-a-Bye Baby and Other Bedtime Rhymes,* Bayley collects twelve rhymes from Mother Goose, along with American and German traditional rhymes. "Toys, angels, animals and grotesques are set in beautifully suggested landscapes or interiors in a little book which is a joy to handle and investigate," concluded Margery Fisher in *Growing Point.*

Bayley's "Copycats" series consists of several small books featuring a cat who imagines himself to be a variety of other animals in such titles as *Crab Cat, Polar Bear Cat,* and *Elephant Cat.* The cat, one of Bayley's favorite animals to illustrate, begins by describing all the benefits of being the other animals. But as soon as he encounters something negative, such as being wet and cold as a penguin cat, he quickly turns back into a regular cat. "A few words serve to link pictures which seem to exist mainly to demonstrate the resilience of cat-nature and the beauty of action and posture, with a

Nico's baby is saved by his cat after a dike bursts and floods a Dutch town in Katje, the Windmill Cat, *written by Gretchen Woelfle and illustrated by Bayley.*

gentle humour to remove any taint of sentimentality," observed Fisher in her *Growing Point* review of the series. Andrew Clements, writing in *New Statesman,* found the series "enchanting," and full of "sequences of ravishing fantastical illustrations."

Annie Ayres, a reviewer in *Booklist,* described Bayley's illustrations in *Fun With Mrs. Thumb* as "charming" and "jewel-like." A reviewer in Publishers Weekly commented that *Fun With Mrs. Thumb* was "a delightful book in doll sized format" with "rich, glowing illustrations." Reviewer T. T. in *School Library Journal* described Bayley's illustrations in *All for the Newborn Baby,* "highly detailed watercolor art," stating it was a "lovely book."

Bayley lives and works in London, creating her illustrations in a studio once used by Arthur Rackham, a renowned English artist and illustrator. She produces her paintings using a technique known as stippling, which consists of dotting paint onto a surface with a brush in thousands of tiny dabs. Preferring to work with water

colors on cartridge paper, Bayley claims that the hardest part of her work is at the rough draft stage: "I use my brain for them," explained Bayley in an essay for *Illustrators of Children's Books: 1967-1976.* "After that it's mindless though absorbing. It's almost painting by numbers. I just fill in what I've drawn."

Biographical and Critical Sources

BOOKS

Illustrators of Children's Books: 1967-1976, Horn Book, 1978.

PERIODICALS

Booklist, January 1, 1994, Annie Ayres, review of *Fun With Mrs. Thumb,* p. 833.
Growing Point, November, 1984, Margery Fisher, "Amusing the Little Ones?," pp. 4332-4335; May, 1985, Margery Fisher, "Nursery Books," pp. 4438-4439.
Junior Bookshelf, February, 1978, review of *One Old Oxford Ox,* pp. 13-14; April, 1985, p. 77.
New Statesman, December 7, 1984, Andrew Clements, "A Serious Business," p. 30.
New York Times Book Review, November 13, 1977, Karla Kuskin, "Picture Books," pp. 57-58; November 13, 1977, Alison Lurie, "The Classics Remain," p. 31.
Publishers Weekly, December 9, 1983, p. 51; November 1, 1993, review of *Fun With Mrs. Thumb,* p. 78.
School Library Journal, December, 1977, Ruth M. McConnell, review of *Nicola Bayley's Book of Nursery Rhymes,* p. 42; February, 1984, pp. 61-62; March, 1985, p. 146; October, 2000, T. T., review of *All for the Newborn Baby,* p. 62.
Washington Post Book World, November 13, 1977, pp. E1-E2.

*   *   *

BLAINE, John
See HARKINS, Philip

*   *   *

BLUE, Zachary
See STINE, R(obert) L(awrence)

*   *   *

BOGAN, Paulette 1960-

Personal

Born October 2, 1960, in Pt. Pleasant, NJ; daughter of Howard (a fishing boat captain) and Lucille (a homemaker; maiden name, Grumo) Bogan; married Charles Johnston, February 29, 1992; children: Sophia, Rachael, Lucille. *Education:* Attended University of Miami (Miami, FL); Parsons School of Design (New York, NY), B.F.A. (illustration), 1983.

Addresses

Home—40 West 11th St., New York, NY 10011.

Career

Freelance illustrator and writer, 1983—. Parsons School of Design, New York, NY, instructor, 1992-95. Her

works have appeared in solo and group gallery shows in New York, NY, 1989-94.

Awards, Honors

Children's Book Council Children's Choice award, 2001, for *Spike in the City,* which was also chosen by the

Paulette Bogan with her cartoon character Spike and pets Mickey and Spike.

Society of Illustrators to be included in their Children's Book, Original Art Show, 2000.

Writings

Spike, Putnam (New York, NY), 1998.
Spike in the City, Putnam (New York, NY), 2000.
Spike in the Kennel, Putnam (New York, NY), 2001.
Spike in Trouble, Putnam (New York, NY), 2003.
Goodnight Lulu, Bloomsbury (New York, NY), 2003.

ILLUSTRATOR

Dad Saves the Day, Silver, Burdett & Ginn, 1992.
Penny Coleman, *One Hundred One Ways to Do Better in School,* Troll Associates (Mahwah, N.J.), 1994.
Helen Lester, *Help! I'm Stuck,* Celebration Press (Glenview, IL), 1996.
Jokes, Riddles and Poems, Scholastic (New York, NY), 1998.
Tracey West, *Teaching Tall Tales Across the Curriculum,* Scholastic (New York, NY), 1998.
Kathleen Weidner Zoehfeld, *Fossil Fever,* Golden Books (New York, NY), 2000.
Kathleen Weidner Zoehfeld, *Amazon Fever,* Golden Books (New York, NY), 2001.

Contributor of numerous illustrations to publications, including *New York Times, Ladies Home Journal, Business Week, Parents, Family Circle, Los Angeles Times Magazine,* and *Billboard.*

Work in Progress

Something to Do and *Under the Bed at Night.*

Sidelights

Paulette Bogan is a long-time illustrator who began a new career in the early 1990s illustrating children's books. The daughter of a fishing boat captain, Bogan grew up in Brielle, New Jersey. Since the second grade, she wanted to be an artist, and Paulette's mother encouraged her interest in art. During a family outbreak of chicken pox, she even allowed Paulette and her siblings to paint a mural on the playroom wall. Paulette continued to paint and went on to graduate from Parsons School of Design.

Early in her career, Bogan contributed illustrations to such periodicals as the *New York Times, Ladies Home Journal, Business Week,* and *Parents.* She also worked for the book publishers Harcourt Brace Jovanovich, Simon & Schuster, and Scholastic. After the birth of her first two children, Bogan decided to make a career change, focusing on children's books. In 1992 she broke into children's book illustration with *Dad Saves the Day.* By 2000 she had illustrated a handful of children's titles, including the nonfiction books *Fossil Fever* and *Amazon Fever* by Kathleen Weidner Zoehfeld, and she had authored her own series of picture books about a dog named Spike. In *Spike,* she told the story of how Spike, dissatisfied with being a dog, tries to change himself.

After trying out the lives of a horse, a bird, and a fish, Spike learns that he is happy being a dog, and Shannon's dog at that. *Spike in the City* shows what kind of adventures a dog might have visiting the city: he rides an elevator, gets messy with gum, and plays Frisbee in the park. In *Spike in the Kennel* readers follow Spike as he stays overnight at a kennel for the very first time. The Spike books caught the attention of reviewers. According to a *Kirkus Reviews* contributor, *Spike* is enlivened with "amiable illustrations with strong lines." Both writing in *School Library Journal,* Shawn Brommer praised the "lively, engaging cartoonlike illustrations" and the pace of narrative and art in *Spike in the City,* and Marlene Gawron noted the accurate portrayal of emotions and humor in *Spike in the Kennel.*

Biographical and Critical Sources

PERIODICALS

Family Life (New York, NY), April, 1998, Christine Loomis, "Children's Hour."
Kirkus Reviews, December 1, 1997, review of *Spike,* p. 1773.
School Library Journal, March, 1998, Christine A. Moesch, review of *Spike,* p. 166; May, 2000, Shawn Brommer, review of *Spike in the City,* p. 130; June, 2001, Marlene Gawron, review of *Spike in the Kennel,* p. 102.

*   *   *

BOLOGNESE, Don(ald Alan) 1934-

Personal

Surname is pronounced "bo-lo-*nay*-see"; born January 6, 1934, in New York, NY; married Elaine Raphael Chionchio (a writer and illustrator), 1954; children: two daughters. *Education:* Graduated from Cooper Union Art School, 1954.

Addresses

Home—New York and Vermont. *Office*—c/o Scholastic, 555 Broadway, New York, NY 10012.

Career

Freelance illustrator, 1954—; Pratt Institute, Brooklyn, NY, instructor in lettering and calligraphy, 1960—; has also taught at Cooper Union Art School, New York University, and the Metropolitan Museum of Art's medieval museum, The Cloisters; author of books for young people; calligrapher.

Awards, Honors

The Colt from the Dark Forest by Anna Belle Loken received the Children's Spring Book Festival Middle Honor Award in 1959; *Plays and How to Put Them On* by Moyne Rice Smith was featured in the American Institute of Graphic Arts Children's Book Show in 1962;

All upon a Stone by Jean Craighead George received the Children's Spring Book Festival Picture Book Award in 1971 and was named an American Library Association Notable Book; *Me, Myself, and I* by Gladys Yessayan Cretan was included in the Society of Illustrators Show in 1971; *The Black Mustanger* by Richard Edward Wormser was named a Western Heritage honor book in 1972; *Fireflies* by Joanne Ryder was honored by the New Jersey Institute of Technology in 1978.

Writings

SELF-ILLUSTRATED

The Miracles of Christ (woodcuts and calligraphy from the exhibit at the Vatican Pavilion at the New York World's Fair), Centurion, 1964.
Once upon a Mountain, Lippincott (New York, NY), 1967.
A New Day, Delacorte (New York, NY), 1970.
Squeak Parker, Scholastic (New York, NY), 1977.
Drawing Horses and Foals, F. Watts (New York, NY), 1977.
Drawing Dinosaurs and Other Prehistoric Animals ("How to Draw" series), F. Watts (New York, NY), 1982.
Drawing Spaceships and Other Spacecraft ("How to Draw" series), F. Watts (New York, NY), 1982.
(With Robert Thorton) *Drawing and Painting with the Computer*, F. Watts (New York, NY), 1983.
Mastering the Computer for Design and Illustration, Watson-Guptill Publications (Toronto, Ontario, Canada), 1988.
Little Hawk's New Name, Scholastic (New York, NY), 1995.

Also contributor of articles to magazines, including *Jubilee*.

SELF-ILLUSTRATED; "HOW TO DRAW YOUR OWN STORY" SERIES

A Safari Adventure, Tor (New York, NY), 1996.
The Dragon, the Knight, and the Princess, Tor (New York, NY), 1996.
Monster Bash, Tor (New York, NY), 1996.
The Haunted House, Tor (New York, NY), 1996.
Monster Truck Demolition Derby, Tor (New York, NY), 2001.
A Circus Adventure, Tor (New York, NY), in press.

"DRAWING AMERICA" SERIES

Drawing History: Ancient Greece, F. Watts (New York, NY), 1989.
Drawing History: Ancient Egypt, F. Watts (New York, NY), 1989.
Drawing History: Ancient Rome, F. Watts (New York, NY), 1990.

"2050: VOYAGE OF THE STARSEEKER" SERIES; WITH WIFE, ELAINE RAPHAEL

Asteroid Alert, Scholastic (New York, NY), 2000.
Rescue in Space, Scholastic (New York, NY), 2000.

WITH WIFE, ELAINE RAPHAEL

The Sleepy Watchdog, Lothrop (New York, NY), 1964.

Sam Baker, Gone West, Viking (New York, NY), 1977.
Donkey and Carlo, Harper (New York, NY), 1978.
Turnabout, Viking (New York, NY), 1980.
Donkey It's Snowing, Harper (New York, NY), 1981.
Drawing Fashions: Figures, Faces, and Techniques, F. Watts (New York, NY), 1985.
Pen and Ink, F. Watts (New York, NY), 1986.
Pencil, F. Watts (New York, NY), 1986.
Charcoal and Pastel, F. Watts (New York, NY), 1986.
Printmaking, F. Watts (New York, NY), 1987.
The Way to Draw and Color Dinosaurs, Random House (New York, NY), 1991.
The Way to Draw and Color Monsters, Random House (New York, NY), 1991.

WITH WIFE, ELAINE RAPHAEL; "DRAWING AMERICA" SERIES

The Story of the First Thanksgiving, Scholastic (New York, NY), 1991.
Pocahontas: Princess of the River Tribes, Scholastic (New York, NY), 1993.
Sacajawea: The Journey West, Scholastic (New York, NY), 1994.
Daniel Boone, Frontier Hero, Scholastic (New York, NY), 1996.

ILLUSTRATOR; RETOLD BY MARGO LUNDELL; BASED ON THE BOOK BY ALBERT PAYSONTERHUNE

Lad, a Dog: Best Dog in the World, Scholastic (New York, NY), 1997.
Lad, a Dog: Lad Is Lost, Scholastic (New York, NY), 1997.
Lad, a Dog: Snake Attack, Scholastic (New York, NY), 1997.
Lad, a Dog: The Bad Puppy, Scholastic (New York, NY), 1997.

ILLUSTRATOR

Anna Belle Loken, *The Colt from the Dark Forest*, Lothrop (New York, NY), 1959.
Moyne Rice Smith, *Plays and How to Put Them On*, Walck (New York, NY), 1961.
Aurora Dias Jorgensen, *Four Legs and a Tail*, Lothrop (New York, NY), 1962.
Edward W. Dolch and Marguerite P. Dolch, *Stories from Spain*, Garrard (Champaign, IL), 1962.
Maryhale Woolsey, *The Keys and the Candle*, Abingdon (Nashville, TN), 1963.
Joan M. Lexau, *Jose's Christmas Secret*, Dial (New York, NY), 1963.
Joan M. Lexau, *Benjie*, Dial (New York, NY), 1964.
William Faulkner, *The Wishing Tree* (text in Japanese), Fuzambo (Tokyo, Japan), 1964, English-language edition, Random House (New York, NY), 1967.
Gaylord Johnson, *The Story of Animals: Mammals around the World*, second edition, Harvey House, 1965.
Jean Ritchie, *Apple Seeds and Soda Straws: Some Love Charms and Legends*, Walck (New York, NY), 1965.
Walter Rollin Brooks, *Jimmy Takes Vanishing Lessons*, Knopf (New York, NY), 1965.
Barbara Walker, *Just Say Hic!*, Follett (Chicago, IL), 1965.

Elizabeth Jane Coatsworth, *The Secret,* Macmillan (New York, NY), 1965.

Roger L. Green, *Tales the Muses Told,* Walck (New York, NY), 1965.

Robert Louis Stevenson, *Treasure Island,* Whitman (Danville, CA), 1965.

Robin Palmer, *Dragons, Unicorns, and Other Magical Beasts,* Walck (New York, NY), 1966.

William Jay Smith, *If I Had a Boat,* Macmillan (New York, NY), 1966.

Joan M. Lexau, *More Beautiful Than Flowers,* Lippincott (New York, NY), 1966.

Beth Greiner Hoffman, *Red Is for Apples,* Random House (New York, NY), 1966.

Irene Hunt, *Up a Road Slowly,* Follett (Chicago, IL), 1966.

Claire H. Bishop, *Yeshu, Called Jesus,* Farrar, Straus (New York, NY), 1966.

Frederick James Moffitt, *The Best Burro,* Silver Burdett (Lexington, MA), 1967.

William Roscoe, *The Butterfly's Ball and the Grasshopper's Feast,* McGraw (New York, NY), 1967.

Beman Lord, *A Monster's Visit,* Walck (New York, NY), 1967.

Lucy Pennell and Jackie M. Smith, *Our Church at Work in the World,* John Knox, 1967.

Clyde Robert Bulla, *Washington's Birthday,* Crowell (New York, NY), 1967.

Michael Mason, *The Book That Jason Wrote,* Funk, 1968.

(With Betty Fraser and Kely Oechsli) *Favorite Stories: A Collection of the Best-Loved Tales of Childhood,* designed by Walter Brooks, Whitman (Danville, CA), 1968.

Clyde Robert Bulla, *The Ghost of Windy Hill,* Crowell (New York, NY), 1968.

William Jay Smith, *Mr. Smith and Other Nonsense,* Delacorte (New York, NY), 1968.

Moyne Rice Smith, *Seven Plays and How to Produce Them,* Walck (New York, NY), 1968.

Thea Heinemann, *Stories of Jesus,* Whitman (Danville, CA), 1968.

Irene Hunt, *Trail of Apple Blossoms,* Follett (Chicago, IL), 1968.

Richard Edward Wormser, *The Kidnapped Circus,* Morrow (New York, NY), 1968.

Mary Chase, *The Wicked Pigeon Ladies in the Garden,* Knopf (New York, NY), 1968.

Robin Palmer, *Centaurs, Sirens, and Other Classical Creatures,* Walck (New York, NY), 1969.

Mary O'Neill, *Fingers Are Always Bringing Me News,* Doubleday (New York, NY), 1969.

Eva-Lis Wuorio, *The Happiness Flower,* World Publishing, 1969.

Jane Hyatt Yolen, *It All Depends,* Funk, 1969.

Just One More, compiled and retold by Jeanne B. Hardendorff, Lippincott (New York, NY), 1969.

Gladys Yessayan Cretan, *Me, Myself, and I,* Morrow (New York, NY), 1969.

Joan M. Lexau, *Benjie on His Own,* Dial (New York, NY), 1970.

Richard Edward Wormser, *Gone to Texas,* Morrow (New York, NY), 1970.

Don Bolognese portrayed the story of the German shepherd police dog that became the first seeing eye dog. *(Illustration from* Buddy: The First Seeing Eye Dog, *written by Eva Moore.)*

Barbara Rinkoff, *Headed for Trouble,* Knopf (New York, NY), 1970.

Jean Craighead George, *All upon a Stone,* Crowell (New York, NY), 1971.

Richard Edward Wormser, *The Black Mustanger,* Morrow (New York, NY), 1971.

Philip Balestrino, *Hot as an Ice Cube,* Crowell (New York, NY), 1971.

Eric Mowbray Knight, *Lassie Come Home,* revised edition, Holt (New York, NY), 1971.

Ernest J. Gaines, *A Long Day in November,* Dial (New York, NY), 1971.

Philip Balestrino, *The Skeleton Inside You,* Crowell (New York, NY), 1971.

Ruth Belov Gross, *What Do Animals Eat?,* Four Winds (New York, NY), 1971.

(With wife, Elaine Raphael) William Jay Smith, *Poems from Italy,* Crowell (New York, NY), 1972.

Doris Gates, *The Warrior Goddess: Athena,* Viking (New York, NY), 1972.

Joan M. Lexau, *The Christmas Secret,* Scholastic (New York, NY), 1973.

Jean Craighead George, *All upon a Sidewalk,* Dutton (New York, NY), 1974.

(With wife, Elaine Raphael) F. N. Monjo, *Letters to Horseface: Being the Story of Wolfgang Amadeus Mozart's Journey to Italy 1769-1770 When He Was a Boy of Fourteen,* Viking (New York, NY), 1975.

(With wife, Elaine Raphael) Margaret Hodges, *Knight Prisoner: The Tale of Sir Thomas Malory and His King Arthur,* Farrar, Straus (New York, NY), 1976.

Nathaniel Benchley, *Snorri and the Strangers,* Harper (New York, NY), 1976.

Ann Himler, *Waiting for Cherries,* Harper (New York, NY), 1976.

Joanne Ryder, *Fireflies,* Harper (New York, NY), 1977.

Nathaniel Benchley, *George, The Drummer Boy,* Harper (New York, NY), 1977.

Betty F. Horvath, *Jasper and the Hero Business,* F. Watts (New York, NY), 1977.

Barbara Brenner, *Wagon Wheels,* Harper (New York, NY), 1978.

(With wife, Elaine Raphael) Robert Penn Warren, *Selected Poems, 1923-1975,* Franklin Library, 1981.

James Preller, *Maxx Trax II: Monster Truck Adventure,* Scholastic (New York, NY), 1988.

William Jay Smith, *Big and Little,* Wordsong (Honesdale, PA), 1991.

Eleanor Coerr, *Buffalo Bill and the Pony Express,* Harper (New York, NY),Collins (New York, NY), 1995.

Eva Moore, *Buddy: The First Seeing Eye Dog,* Scholastic (New York, NY), 1996.

George Shea, *First Flight: The Story of Tom Tate and the Wright Brothers,* Harper (New York, NY),Collins (New York, NY), 1997.

Avi, *Abigail Takes the Wheel,* Harper (New York, NY), Collins (New York, NY), 1999.

Lynda Jones, *Abe Lincoln,* Scholastic (New York, NY), 1999.

Eva Moore, *Good Children Get Rewards,* Scholastic (New York, NY), 2000.

Also contributing illustrator for various publications, including the *New York Herald Tribune.*

Adaptations

All upon a Stone was adapted as a filmstrip with cassette by Miller-Brody Productions in 1976.

Sidelights

Don Bolognese is an author and illustrator who has designed the graphics for over one hundred children's books. Often collaborating with his wife, artist and writer Elaine Raphael, Bolognese has penned and designed popular stories like *The Sleepy Watchdog* and *Sam Baker, Gone West,* has produced books describing various artistic mediums, and has created volumes explaining the art of ancient cultures and how to draw it. Bolognese's solo and joint efforts have been recognized by critics who applaud his work for its attractive and vivid presentation. For example, Mary B. Mason in a review for *School Library Journal* asserted that Bolognese's pictures in Gladys Yessayan Cretan's award-winning book *Me, Myself, and I* "create a beautiful kaleidoscopic effect appropriate to the theme."

Bolognese was born and raised in New York City. Pursuing an interest in design, he attended Cooper Union Art School, graduating in 1954. That same year he married fellow student Raphael, an artist he had worked with during his studies. Bolognese also began his career as a freelance illustrator that year. His artwork was first published in book form in Anna Belle Loken's *The Colt from the Dark Forest* in 1959. More design work for other authors' stories followed before he teamed with Raphael to write and illustrate *The Sleepy Watchdog* in 1964. Also published that year was a volume containing reproductions of the woodcuts and calligraphic text that the artist had prepared for "The Miracles of Christ" exhibit for the Vatican Pavilion at the New York World's Fair. His first solo, self-illustrated children's book, *Once upon a Mountain,* appeared in 1967.

Illustration from Rescue in Space, *book two of the "2050: Voyage of the Starseeker" series for early-grade readers. (By Bolognese and Elaine Raphael.)*

In this work, Bolognese tells the story of a young shepherd boy who mischievously yells for help one day, only to receive the taunting reply "he haw haw" from someone on a nearby mountain. Angered, he informs his king of the insulting rebuttal, and the ruler declares war on the people of the neighboring peak. But when the monarch's army invades the foreign land, the soldiers find their adversaries to be nothing more than an old hermit and a loud-braying donkey. Noting that the artist used an array of paper colors, *Library Journal* contributor Della Thomas asserted that Bolognese's "scratchy drawings ... swarm with activity."

Bolognese has also received critical recognition for his artistic contributions to award-winning books such as Jean Craighead George's *All upon a Stone,* which describes the adventures of a young mole cricket who climbs from beneath a rock one day. The illustrator's design work with Raphael has also received positive reviews. Their work in F. N. Monjo's *Letters to Horseface: Being the Story of Wolfgang Amadeus Mozart's Journey to Italy 1769-1770 When He Was a Boy of Fourteen,* for example, was deemed "elegantly and imaginatively designed," by a *Horn Book* magazine contributor. The critic also pointed out that the couple had visited Italy in order to conduct research for their sketch work.

Bolognese has also concentrated on preparing a variety of "how-to-illustrate" books, many with Raphael. The works range from describing the techniques involved in drawing horses, dinosaurs, and spacecraft, to designing and painting with computers, to learning to create figures and faces. Among these volumes are *Pen and Ink, Pencil,* and *Drawing Fashions: Figures, Faces, and Techniques.* The first two books, according to a *Bulletin of the Center for Children's Books* reviewer, feature "unusually articulate discussion[s] of the materials, techniques, practice, and vision" needed to succeed in these mediums. While some critics were quick to note the duo's effective use of illustration to present a concept or describe an effect, other commentators thought the books showed readers how to appreciate art as well as its creation. *Drawing Fashions* received similar praise. Eleanor K. MacDonald, in a review for *School Library Journal,* called the volume "well-written, the advice sound and the sketches attractive." Later solo efforts by Bolognese about illustration instruction include books in the "How to Draw Your Own Story" series. In the series, Bolognese shows readers how to provide pictures for stories about safaris, fairy tales, monsters, haunted houses, automobiles, and the circus.

Many of Bolognese's illustrations have represented a particular era in American history, including depictions of 1880s New York in Avi's *Abigail Takes the Wheel,* American pioneer life in the 1860s in Eleanor Coerr's *Buffalo Bill and the Pony Express,* and early-twentieth-century Kitty Hawk, North Carolina, in George Shea's *First Flight: The Story of Tom Tate and the Wright Brothers,* In *Abigail Takes the Wheel,* schoolgirl Abigail must take control of her father's freight boat, the *Neptune,* and tow a second ship to safety. *Horn Book* reviewer Marilyn Bousquin commented, "Bolognese creates a turn-of-the-century nautical atmosphere with subdued watercolors that never overwhelm the text." In *Buffalo Bill and the Pony Express,* Coerr tells the story of fifteen-year-old Bill Cody and his experiences as a mail carrier in the Old West. Narrowly escaping a pack of wolves, Indians who take interest in his horse, and local outlaws, Billy makes a name for himself as a brave rider. *Horn Book* critic Maeve Visser Knoth observed, "Bolognese's watercolors, ... set the historical time period and give readers additional details about pioneer life in the 1860's." *First Flight* tells the story of Tom Tate, a young boy enchanted with the Wright brothers and their flying experiments. After flying on the Wright brother's glider and seeing their first successful airplane take to the sky, Tom predicts to his friends that one day, he will fly to the moon. "Bolognese's loose-line watercolor illustrations convey the particularities of turn-of-the-century Kitty Hawk," wrote *Horn Book* reviewer Martha V. Parravano, "as well as the moments of both tension and freedom involved in the creation of the first flying machine."

During the course of his career, Bolognese has self-illustrated sixteen books, has collaborated with Raphael on over twenty more, and has illustrated the texts of over seventy other stories. An instructor of lettering and calligraphy at Brooklyn's Pratt Institute, he has also served as an educator at Cooper Union Art School, New York University, and the Metropolitan Museum of Art, sometimes teaching in conjunction with Raphael.

Biographical and Critical Sources

PERIODICALS

Booklist, April 15, 1995, Stephanie Zvirin, review of *Buffalo Bill and the Pony Express,* p. 1509; November 15, 1996, Stephanie Zvirin, review of *Buddy: The First Seeing Eye Dog,* p. 597; November 15, 1996, Carolyn Phelan, review of *First Flight: The Story of Tom Tate and the Wright Brothers,* p. 597; April 1, 1999, Hazel Rochman, review of *Abigail Takes the Wheel,* p. 1424.
Bulletin of the Center for Children's Books, May, 1970, p. 142; April, 1971, p. 118; July, 1986, review of *Pen and Ink* and *Pencil;* February, 1988.
Horn Book, April, 1971, p. 163; February, 1976, review of *Letters to Horseface: Being the Story of Wolfgang Amadeus Mozart's Journey to Italy 1769-1770 When He Was a Boy of Fourteen,* pp. 51-52; July-August, 1995, Maeve Visser Knoth, review of *Buffalo Bill and the Pony Express,* p. 456; March-April, 1997, Martha V. Parravano, review of *First Flight: The Story of Tom Tate and the Wright Brothers,* p. 214; March, 1999, Marilyn Bousquin, review of *Abigail Takes the Wheel,* p. 206.
Library Journal, November 15, 1967, Della Thomas, review of *Once upon a Mountain,* p. 4241; May 15, 1971, p. 1795.
School Library Journal, January, 1970, Mary B. Mason, review of *Me, Myself, and I,* p. 48; April, 1986,

Eleanor K. MacDonald, review of *Drawing Fashions: Figures, Faces, and Techniques,* p. 96; October, 1986; January, 1987, p. 71.

* * *

BOUCHER, (Clarence) Carter 1954-
(Uncle Carter)

Personal

Born August 20, 1954, in Fort Jackson, SC; son of George H. and Annie Laurie Boucher; married Sherry Lawson (an artist); children: Mary; stepchildren: Lauren Grubb, Sarah Grubb. *Education:* University of South Carolina, B.A. *Religion:* Baptist. *Hobbies and other interests:* Wildlife art.

Addresses

Home—Anderson, SC. *E-mail*—boucher@carol.net.

Career

Financial planner in Anderson, SC, 1998—. Also writer and painter.

Writings

Tiger Dave, illustrated by Leo Dunbar, Richard C. Owen Publishers (Katonah, NY), 1999.
Camel Ben, Richard C. Owens Publishers (Katonah, NY), 2001.

Some writings appear under the pseudonym Uncle Carter.

Work in Progress

Short stories.

Sidelights

Carter Boucher told *SATA:* "One of my greatest joys is to see children's eyes filled with wonder as they listen to a story that takes them to the world of imagination. I know it's been said many times, but the most magical sound in the world is laughter.

"My children's stories began simply when I made up stories to amuse children I worked with as a visual artist in residence. They then evolved into amusement and bedtime stories for my own children, my stepdaughter Sarah and then my own daughter Mary.

"Although I have stories come to me at all times of the day, my basic work habit is to make up one to five stories a night to tell my daughter. We record the stories on a micro-cassette recorder. The stories that get the best reaction from Mary are sent to Richard C. Owens publishers for consideration.

"As for advice to aspiring writers and illustrators, I would say to try to go beyond having a thick skin to the point where you actually consider whether you can grow from criticism."*

* * *

BROWN, Ken (James)

Personal

Born in Birmingham, England; married to Ruth Brown (a children's book author and illustrator); children: two sons. *Education:* Attended Birmingham Art College.

Addresses

Home—London, England. *Agent*—c/o Author Mail, Peachtree Publishers, 494 Armour Circle NE, Atlanta, GA 30324.

Career

Writer. Formerly art director in two advertising firms, LPE and J. Walter Thompson, both in London, England; graphic designer for the BBC, contributor to such programs as *Dad's Army* and *Watch;* director of television commercials; manager of his own production company; illustrator for Gallimard (publisher).

Awards, Honors

Mucky Pup was shortlisted for the Kate Greenaway Medal and winner of the Sheffield Children's Book Award.

Writings

SELF-ILLUSTRATED

Why Can't I Fly?, Anderson Press (London, England), 1990.
Nellie's Knot, Anderson Press (London, England), 1991, Macmillan (New York, NY), 1993.
Mucky Pup, Dutton (New York, NY), 1997.
Mucky Pup's Christmas, Dutton (New York, NY), 1999.
The Scarecrow's Hat, Peachtree Publishers (Atlanta, GA), 2001.
What's the Time, Grandma Wolf?, Peachtree Publishers (Atlanta, GA), 2001.

ILLUSTRATOR

David Day, *King of the Woods,* Four Winds Press (New York, NY), 1993.
Stephen Wyllie, *A Flea in the Ear,* Dutton (New York, NY), 1996.
(With others) Cheryl Willis Hudson, adaptor, *Many Colors of Mother Goose,* Just Us Books (East Orange, NJ), 1997.
Elizabeth MacDonald, *The Wolf Is Coming!,* Dutton (New York, NY), 1998.
Elizabeth MacDonald, *Dilly-Dally and the Nine Secrets,* Dutton (New York, NY), 1999.

Grandma Wolf cleans her cooking pot in Ken Brown's self-illustrated **What's the Time, Grandma Wolf?**

Sidelights

Ken Brown's realistic, yet luminously colored paintings are the highlight of both his own stories for children, and of the books he contributes to. His own stories for the young often have a slight air of mystery about them, as in *Nellie's Knot,* which centers on a young elephant whose trunk is tied in a knot to help her remember something important ... if only she could remember what it was. Brown's lush illustrations artfully combine realism and fantasy as Nellie's friends are seen preparing for her birthday party against a detailed jungle backdrop. Betty Roots called this "a friendly, happy jungle story full of love and fun" in *Books for Keeps.* Similarly, in *Why Can't I Fly?,* a hapless ostrich searches in vain for a reason why she remains earth-bound, and is rescued from despair by her friends. As in *Nellie's Knot,* the illustrations for *Why Can't I Fly?,* featuring "the African landscape, which he depicts in radiant watercolours," as Jeff Hynds put it in *Books for Keeps,* were singled out for praise by the critics. There is also a mystery at the heart of Brown's *What's the Time, Grandma Wolf?,* a picture book version of a tag game known as "What's the Time, Mr. Wolf?." Here, the author depicts Grandma Wolf as a possibly frightening newcomer to the woods, whose mysterious activities are either a threat to the other animals, or an invitation to join her for dinner. *Booklist* reviewer Ilene Cooper singled out the illustrations for special praise, calling

them "topnotch, with every character humorously distinctive."

For *The Scarecrow's Hat,* Brown employs a cumulative plot structure in which a chicken sets out to get the scarecrow's hat, and resorts to a long and complicated set of barters with most of the barnyard animals in order to gain it. The result is "a fun story, lavishly illustrated with Brown's delightful, light-drenched watercolors," proclaimed a reviewer in *For Kids—Teacher Magazine.* "Children will enjoy the repetition and refrain," added Wanda Meyers-Hines in *School Library Journal.* A reviewer for *Publishers Weekly* concluded: "The true standout here ... is Brown's artwork—his airy, sun-dappled watercolors evoke a pleasant summer day."

Pure entertainment is the successful aim of Brown's picture books featuring Mucky Pup. In the first, *Mucky Pup,* a playful puppy gets into trouble with the farmer's wife when he knocks over the trash bin, rolls in the coal dust, and otherwise makes a mess of her house. He is promptly deposited out of doors, where he meets up with a game little piglet, who likes to have the same kind of messy fun as the pup. Then the pup tumbles down a hill and falls into some water, from which he emerges spotlessly clean and is welcomed back into the house. *Booklist* reviewer Ilene Cooper noted that Brown's "pithy" text, combined with his energetic illustrations, make this "a good story-hour choice." A holiday setting gives the reason for re-playing this simple story in *Mucky Pup's Christmas.* Here, the hapless dog is banished to the barn after knocking over the Christmas tree among other things, and hooks up with his buddy the pig again for a roll in the first snow of the season. Cooper was again pleased by the warmth of Brown's simple text and the artistry of his watercolors, dubbing this "a merry addition to holiday shelves."

Brown is also much sought-after as an illustrator for others' stories. In David Day's *King of the Woods,* a small bird finds an apple and claims it for her own, until a larger animal asserts his rights as king of the woods, and claims the apple for his own. Each animal's claim is quickly superceded, however, by another, larger animal's appearance with the same claim of superiority. "Brown's watercolor beasts and birds gain in jocularity and puffed-up foolishness as the book progresses," noted a contributor to *Publishers Weekly.* In Stephen Wyllie's *A Flea in the Ear,* another bully gets his comeuppance when a fox tricks a dog into leaving the hen house, and then the kindly dog enlists his fleas to help him get revenge, and the return of the chickens, from the fox. Again, critics credited Brown's illustrations with turning a simple story into something extraordinary. "The cast of characters is expressively drawn, full of nuance and wit," remarked Ilene Cooper in *Booklist.* A reviewer for *Publishers Weekly* made similar remarks, concluding that *A Flea in the Ear* is "a fun jaunt of a picture book."

A favorite childhood game, this time hide-and-seek, is at the heart of *The Wolf Is Coming!,* written by Elizabeth MacDonald. This farce of a story begins with the rabbits, who go to the hen to hide from the wolf. Then they and the hen and her chicks go to the pigsty to hide from the wolf there. Then the pigs, chickens, and rabbits all rush to hide with the cows, and so on, until they all decide they must somehow squeeze into the stall with the donkey. *Booklist* contributor Hazel Rochman recommended the book for all those preschoolers who love a good game of hide-and-seek. Less frenetic is MacDonald's counting book, *Dilly-Dally and the Nine Secrets,* also illustrated by Brown. Here, Dilly Dally the Duck refuses to leave her place among the reeds of a little island no matter how many friends float by with enticing invitations to come and play. The resulting book offers "a little information, an affirmation of mother love, and plenty of counting practice," according to John Peters in *Booklist.*

Biographical and Critical Sources

PERIODICALS

Booklist, April 15, 1993, Kay Weisman, review of *Nellie's Knot,* p. 1522; June 1, 1996, Ilene Cooper, review of *A Flea in the Ear,* p. 1737; December 15, 1997, Ilene Cooper, review of *Mucky Pup,* p. 701; February 1, 1998, Hazel Rochman, review of *The Wolf Is Coming!,* p. 922; September 15, 1999, Ilene Cooper, review of *Mucky Pup's Christmas,* p. 265; February 1, 2000, John Peters, review of *Dilly-Dally and the Nine Secrets,* p. 1029; March 15, 2001, Connie Fletcher, review of *The Scarecrow's Hat,* p. 1402; July, 2001, Ilene Cooper, review of *What's the Time, Grandma Wolf?,* p. 2012.

Books for Keeps, May, 1990, Jeff Hynds, review of *Why Can't I Fly?,* p. 27; May, 1991, Betty Roots, review of *Nellie's Knot,* p. 29.

Horn Book Guide, fall, 1993, Amy Quigley, review of *Nellie's Knot,* p. 251.

Publishers Weekly, July 12, 1993, review of *King of the Woods,* p. 77; June 17, 1996, review of *A Flea in the Ear,* p. 63; September 27, 1999, review of *Mucky Pup's Christmas,* p.55; March 12, 2001, review of *The Scarecrow's Hat,* p. 88.

School Library Journal, January, 1991, Regina Pauly, review of *Why Can't I Fly?,* p. 68; March, 1994, Jacqueline Elsner, review of *King of the Woods,* p. 192; July, 1996, Barbara Kiefer, review of *A Flea in the Ear,* p. 75; December, 1997, Patricia Pearl Dole, review of *Mucky Pup,* p. 87; March, 1998, Barbara Elleman, review of *The Wolf Is Coming!,* p. 184; October, 1999, Lisa Falk, review of *Mucky Pup's Christmas,* p. 65; March, 2000, Susan Scheps, review of *Dilly-Dally and the Nine Secrets,* p. 210; April, 2001, Wanda Meyers-Hines, review of *The Scarecrow's Hat,* p. 99; September, 2001, Susan Hepler, review of *What's the Time Grandma Wolf?,* p. 183.

OTHER

For Kids—Teacher Magazine, http://www.edweek.org (July 18, 2001), review of *The Scarecrow's Hat.*

BYMAN, Jeremy 1944-

Personal

Born February 26, 1944, in Chicago, IL; son of Leonard (in sales) and Eleanor (a librarian; maiden name, Lesser) Byman; married Aline Sydney Faben, December 29, 1968 (divorced, September 12, 1977); married Elizabeth Lynn Hamilton (a college instructor), May 22, 1993. *Education:* Carleton College, B.A. (government and international relations), 1965; University of Chicago, M.A., Ph.D. (political science), 1975; New York University, M.A. (cinema studies), 1982.

Addresses

Home—10-F Park Village Lane, Greensboro, NC 27455. *E-mail*—jbyman@triad.rr.com.

Career

SUNY College—Buffalo, Buffalo, NY, assistant professor of political science, 1972-74; Illinois State University, Normal, IL, assistant professor of political science, 1974-76; University of North Carolina—Greensboro, Greensboro, NC, assistant professor of political science, 1976-84; Guilford Technical Community College, Jamestown, NC, instructor of political science, 1988-97; freelance writer, 1984—.

Writings

YOUNG ADULT BIOGRAPHY

Madam Secretary: The Story of Madeleine Albright, Morgan Reynolds (Greensboro, NC), 1998.

Ted Turner: Cable Television Tycoon, Morgan Reynolds (Greensboro, NC), 1998.

Andrew Grove and the Intel Corporation, Morgan Reynolds (Greensboro, NC), 1999.

Tim Duncan, Morgan Reynolds (Greensboro, NC), 2000.

J. P. Morgan: Banker to a Growing Nation, Morgan Reynolds (Greensboro, NC), 2001.

Carl Sagan: In Contact with the Cosmos, Morgan Reynolds (Greensboro, NC), 2001.

Author of numerous film reviews for *Triad Style* magazine, 1984—, and articles for local, regional, and national periodicals.

Work in Progress

"High Noon" and Its Enemies, expected in 2002.

Sidelights

Jeremy Byman began his career as a writer for young adults with a biography of the first female secretary of state in United States history. In *Madam Secretary: The Story of Madeleine Albright,* Byman recounts Albright's life story, from her parents' escape from Czechoslovakia during World War II, to her years as a student at a private girls' school and at Wellesley College. After

Wellesley, Albright married and began graduate school in political science. With her Ph.D. in hand, Albright joined the staff of U.S. Senator Edmund Muskie, who was a member of the Senate Foreign Relations Committee. This work put Albright into a position where she eventually was chosen to represent the United States at the United Nations, and later, to be secretary of state under President Clinton. The result is "a candid look at a woman who used her intelligence and political savvy to become one of the most influential players in what has been traditionally a game played only by men," concluded Maura Bresnahan in *Voice of Youth Advocates.* Although Hazel Rochman, writing in *Booklist,* cared less for Byman's detailed recounting of Albright's political maneuverings, Rochman, like Bresnahan, also concluded that "students will be interested in her breakthroughs as a woman."

Madam Secretary was quickly followed by *Ted Turner: Cable Television Tycoon,* a biography of a man who turned his father's billboard business into a huge media conglomerate including television and radio stations, a baseball team, and Cable News Network (CNN), which Turner created in 1980. Another remarkable business entrepreneur was the subject of Byman's next biography: *Andrew Grove and the Intel Corporation.* This work alternates chapters on Grove's life story with those on the life of the company he created, Intel, which is credited with pioneering work in microprocessors that paved the way for the home computer revolution. Like Albright, Byman's earlier subject, Grove began his life as a Jewish refugee from World War II, and went on to a successful college career that set him up for later success in business. Byman's focus on Intel over the course of thirty years "will interest computer enthusiasts and should prove an excellent resource for business students," concluded Roger Leslie in *Booklist.*

Jeremy Byman

Tim Duncan, a rising star in the National Basketball Association (NBA), is the subject of another Byman biography. Here, the author focuses on Duncan's achievements in college, when every year his abilities brought the suspicion that he would drop out of college to play professionally and every year he decided to remain in school until he finished his degree. In 1998, Duncan was named NBA Rookie of the Year, and his team won the championship the following year.

Byman is also the author of *Carl Sagan: In Contact with the Cosmos,* a biography of one of the most famous scientists of the late twentieth century. *Booklist* reviewer Carolyn Phelan praised the author for offering "a balanced picture of Sagan's sometimes controversial life and ideas," which included a sincere belief in the search for life outside our solar system. Byman also garnered praise for *J. P. Morgan: Banker to a Growing Nation,* in which he makes clear why Morgan was both beloved and reviled during his lifetime, according to Marilyn Heath in *School Library Journal.*

Byman told *SATA:* "I backed into a writing career. I had been a college teacher for many years, and thought I would do that until I retired. But I discovered that I was more interested in writing for general audiences than for scholarly ones, and started writing movie reviews and articles for local magazines, as well as advertising copy. Quite by accident, I met a publisher of books for young adults, and he invited me to write a biography of Secretary of State Madeleine Albright. I did, and though I didn't know it at the time, I was off and running. I've since written five more biographies for middle and high school students. I'm currently working on my first book for adults (not counting an unpublished doctoral dissertation). It's about the classic western *High Noon*—how it came to be made, how it changed the course of both films and filmmaking, and how it came to be at the center of an on-going argument about the proper way to make movies. I expect I'll continue to do a bit of everything in the future—adult books, young adult, and magazines."

Biographical and Critical Sources

PERIODICALS

Booklist, December 15, 1997, Hazel Rochman, review of *Madam Secretary: The Story of Madeleine Albright,* p. 688; April, 1998, Anne O'Malley, review of *Ted Turner: Cable Television Tycoon,* p. 1309; March 15, 1999, Roger Leslie, review of *Andrew Grove and the Intel Corporation,* p. 1322; June 1, 2000, Carolyn Phelan, review of *Tim Duncan,* p. 1883; November 1, 2000, Carolyn Phelan review of *Carl Sagan: In Contact with the Cosmos,* p. 528.
Horn Book Guide, fall, 1999, Jack Forman, review of *Andrew Grove and the Intel Corporation,* p. 377.
Kirkus Reviews, March 15, 1998, review of *Ted Turner,* p. 399.
School Library Journal, April, 1998, Rebecca O'Connell, review of *Madam Secretary,* p. 142; August, 1998,

Jennifer Ralston, review of *Ted Turner,* p. 171; May, 1999, Todd Morning, review of *Andrew Grove and the Intel Corporation,* p. 135; August, 2000, John Peters, review of *Carl Sagan,* p. 196; July, 2001, Marilyn

Heath, review of *J. P. Morgan: Banker to a Growing Nation,* p. 120.

Voice of Youth Advocates, June, 1998, Maura Bresnahan, review of *Madam Secretary,* p. 140.

C

CALHOUN, Dia 1959-

Personal

Born January 4, 1959, in Seattle, WA; daughter of James (a small business owner) and Eva Alaire (a homemaker; maiden name, Sneed) Calhoun; married Shawn Richard Zink (a cabinetmaker), February 17, 1990. *Education:* Mills College, B.A. (English), 1980. *Hobbies and other interests:* Fly fishing, canoeing, hiking, gardening, sopranos, yoga, fairy goddaughter.

Addresses

Home and office—2712 North Tenth St., Tacoma, WA 98406.

Career

Writer. Freelance lettering artist and logo designer, 1984-1999 (designed the logotype for Alaska Airlines). *Member:* Society of Children's Book Writers and Illustrators, Phi Beta Kappa.

Awards, Honors

Editors' Choice for Top Ten Best First Novels, *Booklist,* 1999, Best Fantasy novel, *Booklist,* 1999, Best Fantasy, Science Fiction and Horror List, *Voice of Youth Advocates,* 1999, Silver Medal Book of the Year Award, *ForeWord* magazine, 2000, Best Book for Young Adults, American Library Association (ALA), 2000, Lone Star Reading List and Garden State Young Adult Reading List, both 2001, and Young Adult's Choice, International Reading Association (IRA), 2001, all for *Firegold;* Best Fantasy, Science Fiction and Horror List, *Voice of Youth Advocates,* 2000, Books for the Teen Age, New York Public Library, 2001, Bronze Medal Book of the Year Award, *ForeWord* magazine, 2001, Teacher's Choice, IRA, 2001, Best Children's Book list, Bank Street College, 2001, Kentucky Blue Grass Award Reading List, 2001, and Best Book for Young Adults, ALA, 2001, all for *Aria of the Sea.*

Writings

Firegold, illustrated by Herve Blondon, Winslow House (New York, NY), 1999.
Aria of the Sea, Winslow House (New York, NY), 2000.

Work in Progress

Prequel to *Firegold,* set four hundred years earlier.

Sidelights

Novelist Dia Calhoun has produced two award-winning fantasy titles for teens, *Firegold* and *Aria of the Sea,* novels that explore other realms but which are grounded in the universal issues facing adolescents and teens. "My novels are about heroes journeying to the true self, the true voice, and who are seeking the strength to speak with that voice," Calhoun told *Authors and Artists for Young Adults (AAYA)* in an interview. "Though my books use fantasy elements, they do not follow the usual forms of the fantasy genre. Primarily, they are coming-of-age stories; secondarily they are fantasy stories. I feel they are unique to the genre." Inspiration for her well-received fantasies also comes from very real sources: in the case of her debut novel, *Firegold,* it was the commercial orchard which her in-laws own in Eastern Washington; for *Aria of the Sea* it was her own experience with ballet.

In an article for *Voice of Youth Advocates,* Calhoun wrote of her "magic scrap bag" of experiences, comparing the writing process to that of quilt-making. "In the old, practical days," Calhoun noted, "a woman made a quilt based on what she had in her scrap bag.... In the same way, I write my books with what is at hand, using whatever comes out of the scrap bag." Yet for Calhoun, such a process of sorting through memory and experience is initially quite prosaic. "All of my scraps are rather ordinary.... No encounters with unicorns, no conversations with wizards; my mother did not croon fairy tales to me in the womb. Ordinary—until I reach into the scrap bag and pull out pieces for a book. Then the magic swoops in. Somehow the ordinary pieces

In Dia Calhoun's first novel, blue-eyed Jonathan leaves the brown-eyed folk of the Valley to search for his heritage and returns with a legendary Firegold apple to bring about reconciliation. (Cover illustration by Herve Blondon.)

transform into magic apples, singing goddesses, and black ships!"

Born in Seattle, Washington, in 1959, Calhoun grew up in ballet slippers. She trained from age five to sixteen to become a professional dancer; her dream was to dance with a New York company. But beyond dance, there was another wish. "I always knew I wanted to write," Calhoun remarked in an author interview on her publisher's Web site. "In fact I knew in the second grade that's what I wanted to do." Calhoun grew up loving to read, dance, write, draw, and play music; as an adult she finally learned how to combine all these diverse interests by using bits and pieces of each in her writing. A self-confessed "dreamy, imaginative, sensitive child who always had her nose in a book," Calhoun had a list of favorite books which included *The Hundred Dresses* by Eleanor Estes, the 'Little House' books by Laura Ingalls Wilder, *Ballet Shoes* by Noel Streatfield, *A Wrinkle in Time* by Madeline L'Engle, and *The Little Lame*

Princess by Dinah Mulock Craik. "My parents encouraged me in everything creative," Calhoun noted in her interview, but she credits a schoolteacher with encouraging her writing proclivities. "My second-grade teacher, Muriel Kennedy, who loved poetry, urged me to be a writer." One of her earliest products, a poem when she was in the fifth grade, was titled "Our Classroom Flag." Of this early work, Calhoun commented on her publisher's Web site: "It was truly terrible, but it rhymed!"

But soon Calhoun had a choice to make—between dance and college. "I enjoyed school and excelled in liberal arts subjects," Calhoun explained. "When I was a teenager, I studied ballet quite seriously, training for at least two hours a day six days a week. This left little time for the usual teenage activities." Calhoun knew that she would soon have to make a decision to opt for either a professional career in dance or to go on to college. At age fifteen, however, she had foot surgery, and recovering from that and unable to dance, she became more interested in academic work. "At sixteen, I completed my senior year in high school at the University of Washington in Seattle. At seventeen, I quit dancing seriously."

After graduation, and deciding to focus on academics rather than dance, Calhoun attended Mills College in Oakland, California. "My years at Mills College were fabulous," Calhoun stated. "What a wonderful place! I studied English and book arts—fine letterpress printing and graphic design. I also took writing classes. After the immensity of the University of Washington, I loved the small liberal arts college atmosphere. Because there were no men in class, I became more assertive." At Mills, Calhoun decided she wanted ultimately to be a writer, but also realized that she would need some way to support herself in the meantime.

"I chose graphic design," Calhoun noted in her interview, of her pragmatic career decision. "Fresh out of college, I worked as an art intern in an advertising agency in San Francisco. Later, after a few months in Europe, I studied commercial art training at the Art Center College of Design in Los Angeles. I focused on lettering and logo design. As soon as my portfolio was ready, I returned to Seattle and began a career as a freelancing lettering artist." In that capacity, Calhoun did, among other projects, lettering for book jackets. One of her biggest coups during her freelance career was the logo for Alaska Airlines.

In her late twenties, once her business was established, she began experimenting with her long-time dream: writing. "I began writing for one hour every morning," Calhoun recalled. "I never consciously decided to write a children's novel, but when I began writing seriously, regularly, that was what emerged. . . . I still had my collection of children's books and still loved reading them. They were a refuge, just as they had been when I was a child—a refuge from study and ballet and the exigencies of the playground—a magical refuge." On her publisher's Web site, Calhoun said, "I never really found my stride [with writing] until I tried novels.

Everyone says to start with short stories but I'm just not a short story person—I'm too long-winded. I like to weave lots of threads together. My first novel was a middle-grade novel; I wrote it after the space shuttle crash. It's about a sixth grade girl who plays the violin, and the crash has a profound effect on her."

Calhoun worked at her new craft for years before making any breakthrough. "Gradually I increased my writing time to three hours a day," Calhoun remarked. "After five years of work and learning, I finished my first publishable novel—*Firegold.* I sent it to slush piles at six houses before the seventh, Winslow House, bought it. I had neither an agent nor any special contacts."

"Almost everything I write starts with a single impression or image," Calhoun noted on her publisher's Web site. "For *Firegold,* that thing was a memory I've had from childhood, a memory of standing beside a river and having that creepy feeling of being watched. My husband's family owns a commercial orchard. I was there one day, heard the river roaring in the distance and thought—aha! That one memory started the whole book."

Firegold tells the story of a thirteen-year-old boy, Jonathon, who feels he is different from everyone else. The Valley folk are all brown-eyed, and Jonathan's blue eyes set him apart and will surely drive him mad by the time he is an adult, according to Valley lore. In fact, Jonathon's family does not really fit in with the other Valley people. His father, Brian Brae, is a fiercely proud man who has, according to Donna Scanlon writing in *Rambles,* "carried on his family's obsession of searching for the legendary Firegold apples." Jonathon's mother, Karena, is from the north and has never really been able to fit in with the other Valley women. The story opens with Jonathon fishing at the river when he suddenly feels he is being watched. There, hiding behind a boulder, is a young girl whose hair is flaming red with golden streaks in the sunlight and whose cap seems to have little horns. Gazing at him, her eyes are as blue as his own. At first Jonathon is terrified, for she is clearly a Dalriada, one of the barbarians from the Red Mountains whom the Valley people fear. Running home to his parents, Jonathon stumbles into the midst of an argument they are having about when he, Jonathon, will be old enough to accompany his father to the same Red Mountains to hunt. The father feels a boy of twelve is old enough, but the mother holds out for fourteen. So Brian leaves without his son, but returns with a wonderful gift for Jonathon: a colt, black with gold streaks in its mane, a prize from the Dalriada's horses. This horse changes Jonathon's life forever. The colt and the Red Mountains begin calling to him, and he wonders why dark ridges have suddenly appeared on his forehead. Saddened at the death of his mother, Jonathon is confronted with more perplexing questions about his origins. When blight begins killing the local orchard trees, Jonathon is blamed, and he is forced to leave the Valley to search for his identity in the Red Mountains. There he discovers that the Dalriadas are neither barbaric nor crazy, and he

decides to stay with them. Yet for Jonathon, this voyage of discovery and coming-of-age will not be complete until he journeys back to the Valley to see his father.

Critical reception to Calhoun's first novel was overwhelmingly positive. Melanie C. Duncan, writing in *School Library Journal,* felt that "Jonathan's quest evokes a timeless struggle for identity amid vivid imagery, heartbreaking loss, and a subtle weave of fantasy." Scanlon noted that Calhoun "has a good eye for detail, and her writing appeals to all senses," and further commented that "Calhoun is off to a flying start." "A writer to watch," is how a reviewer for *Voice of Youth Advocates* described Calhoun, while also remarking that *Firegold* "is a promising first novel with depth and subtlety in its development." A contributor for *Bulletin of the Center for Children's Books* wrote, "Calhoun has created a compelling mythology for two warring cultures, once one but now separate, and the boy who seeks to reunite them." A writer for *ForeWord* magazine noted, "An intriguing debut novel, Calhoun's *Firegold* captures the imagination as readers follow the

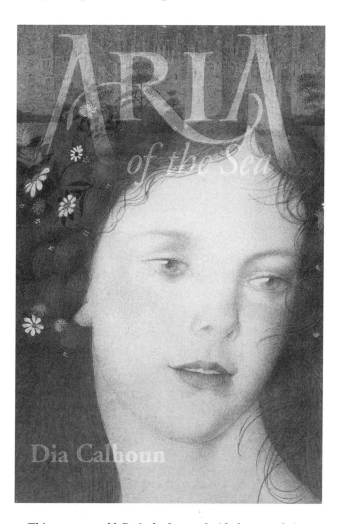

Thirteen-year-old Cerinthe has to decide between being a dancer or healer at the Royal Dancing School in the kingdom of Windward in Calhoun's fantasy story inspired by her training as a classical ballet dancer. (Cover illustration by Gennady Spirin.)

adventure-filled story of Jonathan Brae." The same reviewer concluded, "This coming-of-age story will give inspiration and courage to those nine to fourteen." Writing in *Kirkus Reviews,* a contributor called *Firegold* a "heartfelt, emotionally trenchant coming-of-age adventure with a lightly mystical bent," and further observed that Calhoun "neatly joins the psychological and adventurous aspects of a boy's journey to adulthood with its more enigmatic side." "This first novel by Calhoun succeeds on many levels," announced a reviewer for *Kliatt,* who numbered "a strong sense of place" among the author's other stylistic achievements. The same critic applauded Calhoun's "realistic" details about farming, horses, hunting with a bow, and life in the mountains. And in a starred *Booklist* review, Holly Koelling wrote that Jonathan "is a finely crafted and immensely sympathetic character who draws the reader into his adventures in self-discovery." Koelling concluded that Calhoun's first book is a "rich and complex first novel for teens, which mixes fantasy, adventure, and coming-of-age." The recipient of numerous awards and honors, including a Best Books for Young Adults citation from the American Library Association and a Young Adult's Choice from the International Reading Association, *Firegold* was an auspicious debut for Calhoun.

Calhoun followed up this promising entry into the young adult market with an equally compelling second novel set in the fantasy maritime kingdom of Windward, a book which she had begun even as her manuscript of *Firegold* was making the rounds of publishers. Drawing on her ballet background as well as the landscape of her native Puget Sound for *Aria of the Sea,* Calhoun tells the story of thirteen-year-old Cerinthe Gale, a commoner from the backward and rustic Northern Reach. The daughter of a sail maker, Cerinthe is torn between her twin ambitions: to become a folk healer or to become a dancer. When her mother dies under her care, Cerinthe is shattered and follows her mother's final wish—to go to the capital of Windward, Faranor, to audition for the esteemed School of the Royal Dancers. As a commoner, she stands little chance, but in fact, she does win entrance to the school. However, this does not end her trials, for she meets a talented and wealthy classmate, Elliana, who becomes her rival and nemesis. Cerinthe does find friends at the school though, including the troubled Sileree and Tayla, one of the housemaids. She is also and ultimately apprenticed by Mederi Grace, a healer whom Cerinthe at first is frightened of because of her supposed magic powers, but who soon enlightens the young girl in the ways of healing. Cerinthe's real challenge comes when she must use her powers as a healer to cure Elliana and thereby learns her true calling.

Again, Calhoun's creative efforts won praise and commendations from critics. A reviewer for *Publishers Weekly* called *Aria of the Sea* a "compelling novel," further noting that "readers will remember ... the exceedingly well drawn atmospheric setting and the winning heroine, torn between her two callings." Bruce Anne Shook, writing in *School Library Journal,* felt that this story about "recognizing and responding to one's true calling" has a "powerful message" without being "didactic." Shook concluded, "This fine story has elements of fantasy ... as well as realistic descriptions of dance practice and performance." A critic for *Kirkus Reviews* also lauded Calhoun's ballet description, which "vividly evokes the school's high-strung atmosphere, as well as the joys and challenges of dance." "Any young adult who dreams of dancing, princesses, and a smashing intellectual career will love this story," declared Melinda Elzinga in a *Book Report* review of *Aria of the Sea.* "Calhoun creates a world that completely pulls the reader into it," wrote a contributor for *Voice of Youth Advocates,* who also applauded the Calhoun's creation of a "strong female protagonist who has a passionate attachment to nature and the sea."

Calhoun, who generally writes five hours a day, six days a week at a home office, has also explored the world of *Firegold* in a prequel, set four centuries before that initial book. Additionally, she is investigating the possibility of a companion novel to her *Aria of the Sea.* "My goal," Calhoun remarked, "is to write better and better books. My favorite thing about writing is the spurt of exhilaration that comes when I suddenly see how an image or idea weaves into the whole tapestry of the novel. I love the moments of epiphany." But for Calhoun, such epiphanies come through hard work. "If you want to be a writer," she told *AAYA,* "don't wait for a perfect idea. Start now and write a little bit every day. That's magic." For the author, "fantasy is a way of talking about serious issues while being removed from them at the same time," as she related on her publisher's Web site. Calhoun added, "I hope that young people will be provoked by my work, provoked to think and dream and wonder and change. After the last page, I hope they go forward with strength, courage, and with eyes in their hearts."

Biographical and Critical Sources

BOOKS

Calhoun, Dia, interview with J. Sydney Jones for *Authors and Artists for Young Adults,* Volume 44, Gale (Detroit, MI), 2002.

PERIODICALS

Booklist, May 15, 1999, Holly Koelling, review of *Firegold,* p. 1690; November 15, 1999, p. 618; April 15, 2000, p. 1546.
Book Report, September-October, 1999, p. 58; November-December, 2000, Melinda Elzinga, review of *Aria of the Sea,* p. 57.
Bulletin of the Center for Children's Books, September 1, 1999, review of *Firegold.*
ForeWord, June 1, 1999, review of *Firegold.*
Kirkus Reviews, May 1, 1999, review of *Firegold;* September 1, 2000, review of *Aria of the Sea.*
Kliatt, May 1, 1999, review of *Firegold.*
Publishers Weekly, August 14, 2000, review of *Aria of the Sea,* p. 356.
School Library Journal, June, 1999, Melanie C. Duncan, review of *Firegold,* p. 126; September, 2000, Bruce Anne Shook, review of *Aria of the Sea,* p. 225.

Voice of Youth Advocates, August, 1999, review of *Firegold,* p. 189; October, 2000, review of *Aria of the Sea,* p. 272; April, 2001, Dia Calhoun, "The Magic Scrap Bag: Why I Write Fantasy for Teens," pp. 16-17.

OTHER

Winslow Press, http://www.winslowpress.com/ (July 17, 2001), interview with Dia Calhoun.
Rambles, http://www.rambles.net/ (July 17, 2001), Donna Scanlon, review of *Firegold.*

*   *   *

CAMERON, Ann 1943-

Personal

Born October 21, 1943, in Rice Lake, WI; daughter of William Angus (a lawyer) and Lolita (a teacher; maiden name, Lofgren) Cameron; married Bill Cherry (a retired congressional committee staff director), 1990; children: Angela, Cristi (stepdaughters). *Education:* Radcliffe College, B.A. (with honors), 1965; University of Iowa, M.F.A., 1972. *Politics:* Democrat.

Addresses

Home—Calle Principal, Panajachel, Solola, Guatemala. *Agent*—Ellen Levine Literary Agency, 15 East 26th St., Suite 1801, New York, NY 10010. *E-mail*—ann@childrensbestbooks.com.

Career

Writer, editor, and teacher. Works with Lake Atitlan Libraries, Inc., a U.S. nonprofit organization that funds book purchases for Central American community libraries. *Member:* Authors Guild, Authors League of America.

Awards, Honors

MacDowell Colony fellow, 1968; guest at Yaddo Colony, 1968; grant from National Endowment for the Humanities, 1974; Irma Simonton Black Award, 1981, for *The Stories Julian Tells;* Parents' Choice Award, 1986, and Selectors' Choice, *Wilson Library Bulletin,* 1988, both for *More Stories Julian Tells;* Children's Book Award, Child Study Children's Book Committee at Bank Street College, 1988, and Jane Addams Award, 1989, both for *The Most Beautiful Place in the World;* Blue Ribbon book, *Bulletin of the Center for Children's Books,* 1995, for *The Stories Huey Tells;* National Books Award finalist, and Parents' Choice Gold Award, both 1998, both for *The Secret Life of Amanda K. Woods;* Parents' Choice Silver Award, 2000, for *Gloria's Way.*

Writings

The Seed, Pantheon (New York, NY), 1975.
Harry, the Monster, Pantheon (New York, NY), 1980.

Ann Cameron

The Stories Julian Tells, illustrated by Ann Strugnell, Pantheon (New York, NY), 1981.
More Stories Julian Tells, illustrated by Ann Strugnell, Knopf (New York, NY), 1986.
Julian's Glorious Summer, illustrated by Dora Leder, Random House (New York, NY), 1987.
Julian, Secret Agent, illustrated by Diane Allison, Random House (New York, NY), 1988.
The Most Beautiful Place in the World, illustrated by Thomas B. Allen, Knopf (New York, NY), 1988.
Julian, Dream Doctor, illustrated by Ann Strugnell, Random House (New York, NY), 1990.
The Stories Huey Tells, Knopf (New York, NY), 1995.
(Adapter) *The Kidnapped Prince: The Life of Olaudah Equiano,* introduction by Henry L. Gates, Knopf (New York, NY), 1995.
More Stories Huey Tells, Farrar, Straus (New York, NY), 1997.
The Secret Life of Amanda K. Woods, Frances Foster Books (New York, NY), 1998.
Gloria's Way, illustrated by Lis Toft, Farrar, Straus (New York, NY), 2000.
Gloria Rising, illustrated by Lis Toft, Farrar, Straus (New York, NY), 2002.

Author of introduction, *The Angel Book,* Balance House, 1978. Contributor of stories to *Iowa Review* and *Northwest Review;* contributor of an essay to *Booktalk,* published by the National Council of Teachers of English; contributor of an essay, "Up the Next Mountain," to *Journal of Youth Services in Libraries,* fall, 1998.

Sidelights

"I try to write about characters who have inner abundance—sympathy, imagination, inventiveness, hope, intelligence—and who make happy lives despite modest outer resources," Ann Cameron once told *Something about the Author* (*SATA*). Known for her award-winning books about Julian and his younger brother Huey, Cameron offers young readers stories about issues common to all children, regardless of background. Critics give the author warm praise for her ability to create characters with whom children can identify, as well as her skills at integrating well-meaning adults into her stories. Unlike many books written for a younger audience where adults play an unimportant role, in Cameron's books, children appreciate their elders for their helpful advice. Reviewers consider this feature a highlight of the author's writing, an element she handles gracefully and effectively, without being didactic.

Although she disliked grade school, Cameron read constantly. She once related to *SATA*, "I loved books about characters who struggled to make a happy life for

Mystically "swapping" hands with her friend before he moves away gives Amanda the power to cope with life in 1950s rural Wisconsin. (Cover illustration by Ruth Marten.)

themselves, and who succeeded. I knew from my own childhood that often I wasn't happy, that often even adults did not lead happy lives. The books I loved best taught me to hope, and helped me to believe life could be, if not all good, at least mostly good and even wonderful. Books—especially fiction and autobiography—gave me energy. They were a kind of magic—nothing but paper and ink and a little glue, and then you opened their covers and found they held life inside them. That's why from a very early age (about third grade) I wanted to be a writer—the person who captures the positive energy of life, wraps it in paper, and gives it, all shimmering and forever bright, to others."

After earning a bachelor's degree with honors at Radcliffe College, she went to New York City to work in publishing, hoping to hone her writing skills along the way. In 1965 she found a job as an editorial assistant in the trade department of Harcourt Brace Jovanovich. Cameron told *SATA:* "It was a thrill to work in publishing, to get a thank-you letter for some reviews of Virginia Woolf's essays from her husband, Leonard Woolf; to read the correspondence in which Alfred Harcourt had rejected Faulkner's *The Sound and the Fury;* to see and meet many famous editors and authors—Lewis Mumford, Paula Fox, Anaïs Nin, Irving Howe; and to learn to edit books. However, after two and a half years in publishing, I thought it was time to take the leap into writing. I began an adult novel and on the basis of my incomplete manuscript received a fellowship for a master's degree in creative writing at the University of Iowa, plus invitations to the artists' colonies MacDowell and Yaddo for the summer of 1968. With fellowship and recognition heaped on me, I told my friend Paula Fox I felt like I was walking on God's hand. Paula responded, 'It's a very narrow hand.' She couldn't have been more right.

"At Iowa I became overwhelmed by all I hadn't read, all I didn't know. My adult novel ground to a halt; I couldn't figure out how to organize my experience. What did I really have to say that other writers hadn't already said much better?

"In the midst of my discouragement, I remembered that children's books were short. 'At least I might be able to get through one,' I thought. My second attempt at a children's book—about a seed in the ground who hears a storm above her head and becomes afraid to grow—was published in 1975."

Completing her M.F.A. at the University of Iowa in 1972, Cameron lived in Berkeley, California, for a year, and then returned to New York City, working freelance as a manuscript reader for literary agents. After a multitude of odd jobs, including editing an archaeologists's thesis, working as a camp cook in the rain forest on a Mayan dig in Belize, Central America, and evaluating the potential movie prospects of books for a Hollywood film company, Cameron found her first book, *The Seed,* published in 1975, followed several years later by *Harry, the Monster.*

In 1981 Cameron scored a breakthrough with *The Stories Julian Tells.* Responding to Julian's stories in the *New York Times Book Review,* Natalie Babbit wrote, "You have to go a long way these days to find a book that leaves you feeling as happy as this one." The African-American hero of the stories is Julian Bates, whom Julie Corsaro described in *Booklist* as "energetic, engaging, and intelligent." His brother Huey, his best friend Gloria, and his wise and loving parents all play important roles in Julian's life. When Julian's creativity and enthusiasm lead him into trouble, his parents help him toward self-discovery, moral growth, and pride in his achievements.

Cameron once explained to *SATA* that *The Stories Julian Tells* "was inspired by some stories a friend of mine, Julian DeWette, told me about his childhood." DeWette, a South African, and his brother had once eaten a pudding his father had made as a special present for their mother. Cameron's version ends with the two boys, who've hidden under their bed to escape their angry father, finding they can make amends by cooking a new pudding. The story reminded Cameron that much of childhood is spent trying to fathom the rules of adults and living up to one's own developing sense of morality.

With *The Stories Julian Tells,* Cameron's work began to receive wide recognition. According to Liz Waterland in *Books for Keeps,* the "Julian stories have been deservedly popular ever since they first appeared." Along with the pudding story, *The Stories Julian Tells* includes tales about making a first friend; cats that do gardening work; and Julian's attempt to grow tall by eating a fig tree's leaves, nearly killing the tree. *More Stories Julian Tells* provides five additional stories which, as David Gale wrote in *School Library Journal,* "sparkle with all the innocence and experience of childhood" and "reflect incidents true to children." In this work, Julian learns the destructive effects of name-calling; discovers that his best friend, Gloria, really can move the sun; and sends a message in a bottle that unfortunately gets stuck very close to home.

Three of the Julian books present longer stories with chapters for young readers. *Julian's Glorious Summer* begins when his friend Gloria offers to help him learn to ride the new bike she received for her birthday. Julian cannot tell her that he is afraid of falling, so he gives a false excuse for not riding. He pretends that his father is putting him to work, nights and days. When Julian persuades his father to give him work so that Gloria will believe his excuse, Dad responds with more work than Julian would prefer. Julian finally confides to his mother that he is afraid of falling off a bicycle. His parents then give him a bike for all the work he has done, and he learns to ride and enjoy it. A *Booklist* critic appreciated Cameron's "well-paced plot" and "fine characterizations of Julian's struggles."

Julian, Secret Agent finds Julian, Gloria, and Huey pretending to be "crimebusters." They decide to track down the criminals on the most-wanted posters they see at the post office, but their visits to the supermarket and

hospital give them opportunities to rescue a dog from a hot car and a child from a fountain instead. When the secret agents visit a café, they are certain the cook is a wanted bank robber. It takes the police chief himself to convince them that the "bank robber" is really his son. A critic for *Junior Bookshelf* praised Cameron's "enviable knack of weaving intriguing stories out of small incidents."

Julian is busy sleuthing again in *Julian, Dream Doctor.* This time, however, Julian is trying to figure out what his father wants for his birthday. Julian and Huey first try to use the brainwave machine they have made, and when that fails, they prompt their sleeping father to tell them his "biggest dream," which turns out to be "two snakes. Big ones." When the boys present Dad with the gift they worked so hard to find, Dad is horrified and must confess that snakes are his biggest nightmare. A critic for *Junior Bookshelf* asserted that "Julian's parents are a bit too good to be true." In her *Booklist* review, however, Corsaro appreciated Cameron's ability to develop "well-realized characters and situations."

In 1983 Cameron traveled to Guatemala to visit New York filmmaker Pablo Zavala, a close friend who was from that country. She told *SATA:* "I had always wanted to immerse myself in another culture. We have such brief, narrow lives and learn so little of all the ways to experience being human. Each culture sees the world and the meaning of life with slightly different eyes. I wanted to grow, to see things more than one way, to find more than one way of seeing myself.

"I went to Guatemala for a short vacation, but with the hope that I might stay. In the highland town of Panajachel, which is on the shore of an enormous lake overshadowed by majestic volcanoes, I found a new home. I was in the garden of a Panajachel restaurant, when I looked down into my coffee cup and saw it full of the golden reflections of flowers, and knew this was the place I wanted to stay."

The Most Beautiful Place in the World is set in a Guatemalan town much like Panajachel, where Cameron now lives. As she wrote in *School Library Journal,* the character of the narrator of this book, a seven-year-old boy named Juan, is based on a boy Cameron knows. In *The Most Beautiful Place in the World,* Juan's father has abandoned the family, and when his mother finds a new husband, she is forced to leave Juan with his grandmother. Grandmother's house is already full of children; Juan must help support the family by working as a shoe-shine boy. Juan works hard, but he cannot help wishing that he could go to school like the children he sees in the morning. He begins to teach himself to read by studying the street signs near the tourist office. After Juan relates his dream of going to school to his grandmother, she grants his wish, and Juan optimistically enters the first grade. As Ethel R. Twichell observed in *Horn Book,* this story provides an "unsentimental picture of Juan's hard life" as well as "a modest hope for his brighter future." Phillis Wilson concluded in *Booklist* that Juan tells his "bittersweet story with warmth and dignity," while a

New Yorker contributor commented, "Genuine and touching, this book has much to tell readers who are only acquainted with a land of plenty."

In *The Kidnapped Prince: The Life of Olaudah Equiano*, a shortened retelling of Olaudah Equiano's 1789 autobiography, Cameron gives children insight into the life of another child suffering hardship. Equiano was brutally kidnaped from Benin, Africa, and separated from his family when he was just eleven years old. Bought in Virginia by an English sea captain, he learned to read and write with the other boys on board the ship and survived horrifying battles during the Napoleonic Wars. Betrayed and re-sold by his captain, Equiano sailed between islands in the West Indies, trading small items, until he earned the money to buy his freedom. Calling it "a gripping story of adventure, betrayal, cruelty, and courage," *The Kidnapped Prince* remains "true to the spirit of the original," claimed to Hazel Rochman in *Booklist*.

In 1995 Cameron allowed Huey, the younger brother of her popular Julian character, to have a voice of his own in *The Stories Huey Tells*. In this chapter book, six-year-old Huey invents banana spaghetti, gets in trouble in a restaurant where he is expected to eat all of a baked trout that keeps staring him in the eye, and plays a clever trick on his older brother. Trying to earn a little respect from Julian, Huey complains about the way his older brother treats him like a little kid, a common refrain of younger siblings. "He always acts like nothing I say is important," the six-year-old says of Julian. "Kids everywhere will recognize their fears, dreams, and jokes in Huey's daily adventures," predicted *Booklist* contributor Hazel Rochman. According to *Horn Book* reviewer Maeve Visser Knoth, Cameron tells about Huey's exploits "with her usual rich language, strong sense of childhood angst, and gentle humor."

Huey returns, one year older, in *More Stories Huey Tells*. This time, Huey tries to resuscitate a dying sunflower plant with coffee, dig for buried treasure, and help his dad to quit smoking, among other things. Throughout the five stories, Cameron "writes without condescension," noted Hazel Rochman in her *Booklist* review. The critic commented positively on the author's attempts to capture the small boy's feelings, finding them "subtle and complicated and sometimes profoundly moving." Other critics remarked upon Cameron's ability to write convincing tales about elementary-school-age children growing up. "In these simple stories," *Horn Book* critic Susan P. Bloom wrote, "Cameron doesn't opt for easy solutions or pat answers."

An eleven-year-old girl from Wisconsin is featured in Cameron's 1998 novel *The Secret Life of Amanda K. Woods*, set in the 1950s. Young Amanda feels lonely after her best friend moves to another state. Wishing for more friends and for acceptance from her overbearing mother, the girl adapts new strategies for fitting in, actions that seem to go against her natural tendencies. Eventually, with help from her caring father and a kind teacher, Amanda charts a new course for herself, one

that is "gracefully conveyed through quiet, contemplative narrative," observed a critic in *Publishers Weekly*. Comparing Amanda's tale to that of Julian, *Booklist* contributor John Peters claimed that Cameron "brings the same warm humor and deep understanding of human nature" to her story about the fifth grader. Peters continued his favorable assessment of the novel, calling *The Secret Life of Amanda K. Woods* a "perceptive, emotionally engaging novel."

Critics also responded positively to the role adults play in Cameron's 2000 chapter book, *Gloria's Way*. The book offers young readers the chance to see "children learn[ing] to address their problems with the help of wise adults who offer them good counsel while respecting the children enough to let them work out their own solutions," according to a *Horn Book* contributor. The friend of Julian and Huey Bates, Gloria tells her own stories in six chapters, showing how the young narrator solves the minor crises in her life with the welcomed advice from well-meaning grown-ups. After a parrot ruins the valentine she made for her mother, Gloria is encouraged by Mr. Bates to make another, while her own mother comforts her when the young girl fears Julian prefers playing with a new neighbor rather than her. Writing in *Publishers Weekly*, a critic noticed that "the parents step in, without seeming intrusive, like guardian angels to smooth out life's little wrinkles." Describing the book, a *Kirkus Reviews* contributor observed, "Gloria, a spunky kid who gets into some strange predicaments, finds out that her friends and wise, loving adults are good to have around when trouble beckons." Gloria's adventures continue in *Gloria Rising*, where a meeting with a female astronaut inspires the youngster to set larger dreams for herself. According to a *School Library Journal* reviewer, "readers will ... identify with all involved and cheer when these satisfying characters are satisfyingly vindicated."

Cameron once described to *SATA* what it was like to be a writer: "Now that I've grown up, and become a writer, people say to me, 'I have a story for you'; or 'You could make a story out of that.' They seem to think that writers are like piggy banks, empty inside, and just waiting for some nice person to come along and put in a coin! But stories are not like that. My story will never be exactly like yours. I could never tell yours for you. Your story, if it's really the way you want to tell it, can never be wrong the way an arithmetic answer is wrong; and even if your mother, your father, your teacher or your best friend doesn't understand it, it's still right for you. Right answers in arithmetic are the same for everybody; but stories are individual, special, and all different—brand new thought-flowers blooming in the garden of your head."

The author added, "This doesn't mean that all stories are born perfect, there's usually a struggle to bring them to birth, to make them true to life, to give them fullness and individuality. Our truest and most interesting thoughts aren't always the ones that first come to mind. Writing is a lot like mining for precious ore. You may have to dig up a lot of valueless material before you hit the vein of something precious underneath—the outer surface of our minds is strewn with cliches, misunderstandings, blurred vision that comes from lack of close observation. We are all born with the capacity to discover and use our own inner abundance, but we have to hold on to the faith in ourselves, and be willing to give life our full attention, to shape stories that are both true and new. I once [said] that 'if we are put down, discriminated against, or abused, we lose access to our inner selves. We don't become who we are meant to be, and unfortunately, we pass our frustration and disappointments on to the next generation.' Now I'm struck by how often it's the person who's been put down, discriminated against or abused who overcomes and uses that very experience to become a great human being who speaks out for justice and truth and betters our world."

As an author, Cameron says she focuses on "characters who haven't lost touch with their own inner abundance," and hopes that her fictional young protagonists "can connect or re-connect children to the richness inside themselves."

Biographical and Critical Sources

BOOKS

Cameron, Ann, *Julian, Dream Doctor,* Random House (New York, NY), 1990.

Cameron, Ann, *The Stories Huey Tells,* Knopf (New York, NY), 1995.

Something about the Author Autobiography Series, Volume 20, Gale (Detroit, MI), 1995.

PERIODICALS

Booklist, December 15, 1987, review of *Julian's Glorious Summer,* pp. 702-703; January 1, 1989, Phillis Wilson, review of *The Most Beautiful Place in the World,* p. 784; May 15, 1990, Julie Corsaro, review of *Julian, Dream Doctor,* p. 1797; January 1, 1995, Hazel Rochman, review of *The Kidnapped Prince,* p. 816; November 15, 1995, Hazel Rochman, review of *The Stories Huey Tells,* p. 559; April 15, 1997, Hazel Rochman, review of *More Stories Huey Tells,* p. 1429; April 15, 1998, John Peters, review of *The Secret Life of Amanda K. Woods,* p. 1444; February, 2000, Carolyn Phelan, review of *Gloria's Way,* p. 1110.

Books for Keeps, July, 1990, Liz Waterland, p. 9.

Bulletin of the Center for Children's Books, June, 1980; January, 1982; December, 1987; December, 1988; December, 1995; July, 1997; May, 1998; August, 1998.

Horn Book, January, 1989, Ethel R. Twichell, review of *The Most Beautiful Place in the World,* p. 66; January-February, 1996, Maeve Visser Knoth, review of *The Stories Huey Tells,* p. 97; July-August, 1997, Susan P. Bloom, review of *More Stories Huey Tells,* p. 452; March, 2000, review of *Gloria's Way,* p. 193.

Junior Bookshelf, April, 1990, pp. 80-81; June, 1990, review of *Julian, Secret Agent,* p. 133; October, 1992, review of *Julian, Dream Doctor,* p. 196.

Junior Literary Guild, March, 1981.

Kirkus Reviews, January 1, 2000, review of *Gloria's Way.*

New Yorker, December 12, 1988, review of *The Most Beautiful Place in the World.*

New York Times Book Review, August 9, 1981, Natalie Babbit, review of *The Stories Julian Tells.*

Publishers Weekly, March 23, 1998, review of *The Secret Life of Amanda K. Woods,* p. 101; March 20, 2000, review of *Gloria's Way,* p. 92.

School Library Journal, April, 1986, David Gale, review of *More Stories Julian Tells,* p. 84; June, 1989, Ann Cameron, "Write What You Care About," pp. 50-51; January, 1996, Maggie McEwen, review of *The Stories Huey Tells,* p. 76; June, 1997, Jackie Hechtkopf, review of *More Stories Huey Tells,* p. 85; May, 1998, Cyrisse Jaffee, review of *The Secret Life of Amanda K. Woods,* p. 138; March, 2000, Anne Parker, review of *Gloria's Way,* p. 189; February 12, 2002, review of *Gloria Rising.*

OTHER

Ann Cameron Web Site, http://www.childrensbestbooks.com (December 12, 2001).

*   *   *

COLIN, Ann
See URE, Jean

*   *   *

COOKE, Trish 1962-

Personal

Born March 22, 1962, in Bradford, West Yorkshire, England; daughter of Abiah Basarbas (a cooper and engineer) and Agnes (a domestic) Cooke; married Devon Ramsden (a residential officer), July 24, 2000; children: Kieron Ramsden, Jermaine Ramsden. *Education:* Attended Leeds Polytechnic, 1980; Ilkley College, B.A. (performing arts), 1983. *Religion:* Roman Catholic.

Addresses

Agent—Caroline Walsh, David Higham Assoc. Ltd., 5-8 Lower John St., Golden Sq., London W1F GHA. *E-mail*—TrishCooke@trish61.freeserve.co.uk.

Career

Writer, actress. Presenter on British Broadcasting Corporation (BBC) children's television program *PlayDays;* has also appeared on *You and Me* and hosted the radio program *12345.*

Awards, Honors

Kurt Maschler Award, 1994, Smarties Book Prize (0-5 category), Highly Commended citation for Kate Greenaway Medal, 1995, and She/W. H. Smith Under Fives Book Prize, 1995, all for *So Much.*

Trish Cooke writes about the visiting relatives who want to squeeze, hug, and dance with the baby "so much." (*From* So Much, *illustrated by Helen Oxenbury.*)

Writings

FOR CHILDREN

Mammy, Sugar Falling Down, illustrated by Alicia Garcia De Lynam, Hutchinson (London, England), 1989.

Mrs. Molly's Shopping Trolley, illustrated by Rhian Nest-James, Collins Educational (London, England), 1991.

When I Grow Bigger, illustrated by John Bendall Brunello, Walker (London, England), Candlewick Press (Cambridge, MA), 1994.

Mr. Pam Pam and the Hullabazoo, illustrated by Patrice Aggs, Walker (London, England), Candlewick Press (Cambridge, MA), 1994.

So Much, illustrated by Helen Oxenbury, Walker (London, England), Candlewick Press (Cambridge, MA), 1994.

The Grandad Tree, illustrated by Sharon Wilson, Walker (London, England), Candlewick Press (Cambridge, MA), 2000.

Zoom!, illustrated by Alex Ayliffe, Collins (London, England), 2000.

Waiting for Baby, illustrated by Nicola Smee, Walker (London, England), 2000.

Full, Full, Full of Love, illustrated by Paul Howard, Candlewick Press (Cambridge, MA), 2003.

OTHER

Just a Spring Chicken (film script), Yorkshire Arts Funding for Pilot Film, 1982.

Shopping People, first produced at the Liverpool Play-house, 1989.

Running Dream, first produced at the Albany Empire, 1989.

Back Street Mammy, first produced at the Lyric Hamer-smith, 1991.

A Social Affair (film script), Illustra Films and Hammer-smith Health Authority Commission, 1991.

We Expect Respect (radio play), BBC Radio, 1991.

Gulp Fiction, first produced at the Civic Theatre, Peckham, 1995.

Ooooops Inside Her Head, first produced at the Royal Court Commission, 1995.

Love Them to Death, first produced at the West Yorkshire Playhouse Commission, 1995.

Mary's Light (radio play), BBC Radio, 1996.

The Harriet Tubman Story (radio play), BBC School Radio Drama, 1997.

Something to Think About (radio play), BBC School Radio, 1997.

Luv Dancin' (radio play), BBC Radio Drama, 1998.

Those Old Metal Things (radio play), BBC Radio, 1999.

Single Plus One (radio play), BBC Radio, 2000.

Author of television scripts for children's television programs, including *PlayDays,* BBC1, 1989-96; *You and Me,* BBC School TV, 1990-91; *Tweenies,* CBBC, 1999; and *Mags and Mo,* 2000; for adult television programs, including *Selecting for Quality,* BBC Open University, 1990; *East Enders,* BBC1, 1991; *The Real McCoy,* BBC1, 1994-95; *Brothers and Sisters,* BBC2, 1996; and comedy sketches for Channel Four, 1997; film scripts, including *Cold Water* and *Where Aeroplanes Go to Die,* both 2000.

Work in Progress

Catch! for Scholastic; *Diary of a West Indian Immi-grant,* for Franklin Watts (Orchard). Currently develop-ing a comedy drama series with Children's BBC New Writers called *Velma Lu.*

Sidelights

Trish Cooke's picture books convey the warmth and comfort of a loving family, often from the viewpoint of the smallest children in the family. In her book, *When I Grow Bigger,* Thomas does not enjoy being the smallest, especially when the older kids tease him with all he cannot do. Then his father steps in, and lifts Thomas up to his shoulders, and for a while, Thomas enjoys being the biggest of them all. A contributor to *Books for Keeps* praised Cooke's dialogue, characters, and storyline as "so true to life" that her preschool audience "cannot fail to recognise themselves." Likewise, Kay Weisman wrote in *Booklist:* "Cooke has a keen ear for children's conversations, and her characters ring true." The tone of Cooke's book, *Mr. Pam Pam and the Hullabazoo,* is that of a jaunty party, accentuating the delicious suspense of waiting for a visit from someone new and exciting, here,

Mr. Hullabazoo, an outlandish creature of rainbow colors with polka dots tossed in for fun. *School Library Journal* reviewer Rosanne Cerny recommended the book for reading aloud at story-hour, where the young audience will be drawn into the excitement of the small child in the story.

Likewise, a much-loved baby and a visit are at the center of *So Much,* Cooke's next book. Here, the author depicts a day when one by one, a little boy's house fills up with relatives who each want to hug, kiss, or play with him because they love him so much. When the house is full, in walks the boy's father and everyone shouts "Surprise!" "Cooke's bubbly language works perfectly with her cumulative structure to take full advantage of the excitement and suspense of each new arrival," remarked a contributor to *Publishers Weekly. Booklist* reviewer Ilene Cooper praised the book enthusiastically, writing: "Full of life, love, and laughter, this outsize picture book is a delight on every level."

In *The Grandad Tree,* her next book, Cooke takes on a more serious subject, the death of a family member, in a comforting manner that young children can understand. The text and pictures depict Grandad playing with his grandchildren in spring and summer, Grandad resting under the tree while the children pick apples in the fall, and watching from the window as they play in the winter. Then Grandad is gone and the children look at photos of him, play his fiddle, and honor his memory by planting an apple tree. "The sentiments conveyed are universal in this quiet, tender story, ripe with meaning and love," remarked Ellen Mandel in *Booklist.* Likewise, Miriam Lang Budin called *The Grandad Tree* "a gentle, thoughtful attempt to explain how loving memories of special people can endure long after they have died," in her review in *School Library Journal.*

Cooke told *SATA:* "I started writing children's books when I was still a child myself. I have older brothers and sisters so I became an aunt while I was still at a young age. My nephews and nieces were my audience and initially I made stories up for them. When I had children of my own I naturally told them stories. My first book was published the same year my eldest son was born.

"My mum and dad have been my greatest influence. They are born storytellers. Mum still tells a good story, although sadly dad died in 1994. They always made an ordinary event sound spectacular by how they told it to us.

"I like writing stories in lots of different forms: stage plays, radio, TV, as well as books. I write for adults and children. I'm also an actress and presented a children's TV programme for nine years for BBC (*PlayDays*). I was able to script some of the programmes too, which was good fun!"

Biographical and Critical Sources

PERIODICALS

Booklist, September 1, 1994, Kay Weisman, review of *When I Grow Bigger,* p. 49; March 1, 1995, Ilene Cooper, review of *So Much,* p. 1240; July, 1996, review of *So Much,* p. 6; June 1, 2000, Ellen Mandel, review of *The Grandad Tree,* p. 1896.

Books for Keeps, March, 1996, review of *When I Grow Bigger,* p. 6; July, 1996, review of *So Much,* p. 6.

Bulletin of the Center for Children's Books, November, 1994, review of *Mr. Pam Pam and the Hullabazoo,* pp. 84-85.

Horn Book Guide, July-December, 1994, review of *When I Grow Bigger* and *Mr. Pam Pam and the Hullabazoo,* p. 30.

Publishers Weekly, July 4, 1994, review of *When I Grow Bigger,* p. 61; November 14, 1994, review of *So Much,* p. 66.

School Library Journal, September, 1994, Nancy Seiner, review of *When I Grow Bigger,* p. 182; November, 1994, Rosanne Cerny, review of *Mr. Pam Pam and the Hullabazoo,* p. 74; January, 1995, Anna DeWind, review of *So Much,* p. 83; June, 2000, Miriam Lang Budin, review of *The Grandad Tree,* p. 104.

OTHER

Jubilee Books Web Site, http://www.jubileebooks.co.uk/ (February 23, 2002), author profile of Trish Cooke.*

*   *   *

CUMMINGS, Priscilla 1951-

Personal

Born April 13, 1951, in Ludlow, MA; daughter of Robert (a farmer and chemistry/physics teacher) and Brenda (a homemaker) Cummings; married John W. Frece (an aide to Maryland's governor), September 17, 1983; children: William Frece, Hannah Frece. *Education:* University of New Hampshire, B.A. (English literature), 1973.

Addresses

Home—3026 Aberdeen Rd., Annapolis, MD 21403. *E-mail*—PrisCummings@aol.com.

Career

Holyoke Transcript-Telegram, Holyoke, MA, newspaper reporter, 1973-75; *Hartford Courant,* Hartford, CT, newspaper reporter, 1975-76; *Richmond News Leader,* Richmond, VA, newspaper reporter, 1976-82; magazine editor and writer, 1982-85; writer of children's books, 1986—. *Member:* Society of Children's Book Writers and Illustrators, Children's Book Guild of Washington, DC.

Priscilla Cummings

Awards, Honors

Pick of the List, American Booksellers Association, 1997, and Maryland Black-Eyed Susan Book List, 1999-2000, both for *Autumn Journey;* International Literacy Award, Metro-Washington Association for Childhood Education, 2001, for "Chadwick" books; Notable Children's Book selection, American Library Association, 2002, for *A Face First.* Recipient of several journalism awards from United Press International (UPI) News Editors of New England, National Federation of Press Women, and Virginia Press Association; Virginia Journalist of the Year, UPI, 1980; Arthur J. Blaney Award, 1982.

Writings

Chadwick the Crab, illustrated by A. R. Cohen, Tidewater Publishers (Centreville, MD), 1986.
Chadwick and the Garplegrungen, illustrated by A. R. Cohen, Tidewater Publishers (Centreville, MD), 1987.
The Chadwick Coloring Book, illustrated by A. R. Cohen, Tidewater Publishers (Centreville, MD), 1988.
Chadwick's Wedding, illustrated by A. R. Cohen, Tidewater Publishers (Centreville, MD), 1989.
Oswald and the Timberdoodles, illustrated by A. R. Cohen, Tidewater Publishers (Centreville, MD), 1990.
Sid and Sal's Famous Channel Marker Diner, illustrated by A. R. Cohen, Tidewater Publishers (Centreville, MD), 1991.

Chadwick Forever, illustrated by A. R. Cohen, Tidewater Publishers (Centreville, MD), 1993.
Toulouse: The Story of a Canada Goose, illustrated by A. R. Cohen, Tidewater Publishers (Centreville, MD), 1995.
Autumn Journey (novel), Dutton (New York, NY), 1997.
Meet Chadwick and His Friends, illustrated by A. R. Cohen, Tidewater Publishers (Centreville, MD), 1999.
Chesapeake ABC, illustrated by David Aiken, Tidewater Publishers (Centreville, MD), 2000.
A Face First (novel), Dutton (New York, NY), 2001.

Sidelights

A former journalist, children's author Priscilla Cummings first tried her hand at writing for young readers in 1986 with the picture book *Chadwick the Crab.* A blue crab who calls the Chesapeake Bay home, Chadwick and his other animal friends are featured in several books about the crustacean, introducing children to the importance of preserving the marine environment from pollution. The author's stories about the crab's adventures have proved popular in the Maryland region, with the "Chadwick the Crab" series selling over 300,000 copies.

After publishing several picture books, Cummings added a new dimension to her literature career, authoring two novels for older readers, *Autumn Journey* and *A Face First.* In an interview with *Washington Post* contributor Holly Smith, Cummings confided that this transition was not easy. "I'm embarrassed to say this, but parts of *Autumn Journey* were written almost ten years before the book was published." Despite this slow start, however, the author persisted with her longer fiction, eventually publishing *Autumn Journey* in 1997 and *A Face First* four years later. In describing Cummings' efforts, Smith claimed that "some authors write children's books with lovable characters and straightforward text. Others create complex novels that connect with tough-to-reach adolescents. A few can do both. Priscilla Cummings is one of them."

Described as presenting "true strength of character and respect for both family and the natural world" by *School Library Journal* contributor Susan Oliver, *Autumn Journey* follows the story of eleven-year-old Will Newcomb as his father loses his job and the family must leave their Maryland home and move in with relatives. Despite the extra chores, the fifth grader enjoys living on his grandfather's farm, but his parents' constant fighting disturbs him. When his grandfather suffers a heart attack, Will fears that his family will fall apart, a concern that intensifies after his father temporarily disappears. A Canada goose Will shoots, but cannot bring himself to kill, ultimately teaches Will about perseverence, as he nurses the wounded creature back to health. Writing in *Kirkus Reviews,* a critic found *Autumn Journey* "less a tale of unmitigated woe than a beautifully told, uplifting story about the power and strength of family."

A Face First deals with a different type of tragedy in its focus on twelve-year-old Kelley, who suffers severe burns to her face, hands, and leg after a car accident. As her memory of the events preceding the accident return, Kelley realizes her mother's carelessness caused the crash and begins to blame her for the disfigurement. Forced to wear protective coverings, including a plastic pressure face mask, to help her skin heal, the sixth grader retreats into her own private world, rejecting efforts by family and friends to help comfort her. However, with the support of other burn victims, Kelley begins to realize that she is not alone in her suffering and starts working to accept the changes in her life. Critics noted Cummings' extensive knowledge of medical treatment for burn victims, evidenced in the author's descriptive passages of Kelley's time spent in the hospital. However, according to *School Library Journal* critic Cindy Darling, the author "really shines in showing the careful balance of push, pull, and nurturing that must be maintained by the dedicated medical staff." *Booklist* reviewer Carolyn Phelan remarked that this "knowledgeable but compassionate tone rings true," going on to call *A Face First* "a thoughtful read that will encourage empathy."

Cummings told *SATA:* "When children at school ask me what advice I have for them, as future authors, I tell them they should be reading at every opportunity: books, magazines, newspapers. I tell them to write—not just stories, but poems, letters, journal entries, essays— whatever. And I tell them this: they should be learning to watch and listen.

"As a newspaper reporter for ten years, I learned that standing back to watch and listen often gave me as much compelling information as asking a question or demanding an answer. As an author, I have discovered that standing back to watch and listen gives me many of the valuable details that bring a character to life and drive a story forward.

"When I was on the burn unit of a local hospital researching my novel, *A Face First,* I stood back to become the eyes and ears of my character, Kelley, a twelve-year-old burn victim, slowly recovering in a hospital bed. Outside the window, I saw how 'the traffic never stopped. At two, three—four o'clock in the morning, headlights came and went steadily in the darkness. Like a pulse, Kelley couldn't help but think. Life outside the hospital went on: People got in their cars, buckled themselves in, and went places, even if it was just to pick up shirts at the cleaners or get a gallon of milk at the 7-Eleven or order a meatball sub at Jerry's.'"

"Inside the hospital, I listened to a burn patient cry as he struggled to eat a canned pear, and heard the sounds of a Medivac helicopter landing outside the window to deliver another patient into the emergency room entrance below. Both of these details also become part of Kelley's story.

"Standing back to watch, and listen, for the telling detail has been just as important to me as watching for the right ideas, and listening to my heart and mind for the story to emerge."

Biographical and Critical Sources

PERIODICALS

Booklist, February 1, 2001, Carolyn Phelan, review of *A Face First,* p. 1052.

Kirkus Reviews, June 1, 1997, review of *Autumn Journey,* p. 871.

Publishers Weekly, August 11, 1997, review of *Autumn Journey,* p. 402; January 22, 2001, review of *A Face First,* p. 325.

School Library Journal, February, 1987, Hayden E. Atwood, review of *Chadwick the Crab,* p. 66; October, 1997, Susan Oliver, review of *Autumn Journey,* p. 132; February, 2001, Cindy Darling, review of *A Face First,* p. 117.

Voice of Youth Advocates, February, 2001, Mary E. Heslin, review of *A Face First,* p. 421.

Washington Post, July 5, 2001, Holly Smith, "Maturing with Her Audience."

OTHER

Priscilla Cummings Web Site, http://www. childrensbookguild.org/ (December 14, 2001).

D–E

DALY, Maureen 1921-
(Maureen Daly McGivern)

Personal

Born March 15, 1921, in Castlecaufield, County Tyrone, Ulster, Ireland; naturalized U.S. citizen; daughter of Joseph Desmond (a salesman) and Margaret (Mellon-Kelly) Daly; married William P. McGivern (a writer), December 28, 1946 (died, November, 1983); children: Megan (deceased), Patrick. *Education:* Rosary College, B.A., 1942. *Politics:* Democrat.

Addresses

Home—73-305 Ironwood St., Palm Desert, CA 92260.

Career

Writer and journalist. Freelance writer, 1938—. *Chicago Tribune,* Chicago, IL, police reporter and columnist, 1941-44; Chicago City News Bureau, Chicago, reporter, 1941-43; *Ladies' Home Journal,* Philadelphia, PA, associate editor, 1944-49; *Saturday Evening Post,* Philadelphia, editorial consultant, 1960-69; *Desert Sun,* Palm Desert, CA, reporter and columnist, 1987—. Screenwriter for Twentieth Century-Fox; has lectured on foreign lands and emerging nations. *Member:* PEN, Mystery Writers of America, Writers Guild of America (West).

Awards, Honors

Scholastic magazine short story contest, 1936, third prize for "Fifteen," 1937, first prize for "Sixteen"; O. Henry Memorial Award, 1938, for short story "Sixteen"; Dodd, Mead Intercollegiate Literary Fellowship Novel Award, 1942, and Lewis Carroll Shelf Award, 1969, both for *Seventeenth Summer;* Freedoms Foundation Award, 1952, for "humanity in reporting"; Gimbel Fashion Award, 1962, for contribution to U.S. fashion industry through *Saturday Evening Post* articles; *Acts of Love* was selected one of *Redbook*'s ten great books for teens, 1987.

Writings

YOUNG ADULT FICTION

Seventeenth Summer, Dodd (New York, NY), 1942, illustrated edition, 1948.
Sixteen and Other Stories, illustrated by Kendall Rossi, Dodd (New York, NY), 1961.
Acts of Love, Scholastic (New York, NY), 1986.
First a Dream, Scholastic (New York, NY), 1990.

YOUNG ADULT FICTION; EDITOR

My Favorite Stories (young adult), Dodd (New York, NY), 1948.
My Favorite Mystery Stories (young adult), Dodd (New York, NY), 1966.
My Favorite Suspense Stories (young adult), Dodd (New York, NY), 1968.

YOUNG ADULT NONFICTION

Smarter and Smoother: A Handbook on How to Be That Way (collection of newspaper columns), illustrated by Marguerite Bryan, Dodd (New York, NY), 1944.
What's Your P.Q. (Personality Quotient)?, illustrated by Ellie Simmons, Dodd (New York, NY), 1952, revised edition, 1966.
Twelve around the World, illustrated by Frank Kramer, Dodd (New York, NY), 1957.
Spanish Roundabout (travel), Dodd (New York, NY), 1960.
Moroccan Roundabout (travel), Dodd (New York, NY), 1961.

JUVENILE

Patrick Visits the Farm (fiction), illustrated by Simmons, Dodd (New York, NY), 1959.
Patrick Takes a Trip (fiction), illustrated by Simmons, Dodd (New York, NY), 1960.
Patrick Visits the Library (fiction), illustrated by Paul Lantz, Dodd (New York, NY), 1961.
Patrick Visits the Zoo (fiction), illustrated by Sam Savitt, Dodd (New York, NY), 1963.
The Ginger Horse (fiction), illustrated by Wesley Dennis, Dodd (New York, NY), 1964.

Spain: Wonderland of Contrasts (nonfiction), Dodd (New York, NY), 1965.

The Small War of Sergeant Donkey (fiction), illustrated by Wesley Dennis, Dodd (New York, NY), 1966, reprinted, Bethlehem Books (Bathgate, ND), 2000.

Rosie, the Dancing Elephant (fiction), illustrated by Lorence Bjorklund, Dodd (New York, NY), 1967.

OTHER

The Perfect Hostess: Complete Etiquette and Entertainment for the Home, Dodd (New York, NY), 1950.

(Editor) *Profile of Youth* (adult), Lippincott (Philadelphia, PA), 1951.

(Under name Maureen Daly McGivern; with husband, William P. McGivern) *Mention My Name in Mombasa: The Unscheduled Adventures of an American Family Abroad* (memoir), illustrated by Frank Kramer, Dodd (New York, NY), 1958.

(With W. P. McGivern) *A Matter of Honor,* Arbor House (New York, NY), 1984.

Also author of "High School Career Series," Curtis Publishing Co., 1942-49. Author, with William P. McGivern, of scripts for television series, including *Kojak,* and of screenplay *Brannigan.* Work represented in several textbooks and anthologies. Contributor of over two hundred articles to numerous periodicals, including *Vogue, Mademoiselle, Cosmopolitan, Woman's Day, Scholastic, Woman's Home Companion,* and *Redbook.*

Daly's papers are housed in a permanent collection at the University of Oregon Library.

Adaptations

Film rights to *Seventeenth Summer* were purchased by Warner Bros., 1949; *The Ginger Horse* was filmed by Walt Disney Studios; Daly's short story, "You Can't Kiss Caroline," has also been dramatized.

Sidelights

An accomplished writer and an award-winning and prolific journalist, Maureen Daly has made a career of successfully bridging genres and print mediums. As the author of the groundbreaking young adult novel *Seventeenth Summer,* Daly is also credited with establishing "Young Adult Literature" as a genre separate from the juvenile or adult publishing markets. With her debut novel in continuous publication since it first appeared in 1942, Daly's name remains recognizable to readers both young and old. In addition to her books for both teens and younger readers, Daly has also written several books of nonfiction for adults, published numerous articles and columns in newspapers and periodicals such as the *Chicago Tribune* and *Desert Sun,* and authored screenplays for films and television.

Born in 1921 in Ireland, Daly and her mother and two sisters eventually moved to Wisconsin to join her father, Joseph Daly, who had immigrated earlier. An avid reader, Daly haunted her local library on a weekly basis, and enjoyed books by Jane Austen, Charlotte Brontë,

Maureen Daly describes how young love really feels in her groundbreaking young adult novel, first published in 1942.

Edna Ferber, and Sinclair Lewis during high school. She also enjoyed writing, and because of her combination of talent and discipline—Daly adopted a strict writing regime at an early age—she was an award-winning writer by the time she reached fifteen in 1936, when a story she entered in *Scholastic* magazine's short story contest won third prize. The next year, Daly's English teacher submitted another of her stories to the contest; "Sixteen," a tale about a boy and a girl who meet at a skating rink, was awarded first prize, and since *Scholastic* first printed it in 1938 has been included in over three hundred anthologies and published in twelve different languages. The story is also in Daly's collection *Sixteen and Other Stories.* "Even now, when I get checks from the reprint of 'Sixteen,' it's like seeing an old friend from 1938," Daly commented to an interviewer for *Publishers Weekly.*

In 1938 Daly enrolled at Rosary College, in River Forest, Illinois. Coming home after her freshman year, she announced that she was going to write her first novel. Making an office in the basement of her parent's home, she went to work, and, after three years of work, she finished *Seventeenth Summer.* The story focuses on seventeen-year-old Angie, who falls in love with a boy from her small town. She submitted the manuscript to New York City publishing house Dodd, Mead during her senior year at college, and the novel quickly became a bestseller, making Daly a successful author at the age of twenty-one. *Seventeenth Summer* has remained in print for nearly half a century, selling more than a million copies worldwide.

Set in a rural Wisconsin town, *Seventeenth Summer* follows the sweet and innocent romance of teenagers Angie Morrow and Jack Daly as they experience all the joys and tribulations universally felt by teens discovering love for the first time. Angie, who narrates the story, and her three sisters are modeled after Daly and her siblings; her mother provides a supportive role as a confidante, while her father remains a distant character. Although the novel's plot is simple, as an essayist in *St. James Guide to Young Adult Writers* noted, "the sensitivity toward adolescent feelings which pervades the [female-oriented] story leads readers to remember the book long after finishing it."

When Daly's novel was published in 1942, there was no Young Adult Novel category for reviewers to pigeon-

From **The Small War of Sergeant Donkey,** *written by Maureen Daly and illustrated by Wesley Dennis.*

hole it into; instead, *Seventeenth Summer* was held up to the standards of an adult novel. Reviewers were quick to praise the book's sensitive portrayal of the many and varied emotions and facets that come into play during an adolescent's experience of first love. "*Seventeenth Summer,* perhaps captures better than any other novel the spirit of adolescence," stated Dwight L. Burton in *English Journal.* "More than just a love story of two adolescents," the critic added, "*Seventeenth Summer,* with its introspection and fine mastery of the scene, portrays the adolescent validly in several of his [or her] important relationships—with his [or her] family, with his [or her] age mates, and, very important, with himself [or herself]. In each of these three aspects, Miss Daly is discerning." Characterizing the novel's tone as "Lyrically young and breathless," Edith H. Walton noted in her review of *Seventeenth Summer* for the *New York Times Book Review* that the novel "deals with one of the oldest themes in the world, the theme of first love, and deals with it in a fashion which is so unhackneyed and so fresh that one forgets how often the same story has been told before.... Completely up to date in its idiom and its atmosphere, vividly authentic in a warm and homely way, it seems to me to be as unpretentiously good a first novel as any one could ask.... Simply, eloquently, Maureen Daly tells one how youth in love really feels— how it felt yesterday and how it feels today."

As the author once explained, *Seventeenth Summer* "was written in a spurt of creativity and emotion because I was so wildly and vividly happy about love and life at a particular time in my existence. I knew that euphoria and hope could not last (and it didn't) and I wanted to get all that fleeting excitement down on paper before it passed, or I forgot the true feelings. Lucky I did. I have never felt so hopeful since. It was not until the reviews came out (and the royalties came in) that I realized I had recorded universal emotions and joys—and people would want to read about them year after year."

Despite her success as a novelist with *Seventeenth Summer,* Daly had decided to pursue a career in journalism. While still in college, she got a job as a reporter covering the police beat for the *Chicago Tribune.* Journalism provided the disciplined writer with a new challenge. As she later recalled in *Publishers Weekly:* "I had to work really hard to keep all the details straight, when I called from the scene of news stories. I was so afraid they would fire a question at me and I wouldn't have the answer. Often I'd be standing in phone booths with sweat pouring down my back."

In addition to reporting on crime for the *Chicago Tribune,* Daly also reviewed books and wrote an advice column for the paper's Sunday magazine. Aimed at teens, Daly's column, "On the Solid Side," was so popular the paper soon ran it three times a week. "On the Solid Side" was eventually syndicated to more than a dozen newspapers, and a collection of Daly's articles was published in 1944 as *Smarter and Smoother.* By the following year, the book had gone into its ninth printing. A *Kirkus* reviewer suggested that "parents should be thankful to Maureen Daly for she gives all the advice and counsel that teenagers think is sermonizing from parents, but that they'll lap up in this form."

Throughout much of her adult life, Daly has worked as a journalist, and has been on staff at such respected publications as *Ladies' Home Journal* and *Saturday Evening Post.* In addition to several awards, she has earned a reputation as a talented and thorough professional. As a freelancer, Daly has also become known for being prolific; she has penned and published hundreds of articles on a wide variety of topics, many of which explore one of her favorite subjects—travel and foreign lands—which she developed after marrying mystery writer William P. McGivern in 1946.

In 1949 Daly left her job as associate editor for *Ladies' Home Journal,* and moved to Europe with her husband and two-year-old daughter, Megan. Working as a freelance writer while raising her growing family—the McGiverns also had a son, Patrick—Daly spent time in Paris, Rome, Dublin, London, and Spain, reported on the important issues of the day, and interviewed such notable people as Eleanor Roosevelt and Harry S. Truman. When her children reached their teen years, Daly and her family returned to the United States, and bought a farm in Pennsylvania. Highway development eventually encroached upon their rural home, and the McGiverns moved to California, where Daly has continued to make her home.

Daly's years traveling and living in Europe were the inspiration for her several books on travel, including her own family's personal experiences in *Mention My Name in Mombasa: The Unscheduled Adventures of an American Family Abroad.* Writing with her husband, Daly introduces readers to the quaint places and captivating people her family encountered during their travels. A *Kirkus* reviewer dubbed *Mention My Name in Mombasa* "charming," and went on to comment: "Writing with intelligence, sympathy and humor, interested in people rather than scenery, the authors tell of fishermen and babysitters, flowers and artists, bulls and bullfighting, friendly servants, food good and bad, palaces and hotels. Lengthy but never dull, neither a guidebook nor a study of social conditions, the book should appeal to all kinds of travelers, ... and to students of social life outside the United States."

Daly also shares her travel experiences with younger readers in *Spain: Wonderland of Contrasts* and with young adults in *Twelve around the World, Spanish Roundabout,* and *Moroccan Roundabout.* In the *New York Times Book Review,* Lavinia R. Davis stated that *Spanish Roundabout* "is not a guide book in the usual sense. It is, rather, a cohesive series of profiles and sketches of Spain drawn from affection, experience and compassion.... [The] emphasis is on people in contemporary Spain. Family life, bull-fighting, religious observances, cooking and teenage mores are described so skillfully and with such a complete lack of condescension that the reader cannot help sharing the author's enthusiasm and eager curiosity."

Daly's husband died in 1983 after a long battle with cancer; her daughter, Megan, died of cancer a year later. Grief-stricken, Daly attempted to write about her feelings, but judged the results too depressing. Then, during a day whale-watching with friends on the Baja, California coast, she found herself in a different frame of mind. She returned home and began a new novel about her daughter, looking back to Megan's "seventeenth summer." That work was published in 1986 as *Acts of Love.* Another young adult novel, *First a Dream,* which focuses on a young woman who moves from Pennsylvania to California during high school, followed in 1990. As in *Seventeenth Summer,* Daly's more recent novels provide her fans with a sensitive love story that involves many of the experiences and emotions young people realize on their road to maturity. Describing Daly as "the spiritual grandmother of the young adult novel," Richard Peck noted in the *Los Angeles Times* that "well before the term 'YA' [Young Adult] was coined [Daly] wrote the perennial best-seller, *Seventeenth Summer.* With *Acts of Love* she returns after 44 years to the sort of love story she pioneered when she was herself a YA."

"I write more than one kind of book," Daly once explained of her writing career. "In travel books I try to put down what I see, feel and learn as vividly and memorably as the experiences that have occurred to me. In fiction I am an entertainer but sometimes a sad one. The stories—fictionalized versions of real life—are often melancholy but sometimes there is a joy, and a relief, in just sharing a human adventure." The disciplined habits she developed as a young woman have continued to guide her life: writing in the early morning, breaking for lunch, then writing into the late afternoon. A popular speaker, she has appeared at a number of conferences, as well as spoken to classes of students in public schools and universities.

"Writing is my kind of freedom, the chance to look outward as well as inward. It is an excellent excuse for curiosity, for traveling, studying, and just staring at other people and other scenes. I am constantly plagued by the 'need to know,' not just to stockpile lists of facts and statistics but to have some understanding of what it is like to be someone else, or live somewhere else. So I travel to 'see' and write to 'think' and find out about myself and other people I meet—or invent." In the late 1980s Daly honored her daughter's memory by endowing a library at the Barbara Sinatra Children's Center at the Eisenhower Medical Complex in Rancho Mirage, California.

Biographical and Critical Sources

BOOKS

Contemporary Literary Criticism, Volume 17, Gale (Detroit, MI), 1981.

Gallo, Donald, editor, *Speaking for Ourselves: Autobiographical Sketches by Notable Authors of Books for Children,* Vol. I, National Council of Teachers of English, 1990.

St. James Guide to Young Adult Writers, 2nd edition, St. James Press (Detroit, MI), 1999.

Something about the Author Autobiography Series, Volume
1, Gale (Detroit, MI), 1986.

PERIODICALS

ALAN Review, spring, 1994, Nancy Vogel, "The Semicen-
tennial of *Seventeenth Summer:* Some Questions and
Answers."
Chicago Tribune, September 1, 1986.
English Journal, September, 1951, Dwight L. Burton, "The
Novel for the Adolescent," p. 15.
Journal of Reading, February, 1993, Lisa Ann Richarson,
"A Retrospective with Maureen Daly," p. 424.
Kirkus Reviews, March 1, 1944, "Fifteen and Up: 'Smarter
and Smoother,'" p. 120; July 15, 1958, review of
Mention My Name in Mombasa, p. 535.
Life, November 7, 1949, "Career Sisters"; May 11, 1959,
"They All Made Good."
Los Angeles Times, October 11, 1986, Richard Peck,
review of *Acts of Love.*
Nebraska English Journal, spring, 1992, Nancy Vogel,
"The Semicentennial of *Seventeenth Summer:* Maureen
Daly's Acts of Love."
New York Times Book Review, May 3, 1942, Edith H.
Walton, review of *Seventeenth Summer,* p. 7; July 12,
1942; July 24, 1960, Lavinia R. Davis, "For Younger
Readers: 'People in Action,'" p. 20.
Publishers Weekly, June 27, 1986, Kimberly Olson Fakih,
"The Long Wait for Maureen Daly," pp. 36, 38-39;
March 30, 1990, review of *First a Dream,* p. 64.
School Library Journal, April, 1990, Joyce Adams Burner,
review of *First a Dream,* p. 139.
Wilson Library Bulletin, February, 1991, Cathi MacRae,
review of *First A Dream,* p. 118.

*   *   *

ELISH, Dan 1960-

Personal

Born September 22, 1960, in Washington, DC; son of
Herber (in business) and Leslie (Rubin) Elish. *Education:* Middlebury College, B.A. (cum laude), 1983.

Addresses

Home—200 West 93rd St., Manhattan, NY 10025.
Agent—Sue Cohen, Writers House, 21 West 26th St.,
New York, NY 10010.

Career

Writer.

Awards, Honors

National Arts Club, scholar; The Bread Loaf Writers
Conference.

Writings

The Worldwide Dessert Contest, illustrated by John Steven
Gurney, Orchard Books (New York, NY), 1988.
Jason and the Baseball Bear, illustrated by John Stadler,
Orchard Books (New York, NY), 1990.
The Great Squirrel Uprising, illustrated by Denys Cazet,
Orchard Books (New York, NY), 1992.
*My Christmas Stocking: Stories, Songs, Poems, Recipes,
Crafts & Fun for Kids,* illustrated by James Bernardin,
Smithmark Publishers (New York, NY), 1993.
Harriet Tubman & the Underground Railroad, Millbrook
Press (Brookfield, CT), 1993.
The Transcontinental Railroad: Triumph of a Dream,
Millbrook Press (Brookfield, CT), 1993.
James Meredith and School Desegregation, Millbrook
Press (Brookfield, CT), 1994.
Vermont, Marshall Cavendish (New York, NY), 1997.
Washington, D.C., Marshall Cavendish (New York, NY),
1998.
The Cherokee Removal: The Story of the Trail of Tears,
Marshall Cavendish (New York, NY), 2001.
Me and the Guy with the Movie Star Gums, Atheneum
(New York, NY), 2002.
*Born Too Short: The Confessions of an Eighth-Grade
Basket Case,* Simon & Schuster (New York, NY),
2002.
New York, Benchmark Books (New York, NY), 2003.

Contributor to children's periodicals, including *3-2-1
Contact* and *Sports Illustrated for Kids.*

Sidelights

Dan Elish is the author of a variety of children's books,
including middle-grade novels, biographies, and geo-
graphical and historical works. Early in his career, he
was inspired by reading Roald Dahl's *Charlie and the
Chocolate Factory* to write a novel about a boy's desire
to win a dessert contest, *The Worldwide Dessert Contest.*
"I remember thinking that writing a children's novel
would probably only take a few months," Elish once
commented. "Instead, it took a year and a half. It took
me four or five months to realize what the story was
about." It's about John Applefeller's eleventh attempt to
win the coveted contest. According to Pam Spencer of
School Library Journal, the tale "skirts close to silliness
on occasion," yet should appeal to many.

Elish wrote several more novels in a humorous, imaginative vein, including *Jason and the Baseball Bear* and
The Great Squirrel Uprising. "I knew I wanted to write
something using zoo animals as characters," Elish once
said, "After months of banging my head against the wall,
I jotted down a conversation between a boy and a polar
bear about baseball." This was the kernel of *Jason and
the Baseball Bear,* about a Little League team that gets
great coaching from an unusual source. Reviewers
commented positively on the tale's humor. James
Witham noted in a review for *School Library Journal* a
"number of witty touches," and Margaret A. Bush of
Horn Book described the work as a "well-constructed

Dan Elish describes the building of the first railroad linking the eastern and western states in **The Transcontinental Railroad: Triumph of a Dream.** *(Photo from The Oakland Museum.)*

and lighthearted account," predicting that "readers will enjoy the drama of the final inning of the game." The idea for *The Great Squirrel Uprising* came to Elish while he was walking in Central Park in New York City. He once commented, "An image of a squirrel riding a skateboard and being chased by the police flashed through my mind." Months later the story developed into the tale of a group of squirrels and pigeons who protest the humans' rudeness and throwing of trash in Central Park by blocking human access to the park. "Populated with endearing, well-developed characters, this light, entertaining story will appeal even to reluctant readers," a *Kirkus Reviews* contributor predicted.

During the mid-1990s, Elish wrote historical and biographical titles for middle-grade readers, such as *Harriet Tubman & the Underground Railroad, The Transcontinental Railroad: Triumph of a Dream,* and *James*

Meredith and School Desegregation, which were generally well received. *Horn Book Guide* reviewer Lois F. Anderson termed *Harriet Tubman* "thoughtful," and Eunice Weech in *School Library Journal* called *James Meredith* "well written." Moreover, "informative, interesting, and attractive" is how George Gleason described *The Transcontinental Railroad* in his collective review for *School Library Journal.*

Elish wrote titles for Marshall Cavendish's middle-grade "Celebrate the States" series: *Vermont* and *Washington, D.C.* Each volume in the series contains sections on geography, history, government, economy, famous citizens, landmarks, and bibliography. "These are easily the longest and most comprehensive books of their type," wrote Kathleen Isaacs about *Washington, D.C.* in her collective review for *School Library Journal.* Likewise, Peter D. Sieruta of *Horn Book Guide* called

Vermont "attractive," "accessible" and "competently written."

Biographical and Critical Sources

PERIODICALS

Booklist, March 1, 1992, Carolyn Phelan, review of *The Great Squirrel Uprising,* p. 1277; February 1, 2002, Carolyn Phelan, review of *Born Too Short: The Confessions of an Eighth-Grade Basket Case,* p. 938.

Horn Book, September-October, 1990, Margaret A. Bush, review of *Jason and the Baseball Bear,* pp. 600-601.

Horn Book Guide, July-December, 1993, Lois F. Anderson, review of *Harriet Tubman and the Underground Railroad,* p. 156, Amy Quigley, review of *The Transcontinental Railroad: Triumph of a Dream,* p. 169; January-June, 1997, Peter D. Sieruta, review of *Vermont,* p. 394; January-June, 1998, Peter D. Sieruta, review of *Washington, D.C.,* p. 427.

Kirkus Reviews, February 15, 1992, review of *The Great Squirrel Uprising,* p. 252.

National Catholic Reporter, November 9, 1990, Sam Cox, review of *Jason and the Baseball Bear,* p. 27.

Publishers Weekly, May 20, 1988, review of *The Worldwide Dessert Contest,* pp. 92-93; January 14, 2002, review of *Born Too Short: The Confessions of an Eighth-Grade Basket Case,* p. 61.

School Library Journal, May, 1988, Pam Spencer, review of *The Worldwide Dessert Contest,* p. 96; June, 1990, James Witham, review of *Jason and the Baseball Bear,* p. 118; January, 1994, George Gleason, review of *The Transcontinental Railroad,* p. 118; May, 1994, Eunice Weech, review of *James Meredith and School Desegregation,* p. 122; August, 1997, Allison Trent Bernstein, review of *Vermont,* pp. 160-161; January, 1999, Kathleen Isaacs, review of *Washington, D.C.,* p. 136.*

*   *   *

ELLIS, Deborah 1960-

Personal

Born August 8, 1960, in Cochrane, Ontario, Canada; daughter of Keith (an office manager) and Betty (a nurse; maiden name, Daugherty) Ellis. *Politics:* "Feminist, anti-war."

Addresses

Home—P.O. Box 75521, 607 Gerrard St., East Toronto, Ontario M4M 1Y2, Canada.

Career

Writer; Margaret Frazer House, Toronto, Canada, mental health worker, 1988—.

Awards, Honors

Book of the Year for Children shortlist, Canadian Library Association, 1999, Governor General's Award,

To avoid Taliban restrictions, eleven-year-old Parvana disguises herself as a boy to help her family survive after her father's arrest in Kabul, Afghanistan. (Cover illustration by Pascal Milelli.)

2000, and Silver Birch Reading Award shortlist, 2001, all for *Looking for X;* Red Maple Reading Award shortlist, 2001, for *The Breadwinner.*

Writings

Haley and Scotia, Frog-in-the-Well, 1995.
Looking for X, Groundwood Books (Toronto, Canada), 1999.
Women of the Afghan War, Praeger Books (Westport, CT), 2000.
The Breadwinner, Groundwood Books (Toronto, Canada), 2001.

Work in Progress

Several books for young readers, adult non-fiction.

Sidelights

Canadian writer Deborah Ellis's political activism has inspired her writings for young adults. In *Looking for X,* an eleven-year-old girl who calls herself Khyber after the famous mountain pass in Afghanistan lives with her single mother and five-year-old autistic twin brothers in a poor section of Toronto. Khyber struggles through the challenges of her days essentially friendless until she meets a mysterious homeless woman named X, whom she befriends. One day, a group of skinheads harasses X and Khyber in the park, and when the school is vandalized at the same time, Khyber is blamed. So the girl goes in search of X, to corroborate her story, and this starts an odyssey through the world of the homeless in Toronto. Anita L. Burkam, writing in the *Horn Book,* noted that while a reader may expect Khyber's life to be bleak, given all her problems, Ellis instead strives to show the joy in the poor girl's life, mainly provided by her love for her mother and brothers. "What you wouldn't expect are the marvelous characterizations and fiercely close family ties Deborah Ellis has created here," Burkam remarked. For Leslie Ann Lacika, writing in *School Library Journal,* Khyber's "quirky" life is not quite believable, but Ellis's rich characterizations make up for the lack. "Khyber is a likable protagonist and readers will appreciate how she copes with her issues," Lacika continued.

Ellis's interest in Afghanistan takes a front-and-center role in her next young adult novel, *The Breadwinner.* Published in early 2001, before the September 11th attack on the World Trade Center and the ensuing war on terrorism conducted by the United States mainly in Afghanistan, *The Breadwinner* provides a child's-eye view of life under the Taliban regime. Ellis's protagonist is Parvana, an eleven-year-old girl whose scholarly father is imprisoned by the Taliban, leaving the family to starve, since women are not allowed to work or even to leave their homes unattended by a male relative. So Parvana decides to disguise herself as a boy and go out into the streets to earn money to feed her mother and small brothers. "*The Breadwinner* is a potent portrait of life in contemporary Afghanistan," John Green claimed in *Booklist.* Likewise, a contributor to *Publishers Weekly* concluded that "the topical issues introduced, coupled with this strong heroine, will make this novel of interest to many conscientious teens."

Ellis donated all profits from the sale of *The Breadwinner* to a charitable organization that funds schools for Afghan girls living in Pakistani refugee camps. The author visited these refugee camps in order to collect stories of the war in Afghanistan as it was fought by the Soviet Union in the early 1990s. The resulting book,

Women of the Afghan War, also contains first-person narratives of Soviet women soldiers, which Ellis traveled to Moscow in order to obtain. It was while she was recording stories among the Afghans that she heard of a young girl who cut off her hair and donned boys' clothing in order to go out onto the streets of Kabul and earn her family's living. "Something just went click in my head and I knew that I had to do a book about that person," Ellis told Debra Huron in *Herizons.*

Deborah Ellis told *SATA:* "I'm fascinated by the capacity of children to cope in a dangerous world, to live in it with joy and dignity. That is the general theme running through my books for young readers.

"Sometimes I enjoy writing, sometimes I hate it because it takes me away from more pleasurable activities, but always I am compelled to do it. There is nothing so satisfying as completing another manuscript, knowing I've gotten through it one more time. Maybe it will sell, maybe it won't—that's up to the gods—but at least I didn't quit, and that feels great."

Biographical and Critical Sources

PERIODICALS

Booklist, May 15, 2000, Anne O'Malley, review of *Looking for X,* p. 1739; March 1, 2001, John Green, review of *The Breadwinner,* p. 1275.

Herizons, summer, 2001, Debra Huron, "Transcending Borders," p. 36.

Horn Book, July, 2000, Anita L. Burkam, review of *Looking for X,* p. 456.

Maclean's, November 12, 2001, Brian Bethune, "Kabul for Kids: A Canadian scores with a tale of Taliban oppression," p. 56.

Publishers Weekly, March 19, 2001, review of *The Breadwinner,* p. 100.

School Library Journal, July, 2000, Leslie Ann Lacika, review of *Looking for X,* p. 104; July, 2001, Kathleen Isaacs, review of *The Breadwinner,* p. 106.

Time International, November 26, 2001, Bryan Walsh, "Veil of Tears: A children's book details life under the Taliban," p. 66.

OTHER

Groundwood Books, http://www.groundwood.com (February 23, 2002), brief biography of Deborah Ellis.

F

FLOOD, William 1942-

Personal

Born November 22, 1942, in Chicago, IL; son of Charles (in real estate sales) and Adele (a housewife; maiden name, Kovar) Flood; married Nancy "Bo" Bohac (a writer), August, 1967; children: Megan, Michael, Elizabeth, Macey. *Education:* University of Illinois, B.S. (chemical engineering), 1964; University of Minnesota, M.D., 1971.

Addresses

Home—P.O. Box 5534 CHRB, Saipan, MP 96950. *E-mail*—flood@gtepacifica.net.

Career

Children's Health Center, Glenwood Springs, CO, pediatrician, 1974-89; Commonwealth Health Center, Saipan, MP, 1989-97; Saipan Health Clinic, Saipan, MP, pediatrician, 1997-2001; Inscription House Health Center, Shonto, AZ, pediatrician, 2001—.

Awards, Honors

James Strain Outstanding Pediatrician (Colorado), 1992.

Writings

(With Bo Flood and Beret E. Strong) *Pacific Island Legends: Tales from Micronesia, Melanesia, Polynesia and Australia,* illustrated by Connie J. Adams, Bess Press (Honolulu, HI), 1998.
Micronesian Island Legends, Bess Press (Honolulu, HI), 2001.

Author of weekly column, "Flood of Information," in the *Marianas Variety,* 1997-2001.

Work in Progress

A chapter titled "Environmental Health," due in 2002.

Sidelights

William Flood told *SATA:* "Living and working many different places (Colorado, Haiti, Samoa, Malawi [Afri-

Woodcut from Pacific Island Legends: Tales from Micronesia, Melanesia, Polynesia, and Australia, *coauthored by William Flood and illustrated by Connie J. Adams.*

ca], and Saipan) has given us special insights into many different people and their cultures.

"Most of my writing has been on medical topics including a textbook chapter and a weekly news column.

"The two collections of legends were collected from many sources over several years and were developed at my author-wife ("Bo" Flood)'s suggestion of the need for books written for the islands, *about* the islands. The stories have been rewritten for modern readers at the fifth-to-eighth grade level. They are fun!"

Biographical and Critical Sources

PERIODICALS

School Library Journal, October, 1999, Mary R. Hofmann, review of *Pacific Island Legends,* p. 168.

*   *   *

FOGELIN, Adrian 1951-

Personal

Born August 28, 1951, in Pearl River, NY; daughter of Carl Edward (a chemical engineer) and Maria (a writer; maiden name, Bontempi) Fogelin; married Raymond S. Faass (a cabinetmaker), August, 1978; children: Josephine Sandberg. *Education:* Rhode Island School of Design, B.F.A., 1974. *Politics:* Democrat. *Hobbies and other interests:* Gardening, birdwatching, butterfly tagging, environmental activism, "managing family land for wildlife conservation."

Addresses

Home—1563 Marcia Ave., Tallahassee, FL 32310. *Agent*—Jack Ryan, Ryan Communications, Inc., 6201 Trolley Square Crossing, Atlanta, GA 30306. *E-mail*—AFogelin@aol.com.

Career

Baltimore Zoo, Baltimore, MD, illustrator, 1972-78; Soft Shell Designs (art gallery), Islamorada, FL, owner, 1982-89; Key Largo Library, Key Largo, FL, branch manager, 1991-93; Jefferson Clay Creations, Islamorada, FL, assistant potter, 1993-95; Florida State University, Tallahassee, FL, library technical assistant, 1995-2001; writer, 2001—. Florida Keys Community College, adjunct instructor in art, 1981-91; also taught at a daycare center. Bay Watch, water quality monitor; Monarch Watch, member of monarch butterfly tagging program. *Member:* Wednesday Night Writers.

Awards, Honors

Citation for "top shelf fiction for middle school readers," *Voice of Youth Advocates,* 2000, honor book, "notable books for a global society," International Reading Association, citation for "best book for young adults," American Library Association, and finalist for Georgia

Adrian Fogelin

Children's Book of the Year award, all 2001, for *Crossing Jordan.*

Writings

Crossing Jordan (novel), Peachtree Publishers (Atlanta, GA), 2000.
Anna Casey's Place in the World (novel), Peachtree Publishers (Atlanta, GA), 2001.

Work in Progress

My Brother's Hero, a sequel to *Crossing Jordan* and *Anna Casey's Place in the World; The Wild Party,* a picture book exploring simple ways for children to attract wildlife to their own backyards.

Sidelights

Adrian Fogelin told *SATA:* "The background music of my childhood was the clatter of typewriter keys punctuated by an occasional ding. The music was made by my mother, Maria Bontempi Fogelin, a fiction writer who left manuscript pages, worked over with a number two pencil, in small piles throughout the house. She wrote many novels, published a couple, one of which was serialized in *Redbook* and translated into half-a-dozen languages. But selling books was not what sustained my mother's lifelong romance with writing. It was always that lightning bug in a bottle, the story. She gleaned material for her stories everywhere: her own childhood, the activities of her children (to our frequent embarrassment), conversations overheard in the checkout line at the store. She was relentless. She never forgot anything.

"Influenced by my mother, I kept diaries, wrote occasional short stories and poems, but chose art as a career. Because fine art was an unreliable field, I worked an astonishing variety of jobs. I spent hours inside animal enclosures as the illustrator for the Baltimore Zoo, ran my own art gallery in the Florida Keys, cleaned condos, managed a public library, taught at a daycare center, made pottery—a meandering career path that has turned out to be rich with material for my own stories.

"At age thirty-five, I began to write seriously. I was working on an adult novel when the eight-year-old next door told me that her family had to move. 'There are getting to be too many black people in the neighborhood. Black people break into your house, they rob you. They shoot you.' Hearing this parroting of ideas that had originated with her parents so galvanized me that I began writing a book for middle-school readers that addressed the question, 'What do you do when the lesson your parents teach you is wrong?' At first the moral issue cast a long shadow over the story, but quickly the characters, many of whom are based on the kids who live and play on the streets of my Tallahassee neighborhood, gave my indignation a more human voice. No one in *Crossing Jordan,* not even the story's racist father, is without merit or the possibility of change.

"A second title, *Anna Casey's Place in the World,* grew out of the first. The characters demanded it. In *Anna* two new children enter foster care in the neighborhood. This story addresses the deep need to find home, and the wider issue of protecting our global home, the environment.

"I admit it, I consider children our best hope for a livable future. In my writing I try to raise the issues that will affect that future, trusting young readers to think them over and do better than we have when they take over from us. But why do it with fiction? Simple. Like my mother, I love a good story."

Biographical and Critical Sources

PERIODICALS

Booklist, October 15, 2001, GraceAnne A. DeCandido, review of *Anna Casey's Place in the World,* p. 389.
Bulletin of the Center for Children's Books, April, 2000, review of *Crossing Jordan.*
School Library Journal, June, 2000, Gerry Larson, review of *Crossing Jordan,* p. 144; December, 2001, Faith Brautigam, review of *Anna Casey's Place in the World,* p. 133.
USA Today, May 25, 2000, Linda Mallon, "For Young Readers: Fitting In, Traveling On," p. 9D.*

*   *   *

FORD, S. M.
See UHLIG, Susan

G

GERAS, Adele (Daphne) 1944-

Personal

Surname begins with a hard "G" and rhymes with "terrace"; born March 15, 1944, in Jerusalem, Palestine (now Israel); daughter of Laurence David (a lawyer) and Leah (Hamburger) Weston; married Norman Geras (a professor and author), August 7, 1967; children: Sophie, Jenny. *Education:* St. Hilda's College, Oxford, B.A., 1966. *Religion:* Jewish. *Hobbies and other interests:* "I enjoy the movies more than anything and read an enormous amount of everything, but my great love is thrillers and detective stories. I am very lazy, and like sleeping in the afternoons."

Addresses

Home—10 Danesmoor Rd., Manchester M20 3JS, England. *Agent*—Laura Cecil, 17 Alwyne Villas, London N1 2HG, England.

Career

Fairfield High School, Droylsden, Lancashire, England, French teacher, 1968-71; writer, 1976—. Actress in *Four Degrees Over* (play), London, England, 1966.

Awards, Honors

Taylor Award, 1991, for *My Grandmother's Stories: A Collection of Jewish Folktales;* National Jewish Book Council Award, 1994, for *Golden Windows, and Other Stories of Jerusalem; Boston Globe-Horn Book* Honor Book, for *Troy.*

Writings

Adele Geras

FICTION; FOR CHILDREN

Tea at Mrs. Manderby's, illustrated by Doreen Caldwell, Hamish Hamilton (London, England), 1976.
Apricots at Midnight, and Other Stories from a Patchwork Quilt, illustrated by Doreen Caldwell, Hamish Hamil- ton (London, England), 1977, Atheneum (New York, NY), 1982.
Beyond the Cross-Stitch Mountains, illustrated by Mary Wilson, Hamish Hamilton (London, England), 1977.

Inspired by a photograph of Geras's mother and four aunts, this story of five Bernstein girls and their mother is a vivid family tale of New York life before World War I. (Cover illustration by Douglas Hall.)

The Painted Garden, illustrated by Doreen Caldwell, Hamish Hamilton (London, England), 1979.

A Thousand Yards of Sea, illustrated by Joanna Troughton, Hodder & Stoughton (London, England), 1980.

The Rug That Grew, illustrated by Priscilla Lamont, Hamish Hamilton (London, England), 1981.

The Christmas Cat, illustrated by Doreen Caldwell, Hamish Hamilton (London, England), 1983.

Little Elephant's Moon, Illustrated by Linda Birch, Hamish Hamilton (London, England), 1986.

Ritchie's Rabbit, illustrated by Vanessa Julian-Ottie, Hamish Hamilton (London, England), 1986, Random House (New York, NY), 1987.

Finding Annabel, illustrated by Alan Marks, Hamish Hamilton (London, England), 1987.

Fishpie for Flamingoes, illustrated by Linda Birch, Hamish Hamilton (London, England), 1987.

The Fantora Family Files, illustrated by Tony Ross, Hamish Hamilton (London, England), 1988, Morrow (New York, NY), 1998.

The Strange Bird, illustrated by Linda Birch, Hamish Hamilton (London, England), 1988.

The Coronation Picnic, illustrated by Frances Wilson, Hamish Hamilton (London, England), 1989.

Bunk Bed Night, Dent (London, England), 1990.

My Grandmother's Stories: A Collection of Jewish Folktales, illustrated by Jael Jordan, Knopf (New York, NY), 1990, Heinemann (London, England), 1990.

Nina's Magic, Hamish Hamilton (London, England), 1990.

Pink Medicine, Dent (London, England), 1990.

A Magic Birthday, Simon & Schuster (London, England), 1992.

The Fantora Family Photographs, illustrated by Tony Ross, Hamish Hamilton (London, England), 1993, Morrow (New York, NY), 1999.

Golden Windows, and Other Stories of Jerusalem, HarperCollins (New York, NY), 1993, Heinemann (London, England), 1995.

Baby's Bedclothes, illustrated by Prue Greener, Longman (London, England), 1994.

The Dolls' House, illustrated by Prue Greener, Longman (London, England), 1994.

Keith's Croak, illustrated by Prue Greener, Longman (London, England), 1994.

Mary's Meadow, illustrated by Prue Greener, Longman (London, England), 1994.

Mimi and Apricot Max, illustrated by Teresa O'Brien, Longman (London, England), 1994.

Josephine, illustrated by Teresa O'Brien, Longman (London, England), 1994.

The Return of Archibald Gribbet, illustrated by Sumiko, Longman (London, England), 1994.

Toey, illustrated by Duncan Smith, Heinemann (London, England), 1994.

Gilly the Kid, illustrated by Sue Heap, Simon & Schuster (London, England), 1995.

Little Swan, illustrated by Johanna Westerman, Random House (New York, NY), 1995.

Stories for Bedtime (with cassette), illustrated by Amanda Benjamin, HarperCollins (New York, NY), 1995.

A Candle in the Dark (part of "Flashbacks" series), A. & C. Black (London, England), 1995.

(Compiler) *A Treasury of Jewish Stories,* illustrated by Jane Cope, Kingfisher (London, England), 1996.

Beauty and the Beast, and Other Stories, Viking Penguin (London, England), 1996.

From Lullaby to Lullaby, illustrated by Kathryn Brown, Simon & Schuster (New York, NY), 1997.

The Random House Book of Opera Stories, Random House (New York, NY), 1998.

The Six Swan Brothers, illustrated by Ian Beck, Scholastic (London, England), 1998.

The Gingerbread House, illustrated by Michael Sheeny, Barrington Stoke, 1998.

Silent Snow, Secret Snow, Puffin (London, England), 1998.

Louisa's Secret, illustrated by Helen Popham, Red Fox (London, England), 1998.

Louisa in the Wings, illustrated by Helen Popham, Red Fox (London, England), 1998.

Louisa and Phoebe, illustrated by Helen Popham, Red Fox (London, England), 1998.

Sun Slices, Moon Slices, illustrated by Karin Littlewood, Scholastic (London, England), 1999.

Sleep Tight, Ginger Kitten, illustrated by Catherine Walters, Penguin Putnam (New York, NY), 2001.

Louisa on Screen, Red Fox (New York, NY), 2001.

Also contributor to periodicals, including *Cricket.*

"MAGIC OF BALLET" PICTURE-BOOK SERIES

(Reteller) *Swan Lake,* illustrated by Emma Chichester Clark, David & Charles (London, England), 2001.
(Reteller) *Sleeping Beauty,* illustrated by Emma Chichester Clark, David & Charles (London, England), 2001.
(Reteller) *Giselle,* illustrated by Emma Chichester Clark, David & Charles (London, England), 2001.
(Reteller) *The Nutcracker,* illustrated by Emma Chichester Clark, David & Charles (London, England), 2001.

FICTION; FOR YOUNG ADULTS

The Girls in the Velvet Frame, Hamish Hamilton (London, England), 1978, Atheneum (New York, NY), 1979.
The Green behind the Glass, Hamish Hamilton (London, England), 1982, published as *Snapshots of Paradise: Love Stories,* Atheneum (New York, NY), 1984.
Other Echoes, Atheneum (New York, NY), 1983.
Voyage, Atheneum (New York, NY), 1983.
Letters of Fire, and Other Unsettling Stories, Hamish Hamilton (London, England), 1984.
Happy Endings, Hamish Hamilton (London, England), 1986, Harcourt (San Diego, CA), 1991.
Daydreams on Video, Hodder & Stoughton (London, England), 1989.
The Tower Room, Hamish Hamilton (London, England), 1990, Harcourt (San Diego, CA), 1992.
Watching the Roses, Hamish Hamilton (London, England), 1991, Harcourt (San Diego, CA), 1992.
Pictures of the Night, Harcourt (San Diego, CA), 1993.
A Lane to the Land of the Dead, Hamish Hamilton (London, England), 1994.
Troy, Harcourt (San Diego CA), 2001.

OTHER

(With Pauline Stainer) *Up on the Roof* (adult poetry), Smith Doorstep (Huddersfield, England), 1987.
Yesterday (memoirs), Walker (London, England), 1992.
Voices from the Dolls' House (adult poetry), Rockingham Press (Ware, England), 1994.

Geras's work has been translated into several languages, including Dutch and German.

Work in Progress

Another entry in the "Louisa" series for Red Fox; an adult novel for Orion Books.

Sidelights

Adele Geras is a British author of children's books as well as the creator of short stories and novels for young adults. While her many picture books deal with largely domestic situations, her works for older readers often deal with spookier topics and also focus on the family and relationships between individuals. Known for telling tales with strong emotional content, Geras also focuses her readers' attention on the nuances of daily life: on clothing, food, and setting. A childhood spent following her father, a British civil servant, on his wide-ranging assignments for the British government while it was still

master over a large colonial empire, greatly influenced her work. Using her experiences of historic Jerusalem, where she was born, exotic Africa, and Great Britain, where she attended boarding school and now lives, Geras weaves a strong sense of place and time into her fiction. Her portraits of vivid characters, also often drawn from recollections of the people she encountered during her childhood years, have been praised by reviewers and readers alike. Sea travel, Jewish culture, and a love of tradition also play a part in shaping her stories for children and teenage readers. "I write because I enjoy it," Geras once told *SATA.* "I write about places and things that have been important to me in one way or another."

"I used to write a lot as a child," Geras once commented, "and then I found that what happened was, as you got more and more educated and had more and more academic work given to you, you had less and less time to do your own stuff. And of course the other thing is that, as you become an adolescent, you become very self-conscious, and you get the idea that if you can't be

An English girl recalls the events leading up to her rape on her eighteenth birthday in Geras's modern version of "Sleeping Beauty." (Cover illustration by S. M. Saelig.)

Tolstoy or Jane Austen, then you're not going to be anybody at all and you should stop. So I did stop when I was about fourteen, and I didn't start again until after my daughter was born. Then I rediscovered what fun it was—which is what every child knows."

Geras's first attempt at writing as an adult was spurred on by a competition in the London *Times*. "As soon as I saw the contest announced . . . I wrote a story and sent it off," she recalled in an essay for *Something about the Author Autobiography Series* (*SAAS*), "and although it did not win, it did become the starting point for *Apricots at Midnight*. It's a ghost story called 'Rose' and the moment I'd finished it, I knew that this was what I wanted to do from now on."

"Rose" would be joined by several other short tales and published by Geras in 1977 as *Apricots at Midnight*, a collection of story "patches" narrated by Aunt Piney, a dressmaker, as she works on a quilt with her young niece. A *Publishers Weekly* reviewer found the collection "unusual and entrancing," while *Horn Book* contributor Kate M. Flanagan praised the tales as "rich in detail and delightfully recounted." Geras's enthusiasm for her newly found craft also found an outlet in writing picture books for young children. The first, *Tea at Mrs. Manderby's*, is a sensitive story about a young girl who resigns herself to taking afternoon tea with an elderly neighbor at her parent's urging. Several more books for young readers would follow, including *A Thousand Yards of Sea*, about a fisherman who releases a mermaid from his net and is rewarded with beautiful sea-colored cloth that the ladies of his village make into swishing skirts and *Toey*, about two children who hope for a new pet and end up with a pair of playful kittens. Geras has also published many short stories in magazines such as *Cricket;* several of her tales have been collected in 1995's *Stories for Bedtime*.

Geras has gone on to produce dozens of picture books and chapter books for younger readers, many of which have also been published in the United States as well as her native England. *Gilly the Kid* features a cowgirl at the Lazy Daisy Ranch whose greatest ambition is to catch a real villain. Ethel E. Ashworth, reviewing the title in *School Librarian*, found it to be a "funny, happy story" that moves "at a brisk pace." *From Lullaby to Lullaby* presents a "magic dream adventure," according to *Booklist* contributor Lauren Peterson, in which a blanket being knit for a young daughter inspires dreams. "Geras's economical text spins this beguiling conceit into a lilting lullaby of words," wrote a critic for *Publishers Weekly*. Geras has also created many popular retellings, including 1997's *Beauty and the Beast, and Other Stories*, "a handsome collection," in the opinion of *School Library Journal* critic Donna L. Scanlon, with "an emphasis on dialogue and . . . original touches." *Booklist* reviewer Hazel Rochman felt that with the "present focus on fractured fairy tales and revisions," she found it "thrilling to return to the old stories and feel their power." A wandering feline is at the center of Geras's 2001 *Sleep Tight, Ginger Kitten*, a tale young-

sters "will relate to," in the opinion of Rosalyn Pierini, writing in *School Library Journal*.

Geras turns to stories from the ballet for titles in the "Magic of Ballet" series. Recounting stories from *Sleeping Beauty* and *Swan Lake* among others, Geras provides retellings along with a brief history of each ballet and its choreography in books which "will be helpful to middle-graders attending a ballet performance," according to *Booklist* contributor Carolyn Phelan. Geras has done much the same for opera with *The Random House Book of Opera Stories*, a "useful and attractive book," as Phelan noted in a *Booklist* review. "Geras's generous use of dialogue and brisk pacing helps make the stories vivid," wrote a contributor for *Publishers Weekly*.

For somewhat older readers, Geras recounts the adventures of a most uncommon family, the Fantoras, in rollicking chronicles maintained by the family pet, one Ozymandias, aka Ozzy the cat. Each member of the family has some sort of magical ability: a grandmother who reads the future in her knitting, a vegetarian vampire aunt with the powers of telekinesis, a father who can grow almost anything, a mother who can fly, and children who can make themselves invisible, change the weather, or make dolls animate. "Originally published in England," noted Michael Cart in a *Booklist* review of the first Fantora book, *The Fantora Family Files*, "the text is sprinkled with British terms that add to the book's cheery oddness." A reviewer for *Publishers Weekly* also praised the series as "Delightfully packed with Briticisms," and deemed it a volume that "launches the Fabulous Fantoras series in high style. . . . Jolly good fun." Reviewing the second title in the series, *The Fantora Family Photographs*, a reviewer for *Horn Book Guide* noted that the "family's outrageous antics are sure to please."

In addition to short stories and picture books for young children, Geras is the author of several collections of short fiction for older readers. In 1982 she wrote *The Green behind the Glass*, a set of eight tales about young love that was released in the United States as *Snapshots of Paradise: Love Stories*. Called "an intriguing departure from the sunny sentimentality of so many romance collections for young adults" by *Booklist* reviewer Stephanie Zvirin, *The Green behind the Glass* includes "Don't Sing Love Songs," narrated by a young woman who is on her own with a friend in Paris until their shared attraction towards handsome Jim threatens their friendship. The title story describes an emotion-laden situation where a young woman's older sister knows herself to be the real object of her sister's now-dead fiancé's true affections, while in "Tea in the Wendy House," a young, pregnant woman laments for her soon-to-be-lost youth as she faces a shotgun wedding and a future as wife and mother in a tiny house. *Horn Book* writer Mary M. Burns hailed the variety of styles and settings of Geras's love stories, calling them "distinguished by perceptive insight into human nature, dexterity in plot construction, and a sense of style remarkable for its readability and its imagery and constraint."

In 1994's *A Lane to the Land of the Dead* Geras uses suspense and elements of the supernatural to add spice and a touch of melancholy to the lives of her young protagonists. "Geras shows her usual lightness of touch," Elspeth S. Scott observed in *School Librarian,* predicting the collection would have wide appeal. In contrast, the five tales in *Golden Windows, and Other Stories of Jerusalem* show readers what life was like in the holy city during the early twentieth century. In "Beyond the Cross-Stitch Mountains," one story from this collection, eleven-year-old Daskeh conspires with friend Danny to escape the care of her aunt Phina and visit his own aunt, despite the danger in leaving the bomb shelter where they routinely spend the nights during Israel's 1948 war for independence. And "Dreams of Fire" shows the after-effects of this experience on young Danny as memories of death and violence return to haunt him in the form of a memorial built to honor the war. Reviewer Ellen Mandel praised *Golden Windows* in *Booklist* as "well-written, laced with subtleties of history, and rich in personal emotion."

In addition to being included in *Golden Windows,* Geras's "Beyond the Cross-Stitch Mountains" evolved into a novel for younger readers that draws on the author's Jewish heritage. Similarly, the 1978 novel *The Girls in the Velvet Frame* takes as its setting the city of Jerusalem as it tells the story of five daughters of a widow whose only son, Isaac, left for the United States, only to be unheard from for months. The year is 1913— just four years before the outbreak of World War I. While the close-knit family has little money, their wealthier Aunt Mimi provides a splash of magic in the lives of the five sisters—Rifka, Chava, Naomi, Dvora, and Shoshie—with her dishes of candy, her comfortable home, and the photograph she arranges to have taken of them as a birthday gift for their mother. At the suggestion of their worldly aunt, the girls send a copy of the finished photograph to New York City, hoping that their brother will see it and contact them. "The appeal of this charming book comes ... from the accurate, penetrating and quite unsentimental portraits of the five children and of their elders," Marcus Crouch noted in the *Times Literary Supplement.* Cyrisse Jaffee similarly acclaimed Geras's characters, adding in *School Library Journal* that "marvelous descriptions of time and place add contours."

Geras's 1983 novel *Voyage* focuses on the history of the Jewish people, describing the passage of those who fled from the poverty of Eastern Europe by enduring the fifteen-day crossing of the Atlantic Ocean aboard a tightly packed ship. In the novel, which takes place just after the turn of the century, readers are introduced to the hopes and fears of several vivid characters: spunky Mina, who must keep up the spirits of her worried mother and her brother; Golda, who is bringing her baby girl to join her husband in New York City; and Yankel, a bully who is making the trip with his mother. The sight of the Statue of Liberty in New York Harbor at journey's end marks the beginning of a new life for these people, as it has for the thousands of actual immigrants whose lives they symbolize. The book's

vignettes "cleverly [reveal] not only the happenings on board but the thoughts, hopes, fears, and memories of the little community," Ethel L. Heins wrote in *Horn Book.* This novel has proved to have relevance decades after its original publication. "*Voyage* is so well-written and well-executed," Michael Thorn wrote in the *Times Educational Supplement,* "that the opportunity ... to obtain this book, which dares to talk seriously to its audience about love, should not be missed."

Geras has written several other novels for young adult readers. Among the most notable are three books that comprise her "Egerton Hall" series. Set in Egerton Hall boarding school in 1963, the stories revolve around three friends—Alice, Bella, and Megan—as the events of their lives take turns that resemble the fairy tales of old. In 1990's *The Tower Room,* Megan becomes a modern-day Rapunzel when she is freed from a lackluster tower room in the boarding school after falling in love with a handsome young laboratory assistant at Egerton Hall. Told in her own words as she looks back over the chain of events leading up to her life with her "Prince Charming" in a small, humble London apartment, Megan realizes that real life doesn't always end "happily ever after."

In 1991's *Watching the Roses,* Geras draws from the Sleeping Beauty legend in telling Alice's story. The reader eavesdrops upon the young woman, lying on her bed in her parent's large house, as she recounts to her diary the events surrounding her eighteenth birthday party. As preparations for the party—actually, a gala ball—are in their final stages, Alice recalls telling friends Megan and Bella stories about her estranged Aunt Violette, who had once dourly predicted that Alice would never live past eighteen. But her anticipation turned to tragedy, the reader soon learns, as the young woman reveals that she was attacked and raped by the uncouth son of her family's gardener on the very night of the ball. She now lies in her room recovering from the shock of the event and silently questioning her own culpability. As in the Sleeping Beauty legend, time seems to stop while Alice attempts to come to terms with these events and deal with both her sexuality and her concerns over how the rape will affect her relationship with Jean-Luc, her own handsome prince. Florence H. Munat praised *Watching the Roses* in *Voice of Youth Advocates,* noting that Geras "has deftly added just the right modern twists and details to lure older readers back to the story that enchanted them as children."

Geras's fairy-tale trilogy is completed with a modern retelling of Snow White's story, casting eighteen-year-old Bella in the lead. Taking place in Paris during Bella's summer vacation from Egerton Hall, *Pictures of the Night* features an evil stepmother, Marjorie, who becomes so jealous of her stepdaughter's budding singing career that she actually tries to kill the beautiful young woman. However, Bella is saved from Marjorie's attempt to poison her—with apple-flavored liqueur—by the quick thinking of Mark, a rich American medical student visiting France. In a *Kirkus Reviews,* a critic called Geras "a writer distinguished for her imaginative power and fresh, vivid writing." "The fairy tale parallels become more apparent as the trilogy proceeds," noted Sheila Ray in _Twentieth-Century Young Adult Writers,_ "gradually moving through the momentous year when the girls fall in love and face their emerging sexuality, creating a powerful tour de force, outstanding in young adult literature."

The Trojan War takes center stage in Geras's 2001 novel, _Troy,_ as she sets her tale in the last ten months of military action and tells it from the point of view of the women of Troy. These women are sick of tending the wounded; the men, too, are tired of the fighting, but the gods and goddesses, growing bored, try to think of ways to stir things up again. Focusing on two orphaned sisters, Xanthe and Marpessa, Geras provides a "feminist perspective," according to a reviewer for _Publishers Weekly_ who also felt that the saga was recreated with "exceptional grace and enormous energy." Xanthe is the caretaker of Andromache's child and also a healer to the injured warriors, while Marpessa is an assistant to Helen and can see the gods. Devoted sisters, they soon fall out when Aphrodite, in a fit of pique, makes them fall in love with the same young man, Alastor. "Mythology buffs will savor the author's ability to embellish stories of old without diminishing their original flavor," wrote the _Publishers Weekly_ contributor, while "the uninitiated will find this a captivating introduction to one of the pivotal events of classic Greek literature." Likewise, _Booklist_ critic Stephanie Zvirin found _Troy_ to be "[s]exy, sweeping, and ambitious."

A prolific author whose work is consistently given high marks by reviewers, Geras once told _SATA:_ "I write very quickly once I get started, but hate getting started—it's like diving from a high board into cold water—terrifying in prospect, but terrific when you've taken the plunge." Geras advised beginning writers: "Read all the time and learn to type. It used to take me almost as long to copy a novel out neatly for the typist as it did to write it."

Biographical and Critical Sources

BOOKS

Something about the Author Autobiography Series, Volume 21, Gale (Detroit, MI), 1996.
Twentieth-Century Young Adult Writers, 4th edition, St. James Press (Detroit, MI), 1994.

PERIODICALS

Booklist, August, 1984, Stephanie Zvirin, review of _Snapshots of Paradise,_ p. 1609; March 1, 1993, p. 1222; October 15, 1993, Ellen Mandel, review of _Golden Windows, and Other Stories of Jerusalem,_ p. 442; July, 1995, p. 1878; November 15, 1996, Hazel Rochman, review of _Beauty and the Beast, and Other Stories,_ p. 582; April 15, 1997, Lauren Peterson, review of _From Lullaby to Lullaby,_ p. 1436; October 15, 1998, Carolyn Phelan, review of _The Random House Book of Opera Stories,_ p. 414; November 1, 1998, Michael Cart, review of _The Fantora Family Files,_ p. 490; July, 2001, Carolyn Phelan, reviews of _Sleeping Beauty_ and _Swan Lake,_ p. 2002; September

1, 2001, p. 104; September 15, 2001, Stephanie Zvirin, review of _Troy,_ p. 225.
Book Report, May-June, 1992, p. 40; March-April, 1994, p. 40.
Books for Keeps, March, 1998, p. 21; November, 1999, p. 49.
Books for Your Children, autumn, 1992, p. 27.
Christian Science Monitor, May 13, 1983.
Horn Book, January-February, 1983, Kate M. Flanagan, review of _Apricots at Midnight, and Other Stories from a Patchwork Quilt,_ pp. 43-44; July-August, 1983, Ethel L. Heins, review of _Voyage,_ p. 452; September-October, 1984, Mary M. Burns, review of _Snapshots of Paradise,_ p. 596; July-August, 1991, pp. 461-462; March-April, 1993, p. 211.
Horn Book Guide, spring, 1999, p. 66; fall, 1999, review of _The Fantora Family Photographs,_ p. 291.
Junior Bookshelf, December, 1976, p. 326; June, 1994, p. 100; August, 1995, p. 134; June, 1996, p. 113.
Kirkus Reviews, September 1, 1984, p. J8; March 15, 1993, review of _Pictures of the Night._
New York Times Book Review, November 11, 1990, p. 31; July 15, 2001, p. 25.
Publishers Weekly, October 15, 1982, review of _Apricots at Midnight, and Other Stories from a Patchwork Quilt,_ p. 66; April 26, 1993, p. 809; September 6, 1993, p. 98; November 25, 1996, review of _Beauty and the Beast, and Other Stories,_ p. 74; March 17, 1997, review of _From Lullaby to Lullaby,_ p. 82; August 10, 1998, review of _The Fantora Family Files,_ p. 388; August 31, 1998, review of _The Random House Book of Opera Stories,_ p. 78; May 7, 2001, review of _Troy,_ p. 248; August 20, 2001, p. 83.
School Librarian, June, 1983, p. 162; November, 1992, p. 157; May, 1994, p. 60; May, 1995, Elspeth S. Scott, review of _A Lane to the Land of the Dead,_ p. 77; August, 1995, Ethel E. Ashworth, review of _Gilly the Kid,_ p. 103; July, 1997, pp. 67-68; spring, 1998, p. 24; autumn, 1998, p. 136; summer, 1999, p. 99.
School Library Journal, September, 1979, Cyrisse Jaffee, review of _The Girls in the Velvet Frame,_ p. 138; November, 1992, p. 121; June, 1993, p. 129; October, 1993, pp. 123-124; February, 1997, Donna L. Scanlon, review of _Beauty and the Beast and Other Stories,_ pp. 90-91; July, 1997, pp. 67-68; October, 1998, p. 153; January, 1999, p. 127; May, 2001, Rosalyn Pierini, review of _Sleep Tight, Ginger Kitten_ p. 115; July, 2001, p. 108.
Times Educational Supplement, September 20, 1991, p. 32; February 19, 1993, p. vi; November 5, 1999, Michael Thorn, review of _Voyage,_ p. 23.
Times Literary Supplement, September 29, 1978, Marcus Crouch, review of _The Girls in the Velvet Frame,_ p. 1083; March 27, 1981, p. 340; January 27, 1984; November 30, 1984; June 6, 1986.
Voice of Youth Advocates, December, 1992, Florence H. Munat, review of _Watching the Roses,_ p. 278.

GOLDIN, Barbara Diamond 1946-

Personal

Born October 4, 1946, in New York, NY; daughter of Morton (an accountant) and Anna (a medical secretary) Diamond; married Alan Goldin (a soil scientist), March 31, 1968 (divorced 1990); children: Josee Sarah, Jeremy Casey. *Education:* University of Chicago, B.A., 1968; Boston University, teaching certificate in primary and special education, 1970; attended Western Washington University, 1980. *Religion:* Jewish.

Addresses

Office—P.O. Box 981, Northampton, MA 01061. *Agent*—Virginia Knowlton, Curtis Brown Ltd., 10 Astor Pl., New York, NY 10003.

Career

Special education teacher at public schools in Gloucester and Ipswich, MA, 1970-72; preschool teacher in Missoula, MT, and Yellow Springs, OH, 1972-75; Children's Bookshop, Missoula, co-owner and operator, 1975-76; Goldendale Public Library, Goldendale, WA, library assistant in children's section, 1976-78; preschool teacher in Bellingham, WA, 1980-82; Congregation B'nai Israel Preschool, Northampton, MA, head teacher, 1986-89; Heritage Academy, Longmeadow, MA, middle school English teacher, 1990—; freelance writer. *Member:* Society of Children's Book Writers and Illustrators.

Awards, Honors

National Jewish Book Award, 1989, for *Just Enough Is Plenty: A Hanukkah Tale;* Association of Jewish Libraries Award, 1992, for *Cakes and Miracles: A Purim Tale;* American Library Association Notable Book, 1995, for *The Passover Journey: A Seder Companion.*

Writings

JUVENILE

Just Enough Is Plenty: A Hanukkah Tale, illustrated by Seymour Chwast, Viking (New York, NY), 1988.

The World's Birthday: A Rosh Hashanah Story, illustrated by Jeanette Winter, Harcourt (San Diego, CA), 1990.

The Family Book of Midrash: Fifty-two Stories from the Sages, J. Aronson (Northvale, NJ), 1990.

Cakes and Miracles: A Purim Tale, illustrated by Erika Weihs, Viking (New York, NY), 1991.

Fire!: The Beginnings of the Labor Movement, illustrated by James Watling, Viking (New York, NY), 1992.

The Magician's Visit: A Passover Tale, illustrated by Robert Andrew Parker, Viking (New York, NY), 1993.

The Passover Journey: A Seder Companion, illustrated by Neil Waldman, Viking (New York, NY), 1994.

Red Means Good Fortune: A Story of San Francisco's Chinatown, illustrated by Wenhai Ma, Viking (New York, NY), 1994.

Night Lights: A Sukkot Story, illustrated by Louise August, Harcourt (San Diego, CA), 1995.

Bat Mitzvah: A Jewish Girl's Coming of Age, illustrated by Erika Weihs, Viking (New York, NY), 1995.

Creating Angels: Stories of Tzedakah, J. Aronson (Northvale, NJ), 1996.

Coyote and the Fire Stick: A Pacific Northwest Indian Tale, illustrated by Will Hillenbrand, Harcourt (San Diego, CA), 1996.

While the Candles Burn: Eight Stories for Hanukkah, illustrated by Elaine Greenstein, Viking (New York, NY), 1996.

The Girl Who Lived with the Bears, illustrated by Andrew Plewes, Harcourt (San Diego, CA), 1997.

Journeys with Elijah: Eight Tales of the Prophet, illustrated by Jerry Pinkney, Harcourt (San Diego, CA), 1999.

Ten Holiday Jewish Children's Stories, illustrated by Jeffrey Allon, Pitspopany, 2000.

A Mountain of Blintzes, illustrated by Anik McGrory, Harcourt (San Diego, CA), 2001.

(Collector and reteller) *One-hundred-and-one-read-aloud Jewish Stories: Ten Readings from the World's Best Loved Jewish Literature,* Black Dog & Leventhal (New York, NY), 2001.

Author of retelling of Tchaikovsky's ballet *The Sleeping Beauty* for boxed editions of compact discs, BMG Music, 1993. Contributor of story to *The Haunted House,* edited by Jane Yolen and Martin H. Greenberg, HarperCollins (New York, NY), 1995. Contributor of articles and reviews to children's magazines and newspapers, including *Highlights, Cricket, Shofar, Seattle's Child, Child Life,* and *Jack and Jill.*

Work in Progress

Kids Talk about Religion, for Viking; *What Is Hidden Is Revealed: Tales of Revelation,* for Aronson.

Sidelights

Barbara Diamond Goldin is an author of children's picture books, novels for older children, story collections, and nonfiction. Her popular picture books deal mainly with holidays and the retelling of folktales, and they often emphasize her Jewish heritage. Her first picture book, *Just Enough Is Plenty: A Hanukkah Tale,* set the tone for much of her subsequent work: well researched stories often set in the "old country" of Eastern Europe, in the shtetls where three of Goldin's grandparents came from. Growing up in New York and Pennsylvania, Goldin was partially cut off from these grandparents because of a language barrier. Yiddish was still their first language, and thus young Goldin was not able to share in their rich heritage. It was only with the research for her first children's book that she began to understand their histories.

This first book was a long time coming, however. Teaching, motherhood, and stints as a bookshop owner and librarian all came first. Then, in 1981, Goldin took a writing workshop with Jane Yolen and spent the next years placing articles and stories in magazines, but also in gathering rejection slips from book publishers. Increasingly, she became fascinated with the Eastern European origins of her relations and researched memoirs as well as the writings of Shalom Aleichem and Isaac Bashevis Singer. Black and white photographs of pre-Holocaust Eastern Europe also aided in this reconstruction, and such research ultimately coalesced into the story of a poor shtetl family who take in a peddler at Hanukkah to share their holiday meal. The peddler repays their kindness by leaving behind a bag of gifts, just as the prophet Elijah does in the traditional stories. The book, *Just Enough Is Plenty,* is a "satisfying tale of traditional values," according to Hanna B. Zeiger in *Horn Book,* and a *Publishers Weekly* reviewer noted that "Goldin's tale and Chwast's vibrant, primitive paintings are masterfully combined." *Junior Bookshelf* critic Marcus Crouch offered a favorable estimation of "this admirable picture-book," commenting that "the simple story is told briefly but with due regard to the importance of its message." *Just Enough Is Plenty* went on to win the National Jewish Book Award.

Goldin continued with holiday themes in her later picture books. *The World's Birthday: A Story about Rosh Hashanah* explores the Jewish New Year, through the story of young Daniel who decides to throw a birthday party for the world and buys a birthday cake for the occasion. Zeiger, writing in *Horn Book,* noted that the blend of text and illustrations created a "tale that captures the spirit of the holiday." *Cakes and Miracles: A Purim Tale* returns to an Eastern European shtetl to tell a story of Purim, a celebration of spring. The young blind boy Hershel finds a place for himself in the life of his village when he helps his mother bake cakes for the holiday, shaping the dough with a special sensitivity he has as a result of his lack of sight. A *Booklist* reviewer stated that *Cakes and Miracles* is "a heartwarming story that is really about using one's special gifts," and Zeiger, in *Horn Book,* concluded that it is a "loving story." Betsy Hearne of the *Bulletin of the Center for Children's Books* called the work a "blessedly unsentimental picture of a blind boy" and also noted that an afterword to the book summarized the origins and customs of Purim.

The important Jewish holiday of Passover is depicted in two books by Goldin. *The Magician's Visit: A Passover Tale* is a picture book in which the prophet Elijah himself comes to provide a feast for a poor couple, while *The Passover Journey: A Seder Companion,* a nonfiction work, looks at the history and customs of this holiday and the ceremonial evening meal, or Seder. Goldin explained that she worked on *The Passover Journey* on and off for four years in an attempt to organize her material and get it exactly right. Betsy Hearne of the *Bulletin of the Center for Children's Books* offered a favorable estimation of Goldin's efforts, stating: "More thorough than many children's books on *Pesach,* this takes great care to explore Jewish tradition and to encourage individual response to it." In a starred review, *Booklist*'s Stephanie Zvirin commended the intricate blending of text and illustration in the work, calling *The Passover Journey* "a beautiful wedding of the work of two talented individuals. . . . A book for family sharing

as well as a rich source of information." Goldin has also compiled a collection of tales and retellings to be read aloud, one each night, for the Hanukkah season. *While the Candles Burn: Eight Stories for Hanukkah* is, according to Janice M. Del Negro of the *Bulletin of the Center for Children's Books,* "a solid addition to collections looking for something a little more unusual than typical holiday fare."

A departure from such picture books with strictly Jewish themes are two short novels for older readers focusing on historical issues such as the labor movement and immigration. *Fire!: The Beginnings of the Labor Movement* is a view of the 1911 Triangle Shirtwaist factory fire through the eyes of eleven-year-old Rosie who wants to quit school and go to work in the garment factory like her older sister. When a fire destroys the building and kills 146 workers, Rosie, the daughter of Russian immigrants, realizes her need for an education and for the labor movement to win strength. "Rosie and her friends will appeal to readers looking for a good story as well as to those needing information on the era," commented *School Library Journal* contributor Joyce Adams Burner.

Goldin explored the lives of Chinese Americans in *Red Means Good Fortune: A Story of San Francisco's Chinatown,* set in 1869. Jin Mun, a twelve-year-old boy, helps out in his father's laundry, but when he discovers a young Chinese girl sold into slavery, he sets a new mission for himself: to free the girl. Carla Kozak, writing in *School Library Journal,* noted that the book was "well-researched and clearly written," while Carolyn Phelan of *Booklist* commented that the "characters and story are involving." Phelan, however, also felt that the book was "too short and the ending will leave the readers wondering what happened next."

Goldin has continued her eclectic mix of story material with a retelling of a Native American tale in *Coyote and the Fire Stick: A Pacific Northwest Indian Tale,* as well as further explication of Jewish tradition and customs in *Bat Mitzvah: A Jewish Girl's Coming of Age.* The former, a retelling of a pourquoi tale explaining the origin of fire, is raised "above the common" variety of such retellings, according to Patricia Lothrop Green in *School Library Journal,* by Goldin's characterization of Coyote and the illustrations of Will Hillenbrand. *Horn Book* reviewer Ann A. Flowers concurs, describing *Coyote and the Fire Stick* as "a well-told story with inventive oil and oil pastel illustrations." With the nonfiction *Bat Mitzvah,* Goldin explains the relatively recent ceremony of the celebration of a girl's coming of age at twelve or thirteen. Ellen Mandel of *Booklist* called the work "relevant, informative, and highly readable," and *School Library Journal* contributor Marsha W. Posner concluded that *Bat Mitzvah* would be "an insightful addition to all collections."

In *The Girl Who Lived with the Bears,* Goldin returned to a tale of the Pacific Northwest. The arrogant daughter of a chief loudly insults the bear people. The bear people soon take her captive to punish her for her pride; the chief's daughter serves them as a slave, but proves her worth. One of the men of the bear people takes her as his wife, and she grows to love him and his people. Critics praised the details that Goldin includes in the text: a reviewer for *Publishers Weekly* noted that the details of every day life of the Native Americans of the Pacific Northwest "ground the fantasy elements." The reviewer called *The Girl Who Lived with the Bears* "a graceful and poignant retelling."

For *Journeys with Elijah: Eight Tales of the Prophet,* Goldin used her skills writing about diverse communities to retell eight stories of visits by the prophet Elijah to Jews living in such areas as China, North Africa, the Caribbean, Israel, and Argentina. Traditionally, Jewish families set a place at their Passover meal for Elijah; Elijah is said to be able to appear to anyone in any guise, and will often reward those who are worthy. Goldin retells stories of these visits from Elijah and creates an "eloquent collection," according to Susan P. Bloom of *Horn Book Magazine.* Stephanie Zvirin, reviewing the collection for *Booklist,* commented that Pinkney's paintings and Goldin's retellings are "vibrant" and note that the characters are reflected in both the illustrations and the prose "with vigor, heart, and color."

Goldin released a new holiday title in 2001 with *A Mountain of Blintzes.* The story, set in the Catskill mountains, tells of a Jewish family preparing for Shavuot. The mother and the father both agree to work a little extra for the two weeks before the holiday, and will use the extra money to buy ingredients for blintzes, the traditional holiday food of Shavout. But neither of the parents actually save any money, assuming that the other is putting enough away. Just when it seems that the family won't have enough money after all, the children explain that they have been secretly working at odd jobs to save the money the family needs. Karen Simonetti of *Booklist* wrote that this tale based on a traditional Jewish folktale of Chelm makes an "ebullient picture book." *School Library Journal* critic Teri Markson called the book "a delightful and satisfying tale." Goldin also included her family's recipe for blintzes at the end of the tale.

Goldin, whose favorite place to work is at a local college library, enjoys the process of research and writing. "I still love to write and research and discover new worlds on paper," she once said. "Writing is still an exciting process for me. I'm never certain when I sit down to write what the next few hours will bring."

Biographical and Critical Sources

PERIODICALS

Booklist, January 15, 1991, review of *Cakes and Miracles,* p. 1062; December, 15, 1993, Carolyn Phelan, review of *Red Means Good Fortune,* p. 754; March 1, 1994, Stephanie Zvirin, review of *The Passover Journey,* p. 1260; September 1, 1995, Ellen Mandel, review of *Bat Mitzvah,* p. 56; April 15, 1997, Karen Morgan, review of *The Girl Who lived with the Bears,* p. 1424; April 15, 1999, Stephanie Zvirin, review of *Journeys with Elijah,* p. 1524; October 1, 2000, Stephanie Zvirin, *Ten Holiday Jewish Children's Stories,* p. 48; March 1, 2001, Karen Simonetti, review of *A Mountain of Blintzes,* p. 1287.

Bulletin of the Center for Children's Books, February, 1991, Betsy Hearne, review of *Cakes and Miracles,* p. 141; April, 1992, p. 206; March, 1993, p. 233; April, 1994, Hearne, Betsy, review of *The Passover Journey,* pp. 257-58; November, 1996, Janice M. Del Negro, review of *While the Candles Burn,* pp. 96-97.

Horn Book, November-December, 1988, Hanna B. Zeiger, review of *Just Enough Is Plenty,* p. 763; November-December, 1990, Hanna B. Zeiger, review of *The World's Birthday,* pp. 718-19; July-August, 1991, Hanna B. Zeiger, review of *Cakes and Miracles,* p. 447.

Horn Book Magazine, November-December, 1996, Ann A. Flowers, review of *Coyote and the Fire Stick,* p. 748; March, 1999, Susan P. Bloom, review of *Journeys with Elijah,* p. 223.

Junior Bookshelf, April, 1989, Marcus Crouch, review of *Just Enough Is Plenty,* p. 60.

Kirkus Reviews, September 15, 1988, p. 1403; July 15, 1990, p. 1011; December 1, 1990, p. 1671; May 15, 1992, p. 677; January 1, 1993, p. 67; January 1, 1994, p. 67.

New York Times Book Review, September 12, 1999, Kevin Kelly, review of *Journeys with Elijah,* p. 37.

Publishers Weekly, September 30, 1988, review of *Just Enough Is Plenty,* p. 66; August 31, 1990, p. 64; December 7, 1990, p. 90; January 4, 1993, p. 72; January 24, 1994, p. 57; February 14, 1994, p. 65; November 13, 1995, p. 65; April 7, 1997, review of *The Girl Who Lived with the Bears,* p. 91; March 22, 1999, review of *Journeys with Elijah,* p. 88; November 1, 1999, review of *Journeys with Elijah,* p. 54.

School Library Journal, July, 1992, Joyce Adams Burner, review of *Fire!,* p. 73; May, 1994, Carla Kozak, review of *Red Means Good Fortune,* p. 114; November, 1995, Marcia W. Posner, review of *Bat Mitzvah;* October, 1996, Patricia Lothrop Green, review of *Coyote and the Fire Stick,* p. 114; April 1997, Pam Gosner, review of *The Girl Who Lived with the Bears,* p. 124; June 1999, Martha Link, review of *Journeys with Elijah,* p. 116; April 2001, Teri Markson, review of *A Mountain of Blintzes,* p. 108.

Sunday Republican (Springfield), September 1, 1996, p. D5.*

*   *   *

Autobiography Feature

Barbara Diamond Goldin

There I was, seven years old, trooping behind my father along with my two younger brothers to the large vegetable garden that grew by the railroad tracks. We each carried paper bags to hold the tomatoes and cucumbers and radishes that we would pick. Not an unusual event, you're thinking, but to us it was. At the time, we lived in the middle of New York City on the fifth floor of a fifteen-floor building that was part of a larger apartment complex. How my father found this garden tended by the railroad workers in their spare time I don't know. Since no one else ventured there, the railroad workers smiled at us when we came and let us pick what we wanted.

My father, who was born on a farm in the Catskill Mountains, was forever "exploring," as he called it, and we children were delighted with his finds. Among other places, he also took us to the Museum of Natural History to look at the Blue Whale and the dinosaur bones, to the Statue of Liberty by ferry, and into whatever woods he could find. To this day I still love the city and the country and "exploring." Thanks to my father, I became just as used to picking blueberries in the woods in upstate New York as I was crossing the busy city streets going to school or falling asleep to the sound of the elevated trains outside my bedroom window.

I took growing up in New York City for granted. My whole family lived there, my grandparents, aunts and uncles and cousins. When we were very little, my grandpa Joe, my mother's father, would come look after my brothers and me on weekdays to give my Mom a "break." He spoke Yiddish and we spoke English, but somehow we got along very well. Sometimes Grandpa Joe would take me along with him to his little shul, his synagogue, a small Orthodox one whose congregants were mainly immigrants from Eastern Europe like my grandfather. I was allowed to sit in the men's section of the synagogue because I was little, and I'd play with the fringes on his prayer shawl while he prayed, swaying gently back and forth. I loved the fuss everyone made over me. And there was always the kiddush, the wine and cake afterwards, and the warm greetings.

Other times Grandpa Joe took me with him to get a big fat kosher hot dog with sauerkraut and mustard at the local deli. I remember the little black-and-white tiles on the floor and the rich smells of the place that made my stomach grumble the minute I walked inside. I remember, too, the old kind of seltzer bottles Grandpa Joe had delivered to his apartment—the kind that spritzed—and the hot tea he drank out of a glass. In his broken English, he taught me how to play cards—one of his great passions.

I don't remember his wife, my grandma Rose, who died when I was one, but I often heard about how wise and ahead of her times she was. She convinced the rabbi and the other men in his Saturday afternoon study group to let her study with them, which was unusual in the Bronx in the early 1930s. She also felt strongly that women had a right to an education and a right to work outside the home, ideas that were also not as common then as they are now. My mother and my aunt Ida often tell me that I look and even talk like my grandma Rose. Over the years I've often wondered—do I really look like her? Talk like her? Sometimes I stare at the few pictures we have of her and try to see the resemblance.

My grandparents on my father's side also lived in the city, in Brooklyn. That's the Diamond side of the family. Part of the lore floating around my family about the Diamond clan includes the idea of what my aunt Helen calls "Diamond luck"—it's the kind of luck where you're unwittingly walking along and fall into it. To this day, if I find a parking space on a busy city street or get the exact kind of job I've been wishing for, I think, it's Diamond luck.

Part of the Diamond lore includes family stories like the one about Great-uncle Haim. He came to the United States from Lithuania on a visit and sold one of his many inventions, the backstitch, to Singer sewing machine and another invention for some kind of bottle cap to some other company. Then he went back to Lithuania because his wife didn't want to move here.

Grandpa Harry Diamond, my father's father, was a jack-of-all-trades, an amateur everything. He was the one who tried farming in the early 1900s in the Catskills where my father was born. Since the land was so rocky, he took to delivering milk and eggs to the neighbors, and my grandma Sarah took in boarders to try to help make ends meet. But they weren't the Grossingers and, when my father was still a boy, his parents had to give up the farm for financial reasons and move back into the city.

Grandpa Harry started all of his grandchildren on hobbies like stamp and coin collections. He was full of "tricks" which we kids loved and our mothers didn't. He would write A, B, C, D, etc., in big black crayon on our piano keys, for instance, to teach us a quick way to play. He always brought with him a big pile of games from

John's Bargain Store whenever he came to visit, and collected old broken radios and phonographs. He would take them apart and hook them up in odd ways to get them to work. He set up a darkroom and showed us the magic of developing pictures. Once again I don't remember his wife, my grandma Sarah, as well. She was kind and quiet and died when I was eight.

I'm telling you all this about my grandparents because these experiences affect me a lot as a writer. Early in my career I went to a conference and heard a children's book writer say "Write what you know." As I work on more and more stories as an adult, these early memories of growing up in a large extended family often come back to me and give me ideas. For example, once, on the holiday of Passover, we opened the door for the Prophet Elijah and a cat walked in. This later became the core of one of the first stories I sold which was called "Elijah's Arrival" and was published by *Jack and Jill* in its April/May 1984 issue.

Much of my interest in researching and writing about Eastern Europe comes from these grandparents I have told you about. Three out of four of them were from the "Old Country." I heard that term a lot while I was growing up, but I realized as an adult that I knew very little about what it was like in Eastern Europe or about how my grandparents lived when they were young. And I couldn't ask them. They were all gone.

So I began to read everything I could on Eastern European life, especially memoirs and fiction by great Yiddish writers like Isaac Bashevis Singer and Shalom Aleichem. I looked at old photographs of small town shtetl life. Quite a few of my picture book stories came from this period of time when I read and thought about Eastern Europe and my grandparents—books like *Just Enough Is Plenty: A Hanukkah Tale, Cakes and Miracles: A Purim Tale,* and *The Magician's Visit: A Passover Tale.* I had a strong urge to capture this way of life in story form for today's young readers, and for myself, because it is a way of life that is gone forever. The Second World War and Hitler's Holocaust saw to that. As a Jew who was born right after the war was over, writing these stories helps me deal with the horrible event of the Holocaust. I can recreate life in Eastern Europe on the page—immortalize it there, at least, and make it live again for young children and myself.

Once I brought my first published book, *Just Enough Is Plenty: A Hanukkah Tale,* to my cousin Sarah to show it to her. By this time, she was my only relative still alive who had lived in Eastern Europe before the war. She looked at the book, looked up at me, and said, "This is just the way it was." Her words made me feel so good.

Besides my grandparents, there were my aunts, uncles, and cousins, who also lived in New York. My mother's brother, my uncle George, was a practical joker. He would give you a huge wrapped-up present, and you'd spend the next hour unwrapping it, only to find box inside of box inside of box. If you were lucky, there'd be something in the middle. (There usually was.) Uncle Lou, who was a bachelor and smoked cigars, took us places in his incredibly clean car. (My parents didn't have a car then.) Between the cigar smoke and the way he drove his stick shift, my brothers and I rarely made it anywhere with him without getting sick to our stomachs. The joke in the family was "Don't give anything to (my mother) Anna's kids to eat if they're going in your car."

Barbara D. Goldin, 1990

Uncle Solly told us stories, including the one I've just told you, about the family and the people he knew, about the daring things he and my uncle George did when they were young, and how they would always "protect" my mother, the baby of the family. Our godmother Aunt Ida often took care of us in her big house in Paterson, New Jersey. She was and still is the keeper of the samovar Grandma Rose brought with her from the Old Country, and of the delicate little wine cups she, my mother, and their brothers used at Passover seders when they were children.

We spent a lot of time with my father's brothers and sisters, too. Uncle Natie can build or repair anything and has an airplane pilot's license besides. Uncle Maxie is an artist who introduced us to pottery wheels, kilns, fusing glass, sculpting paper, all kinds of things. There is such a resemblance between my father and Maxie and Natie that often one of us young children would mistake an uncle for a father and beg to be lifted up, only to discover at face level that he or she had the wrong Diamond. My dad's sister, Aunt Bessie, has a beautiful singing voice and is under strict orders to bring her cheesecakes to every family get-together. Aunt Frances's fame is due to her husband Howie, who did all sorts of odd things like hypnotize you if your mother let you.

Diamond clan gatherings were and still are busy, noisy affairs, always erupting into a jam session. Uncle Maxie will whip a harmonica out of his pocket and start to play. Aunt Helen, Aunt Bessie, Aunt Estelle, and Uncle Morris—then everyone—will start to sing. My cousins David, Jerry, Nancy, Shari and more, and brother Bert drag out guitars, kazoos, whatever. With all the new little cousins here now, we've added a box of dress-ups to the fun.

My place in this big extended family is as the oldest of three children born to Anna (daughter of Joe and Rose) and Morton (son of Harry and Sarah). I don't remember very much from those very early years, but my mother does. She tells a story about me when I was about two years old. She'd lost me in a big store and was frantically looking for me when she saw a large crowd by the cash registers. She feared the worst—that I had hurt myself. But when she reached the circle, she saw me in the center, dancing around and putting on a show. I must have thought I was at a Diamond clan gathering.

Another story she tells is that I loved going to the movie theater. In those days, the theater played the same movie over and over again, and you paid one admission and could sit there all day long. Once when I was around six, she had to send Uncle Lou after me to drag me out of the theater. I had sat through *Elephant Walk* about five times. It's no wonder that, to this day, I have a vivid image in my mind of a huge herd of elephants stampeding through a villa with Elizabeth Taylor looking on in terror.

When I was two and a half, my brother Robert was born. I must have been a bit jealous because there's a story about me squeezing cherry juice right into his eyes. Bert was born a few years later. For years I was the "big" sister, until Robert and Bert grew to be over six feet tall and I stayed a shrimp of five feet two and a half inches.

My mom read lots of books to us when we were little, and this must have helped give me my love of books. But I had trouble when I went to first grade where they taught reading by emphasizing sight recognition of whole words. As soon as my mother saw my very poor grade in reading, she took over and taught me to read using phonics, which emphasizes learning the alphabet, the sounds of the letters, and blending the letters together. I did much better in school after that.

Another memory I have of these years in the New York City apartment house was coming home from school and seeing fire trucks in front of my building. Immediately

Maternal grandparents, Joe and Rose Friedman, with daughter, Ida, and son Lou, 1912 (not pictured are children Solly, George, and Anna

I worried that the fire was in my apartment. It was. A fire had started in the kitchen and smoke filled the whole place. By the time I arrived, my brothers were hiding under their beds and my mother was trying to convince the firemen not to chop up the furniture.

I also remember one Halloween when all the lights went out suddenly. Was it a quirky electric failure or the custodian playing a Halloween prank? I never found out. We ended up using candles to see by and, when the lights came on, we discovered that the cake my mother had been making had pink frosting instead of orange. We ate it anyway, of course.

Sometimes I liked being the oldest child and sometimes I didn't. I liked being the one to get a watch first and go to bed later than my brothers, but I didn't always like being in charge of them. Robert and Bert could be a handful. Once my mother sent me off with Robert to try out the brand-new wading pool in the nearby park. It didn't take us long to find out, however, that the pool didn't actually have any water in it. Its cement cracks had recently been filled with a black tar which was still drying. Of course my brother Robert found the tar and smeared it all over his hair. When I brought him home, my mother had to cut a good portion of his hair off, and she wasn't too happy with me either.

When I was eight years old everything changed. My father, who was an accountant for the federal government, accepted a job transfer to Philadelphia. Philadelphia was only ninety miles from New York, but it was worlds away to me. We moved midway through the school year, my third grade year. Besides leaving my extended family in New York, my school, and my friends, I suddenly found out that I was different. I was the new kid in the class, the school, and the neighborhood. I was teased and bullied because I was new and had a New York accent. Practically everything I said made the other kids laugh at me. The rest of that third grade year was a very hard one for me. Looking back, I feel that during that year I went from being an outgoing secure kid to an insecure, shy one. And I acquired this new feeling—of being an outsider, someone different from everybody else.

I developed low grade fevers and, fortunately, our new family doctor guessed their cause—homesickness. He told my mother to take me on a visit to our old apartment building in New York. On returning there, I found out that a lot of people I knew had also moved away. The building looked much shabbier than I remembered, and our little house in Philadelphia looked better and better to me. After that trip, my fevers disappeared and I slowly adjusted to my new life.

In fourth grade things improved. I had a wonderful teacher named Mrs. Chambeau who supplied us all with books from her own lending library. That was the year I really began to lose myself in books. We also moved to a house on a street full of kids of all ages. I roller-skated with them in the street, jumped hopscotch and rope, and swapped secrets. In summer, everyone moved outside. It was too hot inside in those days before every house had air conditioning. Parents dragged television sets out onto the stoop, the steps in front of our attached "row" houses. They watched favorite shows like *Ed Sullivan* and *The Honey-*

Paternal grandparents, Harry and Sara Diamond, with children (first row, left) Natie, Frances, (second row) Bess, (third row) the author's father, Morton ("Moe"), and Maxie, New York City, 1937

mooners, chatted with neighbors, and kept an eye on all the kids. We, the kids, played hide-and-seek among the bushes, jacks on the steps, bottle caps in the street, and ball bouncing games against the brick walls. We played until the last possible moment, until we heard our name called for the third or fourth time by an exasperated parent whose voice was getting thin.

So things did get better, but things had also changed forever. And I had changed. I still saw my relatives often and grew up feeling close to them. But a part of me always felt like a stranger where I lived—the kid who just couldn't say "chocolate" quite right.

Later on, much later, I wrote a short story based on this time of my life called "Ketsele's Gift," which was published in *Cricket,* in April of 1989. The girl in the story is based on me and the grandfather on my grandpa Joe. When I do school visits, I like to read this story and talk about what is true in it and what is fiction. I learned a lot about myself and my relationship with my grandfather from writing this story. And I find that the discoveries I make when I write are one of the most exciting parts of being a writer.

This incident—making a present for my grandfather for his first visit to my new house—was a memory that had stuck in my mind for many years. By writing the story, I discovered it had stayed with me for a reason—there had been something unresolved that continued to bother me over the years, something I did not understand. I had worked for days on the present—a notebook full of Hebrew words—and thought my grandfather would be so pleased and would love the fact that I was learning his language in my new Hebrew school. But when I gave him the notebook, he hardly paid any attention to it. I was very disappointed and never knew why he didn't react the way I had expected.

In writing the story, I realized that as a nine year old I hadn't understood that he spoke Yiddish and not Hebrew. They are two very different languages that use the same alphabet. I wondered if he would have been excited if I had done the notebook in Yiddish instead. So, in my story, the girl figures out this difference in the two languages herself and starts a new notebook for her grandfather with Yiddish words. He is very pleased and ends up teaching her more and more Yiddish. Much to my surprise, this story turned out to be all about communication between a girl and her grandfather, and the frustrations of a granddaughter who can't speak to her grandfather in his language. "Ketsele's Gift" has a happy ending and I felt a lot better after writing it. I couldn't change the past by writing about it, but I could certainly understand it better. I find I often work out

With father, 1946

questions I have, and problems I am thinking about, through my writing.

All the way through the twelfth grade, I continued to live on this same street in Philadelphia. I worked hard in school, "hung out" with my friends, and enjoyed my family. My father still took us "exploring," now to Pennsylvania Dutch farm auctions where we'd get stuck behind horse-drawn Amish wagons and eat shoofly pie at farmers' markets. Or he would take us to help him search for certain towers to climb or waterfalls to swim under that he'd read about in his piles of AAA (American Automobile Association) maps and brochures that kept spilling out of the night table by my parents' bed.

My mom, who had been a medical secretary, stayed home to take care of us. She loves to cook and her specialty was and is delicious cakes. These cakes never lasted long. She'd put a just-baked cake out on the kitchen table to cool, make a phone call, and one of us, most likely Bert, would eat a piece out of the middle, the moistest part. If Mom did get a chance to frost the cake, one of us would invariably come along and gobble up fingerfuls of frosting off the cake, thinking that no one would notice.

The three of us together could be quite a force. We regularly scared away baby-sitters by teasing them and spying on them when they brought their boyfriends over. But we soon found out that baby-sitterless, we were also very good at scaring ourselves. When our parents went out at night, we loved to watch all those scary movies on TV. The tricky part came when the movie was over. We'd all three make a mad dash for the stairs at the same time, pushing and shoving. Not one of us wanted to be the last one to reach those stairs, because, by an unwritten rule, that person had to turn off the TV and all the downstairs lights, and mount the stairs in *the dark!*

My room was at the top of the stairs and oh how I hated that. I knew that if a burglar entered the house, he'd climb those stairs and see my room first. So I had all these tricks. I had a way of closing the regular door to my room and then opening the closet door so the two doors would form a sort of double barrier. Sometimes I'd add a chair piled high with things that would clang in the night. That way, at least, the imagined burglar would make a lot of noise trying to get to me. Luckily, my various tricky systems were never put to the test.

My family was particularly good friends with another family on our street—the Freimarks. Both our family and theirs were a little different from the other families in the neighborhood, a little quirkier. Fred was a gifted wood-worker who, as a child, had fled Nazi Germany with his family and gone to live in Haiti. Eventually he and his family moved to the United States. Fred carved amazing wood sculptures for their house, probably influenced by his years in Haiti. In addition, instead of painting, wall papering, or panelling their living room wall, Fred covered the wall with different shapes and kinds of wood in a wonderful mosaic, certainly the only one like it in the neighborhood. His wife Eva was Hungarian with her own story of how she, her sister, and mother made a narrow escape by train just as the Nazis were moving into Hungary. Eva made the best apple strudel from scratch, rolling the thin layers of dough on her kitchen table; and she loved all kinds of music, including Christmas carols. She would play these on the family record player all through December, surprising people like me who only heard these carols on TV, at school, or in the homes of my friends who weren't Jewish.

Fred and Eva's children, Bob and Sue, were like a brother and sister to us. They were a funny and even outrageous family. Just going over to their house could be an event. Once, on Passover, my father, whose Hebrew name is Moses, went there during the Passover meal, the seder, for some reason. When he walked inside, they all stood up from the table in unison, pointed at my astonished father, and sang "Go Down Moses" to him. He came back bewildered and couldn't remember what he had gone over there to ask about.

During these growing-up years, I read all the time, but especially in summer. And went on endless walks to the library to replenish my supply, especially any book by Enid Blyton I could find. I loved her adventure stories. My mother would try and get me out of my room into the "fresh air," but if my friends were at camp or "down the shore," she didn't succeed.

I didn't really think of myself as a writer when I was growing up. I didn't write stories or poems except in school. But I loved to tell stories. I'd often make up stories in my head before I went to sleep. And when I baby-sat, which was very often because I liked making my own money, I figured out a way to get the parents to ask me back. I'd tell the kids a story, often an outer-space adventure, using the kids as the main characters, and leave it hanging in the middle. They would beg to have me as their sitter. I also loved writing letters, keeping journals, and doing my own research that had nothing to do with school.

My dad loves to read about history, including ancient history. Maybe that's why I chose ancient Egypt as my passion. Or it could have been that I fell in love with an historical fiction book called *Mara: Daughter of the Nile,* but for a few years I read everything at the library about Ancient Egypt and kept lots of notes. I even thought I wanted to be an archaeologist until I went to college and fell asleep at the archaeology club meetings. My friend Kathy, who also thought she wanted to be an archaeologist, told me I snored.

A big part of my life growing up in Philadelphia was my synagogue. My family belonged to a small one that started in a house and grew larger over the years as more and more families joined. For the most important holidays of the year, the fall High Holidays, we had services in the movie theater because the synagogue was too small to fit all the people who wanted to come. We got to sit in those plush velvet seats and smell popcorn while the rabbi and cantor were up where the movie usually was.

Since it was a small synagogue at first, the families were all very close and I got to know the kids around my own age very well. We went to public school and Hebrew school together, and some of us even went on to Hebrew high school where we commuted to another part of the city for after-school Hebrew classes.

I never had a bat mitzvah ceremony, though, because when I was thirteen, girls were not allowed to have the same coming-of-age ceremony that boys did in my fairly traditional synagogue. My attitude was, if I can't do what

Barbara at age five

the boys do, I didn't want to do anything at all, certainly not the token Friday night service that was offered to me. Years later, I wrote a book called *Bat Mitzvah: A Jewish Girl's Coming of Age* in which I was able to explore the possibilities that were available to girls when I was young and what is happening in the Jewish community today for girls of thirteen. I loved working on this book and learning all about Jewish women's history and the growth of the bat mitzvah ceremony for girls. I was also pleased to be able to include my own daughter Josee in this book, who had become a bat mitzvah about a year before I started working on it.

When it was time for me to go to college, I knew I wanted to go away from home, to another big city. I had done well in school and qualified for scholarships at the schools I applied to. My parents were wonderful in that they let me make my own choices about college and career. I took the decision about college very seriously and agonized for months during my senior year about which school to go to. It was hard to decide since I wasn't able to visit all the schools. I finally did choose, though, and in the fall of 1964, set out by car with a high school classmate, Lon Bannett, and his parents for Chicago, a city neither one of us had ever seen. We were both entering the University of Chicago and my mother had sewn a pocket in my underwear for me to hide all my money until I got there.

In a way, the University of Chicago was an ideal school for me, although I wasn't always sure of it at the time. The courses and professors were exciting and challenging, and I learned how to really do research, about everything. I am often thankful for my education there, because it has helped me so much in my work as a writer now.

No experience is perfect, though, and there was one teacher there with whom I had a problem—my freshman English Composition teacher. For some reason, he did not like my writing, though I had been an outstanding writer all through my high school career. I struggled to please him all year long. It wasn't until years later, when I worked with Dr. Flora Fennimore at Western Washington University, that I finally overcame those negative feelings about my writing left over from my freshman college English course. Only then did I go on to pursue my writing career. Now I teach English to middle school students and am often reminded of the college English teacher I had; of how damaging one teacher can be, and of how encouraging

Barbara with mother and brothers, Bert (front) and Rob, 1955

another one is when it comes to the sometimes fragile creative efforts we put on paper.

It was during college that I settled on my career choice of teaching. I was especially influenced by some volunteer work I did on the south side of Chicago through a student tutoring project called STEP. I worked with the same boy Gregory for three years and helped him with his reading. I got to know a group of his friends and would often take them all over the city, to the museums, parks, downtown. One Halloween I took them trick-or-treating in my neighborhood where, to their delight, they collected bags and bags of candy. The problem came at the end of the night. They had to figure out how to get that candy back home without it getting stolen by the gangs in their neighborhood. Their solution was to stuff the bags under their coats and brave the walk home, luckily successfully.

The year I graduated from college, 1968, was also the year I married my high school sweetheart, Alan Goldin. For three years we were both teachers and spent our summers traveling—all over Europe, the United States and Canada. During this time of my life, I avidly explored various art forms like pottery and weaving, which I would later give up to devote to the one I find most fulfilling—writing.

One summer we traveled to western Canada and the Banff School of Fine Arts, where Alan took photography and I studied weaving. We lived in a tent, wove and took pictures, swam in natural hot springs, and hiked to tea houses in the Canadian National Parks. We were as likely to meet a bear on the trail from the campground to the studio as we were to meet a fellow artist. In Banff I developed a long-lasting relationship with my weaving teacher Lilly Bohlin and studied with her several more times at her studio in Victoria, British Columbia. Later on I even bought a sixty-inch-wide Swedish loom, which took up most of our living room.

During the school year, we taught in public schools in the Gloucester, Massachusetts, area and lived by the sea. Gloucester was full of "atmosphere," and I loved waking up very early, walking along the harbor to Bear Skin Neck to have breakfast at Ellen's. That's where the local fishermen gathered before they went out on their boats to start their day's work.

After a year of course work at Boston University, I taught the educably retarded one year and the emotionally disturbed another and found it all a real challenge. To give you an idea, once a student of mine disappeared from the classroom and was found in a basketball hoop in the gym a little while later by my supervisor. How he got up into the hoop I don't know, except that he was extremely agile. This particular boy was intent on being in the classroom when he wasn't supposed to be, and outside of it when he was supposed to be in it. During a home visit, this same boy's stepfather pulled a gun on my assistant.

When I worked with students whose home situations were like this boy's, I felt that my efforts as a teacher were lost as soon as the child went home from school. It was around this time that I decided to concentrate on teaching preschool. Perhaps, I reasoned, if we got to kids in the early years ... we could prevent, diagnose, and work with the kinds of problems I had seen in the older students. I remembered the dedicated staff and wonderful work of the Chicago Child Care Society where I had volunteered in a preschool class as a college student. As I went into teaching preschoolers, I found that my special education background was an enormous resource for me in working with the children and their parents.

At this point, Alan decided he wanted to leave teaching altogether and study forestry out west. This news was a shock to me, since I felt very at home in New England and didn't have any desire to move so far away. But Alan was very set on his idea and we soon left for Missoula, Montana, where, on my first day in our new apartment, I ran into another tenant skinning a black bear in our joint backyard.

At first I felt very disoriented in Missoula, an outsider once more. But I did find a teaching job in a preschool, and decided to train in the Montessori method with a wonderful teacher and friend Valeska Appleberry. Spending a year away from Montana to do that, I immersed myself in a training course in Michigan for a summer, and in Valeska's school in Yellow Springs, Ohio, for the school year. I lived with her and her husband Lynton and learned much more from them than methods of teaching. The Appleberries have many stories to tell about living on the land, growing your own (food and children and morality), about people and human nature, about music and world politics.

When I returned to Montana, I not only went to work in a Montessori school there, but also opened up a children's bookstore with a friend, Georgia Johnson, who had been trained as a children's librarian. We both loved children's books and jumped into this business endeavor with much enthusiasm. But before long, Alan had finished his course of study in forestry and soils, and took a job with the Soil Conservation Service in Goldendale, Washington. Alan didn't have the same feelings of wanting to set down roots and hating the feeling of always being the outsider that I had. Rather reluctantly, I sold my share of the bookstore to Georgia and moved to eastern Washington.

I tried to make the most of the move to this town of three thousand and, luckily, got a job as a children's librarian in the quaint public library. We lived seven miles out of town up a dirt road in one of three A-frame houses on some land owned by Glen, an ex-rodeo star. Glen used to threaten to hide his wife's shoes so she couldn't go into town to the church so much! We had deer on our front lawn—real ones—and miles and miles of forest behind our house.

While we lived in Goldendale, we came to know the Columbia River area and Mt. Adams, and picked and canned all the peaches we could stand. I got an even better education in children's books at my job in the library. We were also able to spend time with my college roommate Kristin Skotheim who lived north of us in the town of Toppenish. She taught at Project Pallatisha for handicapped pre-schoolers on the Yakima Indian reservation and took us to our first real pow wow. Later on I would do a retelling of a Native American story from this area of the country called *Coyote and the Fire Stick.*

After two years in Goldendale, Alan was offered a job transfer to the western part of the state, to Bellingham, Washington, and I was glad. I had felt very isolated in this small town, and Bellingham was midway between the two lively cities of Seattle and Vancouver. Also, Kristin had just moved there to teach in a head start classroom on the Lummi reservation. The nearest synagogue to Goldendale that I knew of had been one hundred miles away, the

High school graduation, 1964

nearest movie theater and bookstore thirty-five miles. Bellingham had all these plus a university.

Though Bellingham didn't feel like home to me, the perpetual outsider, I was very drawn to the awesome landscape of water, mountains, and trees, and to the lifestyle and myths of the Northwest Coast native peoples. Alan and I traveled up and down the coast where it was an everyday experience to watch tens of eagles circling overhead. We traveled to the interior of British Columbia where native villages dotted with impressive totem poles stood along the rivers. I volunteered in my friend Kristin's Lummi Head Start classroom and searched through local libraries hunting for information and stories. Besides *Coyote and the Fire Stick,* another one of my books has come out of this period of my life—*The Girl Who Lived with the Bears,* a Haida-Tlingit tale.

It was while living in Bellingham that I became a writer. During all my years of preschool teaching (eleven as of now), in all sorts of schools in all kinds of places, I told stories I made up on the spot to the children. I remember one school especially that had a large closet off the main room. Sometimes we'd go in there for a story. There's nothing like a dark closet for effect, especially around Halloween. A turning point came for me when one little girl asked for a particular story over again—one that I had told the year before. Much to my dismay, I couldn't remember it. I decided that I had better start writing down some of these stories.

And so I began taking classes in writing books for children from Dr. Flora Fennimore at Western Washington

University. She emphasized the joy of the process, not the focus on the end product, as my college English composition teacher had. I learned that by writing more and more, my end product improved over time with practice. Listening to feedback from others and revising a lot helped. I found out that I loved to write and was reminded of my father's efforts. Before I was born, and off and on while I was growing up, he had written poems and stories. He even had a short story published in *Boy's Life* during his Boy Scout leader's days, of which he is very proud.

This was also about the time that I had our first child, Josee, named after my grandpa Joe. She was a lively and alert baby, loved getting into things and pulling everything out—from purses, drawers, and clean folded laundry hampers. She loved music and fell asleep to the beat of Buddy Holly songs. Taking things apart and putting them back together was a delight to her. To this day, she still loves to do puzzles! I timed my writing sessions with her nap times and became a very disciplined writer. The minute she fell asleep, I would head for my tiny study. A lot of my early stories (never published) were about my experiences with Josee—berry picking, camping, carving pumpkins.

When Josee was a toddler, I found out about a course in writing for children given by Jane Yolen at Centrum in nearby Port Townsend, Washington. I couldn't believe it! I had read every single one of Jane Yolen's books I could find while I was working at the Goldendale Public Library. She had been a favorite of Georgia's, my old bookstore partner, who first pointed out *The Girl Who Cried Flowers* to me.

And so I left Josee in the care of her father and a friend's teenage daughter, and took the ferry boat to Port Townsend for the workshop, feeling excited and a bit scared. From the moment I left my car in the parking lot at Centrum (I didn't see it for the next ten days!), I was immersed in the writing life. I actually met Jane Yolen, who turned out to be a down-to-earth and charming person, and a most helpful and perceptive teacher. She not only listened to our stories, taught us how to critique each other's work, and inspired us to write and rewrite (we even had the local bakery decorate our final party cake with the words Revise! Revise!), but she also taught us about the nitty gritty aspects of writing and marketing—how to

"We always put on my Dad's hats and took a 'stoop' picture at every family get-together. These are relatives from both sides of the family. (Back row, from left) Aunt Ida, Aunt Helen, Jesse, me, Uncle Solly, Aunt Kay; (front row, from left) Dad, Shari, Mom, Nancy, and Al," Philadelphia, about 1974

Behind the counter in The Children's Bookshop, the bookstore Goldin established with her friend, Missoula, Montana, 1976

organize our files, how to keep track of where we sent our stories, and where to send them.

I also met a whole group of people who were writing for children, including Nancy White Carlstrom, who turned out to be a kindred spirit. Our paths had crisscrossed all our lives from Pennsylvania to Gloucester to the Seattle area, and we had never met. After the workshop, we both joined an ongoing Society of Children's Book Writers critique group in Seattle, which I drove to each week from Bellingham—an hour and a half away.

The group was a great support during all the years when rejection letters were the norm. We all accumulated so many of these rejection letters that our writing group decided to have a rejection letter contest to perk up our spirits. The person with the most rejection letters (which meant the person who actually was the most active at writing and sending out their stories) would win a bag of Hershey kisses. Nancy White Carlstrom got the prize. (She later went on to write the very popular Jesse Bear books.) Over half of that original Seattle writing group has had publishing success, though it may have taken years, in my case five, to sell that first book to a publisher.

We lived for a total of eight years in Bellingham and saw Josee in a new light as a big sister to a sweet and (at

the time he seemed to be a) very mild tempered baby brother. We watched Josee line up all her dolls on our bed and then place Jeremy at the end of the row, all smiling and willing. They climbed in and out of my loom like it was the latest in jungle gym equipment. (Who had time to weave anymore?) I got into sewing Halloween costumes as Josee and Jeremy turned into clowns and then caped and masked mystery super heroine and hero. I became adept at making birthday parties with a theme—fire engines, unicorns, cookie decorating, and roller skating. And for hours I waited in line to buy a Cabbage Patch doll, finally ending up with a preemie which was better than nothing.

I continued going to my writing group in Seattle, taking baby Jeremy in a basket to the meetings where he would sleep through all the critiquing. I adapted my writing to Josee and Jeremy's schedules, grabbing writing time when I could. Often I woke up early to write before anyone else was awake.

I had lots of writing ideas by this time, one specifically inspired by being in Bellingham called *Red Means Good Fortune: A Story of San Francisco's Chinatown.* The idea for this story came from a conversation I had with a friend there about prejudice and minorities in the Northwest. She related some stories her grandmother, a native Bellinghamster, told her about the Chinese who worked on the railroad line that ended in Bellingham. Her grandmother said that when they finished the line, the opening to one of their tunnels was purposely blocked up so that the whole crew was killed. I was horrified by this story and always meant to look up the incident in old newspaper files in Bellingham to see if it was a true story. I never did. But her story led me to do research on the Chinese immigrants on the West Coast. I was curious to find out if there had been this much prejudice against the Chinese and discovered that there had. I wove this research into the story for *Red Means Good Fortune* about a boy Jin Mun who lives in San Francisco's Chinatown, whose father owns a laundry, and whose brother helps build the railroad. The plot revolves around Jin Mun's accidental meeting with a Chinese slave girl Wai Hing and his plans to buy her freedom.

As it happens, I knew nothing about Chinese slavery until I came across stories about it in the books I read. Originally, I thought my book would be about a boy who worked on the railroad. Only after doing all the research did I decide to focus the story on Jin Mun and Wai Hing. This is one of the interesting aspects of researching an

With her children, Josee and Jeremy, Lake Louise, Canada, 1983

historical fiction story—the research can influence the plot and change its direction.

In looking back now after I've written a number of books, I realize that much of my writing grows out of my interest in my own cultural background and religion, and in others'. When I think of myself as that sixth grader who read every book I could find on ancient Egypt, I realize that it wasn't archaeology that I was interested in so much as people and the way they have lived and do live in different times and places, and how they do when they're transplanted from one place to another, just as I seemed continually destined to be.

This interest periodically pops up in my life in the form of actually "exploring" (to use my father's term) different people's neighborhoods or villages, attending a variety of places of worship, and talking to a mix of spiritual leaders. Never having taken a formal comparative religions course, I have often created my own. During my first year of college, I remember dragging my poor but willing friends Lon and Kristin to different kinds of services—Lutheran one week, Ethical Culture or Quaker another, once even to a mission on skid row in downtown Chicago where we were given free doughnuts and coffee and preaching besides. I still am very much interested in religions, my own and others', in what people believe, how they pray, how they celebrate, how they try to answer the "big" questions.

For the book project I am currently working on, I am able to explore this area even further. I am interviewing children and teenagers of all different backgrounds about their religion—what they believe, their holidays, customs, how their religion impacts on their life, if their beliefs are different from their parents'. The book is tentatively called *Kids Talk About Religion* and will be published by Viking. But here I'm jumping ahead. Back in Bellingham I picked up on this "exploring" of religion again, this time within Judaism. I had lived in places that were very isolated as far as my own religion was concerned, places that did not even have a synagogue. Now I lived close to cities like Seattle and Vancouver, British Columbia, which had many choices.

One Saturday, I drove up to Vancouver to "try" a service at Or Shalom, a Jewish group that I had heard about. I remember entering a dark hallway, standing there transfixed, as I listened to a man with a deep and rich voice tell a story from the Old Country, a story about faith and magical prophets and charity.

Over the next eight years, I heard many more stories from Rabbi Daniel Siegel and his wife Hanna Tiferet Siegel. As it turned out, the Siegels and Or Shalom opened a whole new world to me within my own religion.

The services the Siegels led and the stories they told drew from many sources, including Talmud and Midrash (terms I wasn't too sure about), Hasidic and contemporary rabbis, and religious leaders of all paths. As I learned more and more stories and commentaries, I decided that someday I would like to collect a group of these stories and retell them in a way that would appeal to children and their families today. This idea was to simmer on the back burner of my mind for years, as I went about learning where and how to find these stories to retell.

One step along the way was my discovery of a library at one of the Seattle synagogues. When I told Kay Crane,

Jeremy, Josee, and Barbara settled down in Northampton, Massachusetts, 1994

the librarian, what I was working on, she showed me many useful books and saved me hours of frustrating research.

Besides searching for wonderful stories to retell from classical Jewish sources, I also began to write my own Jewish holiday stories—stories that weren't too informational, too teachy. I knew from all my submitting and rejection letters that editors were looking for Jewish holiday stories, but not ones "bogged down" with information. I worked hard on trying to make a story move, not just telling about a holiday, but telling a good story that happened to involve a holiday. When I finally started to sell to children's magazines, I knew my stories were getting better. I was also writing articles for Jewish newspapers about how to celebrate the Jewish holidays with children. These articles fed into my fictional holiday stories as background information and a source for ideas.

About this time, my personal life went through some major changes, some good, some not so good. My husband Alan's job came to an end in Bellingham after eight years there. Our choices were to be transferred back to the eastern part of Washington state or look for other jobs. Through a friend, we heard of an opening in soil science at the University of Massachusetts in Amherst, right near where Jane Yolen, my Centrum teacher, lives.

I was thrilled about the possibility. I had wanted to move back to the East Coast for a long time. I missed my family and wanted to see them more often than living on the West Coast allowed. Plus I missed the east, the seasons as I knew them, the places and people, even the more hectic way of life, the bustling crowded cities, and the ethnic neighborhoods. In a way, I had felt much like the girl in the story I retold called *The Girl Who Lived with the Bears* all the time I lived out west. That is probably the reason I was so drawn to that story when I first came across it. I totally identified with her—coming from one village and being taken to live in another very different one. I had come to appreciate my new village and learn from it and grow, but I yearned for my old one.

Alan applied for the job, got it, and we moved. One big garage sale, lots of good-bye parties and farewells, frantic packing, and we were in Northampton, Massachusetts. Happy to be back east, I loved life in Northampton. I found many other writers and writing groups and no longer felt like an outsider. Besides my teacher Jane Yolen, a fellow student from the Centrum workshop, Lauren Mills, lived here, too. And a year later Rabbi Daniel and Hanna Tiferet Siegel moved to New Hampshire from Vancouver, so I was able to continue my relationship with them. Josee and Jeremy, who were seven and four years old respectively at the time of the move, adjusted well also.

But Alan was not so happy. He wanted to take a different job and move again just a year later. I had had too much of moving and very much wanted to set down roots. The little girl in me, who had moved from New York to

Philadelphia and been picked on for being different, had had enough of being the new kid on the block. I wanted a home and felt that Northampton could be a very good one. Eventually Alan and I separated and then divorced. After twenty-four years of marriage, we went through several very painful years, painful for our two children, as well as for us.

As difficult as my personal life was at that time, my writing life blossomed. I continued to work hard at my writing while teaching in a synagogue preschool. Deborah Brodie at Viking liked my Hanukkah story *Just Enough Is Plenty* and accepted it for publication. I was thrilled! We worked together on the manuscript, and she helped me make it a much stronger story. She also accepted my Purim story *Cakes and Miracles,* which is about a blind boy who realizes in a dream that he can "see" in his mind—and that he should act on what he "sees." He uses his skills with his hands to shape Purim cakes and cookies that sell well in the marketplace. I dedicated this book to my son Jeremy because, as he says in his own words, "I like to make cookies and I like to eat them."

Deborah Brodie and I have continued to enjoy working together on books—sometimes the idea comes from me, sometimes from her, and sometimes from a collaboration. One book that she asked me to do was a book about the holiday of Passover that could be used at the festival meal called a seder. This book took a long time because first I read many books about Passover and many Haggadot, the books used at the seder. I still have a whole shelf in my study filled with these Haggadot. Then I wrote and wrote and wrote, and we cut and cut and cut. The hardest part of doing this book was figuring out how to organize all the material that I had accumulated in an interesting way. At last, I had the idea of looking at the book as being about two journeys, and so I divided *The Passover Journey: A Seder Companion* into two sections. The first is about the Israelites' journey from Egypt through the desert to the Promised Land. The second is about our own journey which we take during the Passover seder when we relive the journey of the ancient Israelites in our own way.

The picture book *The Magician's Visit* was originally part of the larger Passover book, but when we cut it, Deborah thought my retelling would make a good picture book on its own.

Another idea Deborah gave me was to write for the Viking series "Once Upon America." She knows how much I enjoy doing historical fiction and research. Two Janes—Jane Yolen and Jane Gronau—gave me the idea for *Fire!: The Beginnings of the Labor Movement,* which is a story based on the Triangle Factory fire in New York City in 1911. This idea seemed a natural for me since my mother's family lived on the Lower East Side of New York City near the factory during the early 1900s. Also, my grandpa Joe had been a garment worker, a presser of ladies' cloaks and suits, and the Triangle Factory was part of that garment industry. Here I was mining my family's past once again, a comfortable feeling.

I loved doing the research for this book—I walked the streets of the Lower East Side, the names of which have not changed over the years. I found the Triangle Factory building, which still stands near New York University and has a plaque on its corner dedicated to the 146 workers who died in the fire. I visited a fire engine museum and a tenement museum, and read many memoirs to create the story about a girl named Rosie whose older sister works in the Triangle Factory on the day of the big fire.

Facts that I read about influenced my plot. For instance, I read that victims of the fire were sometimes identified by their jewelry. So early in the book I introduce Rosie's cousin Celia who has just become engaged. Later, it is this cousin who perishes in the fire and is identified by her engagement ring.

At about the same time that Deborah Brodie accepted *Just Enough Is Plenty,* I met a bookstore owner named Sondra Botnick at my local synagogue bookfair. Remember that idea for a book of stories from Midrash? Well, this is where Sandra fits in. She guided me through her bookstore, helping me select those books that would teach me more about Midrash and how and where to find these classical rabbinic stories. I learned that Midrash are those stories rabbis and others told and still tell about the Bible—to explain or explore the characters, events, and laws found there.

One of the most helpful articles about finding your way through Talmud that I read was by Arthur Kurzweil, who turns out to be an editor at Jason Aronson Inc., Publishers. I met Arthur at a CAJE (Coalition for the Advancement of Jewish Education) conference, asked him if he would be interested in a book of Midrash retold for children, sent him a proposal, and got a positive response. I tremendously enjoyed working on the book that resulted from this proposal. It is *A Child's Book of Midrash,* most recently reissued with the new title of *The Family Book of Midrash.* I dedicated this book to my daughter, Josee, since it was she who partly started me on this search to begin with—to find a book like this to read my own children.

I have also written a second book for Jason Aronson called *Creating Angels: Stories of Tzedakah* in which I have retold stories from classic sources as well as from Hasidic rabbis and folklore. All the stories are about some aspect of charity, or acts of giving, of loving-kindness.

Besides Viking and Aronson, I have also been fortunate to have had books published by Harcourt Brace, including the two retellings of Native American stories I've already mentioned. Jane Yolen, who at one time had her own imprint at Harcourt, was my editor for *The World's Birthday: A Rosh Hashanah Story.* The idea for this story began years before at an Or Shalom Rosh Hashanah children's service. As part of the service, Hanna Tiferet Siegel presented the children with a round challah birthday cake for the world that they loved. Emphasizing that Rosh Hashanah is the world's birthday struck me as an appealing start for a picture book story. The characters in the book evolved from earlier stories I had written and never sold.

Years before, when my children were young, I had come across Sydney Taylor's *Danny Loves a Holiday.* I loved Danny—his honest emotions, humor, warmth, and love of the Jewish holidays. Inspired by Taylor's stories, I developed my own characters, a brother and a sister, and wrote a collection of Jewish holiday stories. As it turned out, this was a practice collection, because it never sold. But I used the characters and some plot ideas in later stories. These characters popped up in a March 1992 *Highlights* story called "Brave Like Mordecai" about the holiday of Purim, in *The World's Birthday,* and in *Night Lights: A Sukkot Story* which I worked on with Elizabeth Van Doren at Harcourt. In *Night Lights,* the idea as well as the characters evolved from this earlier collection. A boy Daniel is both eager and afraid to sleep outside in the family's sukkah, a temporary shelter set up for the holidays, with only his big sister Naomi.

I've also worked with Liz at Harcourt on *Coyote and the Fire Stick,* with Anne Davies at Harcourt on *The Girl Who Lived with the Bears,* and with both on a story about my cousin Sarah, who grew up in Eastern Europe in the early 1900s. This story, which is still in progress, is based on a visit my daughter Josee, then four or five, and I made to Cousin Sarah in Florida. Sarah, always so lively, enthusiastic, and giving, was showing me the family pictures on her walls and in albums. Some of the photos were of her brother and his sons who died in the Holocaust. They were doctors who refused to go along with Nazi experiments and so were killed. There was an even more painful part to the story that she told—the Nazi soldiers made her brother watch his sons die first before he was killed.

Our visit with Sarah was very moving for me. She shared so much. And despite the sad stories, she also told many happy ones about her life in America, about how happy she was to be here, and about her life with her husband Max. All the time I talked with Sarah, Josee played with the dolls Sarah crocheted as a hobby and donated to charities. I did not know until later, after we left, that Josee was listening to much of what Sarah had told me. I found this out in the car on the way home, when Josee started asking me questions about the Holocaust and Sarah's brother and I had to find a way to answer her. Ever since then, I have been working on this story, which grew out of this very real visit with my cousin.

As you can see from all that I've written, the ideas for my stories come from many sources—from real life incidents, experiences with my children, childhood experiences, family stories, from my readings and research, from things that fascinate me that I hear, come across or read about, from dreams, day dreams, conversations, and issues that concern me—what it's like to be the outsider, why people pick on or bully others, why there is prejudice, what people believe in, what I believe in.

You can also see that I like to do a variety of different kinds of writing. I love finding wonderful stories and retelling them. I enjoy writing original picture book stories, as well as stories for older children. Historical fiction, nonfiction, and books based on interviews as well as research are all a welcome challenge for me. My editors stretch me and I stretch myself to try new things. And since my move to Northampton, I have also found an agent Virginia Knowlton, who helps me make sense of the business as well as the creative side of being a writer. With all the wonderful writers here, I am now part of two writing groups and enjoy their critique sessions, retreats, camaraderie, and support.

My writing life is a full one—rewarding and busy. But I have also continued teaching. After eleven years with classes of pre-schoolers, I am now teaching middle school. Perhaps I wanted this change because my own children were growing up, or because I was just ready for something different. I teach English part-time to sixth through eighth graders and all subjects to fifth graders at Heritage Academy, a Jewish Day School in Longmeadow, Massachusetts. I enjoy working with this age group in all subjects but especially in creative writing and literature—the world of words. My students and I work together on their stories, poems, essays; on brainstorming ideas, following through, revising, and forming their own peer critique groups.

Over the past eight years that I have been teaching at Heritage Academy, I have taught many students who now consider themselves writers and are serious about it, write a lot, and want to become professional writers. My students put together yearbooks, share their poetry in classroom "cafes," teach me how to use computers, write graduation speeches, argue with me about books and grammar rules. I see them work together with a friend or two on a story and think of how I would love to do that, too. We go through the ups and downs of submitting stories to magazines and writing contests, since some of them choose to pursue the process of trying to get their own work published.

My own children are now teenagers, too. Jeremy is sixteen years old and Josee eighteen. Jeremy loves sports—first karate, then Little League, and now downhill skiing. He plays drums and bass guitar, and is in a band with his friends called Haggis. His other passions include Dungeons and Dragons and other role-playing games, and computers. He is lively, thoughtful, and good company on trips to ski areas. Josee is a freshman at George Washington University and is very busy volunteering in homeless shelters, working part-time in the Office of Admissions, being an intern for a Congressman and a cadet in Army ROTC, besides studying engineering.

Because of Josee and Jeremy, I find myself writing in odd places. I've become adept at packing my bags with research materials, rough drafts, tablets, and setting up a temporary work area in a chilly ski resort restaurant and other unlikely spots.

One summer, for her sixteenth birthday present, Josee wanted me to take her and three friends on a camping-hiking trip to Acadia National Park in Maine. At the same time, I had a deadline for my Hanukkah collection called *While the Candles Burn.* All the stories were complete for the collection, but the long introduction to the book and the shorter introductions for each story were not yet written. Undaunted, we packed up the car and off we went, Josee, three friends, me, tents, sleeping bags, cookstove, clothes, rain and writing gear. We set up in a campground near Southwest Harbor, Maine, and I cased the small town nearby for a possible writing spot. I found it—a restaurant called the Deacon's Bench that opened up early, very early. Each morning, while the girls slept in, I drove into town and set up at one of the tables in the homey restaurant. I felt like I was in someone's living room. I learned all the local gossip, even got included in a couple of conversations, and wrote all those introductions. Now, whenever I look at the book *While the Candles Burn,* I think of Maine and harbors and fishing boats, of homemade muffins, and a wonderful vacation by the sea.

As I turn that awesome sounding half century mark in age, I am happy to say I no longer feel like the perpetual outsider. For over eleven years now, I have lived in Western Massachusetts. I enjoy my exploring, searching, researching, writing and living in a comfortable and very rooted spot, a place I feel very much is home.

GREENWOOD, Barbara 1940-

Personal

Born September 14, 1940, in Toronto, Ontario, Canada; daughter of George A. (a manufacturing jeweler) and Anne (Fisher) Auer; married Robert E. Greenwood (a physicist and professor), July 16, 1966; children: Edward, Martha, Adrienne, Michael. *Education:* Attended Toronto Teachers College, 1960-61; University of Toronto, B.A., 1971. *Religion:* United Church of Canada. *Hobbies and other interests:* Reading, choral singing.

Addresses

Home—59 Leacroft Crescent, Don Mills, Ontario M3B 2G5, Canada. *E-mail*—bgrwood@interlog.com.

Career

Teacher and author. Leaside Board of Education, Toronto, Canada, classroom teacher, 1961-66; freelance teacher for the gifted, 1975-85; freelance writer, 1980—; Ryerson Polytechnic University, creative writing instructor for department of continuing education, 1986—. Writer-in-residence, Markham Library System, 1989-90. Workshop leader at Maritime Writers' Workshop and University of Toronto Summer Program. Member of board of directors, Orpheus Choir of Toronto, 1989-94. *Member:* Writers' Union of Canada (second vice president, 1989-90), Canadian Society of Children's Authors, Illustrators, and Performers (president, 1985-87).

Awards, Honors

Vicky Metcalf Short Story Award, Canadian Authors Association, 1982, for "A Major Resolution"; White Raven Award, International Youth Library, 1992, for *Spy in the Shadows;* Ruth Schwartz Foundation Children's Book Award, Mr. Christie's Book Award, Canadian Children's Book Centre and Communications Jeunesse, and Children's Literature Roundtables of Canada Information Book Award, all 1995, all for *A Pioneer Story: The Daily Life of a Canadian Family in 1840; A Pioneer Sampler: The Daily Life of a Pioneer Family in 1840* was chosen a Notable Children's Trade Book in the Field of Social Studies by the Children's Book Council and the National Council for Social Studies, and named to the Utah Children's Informational Book Award Master List, both 1996; Information Book Award, Children's Literature Roundtables of Canada, 1999, and Notable Book selection, *Smithsonian* magazine, both for *The Last Safe House: A Story of the Underground Railroad.*

Writings

FICTION

A Question of Loyalty, Scholastic Canada (Richmond Hill, Canada), 1984.

Spy in the Shadows, Kids Can Press (Toronto, Canada), 1990.

A Pioneer Story: The Daily Life of a Canadian Family in 1840, illustrated by Heather Collins, Kids Can Press (Toronto, Canada), 1994, published as *A Pioneer Sampler: The Daily Life of a Pioneer Family in 1840,* Ticknor & Fields (New York, NY), 1995.

The Last Safe House: A Story of the Underground Railroad, illustrated by Heather Collins, Kids Can Press (Toronto, Canada), 1998.

A Pioneer Thanksgiving: A Story of Harvest Celebrations in 1841, illustrated by Heather Collins, Kids Can Press (Toronto, Canada), 1999.

Gold Rush Fever: A Story of the Klondike, 1898, illustrated by Heather Collins, Kids Can Press (Toronto, Canada), 2001.

NONFICTION

(With Audrey McKim) *Her Special Vision: A Biography of Jean Little,* Irwin (Toronto, Canada), 1987.

Jeanne Sauvé (biography), Fitzhenry & Whiteside (Markham, Canada), 1988.

Klondike Challenge: Rachel Hanna, Frontier Nurse (biography), Grolier (Toronto, Canada), 1990.

Barbara Greenwood

(With Patricia Hancock) *The Other Side of the Story* (creative writing handbook), Scholastic Canada (Richmond Hill, Canada), 1990.

(With husband, Bob Greenwood) *Speak Up! Speak Out!: A Kid's Guide to Public Speaking,* illustrated by Graham Pilsworth, Pembroke (Markham, Canada), 1994.

The Kids Book of Canada: Exploring the Land and Its People, illustrated by Jock McRae, Kids Can Press (Toronto, Canada), 1997, revised, 1999.

Pioneer Crafts, illustrated by Heather Collins, Kids Can Press (Toronto, Canada), 1997.

Some of the author's books have been translated into French.

EDITOR

Presenting ... Children's Author's, Illustrators, and Performers, Pembroke (Markham, Canada), 1990.

(And abridger) Lucy Maud Montgomery, *Anne of Green Gables,* illustrated by Muriel Wood, Key Porter (Toronto, Canada), 1991.

(And abridger) Louisa May Alcott, *Little Women,* Key Porter (Toronto, Canada), 1992.

The CANSCAIP Companion: A Biographical Record of Canadian Children's Authors, Illustrators, and Performers, Pembroke (Markham, Canada), 1994.

(And abridger) Johanna Spyri, *Heidi,* Key Porter (Toronto, Canada), 1994.

Behind the Story: The People Who Create Our Best Children's Books and How They Do It, Pembroke (Markham, Canada), 1995.

(And abridger) Anna Sewell, *Black Beauty,* illustrated by Rene Benoit, Key Porter (Toronto, Canada), 2001.

(And abridger) Frances Hodgson Burnett, *The Secret Garden,* Key Porter (Toronto, Canada), 2001.

OTHER

Also author of articles and short stories appearing in educational anthologies, including *Contexts I,* Nelson Canada, 1981; editor of the *Canadian Society of Children's Authors, Illustrators, and Performers News;* contributor of a monthly column to *City Parent Magazine.*

Sidelights

Barbara Greenwood is the author of several children's books which explore the lives of Canadian settlers in the 1800s. With titles such as *A Pioneer Sampler: The Daily Life of a Pioneer Family in 1840, The Kids Book of Canada,* and the biography *Klondike Challenge: Rachel Hanna, Frontier Nurse,* she conveys her fascination with the history of her native country, using mining journals, letters, museum archives, and other sources for the many details that she presents to readers of her fiction and nonfiction.

"I have always loved the feeling of sinking into a story, living in its world, becoming in my imagination each of the characters in turn," Greenwood once told *SATA.* "I was quite young when my voyages into stories also

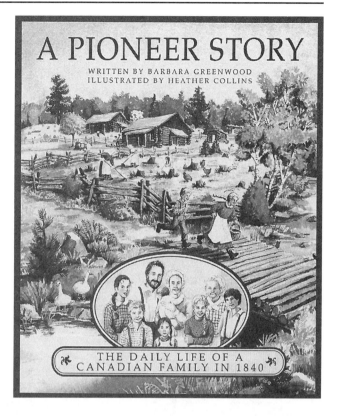

In this work, Greenwood describes what pioneer life was like for a Canadian family. (Cover illustration by Heather Collins.)

became voyages into the past. I traveled from the worlds of *Heidi* and *The Secret Garden* back through adventures in Elizabethan England, Roman England, and ancient Egypt. Through stories, those times became as real for me as my own home, neighborhood, and classroom. I was about twelve before I realized that I wanted to be in charge of the time travel ship—not just experience adventures in books but actually write my own."

While as a child Greenwood enjoyed reading books set in the past, by the time she was a teenager, as she once told *Canadian Children's Literature,* she realized that "one place I never found myself on these story-trips was in Canada's past." After her youngest child started elementary school, Greenwood decided to pursue a long-held interest in writing. Hoping to expose young readers to the rich and varied experiences of Canada's past, she began searching for information about the lives of important historical figures about which children would be interested. The result of that research was *A Question of Loyalty,* a book about the Mackenzie Rebellion in 1837 during which an armed group of Canadian farmers and mechanics led by William Lyon Mackenzie began an unsuccessful rebellion against British colonial rule.

In her multi-award-winning 1994 book *A Pioneer Story: The Daily Life of a Canadian Family in 1840,* Greenwood focuses on the everyday life of settlers in the mid-1800s. By following the events of a fictional pioneer

In 1856, a Canadian family helps a young girl escape from slavery in a story of the Underground Railroad in Canada, **The Last Safe House.** *(Written by Greenwood and illustrated by Heather Collins.)*

family, Greenwood carefully recreates what life was like in a pioneer household and explains how settlers farmed, went to school, and made everything they needed, including butter, maple sugar, and candles. Hands-on activities, such as making ink, toys, and honey butter, are also included. Calling it "an ideal book for all Canadian schools and libraries," Ken Setterington, writing in *Quill & Quire,* praised Greenwood for her skill in weaving factual information into her narrative. Reviewing the book in its retitled U.S. version—*A Pioneer Sampler: The Daily Life of a Pioneer Family in 1840*—a critic in *Publishers Weekly* applauded Greenwood's narrative passages, saying they "convey a lively sense of character and place." For schools and libraries in need of books about pioneer life, *School Library Journal* critic Elaine Fort Weischedel recommended *A Pioneer Sampler,* saying it is "a welcome and useful addition" for children interested in the subject.

A Pioneer Story was the beginning of Greenwood's writing about the life of Canada's early settlers, and was also the fulfilment of one of its author's childhood dreams. "Although my earliest adventures in books were based on ones I'd read, I soon realized that I wanted to write about life as it was lived long ago in my neighborhood," Greenwood recalled. "That impulse led me to the reference library and many fascinating diaries and letter collections by early settlers." This uncovered wealth of original source material has served as the basis for several more books, including *A Pioneer Thanksgiving: A Story of Harvest Celebrations in 1841,* which follows the traditional mid-nineteenth-century celebration of Thanksgiving. Instructions for corn-husk dolls, baskets, and simple weathervanes are included within the fictional story of the Robertson family, along with information about native crops used in the fall feast and recipes for dishes that are truly time-tested.

A *Kirkus Reviews* critic deemed *A Pioneer Thanksgiving* a "perfect book" with which to "help while away the hours before dinner is ready," while in *School Library Journal* Linda Greengrass noted that Greenwood's text is "carefully crafted to make the experiences described equally valid for Canadians and for residents of the northern United States." *Pioneer Crafts* contains directions for authentic crafts such as molded candles, woven textiles, soaps, baskets, quilts, and braided rugs, as well as more unusual items such as silhouettes, punched tin, and toys. "The author has avoided falling into the trap of excessive authenticity, substituting modern materials and tools as needed," according to *Quill & Quire* contributor Sheila McGraw. The seventeen craft projects included are "suitable for middle-graders," according to *Booklist* contributor Kay Weisman.

Continuing her examination of the history of North America, Greenwood's *The Last Safe House: A Story of the Underground Railroad* is the fictional tale of a slave named Eliza Jackson, who escapes with her brother Ben from a Virginia plantation and together the two travel

north. Now one of the "midnight visitors" who travel along the Underground Railroad, Eliza eventually arrives at the Ontario home of Johanna Reid and her abolitionist parents. While Eliza and Ben wait to be reunited with their mother, Johanna overcomes her initial resentment over the presence of the two black children, and teaches Eliza to read and write. "This fictional story, based on the experiences of many real slaves and their helpers, is filled with drama and pathos and grips the reader from beginning to end," noted *Quill & Quire* contributor Joanne Findon. As she did with *A Pioneer Sampler,* Greenwood interweaves factual information about the Underground Railroad, plantation life, and other aspects of nineteenth-century life into her story, achieving a book that *School Library Journal* contributor Carol Fazioli characterized as "part novel, part history lesson, and part activity guide. Surprisingly," the critic added, "Greenwood succeeds on all counts."

Biographical and Critical Sources

PERIODICALS

Black Enterprise, February, 1999, Sonja Brown Stokely, review of *The Last Safe House: A Story of the Underground Railroad,* p. 211.

Booklist, April 1, 1995, Carolyn Phelan, review of *A Pioneer Sampler: The Daily Life of a Pioneer Family in 1840,* p. 1390; September 15, 1997, Kay Weisman, review of *Pioneer Crafts,* p. 228; September 1, 1999, Lauren Peterson, review of *A Pioneer Thanksgiving: A Story of Harvest Celebrations in 1841,* p. 145.

Books for Young People, April, 1988, p. 7.

Books in Canada, February, 1995, p. 50.

Canadian Children's Literature, no. 48, 1987, "Barbara Greenwood," pp. 66-68; no. 63, 1991, p. 79; no. 78, 1995, p. 83.

Canadian Materials, July, 1988, p. 121; July, 1989, p. 167; November, 1990, p. 276; May, 1991, p. 163; November, 1994, p. 211.

Children's Book Review Service, May, 1995, p. 117.

Horn Book, May-June, 1995, Elizabeth S. Watson, review of *Pioneer Crafts,* p. 341.

Horn Book Guide, fall, 1998, Carolyn Shute, review of *The Kids Book of Canada,* p. 430.

Kirkus Review, November 15, 1998, review of *The Last Safe House,* p. 1669; September 1, 1999, review of *A Pioneer Thanksgiving,* p. 1417.

Library Times, September, 1995, p. 48.

New York Times Book Review, June 4, 1995, review of *A Pioneer Sampler,* p. 25; December 20, 1998, review of *The Last Safe House,* p. 25.

Publishers Weekly, January 16, 1995, review of *A Pioneer Sampler,* p. 455; March 16, 1998, review of *The Kids Book of Canada,* p. 67.

Quill & Quire, October, 1990, p. 16; June, 1991, p. 27; September, 1994, Ken Setterington, review of *A Pioneer Story: The Daily Life of a Canadian Family in 1840,* p. 74; February, 1997, Sheila McGraw, review

Thirteen-year-old Tim discovers the harshness of gold mining in the Klondike when he sets out with his brother vand dog to seek his fortune. (From Gold Rush Fever, *written by Greenwood and illustrated by Heather Collins.*)

of *Pioneer Crafts,* pp. 53-54; July, 1998, Joanne Findon, *The Last Safe House,* pp. 41-42.

School Library Journal, April, 1995, Elaine Fort Weischedel, review of *A Pioneer Sampler,* p. 142; September, 1997, Rosie Peasley, review of *Pioneer Crafts,* p. 230; June, 1998, Ronald Jobe, review of *The Kids Book of Canada,* p. 160; January, 1999, Carol Fazioli, review of *The Last Safe House,* p. 142; September, 1999, Linda Greengrass, review of *A Pioneer Thanksgiving,* p. 234.

*   *   *

GREGORY, Jean
See URE, Jean

H

HAGUE, Michael R. 1948-

Personal

Born September 8, 1948, in Los Angeles, CA; son of Riley Herbert (a truck driver) and Daisy Marie (King) Hague; married Susan Kathleen Burdick (an artist and author of children's books), December 5, 1970; children: Meghan Micaela, Brittany Michael, Devon Heath. *Education:* Art Center College of Design, B.F.A. (with honors), 1972.

Addresses

Home—Colorado Springs, CO. *Agent*—c/o Henry Holt & Co., Author Mail, 115 West 18th St., New York, NY 10011.

Career

Hallmark Cards, Kansas City, KS, illustrator, 1973-75; Current, Inc., Colorado Springs, CO, illustrator, 1975-77; author and illustrator of children's books, 1977—. Work has been exhibited at the Port Washington, Long Island, public library, 1986, and at the "Children's Books Mean Business" group show, 1984; illustrations appeared on the television series *thirtysomething,* 1989.

Awards, Honors

Dream Weaver was chosen for the American Institute of Graphic Arts Book Show (formerly known as Fifty Books of the Year), 1980; International Reading Association children's choices citation, 1982, for *The Man Who Kept House;* Colorado Children's Book Award, University of Colorado, 1984, and Georgia Children's Picture Storybook Award, University of Georgia, 1986, both for *The Unicorn and the Lake;* Parents' Choice Award for children's books, Parents' Choice Foundation, 1984, for *The Frog Princess; Aesop's Fables, The Legend of the Veery Bird,* and *Alice's Adventures in Wonderland* were all selected as children's books of the year, Child Study Association of America, 1985; Graphic Arts Award for

Michael R. Hague

best juvenile book, Printing Industries Association, 1986, for *A Child's Book of Prayers.*

Writings

SELF-ILLUSTRATED CHILDREN'S BOOKS

(Reteller with wife, Kathleen Hague) *East of the Sun and West of the Moon,* Harcourt (New York, NY), 1980.

(Reteller with Kathleen Hague) *The Man Who Kept House,* Harcourt (New York, NY), 1981.

(Editor) *Michael Hague's Favorite Hans Christian Andersen Fairy Tales,* Holt (New York, NY), 1981.

(Editor) *Mother Goose: A Collection of Classic Nursery Rhymes,* Holt (New York, NY), 1984.

(Editor) *Aesop's Fables,* Holt (New York, NY), 1985.

A Child's Book of Prayers, Holt (New York, NY), 1985.

Unicorn Pop-Up Book, Holt (New York, NY), 1986.

Michael Hague's World of Unicorns, Holt (New York, NY), 1986.

(Editor) Robert Louis Stevenson, *The Land of Nod and Other Poems for Children,* Holt (New York, NY), 1988.

My Secret Garden Diary, Arcade (New York, NY), 1990.

Magic Moments: A Book of Days, Arcade (New York, NY), 1990.

Our Baby: A Book of Records and Memories, Arcade (New York, NY), 1990.

A Unicorn Journal, Arcade (New York, NY), 1990.

Michael Hague's Family Christmas Treasury, Holt (New York, NY), 1995.

The Perfect Present, Morrow (New York, NY), 1996.

Michael Hague's Family Easter Treasury, Holt (New York, NY), 1998.

Michael Hague's Magical World of Unicorns, Simon & Schuster (New York, NY), 1999.

(Editor) *The Book of Fairies,* HarperCollins (New York, NY), 2000.

Teddy Bears' Mother Goose, Holt (New York, NY), 2001.

Kate Culhane: A Ghost Story, North-South/SeaStar Books (New York, NY), 2001.

ILLUSTRATOR; CHILDREN'S BOOKS

Ethel Marbach, *The Cabbage Moth and the Shamrock,* Star & Elephant Books, 1978.

Beth Hilgartner, *A Necklace of Fallen Stars,* Little, Brown (Boston, MA), 1979.

Jane Yolen, *Dream Weaver,* Collins (New York, NY), 1979, revised edition, Philomel Books (New York, NY), 1989.

Deborah Apy, reteller, *Beauty and the Beast,* Green Tiger, 1980.

Eve Bunting, *Demetrius and the Golden Goblet,* Harcourt (New York, NY), 1980.

Julia Cunningham, *A Mouse Called Junction,* Pantheon (New York, NY), 1980.

Kenneth Grahame, *The Wind in the Willows,* Holt (New York, NY), 1980.

Lee Bennett Hopkins, editor, *Moments: Poems about the Seasons,* Harcourt (New York, NY), 1980.

Clement C. Moore, *The Night before Christmas,* Holt (New York, NY), 1981.

Marianna Mayer, *The Unicorn and the Lake,* Dial (New York, NY), 1982.

L. Frank Baum, *The Wizard of Oz,* Holt (New York, NY), 1982, redesigned as *The Wizard of Oz, 100th Anniversary Edition,* Holt (New York, NY), 2000.

Margery Williams, *The Velveteen Rabbit; or, How Toys Became Real,* Holt (New York, NY), 1983.

Kenneth Grahame, *The Reluctant Dragon,* Holt (New York, NY), 1983.

C. S. Lewis, *The Lion, the Witch, and the Wardrobe,* Macmillan (New York, NY), 1983.

Nancy Luenn, *The Dragon Kite,* Harcourt (New York, NY), 1983.

Hague illustrated a 1984 edition of J. R. R. Tolkien's classic **The Hobbit; or, There and Back Again.**

Jakob Grimm and Wilhelm Grimm, *Rapunzel,* Creative Education (Mankato, MN), 1984.

Kathleen Hague, *Alphabears: An ABC Book,* Holt (New York, NY), 1984, published with cassette, Live Oak Media, 1985.

Elizabeth Isele, reteller, *The Frog Princess: A Russian Tale Retold,* Crowell (New York, NY), 1984.

J. R. R. Tolkien, *The Hobbit; or, There and Back Again,* Houghton (Boston, MA), 1984.

Lewis Carroll, *Alice's Adventures in Wonderland,* Holt (New York, NY), 1985.

Kathleen Hague, *The Legend of the Veery Bird,* Harcourt (New York, NY), 1985.

Kathleen Hague, *Numbears: A Counting Book,* Holt (New York, NY), 1986.

Kathleen Hague, *Out of the Nursery, Into the Night,* Holt (New York, NY), 1986.

Frances Hodgson Burnett, *The Secret Garden,* Holt (New York, NY), 1987.

J. M. Barrie, *Peter Pan,* Holt (New York, NY), 1987.

Carl Sandburg, *Rootabaga Stories,* two volumes, Harcourt (New York, NY), 1988-89.

Charles Perrault, *Cinderella, and Other Tales from Perrault,* Holt (New York, NY), 1989.

Marianna Mayer, *The Unicorn Alphabet,* Dial (New York, NY), 1989.

William Allingham, *The Fairies: A Poem,* Holt (New York, NY), 1989.

Kathleen Hague, *Bear Hugs,* Holt (New York, NY), 1989.

Thornton W. Burgess, *Old Mother West Wind,* Holt (New York, NY), 1990.

(With Joe Krush) Carl Sandburg, *Prairie-Town Boy,* Harcourt (New York, NY), 1990.

Mary Norton, *The Borrowers,* Harcourt (New York, NY), 1991.

Twinkle, Twinkle, Little Star, Morrow Junior Books (New York, NY), 1992.

Michael Hague's Illustrated "The Teddy Bears' Picnic", Holt (New York, NY), 1992.

South Pacific, Harcourt (New York, NY), 1992.

The Fairy Tales of Oscar Wilde, Holt (New York, NY), 1993.

Teddy Bear, Teddy Bear: A Classic Action Rhyme, Morrow (New York, NY), 1993.

The Little Mermaid, Holt (New York, NY), 1993.

Little Women or Meg, Jo, Beth and Amy, Holt (New York, NY), 1993.

(And selector) *The Rainbow Fairy Book,* Morrow (New York, NY), 1993.

(And selector) *Sleep, Baby, Sleep: Lullabies and Night Poems,* Morrow (New York, NY), 1994.

The Children's Book of Virtues, edited by William J. Bennett, Simon & Schuster (New York, NY), 1995.

Edward Lear, *The Owl and the Pussy-Cat, and Other Nonsense Poems,* North-South/SeaStar (New York, NY), 1995.

(And selector) *The Book of Dragons,* Morrow (New York, NY), 1995.

Kathleen Hague, *Calendarbears: A Book of Months,* Holt (New York, NY), 1997.

The Story of Doctor Dolittle, Morrow (New York, NY), 1997.

The Children's Book of Heroes, edited by William J. Bennett, Simon & Schuster (New York, NY), 1997.

The Children's Book of America, Simon & Schuster (New York, NY), 1998.

The 23rd Psalm: From the King James Bible, Holt (New York, NY), 1999.

Kathleen Hague, *Ten Little Bears: A Counting Rhyme,* Morrow (New York, NY), 1999.

Kenneth Grahame, *A Wind in the Willows Christmas,* North-South/SeaStar Books (New York, NY), 2000.

The Children's Book of Faith, edited by William J. Bennett, Doubleday (New York, NY), 2000.

Beatrix Potter, *The Tale of Peter Rabbit,* North-South/SeaStar Books (New York, NY), 2001.

Kathleen Hague, *Goodnight, Fairies,* North-South/SeaStar Books (New York, NY), 2001.

ILLUSTRATOR; CHRISTMAS CAROLS

We Wish You a Merry Christmas, Holt (New York, NY), 1990.

Jingle Bells, Holt (New York, NY), 1990.

Deck the Halls, Holt (New York, NY), 1991.

O Christmas Tree, Holt (New York, NY), 1991.

OTHER

Unicorn Calendar, Holt (New York, NY), 1989.

Also illustrator of several calendars, including a series based on C. S. Lewis's "Chronicles of Narnia" books.

Sidelights

One of the foremost illustrators of children's books in America, Michael R. Hague claims to have known he possessed the ability to draw as far back as kindergarten. "My mother had been to art school in England and encouraged me greatly by bringing home art books from which I could copy paintings and drawings," Hague once commented. "She never gave me lessons. I knew as a child that I wanted to illustrate books. I was always reading and rendering illustrations of my own creations for the King Arthur books as well as making portraits of such baseball heroes as Duke Snider of the Los Angeles Dodgers."

Books filled Hague's childhood home and he believed everything he read. "I *still* have a hard time accepting that Prince Valiant is not a real character from English history," professed Hague. Comic books and Disney books were among his favorites, and his most treasured book demonstrated how to draw and animate the Disney characters. "I'm still a great Disney fan—I hold documents as one of the first Mickey Mouse Club members," Hague once stated. "To this day I remember an enormous man named Roy, a Disney animator often featured on the *Mickey Mouse Club* television show. I used to think to myself, 'One day he'll retire, and then....'"

Hague had many friends as he was growing up and was also involved in numerous sports, his favorite being baseball. He continued drawing throughout high school and dreamed of playing professional baseball, all the while realizing that he was not talented enough to do so. After high school Hague briefly attended junior college, transferring to the Art Center College of Design in Los Angeles. His original major was illustration and he hoped for a career in children's books. However, the college directed its illustration majors toward more promising careers, such as advertising, so Hague changed his major to painting. His wife was also a painting major and the two married while still students.

Although Hague retained a strong interest in doing children's books by the time he graduated, he was convinced that he could not earn a living at it and decided to teach. When he discovered that teaching was not the career for him, Hague applied for a job at Hallmark Cards and worked for two years in their Kansas City studio. "It was great to get paid for drawing every day," he recalled. Although he was glad to have a job, Hague still refused to give up on the publishing industry. He put together a portfolio during his first week at Hallmark and sent it out to numerous publishers. "Many of the comments I received early were quite discouraging," noted Hague. "Some editors said my work was 'too weird' for children. Many art directors sent back my portfolio with *no* comment. Silence was the worst response, and alas, the most frequent. How did I keep my morale up? I just assumed they were idiots. Dr. Seuss went to twenty-nine publishers before he had his first book published. After five years, I finally was

Stories, sacred texts, and poems celebrating Easter are included in **Michael Hague's Family Easter Treasury.**

offered illustration work and then it all seemed to come at once."

The first illustration job Hague did was a cover and an inside story for *Cricket* magazine; and his first published book illustration was a pop-up book version of *Gulliver's Travels.* Meanwhile, Hague had begun working for Current, Inc., another greeting card company located in Colorado Springs. "While I was working at Current I contacted Green Tiger Press," Hague once commented. "To my delight, they asked what *I* would like to illustrate. The first thing that came to my mind was *Beauty and the Beast,* which they agreed to. My illustrations for the book were influenced by the Cocteau film. It took a long time before I had another opportunity to propose what *I* wanted to illustrate to a publisher. When you're getting started, it's the publishers who make suggestions, and illustrators tend to accept everything and anything. It still takes me a long time to say 'no' to a project that doesn't interest me. But after the publication and success of *The Wind in the Willows* in 1980, I was in a position to suggest books I like to illustrate."

Hague's maternal grandmother was born in 1908, only two years before *The Wind in the Willows* was published for the first time. "She can recall with delight her father reading aloud to her about the adventures of Mr. Toad and his friends," related Hague. "The book was her father's favorite, and indeed became hers as well. My grandmother passed on a love of 'Willows,' as she refers to it, to my mother; and so when the story reached me it had already claimed three generations and captivated its fourth generation in me." The book's main characters include Mole, Ratty, Badger, and Mr. Toad; and they, along with their surroundings, have inspired an immense following over the years. "With such a loyal and affectionate following, from young children to their great-grandparents, I felt a great responsibility in illustrating the book," explained Hague. *The Wind in the Willows* had also been illustrated by two of Hague's idols, Ernest Shepard and Arthur Rackham, so when he was first approached about the project he was "thrilled, honored, and a bit frightened. I love the book," Hague once noted. "I love the dependable Water Rat, the kindly Mole, the sturdy Badger, and especially Mr. Toad. And so it is, as when one is in love, one forgets all obstacles and fears. That is what happened to me. I've not tried to create a new visual style or interpretation of the story," continued Hague. "I have instead tried to infuse my illustrations with the same spirit Kenneth Grahame's magic words convey. There is, I think, a bit of Toad in all of us. Certainly there must have been some of Mr. Toad in me when I agreed to illustrate this book." Hague later published a slightly altered version of the fifth chapter of that book in *A Wind in the Willows Christmas,* with "vibrant, cozy, and charming" gouache paintings, according to a *School Library Journal* reviewer.

Hague tries to imbue all his illustrations with the same essence the author or the story itself originally creates in his imagination. "I begin with character studies and try to capture on paper what I see in my mind's eye," explained Hague. And to avoid making a book repetitious, he places his characters in a variety of light sources. "Light is one of the elements which makes a painting real," he once commented, "especially when you are painting the fantastic. The more real a tree looks, or the light appears, the more believable the fantasy elements will be. One can't afford to be vague when illustrating fantasy. Ninety per cent of a fantasy book should be based on the real world; you don't need many strange elements to make a story work. In a good illustration of a knight riding on a horse, for example, the viewer will ride over the next hill with him, even though the artist hasn't illustrated what's over there. It's not hard to animate or give gesture to fantasy creatures once you have principles of drawing. I try to make movement and gesture look believable, and one way to do that is to be sure that the backgrounds are realistic. It adds emphasis. Once again, I build a concrete world—not a fuzzy, dream-like place—where kids can see real sky or walls or cities. Then a dragon can become believable."

Kate Culhane: A Ghost Story, *a retelling of a traditional Irish tale set in the mid-1800s, was written and illustrated by Hague.*

Hague claims to have no special tricks or secret answers when it comes to illustrating. If something doesn't look right he merely plays around with it until it does. "Sometimes I'll have a bad day, when nothing seems to come easy," Hague once observed. "People ask me how long it takes to do a painting, and I can't really say because it changes from painting to painting from day to day. I've done some paintings in one day, others in two weeks. I couldn't say why that is." And while working on his illustrations, Hague creates for himself, not for a particular audience: "When I illustrate, I don't think about kids, or what age group the book is aimed toward. I don't like to generalize or second guess my audience. I try to please myself. I am still in touch with my childhood, with the child that still exists in me."

A favorite story of the child that still exists in Hague, in addition to *The Wind in the Willows,* is *The Wizard of Oz.* "When I was a child, there were three places I would have given anything to visit," he once stated. "One was England in the days of King Arthur; another was the Wild West of Hopalong Cassidy; the third, quite different, was the Wonderful Land of Oz. Arthur's England and Hoppy's West were confined to earthly borders. The landscape of Oz was as large or as small as I wished it to be. And, like Alice's Wonderland, it was populated with such extraordinary creatures that I knew anything might happen there. It was a place where the laws of our universe seldom applied." His desire to visit the land of Oz never waned over the years, so it was with much enthusiasm and joy that Hague accepted the job of painting his own Oz. "I count myself as one of the most fortunate of beings," he once said. "For as an artist I have not only the pleasure but the duty to daydream. It is part of my work. I have been a contented daydreamer all of my life, often to the exasperation of those around me. While creating the illustrations for *The Wizard of Oz,* I would slip away. My hands went about their business while my mind walked among the Quadlings and the fierce Kalidahs." Reviewing the hundredth anniversary edition of that book, Lynne T. Burke wrote in *Reading Today* that "Hague's old-fashioned style and muted watercolor palette are the perfect foil for this full-length version of America's best-known fairy tale."

Hague is well known for dozens of other titles for which he collaborated. Working with his wife, the children's author Kathleen Hague, he has produced several volumes, including the popular idea books, *Alphabears, Numbears,* and *Calendarbears.* Reviewing *Calendarbears* in *Booklist,* April Judge dubbed it a "playful collection of bouncy rhymes." Hague has also illustrated other classics of children's literature, including Beatrix Potter's *Peter Rabbit,* Frances Hodgson Burnett's *The Secret Garden,* Margery Williams's *The Velveteen Rabbit,* J. M. Barrie's *Peter Pan,* Carl Sandburg's *Rootabaga Stories,* Charles Perrault's *Cinderella,* and Edward Lear's *The Owl and the Pussy-Cat. Booklist's* Shelley Townsend-Hudson declared that in *The Owl and the Pussy-Cat* "Hague plays off the sensual and grotesque elements of the poetry and uses rich texture and imagination to extend the text's foolishness."

Among the author-illustrator's more popular self-illustrated titles are books full of furry forest creatures and teddy bears. Many of these self-illustrated titles are compilations of works culled from nursery rhymes, Irish legends, and even the Bible, to which Hague adds his signature, detailed drawings. In *Michael Hague's Family Easter Treasury,* for example, he selects from works including Mother Goose, the Bible, and from the poets William Blake and Emily Dickinson, among others. In *Teddy Bears' Mother Goose,* Hague compiled fifty-five nursery rhymes illustrated with "precise detail" which "adds to the charm" of the rhymes, noted *Booklist's* Townsend-Hudson. *The Perfect Present* deals with the adventures of a rabbit named Jack in a shop full of old-fashioned toys. "Fans of Hague's extravagant, nostalgic style will have a feast," commented Susan Dove Lempke in a *Booklist* review of that book. Reviewing the same title, a contributor for *Publishers Weekly* concluded, "Hague's sumptuous wintry watercolors are among his strongest work." An Irish folktale is served up in *Kate Culhane: A Ghost Story,* and fairies take center stage in *The Book of Fairies,* a tale complemented by "Hague's lush, highly detailed artwork," according to *Booklist's* Ilene Cooper.

Imagining and believing were important factors in Hague's childhood, and he maintains that they are "the only forms of magic left. When I was a kid, I thought that magicians actually did work magic—the power to cut a woman in two and put her back together again. As I got older I, of course, realized that these were optical illusions. After a while one draws a distinction between doing tricks and imagination. Our imagination is real magic. And while imagination may change in our increasingly technological world, it is still magic—it's what got us to the moon! Without it, we'd still be living in trees."

Biographical and Critical Sources

BOOKS

Authors and Artists for Young Adults, Volume 18, Gale (Detroit, MI), 1996.

PERIODICALS

Booklist, September 1, 1992, pp. 60-61; April 1, 1993, p. 1425; June 1, 1994, p. 1815; October 1, 1995, p. 313; December 1, 1995, Shelley Townsend-Hudson, review of *The Owl and the Pussy-Cat and Other Nonsense Poems by Edward Lear,* p. 638; September 1, 1996, Susan Dove Lempke, review of *The Perfect Present,* p. 136; March 15, 1997, April Judge, review of *Calendarbears: A Book of Months,* p. 1247; March 15, 1999, p. 1328; May 15, 1999, p. 1702; December 15, 2000, Ilene Cooper, review of *The Book of Fairies,* p. 812; July, 2001, Shelley Townsend-Hudson, review of *Teddy Bears' Mother Goose,* p. 2013.

Books of Wonder News, November, 1988.

Horn Book Guide, July, 1990.

New York, December 12, 1988.

Newsweek, November 13, 1995, p. 86.

Publishers Weekly, October 31, 1986; January 20, 1989, p. 103; April 28, 1989, p. 75; September 28, 1990,

p. 99; September 14, 1992, p. 123; March 14, 1994, p. 70; September 18, 1995, p. 96; November 13, 1995, p. 61; September 30, 1996, review of *The Perfect Present*, p. 88; February 22, 1999, p. 85; October 4, 1999, p. 79; October 9, 2000, p. 90; July 2, 2001, p. 76; July 16, 2001, p. 149.

Reading Today, December, 2000, Lynne T. Burke, review of *The Wizard of Oz, 100th Anniversary Edition,* p. 35.

School Library Journal, March, 1986; January, 1987; June-July, 1987, p. 64; February, 1989, p. 82; June, 1989, p. 109; December, 1989, p. 114; February, 1990, p. 84; October, 1990. P. 37; June, 1992, p. 108; November, 1992, p. 112; May, 1993, p. 102; October, 1993, p. 144; June, 1994, p. 124; October, 1994, p. 110; October, 1995, p. 148; July, 1997, p. 68; March, 1999, p. 198; June, 1999, p. 96; October, 2000, review of *A Wind in the Willows Christmas,* p. 59; December, 2000, p. 130; April, 2001, p. 94.

Times Educational Supplement, November 21, 1986; February 5, 1988, p. 53.

Washington Post Book World, February 9, 1986.

Wilson Library Bulletin, May, 1987, p. 48; February, 1990, p. 91.

OTHER

Michael Hague, http://www.friend.ly.net/ (September 1, 2001).

A Profile of Michael Hague, http://www.northsouth.com/ (September 1, 2001).*

*   *   *

HARKINS, Philip 1912-1997
(John Blaine, a joint pseudonym)

OBITUARY NOTICE—See index for *SATA* sketch: Born September 29, 1912, in Boston, MA; died April 26, 1997, in Santa Barbara, CA. Writer. Harkins attended the University of Grenoble, and the School of Political Science in Paris. Upon finishing high school, he became a world traveler, and worked as a reporter, and as a semi-pro hockey player. For most of his life, however, he was a freelance writer, mostly of works for children. His first book, *Coast Goard, Ahoy!,* was published in 1943. His titles also included *Center Ice, The Day of the Drag Race,* and *Blackburn's Headhunters,* which was filmed as *Surrender—Hell!* in 1959. His last book (with Harold L. Leland under the joint pseudonym John Blaine) was *Danger Below,* the final novel "Rick Brant Science-Adventure Stories," a children's science fiction series.

OBITUARIES AND OTHER SOURCES:

OTHER

Obituary research by Robert Reginald.

HEST, Amy 1950-

Personal

Born April 28, 1950, in New York, NY; daughter of Seymour Cye (a businessman) and Thelma (a teacher; maiden name, Goldberg) Levine; married Lionel Hest (a lawyer), May 19, 1977; children: Sam, Kate. *Education:* Hunter College of the City University of New York, B.A., 1971; C. W. Post College of Long Island University, M.L.S., 1972.

Addresses

Home—450 West End Ave., New York, NY 10024.

Career

New York Public Library, New York, NY, children's librarian, 1972-75; Viking Press, Inc., New York, NY, assistant editor, 1977; full-time writer, 1977—. *Member:* Society of Children's Book Writers and Illustrators.

Awards, Honors

Parents' Choice Award, 1984, for *The Crack-of-Dawn Walkers;* Christopher Award, 1987, for *The Purple Coat; Pete and Lily* was selected one of Child Study Association of America's Children's Books of the Year, 1987, an American Library Association Notable Children's Book, and a *Booklist* Editor's Choice.

Writings

FOR CHILDREN

Maybe Next Year . . . , Morrow (New York, NY), 1982.

The Crack-of-Dawn Walkers, illustrated by Amy Schwartz, Puffin (New York, NY), 1984.

Pete and Lily, Morrow (New York, NY), 1986.

The Purple Coat, illustrated by Amy Schwartz, Four Winds Press (New York, NY), 1986.

The Mommy Exchange, illustrated by DyAnne DiSalvo-Ryan, Four Winds Press (New York, NY), 1988.

Getting Rid of Krista, illustrated by Jacqueline Rogers, Morrow (New York, NY), 1988.

The Midnight Eaters, illustrated by Karen Gundersheimer, Aladdin Books (New York, NY), 1989.

Travel Tips from Harry: A Guide to Family Vacations in the Sun, illustrated by Sue Truesdell, Morrow (New York, NY), 1989.

Where in the World Is the Perfect Family?, Clarion (New York, NY), 1989.

The Best-Ever Good-Bye Party, illustrated by DyAnne DiSalvo-Ryan, Morrow (New York, NY), 1989.

The Ring and the Window Seat, illustrated by Deborah Haeffele, Scholastic (New York, NY), 1990.

Fancy Aunt Jess, illustrated by Amy Schwartz, Morrow (New York, NY), 1990.

A Sort-Of Sailor, illustrated by Lizzy Rockwell, Four Winds Press (New York, NY), 1990.

Love You, Soldier, Four Winds Press (New York, NY), 1991.

Pajama Party, illustrated by Irene Trivas, Morrow (New York, NY), 1992.

The Go-Between, illustrated by DyAnne DiSalvo-Ryan, Four Winds Press (New York, NY), 1992.

Nana's Birthday Party, illustrated by Amy Schwartz, Morrow (New York, NY), 1993.

Weekend Girl, illustrated by Harvey Stevenson, Morrow (New York, NY), 1993.

Nannies for Hire, illustrated by Irene Trivas, Morrow (New York, NY), 1994.

Ruby's Storm, illustrated by Nancy Cote, Four Winds Press (New York, NY), 1994.

Rosie's Fishing Trip, illustrated by Paul Howard, Candlewick Press (Cambridge, MA), 1994.

How to Get Famous in Brooklyn, illustrated by Linda Dalal Sawaya, Four Winds Press (New York, NY), 1994.

The Private Notebook of Katie Roberts, Age Eleven (sequel to *Love You, Soldier*), illustrated by Sonja Lamut, Candlewick Press (Cambridge, MA), 1995.

In the Rain with Baby Duck, illustrated by Jill Barton, Candlewick Press (Cambridge, MA), 1995.

Party on Ice, illustrated by Irene Trivas, Morrow (New York, NY), 1995.

Jamaica Louise James, illustrated by Sheila White Stanton, Candlewick Press (Cambridge, MA), 1996.

Baby Duck and the Bad Eyeglasses, illustrated by Jill Barton, Candlewick Press (Cambridge, MA), 1996.

The Babies Are Coming, illustrated by Chloe Cheese, Crown (New York, NY), 1997.

You're the Boss, Baby Duck, illustrated by Jill Barton, Candlewick Press (Cambridge, MA), 1997.

When Jessie Came across the Sea, illustrated by P. J. Lynch, Candlewick Press (Cambridge, MA), 1997.

The Great Green Notebook of Katie Roberts: Who Just Turned Twelve on Monday, illustrated by Sonja Lamut, Candlewick Press (Cambridge, MA), 1998.

Gabby Growing Up, illustrated by Amy Schwartz, Simon & Schuster (New York, NY), 1998.

Off to School, Baby Duck!, illustrated by Jill Barton, Candlewick Press (Cambridge, MA), 1999.

Mabel Dancing, illustrated by Christine Cavenier, Candlewick Press (Cambridge, MA), 2000.

The Friday Nights of Nana, illustrated by Claire A. Nivola, Candlewick Press (Cambridge, MA), 2001.

Kiss Good Night, illustrated by Anita Jeram, Candlewick Press (Cambridge, MA), 2001.

Don't You Feel Well, Sam?, illustrated by Anita Jeram, Candlewick Press (Cambridge, MA), 2002.

Baby Duck and the Cozy Blanket, illustrated by Jill Barton, Candlewick Press (Cambridge, MA), 2002.

Make the Team, Baby Duck!, illustrated by Jill Barton, Candlewick Press (Cambridge, MA), 2002.

Sidelights

An award-winning author of picture books and juvenile novels, Amy Hest is known for her sensitive and insightful depictions of family relationships. Many of her books focus on children and their grandparents, although parents, annoying siblings, and fabulous aunts also make frequent appearances. Many of the stories are set in New York City and illustrate how love and support of family and friends can get one through trying

Gabby begs her grandfather to make her a purple coat, not the usual navy blue, in Amy Hest's **The Purple Coat.** *(Illustrated by Amy Schwartz.)*

times as well as the ordinary ups and downs of everyday existence.

Hest grew up in a small suburban community about an hour's drive from New York City. As a child, her favorite things to do were biking, reading, and spying. "I spied on everyone, and still do," Hest said in a Four Winds Press publicity release. "All writers, I suspect, are excellent spies. At least they ought to be. My parents took me to the city quite often, and by the time I was seven, I was certain of one thing, that I would one day live there. Many years later, after graduating from library school, I moved to the Upper West Side of Manhattan, and I live here still, with my husband and two children, Sam and Kate."

Hest often uses her children's names for the main characters in her books. *Maybe Next Year ...,* Hest's first published book, features a twelve-year-old named Kate who lives with her grandmother on the Upper West Side of New York City. Two major events unfold in Kate's life during the course of the story, and she must sort out her feelings about both. First, Mr. Schumacher, a widower friend of her grandmother's, moves in to share their apartment. Kate also has to decide whether she is ready and willing to audition for the National Ballet Summer School, as her best friend, Peter, feels she should.

In *The Crack-of-Dawn Walkers,* Hest again portrays a young girl's relationship with a grandparent. Every other Sunday, Sadie gets to go with Grandfather on his traditional morning walk. On the other Sundays, her little brother gets to spend time alone with Grandfather. Millie Hawk Daniel, in a review for the *New York Times Book Review,* praised Hest's combination of the two themes, "the validity of intergenerational camaraderie and the understanding that each child needs his or her own private time with a grandparent."

Children and their grandparents are the primary focus in five more of Hest's books. In a story Ellen Feldman

Grandpa convinces Baby Duck that her new glasses are not so bad in **Baby Duck and the Bad Eyeglasses.** *(Written by Hest and illustrated by Jill Barton.)*

dubbed a "triumph of imagination, resourcefulness and hope" in her *New York Times Book Review* appraisal, *The Purple Coat* tells how Gabrielle and her mother go on their annual trip to Grampa's tailor shop so that Gabby can get a new coat. Up until now, Grampa has always made Gabby a navy blue coat with "two rows of buttons and a half belt in the back"—just the way Mama likes it. This time, Gabby wants a purple coat, but Mama says no. Fashioning an imaginative reversible coat, Grampa manages to please them both. Hest and illustrator Amy Schwartz teamed up again in 1998's *Gabby Growing Up,* in which the eponymous protagonist, now eight or nine years old, once again helps to celebrate the warm relationship between a girl and her grandfather. Gabby has knitted mittens to give to Grampa for his birthday, and when she and her mother come to Manhattan to meet him at a skating rink, she first gets a new hairdo among other surprises en route. Finally the question arises whether Grampa will like Gabby's new braidless look and the bright orange mittens she has knitted for him. Once again, as with *The Purple Coat,* reviewers responded warmly to this intergenerational tale. "Hest and Schwartz lovingly recreate postwar New York City," wrote a reviewer for *Publishers Weekly,* "but the issues they address are timeless.... A thoughtful, effective collaboration." Writing in *Booklist,* Ilene Cooper felt the tale had something for both adults and children: "Although the setting may evoke nostalgia for adults, Gabby's story of universal hopes and worries will easily appeal to today's children." And Virginia Golodetz, reviewing *Gabby Growing Up* in *School Library Journal,* wrote, "Art and text together tell a totally satisfying story of a youngster making choices about herself, with the love and support of her family."

A young girl's relationship with her grandmother is explored in *The Midnight Eaters* and *The Go-Between.* In the first book, Samantha Bluestein and her ill-but-recovering Nana share a bedroom, a cold midnight snack, and some warm conversation in what Heide Piehler of *School Library Journal* called an adept portrayal of "the special love and understanding between generations." *The Go-Between* is also the story of granddaughter-grandmother roommates. Lexi and Gran share a room and enjoy looking out the window at the bustling New York City street below. There, they spy Murray Singer, who runs the newsstand and used to be a good friend of Gran's. Lexi plays matchmaker until she fears that Gran's budding romance with Murray may change her own cherished relationship. All ends happily, however, in this story that, as a *Publishers Weekly* reviewer noted, "blends nostalgia and contemporary family dynamics."

New York City plays a particularly large role in two of Hest's books about grandparents. In *Weekend Girl,* Sophie's parents take a "private, no-kid" vacation, leaving Sophie and her dog to spend the weekend with Gram and Grampa. Although Sophie is sad to be without her parents, she enjoys her grandparents' special surprise of a picnic and concert in Central Park. The city streets and a brewing storm are the background against which Ruby must make her way to keep a checkers date with

Grandpa in *Ruby's Storm.* This book not only explores the intergenerational relationship, but also conveys what Joyce Richards called in *School Library Journal* the "allegorical message that nurturing family relationships often means weathering storms along the way."

Aunts provide nurturing family relationships in Hest's *Fancy Aunt Jess* and *The Ring and the Window Seat.* The title character of *Fancy Aunt Jess* has luxurious blonde hair, dresses stylishly, and loves to host her niece Becky at sleepovers in her Brooklyn apartment. Whenever anyone questions Aunt Jess about her unmarried status, she replies that she is waiting for someone special, someone who will give her goose bumps. Goose bumps appear when she meets the father of Becky's new friend. Eleanor K. MacDonald wrote in *School Library Journal* that this story of a special friendship would "appeal to any child who has pondered the mysteries of adult romance."

Another aunt is featured in Hest's *The Ring and the Window Seat,* a "low-key introduction" to the story of the Holocaust, according to Leone McDermott in *Booklist.* In this graceful tale, Annie's Aunt Stella recalls a birthday she had many years ago. Stella had been saving her money to buy a beautiful golden ring, but one day a carpenter knocked on her door, asking for work. As he was building a window seat for Stella, he told her how he needed the work so he could earn money to send for his daughter, who was hiding from the Nazis. After she heard this, Stella silently slipped her ring money into the carpenter's bag. A few weeks later, she unexpectedly received a gift of a golden ring from the carpenter's daughter. Now, Stella passes the ring on to Annie as a special birthday surprise.

Hest's focus shifts from relatives to friends and their relationships in *Pete and Lily.* These two twelve-year-old girls, neighbors in the same apartment building in New York, form an "Anti-Romance Mission" when Pete—whose real name is Patricia—finds out that her mother and Lily's father have begun dating. Cynthia Percak Infantino praised the author's "convincing portrait of adolescent jealousy" in *School Library Journal,* noting that it also shows the "need to let go of the past and adapt to life's changes." *Getting Rid of Krista* also deals with the themes of jealousy and adaptation. When eight-year-old Gillie's father loses his job, her big sister Krista has to come back home from college. Gillie wants her self-centered, preening sister out of the house as soon as possible. With the help of her best friend and a coincidental meeting with a famous Broadway producer, Gillie gets her wish.

In all of Hest's books, an underlying theme is the incredible variety of family relationships that exist in society. Large families, small families, single-parent families, families with step-parents and step-siblings, are all seen as having their own special charm, as well as their own special difficulties. Another type of special family arrangement is depicted in *Where in the World Is the Perfect Family?,* in which complicated problems face eleven-year-old Cornie Blume. Cornie is adjusting well to the joint-custody arrangement of her divorced parents, shuttling between the East and West sides of New York. But then Cornie's father announces that his new wife is about to have a baby, and her mother begins mentioning a possible move to California. Roger Sutton noted in the *Bulletin of the Center for Children's Books* that these complications give the story "texture" and that "Cornie's a likable, one-of-us heroine whom readers will enjoy."

While the problems in *The Mommy Exchange* are not quite as complex as Cornie's situation in *Where in the World Is the Perfect Family?,* they do demonstrate that differences in families have their good and bad points. Hest's story compares and contrasts two families who live in the same apartment building. Jessica lives upstairs with her parents and her twin siblings; Jason lives downstairs, in peace and quiet with only his mother and father. The two friends envy each other's lives, and they decide to make a weekend switch. After they each experience how the other lives, Jessica and Jason

discover the blessings their own environments have to offer. Hest continues the young duo's friendship in *The Best-Ever Good-Bye Party,* as the two children adapt to the fact that Jason is moving away. Jason seems to be looking forward to the move, which hurts Jessica's feelings, and the two have a fight the day before the move. However, at the good-bye party arranged by Jessica's mother, Jason and Jessica realize that they are still best friends despite everything.

The ups and downs of friendship take the stage in *Pajama Party* and *Nannies for Hire,* which focus on three best friends, eight-year-old Casey and her pals Jenny and Kate. In *Pajama Party,* the girls decide to have their own pajama party when they are excluded from Casey's thirteen-year-old sister's party. Although Kate gets homesick and does not make it through her first night away from home, all ends happily when the girls are reunited in the morning with special breakfast treats. In what Hanna B. Zeiger characterized in *Horn Book* as "a warm-hearted tale of friendship," *Nannies for*

Thirteen-year-old Jessie immigrates to New York City and works sewing lace to earn money to bring her grandmother to the United States in Hest's **When Jessie Came across the Sea.** *(Illustrated by P. J. Lynch.)*

Hire finds the three friends collaborating on a baby-sitting job taking care of Jenny's new baby sister. Not surprisingly, things do not go quite as smoothly as planned, and at the end of what becomes a very stressful day, all three girls appreciate why Jenny's Mom has been so tired and frazzled lately.

In addition to picture books, Hest also writes middle-grade novels. Her most popular books of this type feature a young Jewish girl, Katie, who lives in New York City and Texas during the 1940s. In the first "Katie" book, *Love You, Soldier,* Katie sees the world change from her seventh to tenth birthdays as World War II affects everyone around her, and she worries about her father, who is fighting overseas. She and her mother pore over his letters and try to keep a sense of normalcy on the home front. When a childhood friend of her mother's moves in, also waiting for a husband to return from the war, Katie helps out with the woman's new baby. Sadly, one day the long-dreaded telegram arrives to tell nine-year-old Katie and her mom that Katie's father will not be coming home. Critical praise greeted publication of *Love You, Soldier.* "Hest's book offers another viewpoint of the hardships of World War II in the United States," wrote Phyllis Kennemer in a *School Library Journal* review, while *Horn Book* contributor Mary M. Burns dubbed the novel a "small gem," concluding, "It isn't often that a story accessible to younger readers has the emotional impact of a much more complex novel. Amy Hest's *Love You, Soldier* belongs in that category."

Katie's story continues in *The Private Notebook of Katie Roberts, Age Eleven,* in which the pre-teen fills the pages of a leather notebook with images of her new life in Texas. Her mother is now remarried to Sam Gold, and the family now lives on his ranch. Katie's diary records her nervousness at entering a new school, her ups when she becomes editor of the class paper, and her downs when she learns of her mother's pregnancy and worries about her place in the new blended family. As before, critics responded positively to Katie. A reviewer for *Publishers Weekly* called her an "unusually exuberant narrator" and noted that the young narrator's humorous takes on life "will win readers as [Katie] surmounts hurdle after hurdle." Writing in *Booklist,* Chris Sherman felt that fans of *Love You, Soldier* "will be delighted with this sequel," and called Katie a "captivating, outspoken protagonist whose concerns will be familiar to many children." *Horn Book* contributor Burns had high praise for the novel, noting that unlike most sequels it stands up well on its own; moreover it distinguishes Hest "as a remarkable writer for a difficult audience." "So lifelike is her characterization," added Burns, "that the reader feels impelled to slip into the narrative to offer [Katie] ... a bit of advice." Burns deemed *The Private Notebook of Katie Roberts, Age Eleven* a "finely crafted story" made even better by the "lively line drawings" of illustrator Sonja Lamut.

Katie's third outing, *The Great Green Notebook of Katie Roberts: Who Just Turned Twelve on Monday,* finds the protagonist entering the seventh grade in Texas. Her new notebook was sent to her by a former New York neighbor, and in it she continues to record her feelings about her life. In this installment, readers learn of her infatuation with David, her frustration when she is prohibited from wearing lipstick to school, and her on-again, off-again friendship with a new kid at school, Rudy, an Italian immigrant. Katie still misses her biological father and has fears that her stepfather's new business—a diner—won't succeed. *Booklist* contributor Michael Cart called Katie an "engaging presence," and also characterized her parents as likable and sympathetic." Burns, once again reviewing Katie's adventures in *Horn Book,* also had positive things to say about the journal-novel, noting that "Katie is a believable, dauntless character, with just the right mix of sass and sympathy." And a *Kirkus Reviews* critic called the tale a "rollicking story that balances humor and pre-adolescent angst with the larger canvas of post-WWII America."

Writing for younger readers, Hest has teamed up with illustrator Jill Barton on several "Baby Duck" picture books, chronicling the adventures and misadventures of this young quacker. Her first outing, *In the Rain with Baby Duck,* blends family and weather when Baby Duck—no fan of rain—must navigate puddles to get to her Grampa's on the other side of town. There she learns that her mother did not much like the rain either as a youngster. "Preschoolers will love the large, bright pages with the funny pencil and watercolor illustrations of the duck family," wrote *Horn Book* reviewer Hanna Zeiger, "and they will easily identify with the joy of splashing in puddles (with boots on)." Spectacles give Baby Duck problems in *Baby Duck and the Bad Eyeglasses,* a story that once again provides a loving relationship between grandfather and grandchild. Baby Duck's Grampa is able to convince her that wearing her new glasses is not only simply okay but actually good for her. More praise greeted this addition to the series. *Booklist* contributor Ilene Cooper wrote that "Hest and Barton combine their considerable talents in a delightful story," while in *Horn Book* Maeve Visser Knoth felt that readers "will be delighted to encounter [Baby Duck] again."

The arrival of a new sibling provides the inspiration for *You're the Boss, Baby Duck.* No longer the youngest in the family, Baby Duck is unsure how she feels about her new sister, Hot Stuff, but a visit to Grampa helps to set things right again. This oft-written-about topic is given a new twist by Hest and Barton, according to *Booklist* contributor Cooper; "Baby is just so ducky," the critic quipped, "that anything she appears in is hardly run-of-the-mill." The first day of school is at the heart of *Off to School, Baby Duck!,* and Baby Duck is none too happy about the prospect. Once again, however, it is a talk with understanding Grampa that reassures her that things will be fine. Cooper, reviewing *Off to School, Baby Duck!,* called the young protagonist a "trailblazer of sorts" for introducing young readers to the pleasures of rain, eyeglasses, a new sibling, and school. While there are many books which deal with the subject, "familiar situations seem new, fresh, and very real when Baby is in the middle of them," Cooper noted, adding that "Baby

Sam won't go to sleep until he gets a good-night kiss from his mother in Hest's **Kiss Good Night.** *(Illustrated by Anita Jeram.)*

Duck continues to be a terrific combination of sugar and spice." "No matter how many going-to-school books you already have, don't miss out on this one," declared Kathleen M. Kelly MacMillan in *School Library Journal.*

Before Hest began writing children's books, she worked for several years as a children's librarian, and then in the children's book departments of several major publishing houses. "All my life, though, I secretly wanted to write children's books," she wrote in her publicity release. "'What? You?' This nasty little voice in the back of my head simply laughed at me. 'What in the world would someone like YOU have to say? Don't you get it, Amy, you're the least exciting person in the universe! Go away and let the writers do the writing!'

"It took me a long time—and I won't tell you how many years—to smash that voice to smithereens . . . but smash it I did, and I'm not a bit sorry. Having done that, I was able to get on with it, with the writing. Amazing! I DID find something to write about, and every single day I find something more."

Biographical and Critical Sources

PERIODICALS

Booklist, April 15, 1984, p. 1190; March 15, 1986, p. 1084; March 1, 1988, p. 1181; September 1, 1989, p. 72; February 1, 1990, p. 1091; January 15, 1991, Leone McDermott, review of *The Ring and the Window,* p. 1063; September 15, 1991, p. 151; February 1, 1992, p. 1040; March 1, 1992, p. 1279; January, 1993, p. 810; May 1, 1993, p. 1603; August, 1993, p. 2060; January 15, 1994, p. 871; March 1, 1994, p. 1270l; July, 1995, Chris Sherman, review of *The Private Notebook of Katie Roberts, Age Eleven,* p. 1879; August, 1996, Ilene Cooper, review of *Baby Duck and the Bad Eyeglasses,* p. 1905; September 1, 1996, pp. 143-144; September 1, 1997, Ilene Cooper, review of *You're the Boss, Baby Duck!,* p. 133; November 1, 1997, p. 481; January 1, 1998, Ilene Cooper, review of *Gabby Growing Up,* pp. 822-823; February 1, 1998, p. 918; November 15, 1998, Michael Cart, review of *The Great Green Notebook of Katie Roberts,* p. 590; September 15, 1999, Ilene Cooper, review of *Off to School, Baby Duck!,* p. 259; January 1, 2000, p. 824; April 15, 2000, p. 1552; October 1, 2001, Gillian Engberg, review of *Kiss Good Night,* p. 325, and Carolyn Phelan, review of *The Friday Nights of Nana,* p. 334.

Bulletin of the Center for Children's Books, February, 1983, p. 109; April, 1984, p. 148; April, 1986, p. 149; May, 1988, p. 179; November, 1989, Roger Sutton, review of *Where in the World Is the Perfect Family?,* pp. 59-60; March, 1990, p. 163; September, 1991, p. 11; March, 1992, p. 182; July, 1992, p. 263; April, 1993, p. 251; October, 1993, p. 46.

Childhood Education, winter, 1990, p. 116; summer, 1993, p. 209.

Children's Book Review Service, May, 1984, p. 101; July, 1986, p. 146; spring, 1988, p. 131; December, 1989, p. 39; spring, 1990, p. 135; October, 1991, p. 19; June, 1994, p. 122.

Emergency Librarian, January, 1992, p. 52; March, 1993, p. 50.

Growing Point, January, 1990, p. 5269.

Horn Book, June, 1984, p. 319; September, 1986, p. 589; July, 1988, p. 494; September, 1989, p. 611; March, 1990, p. 189; September-October, 1991, Mary M. Burns, review of *Love You, Soldier,* pp. 591-592; July, 1992, p. 448; May-June, 1994, Hanna B. Zeiger, review of *Nannies for Hire,* pp. 339-340; September-October, 1995, Mary M. Burns, review of *The Private Notebooks of Katie Roberts, Age Eleven,* pp. 599-600; March-April, 1996, Hanna B. Zeiger, review of *In the Rain with Baby Duck,* pp. 188-189; September-October, 1996, Maeve Visser Knoth, review of *Baby Duck and the Bad Eyeglasses,* pp. 577-578; January-Febru-

ary, 1998, p. 65; January-February, 1999, Mary M. Burns, review of *The Great Green Notebook of Katie Roberts,* p. 62.

Horn Book Guide, July, 1989, p. 44; January, 1990, p. 213; spring, 1992, p. 59; fall, 1992, p. 233; fall, 1993, p. 286.

Junior Bookshelf, December, 1989, p. 238.

Kirkus Review, July 1, 1989, p. 990; August 1, 1989, p. 1158; March 1, 1990, p. 342; August 1, 1991, p. 1011; February 1, 1992, p. 184; July 15, 1993, p. 934; February 15, 1994, p. 226; August 15, 1998, review of *The Great Green Notebook of Katie Roberts;* August 15, 2001, p. 1213

New York Times Book Review, May 13, 1984, Millie Hawk Daniel, review of *The Crack-of-Dawn Walkers,* pp. 20-21; November 9, 1986, Ellen Feldman, review of *The Purple Coat,* p. 60; November 21, 1999, p. 39; March 11, 2001, p. 27.

Parents, November, 1984, p. 53.

Publishers Weekly, November 5, 1982, p. 70; February 24, 1984, p. 140; May 30, 1986, p. 67; April 8, 1988, p. 94; July 28, 1989, p. 219; March 15, 1991, p. 59; March 30, 1992, p. 105; April 13, 1992, review of *The Go-Between,* pp. 57-58; February 8, 1993, p. 88; July 28, 1993, p. 77; December 6, 1993, p. 72; June 5, 1995, review of *The Private Notebook of Katie Roberts, Age Eleven,* p. 64; September 22, 1997, p. 79; October 27, 1997, p. 76; December 1, 1997, review of *Gabby Growing Up,* p. 53; June 12, 2000, p. 73; June 16, 2001, p. 145; August 6, 2001, p. 88.

School Library Journal, November, 1982, p. 86; August, 1984, p. 60; August, 1986, Cynthia Percak Infantino, review of *Pete and Lily,* p. 92; August, 1988, p. 95; October, 1988, p. 121; August, 1989, p. 122; October, 1989, Heide Piehler, review of *The Midnight Eaters,* p. 86; June, 1990, Eleanor K. MacDonald, review of *Fancy Aunt Jess,* p. 100; December, 1990, p. 79; August, 1991, Phyllis K. Kennemer, review of *Love You, Soldier,* p. 166; April, 1992, pp. 92, 93; August, 1993, p. 145; October, 1993, p. 100; April, 1994, Joyce Richards, review of *Ruby's Storm,* p. 106; May, 1994, p. 339; February, 1995, p. 74; September, 1995, pp. 178, 200; December, 1995, p. 81; October, 1996, p. 98; December, 1996, p. 94; October, 1997, p. 98; November, 1997, pp. 82-83; January, 1998, p. 87; March, 1998, Virginia Golodetz, review of *Gabby Growing Up,* p. 180; September, 1998, p. 146; September, 1999, Kathleen M. Kelly MacMillan, review of *Off to School, Baby Duck!,* p. 183; June, 2000, p. 114; October, 2001, Amy Lilien-Harper, review of *The Friday Nights of Nana,* p. 120; November, 2001, Susan Weitz, review of *Kiss Good Night,* p. 124.

Smithsonian, November, 1992, p. 202; November, 1993, p. 182.

OTHER

Four Winds Publicity Release, 1993, "Amy Hest."*

HINTZ, Stephen V. 1975-

Personal

Born July 27, 1975, in Milwaukee, WI; son of Martin (a writer) and Sandra (a consultant; maiden name, Wright) Hintz. *Ethnicity:* "Caucasian." *Education:* Attended University of North Carolina—Charlotte; University of Wisconsin—Milwaukee, B.A. *Politics:* Independent. *Religion:* "All." *Hobbies and other interests:* Bodhran, basketball.

Addresses

Home—2525 North Weil St., Milwaukee, WI 53216. *Office*—Peacemakers Mentoring Service, Inc., 2821 North Fourth St., Suite 203, Milwaukee, WI 53212. *Agent*—Martin Hintz, 301 North Water St., Third Floor, Milwaukee, WI 53212. *E-mail*—steve@peacemakers-mentoring.com.

Career

Executive director of a social service provider in Milwaukee, WI, 1998—. National Mentoring Partnership, member.

Awards, Honors

Second place award, Society of American Travel Writers.

Writings

WITH FATHER, MARTIN HINTZ

Wisconsin: A Family Travel Guide, Globe Pequot (Old Saybrook, CT), 1995, reprinted as *Fun with the Family in Wisconsin: Hundreds of Ideas for Day Trips with the Kids,* 1998.
Bahamas, Children's Press (New York, NY), 1997.
North Carolina, Children's Press (New York, NY), 1998.
Israel, Children's Press (New York, NY), 1999.

Work in Progress

Freedom Breeze, a screenplay with a racial theme; *In Life and Letters,* a screenplay; a book of poems.

Sidelights

Stephen V. Hintz told *SATA:* "My motivation for writing comes from my genes. It also comes from the need to express things that are difficult for me to express verbally. I like to see what I think. My dad and brother influence my work. Strangers influence my work. My writing process is to build up thoughts and energy until I either get sick and need to write or catch myself building up and release. Obviously my life has inspired me to write. I choose many topics having to do with race and people because I was raised with the issue. The money and 'get it' mentality of the eighties I knew took precedence over social topics during much of my childhood, and when social topics came back into the picture, it was interesting to explore."*

*   *   *

HOUSTON, Juanita C. 1921-

Personal

Born April 6, 1921, in Greeley, CO; daughter of Ralph C. (a minister) and Florence J. (a homemaker; maiden name, Sahl) Crouse; married William A. Houston (a realtor), September 27, 1952; children: Richard, William A., Jr., Mary Houston Thompson. *Education:* Stanford University, B.A., M.Ed. *Politics:* Republican. *Religion:* Southern Baptist.

Addresses

Home—24701 Raymond Way, No. 222, Lake Forest, CA 92630. *E-mail*—houston1222@hotmail.com.

Career

Public school teacher in Long Beach, CA, 1947-52; elementary teacher at a Christian school in California, 1965-86; writer.

Writings

Our Golden California, ETC Publications (Palm Springs, CA), 1999.
Our Beautiful America, ETC Publications (Palm Springs, CA), 2000.

Work in Progress

Revising *Our Golden California.*

Sidelights

Juanita C. Houston told *SATA:* "For many years I have enjoyed writing of various kinds—devotional, expository, even a little children's fiction and poetry, but none of it has been published.

"The writing of the two books—*Our Golden California* and *Our Beautiful America*—was an outgrowth of my teaching in Christian schools. I taught fourth grade for many years, where we studied the history of our state—California. There was not available to us a good text, so when I retired I set about the task of putting ideas and materials which I had used in the classroom into a book; hence, *Our Golden California.*

"The American history book came about because my attention was called to the need for a Christian text which would teach the truth about our Christian heritage as Americans—something children are not learning in our public schools. My objective was not merely to furnish another American history, but to give students an appreciation for the struggle and sacrifice required to make America a great nation. It is a tribute to God's goodness to this great land."*

*   *   *

HUNECK, Stephen 1949(?)-

Personal

Born c. 1949; married; wife's name, Gwen.

Addresses

Home—St. Johnsbury, VT. *Office*—Stephen Huneck Gallery, 49 Central St., Woodstock, VT 05091.

Career

Artist, illustrator, and writer in Vermont. Operator of galleries in Woodstock, VT, Nantucket, MA, Martha's Vineyard, MA, Santa Fe, NM, and Key West, FL. Sculptures and hand-carved furniture represented in collections, including work at Museum of American Folk Art and Smithsonian Institution. Creator of a chapel dedicated to dogs, St. Johnsbury, VT.

Writings

SELF-ILLUSTRATED; FOR CHILDREN

Sally Goes to the Beach, Abrams (New York, NY), 2000.
Sally Goes to the Mountains, Abrams (New York, NY), 2001.
Sally Goes to the Farm, Abrams (New York, NY), 2002.
Sally's Fun in the Sun, Abrams (New York, NY), 2002.

OTHER

My Dog's Brain, Penguin Studio (New York, NY), 1997.

Also illustrator of *Dog Days 2002 Calendar,* Abrams (New York, NY), 2002.

Biographical and Critical Sources

PERIODICALS

Booklist, December 15, 1997, Mary Carroll, review of *My Dog's Brain,* p. 678; May 15, 2000, John Peters, review of *Sally Goes to the Beach,* p. 1748.
Boston, January, 1993, Jules Older, "Animal House," p. 128; May, 2000, Mark Zanger and Jessika Bella Mura, review of *Sally Goes to the Beach,* p. 264.
Country Living, September, 1991, "Carving Out a Niche," p. 83; August, 2000, Matthew Holm, "Dog Days," p. 30.
New York Times, September 11, 1988, Jules Older, "Artist's Life: The Making of a 'Miracle'," p. 53; August 7, 2001, Carey Goldberg, "A Chapel That Welcomes Dogs, but Not Dogmas," p. A8.
Publishers Weekly, May 29, 2000, review of *Sally Goes to the Beach,* p. 82; June 25, 2001, "Welcome Additions," p. 74.
School Library Journal, June, 2000, Virginia Golodetz, review of *Sally Goes to the Beach,* p. 115; July, 2001, Linda M. Kenton, review of *Sally Goes to the Mountains,* p. 83.
Yankee, March, 1988, Polly Bannister, "Best in Show," p. 108.

OTHER

Stephen Huneck Web Site, http://www.huneck.com (March 2, 2002).*

J–K

JOHANSEN, K(rista) V(ictoria) 1968-

Personal

Born May 19, 1968, in Kingston, Ontario, Canada; daughter of Peter H. (a professor of biology) and Noreen (Bateman) Johansen; married Chris Paul (a Web site designer). *Education:* Mount Allison University, B.A. (with honors), 1990; Centre for Mediaeval Studies, University of Toronto, M.A., 1991; McMaster University, M.A. (English), 1994. *Hobbies and other interests:* Gardening, "growing exotic trees indoors."

Addresses

Home—New Brunswick, Canada. *Agent*—c/o Author Mail, Kids Can Press Ltd., 29 Birch Ave., Toronto, Ontario M4V 1E2, Canada.

Career

Writer. Presenter of children's writing workshops.

Awards, Honors

New Brunswick Lieutenant-Governor's Award for Early Childhood Literacy, 2000, for *Pippin and the Bones;* Eileen Wallace Research Fellowship in children's literature, University of New Brunswick, 2001.

Writings

Torrie and the Dragon, Roussan Publishing, 1997.
The Serpent Bride: Stories from Medieval Danish Ballads, Thistledown Press (Saskatoon, Canada), 1998.
Pippin Takes a Bath, illustrated by Bernice Lum, Kids Can Press (Toronto, Canada), 1999.
Pippin and the Bones, illustrated by Bernice Lum, Kids Can Press (Toronto, Canada), 2000.
Pippin and Pudding, illustrated by Bernice Lum, Kids Can Press (Toronto, Canada), 2001.

Contributor of articles and short fiction to magazines, including *Phantastes, On Spec, Rural Delivery, Atlantic Horse and Pony, Farm Woman, Resource Links,* and *Atlantic Forestry Review.*

K. V. Johansen

Sidelights

K. V. Johansen told *SATA:* "I've always told stories. When I was eight or nine I started writing them down, and I find it hard to imagine myself doing anything else. My favorite type of literature is fantasy. The 'Pippin and Mabel' books are actually an aberration; they're quite 'realistic,' not a dragon, demon, or troll in sight. Pippin is based on my own dog, Pippin, who is a Husky/ German Shepherd/Labrador mix. But in [the real] Pippin's case, life usually imitates art, rather than the other way around. He was never sprayed by a skunk until after I wrote *Pippin Takes a Bath,* and a few months after *Pippin and Pudding* (in which Pippin finds a kitten) was published, a stray cat showed up and adopted us. Pippin still hasn't found any ancient bones, so far as I know. The three 'Pippin and Mabel' books are published in French as the 'Coquine et Mabelle' stories."

Biographical and Critical Sources

PERIODICALS

Atlantic Books Today, summer, 1997, Catherine Wilcox, "Tale for a Midsummer's Night," p. 13; fall, 1998, "Time, Travel, Thrills, and Trolls: New Novels for Young Adults."

Kids' Home Library, September 8, 1999, review of *Pippin Takes a Bath.*

Resource Links, April, 1999, Connie Hall, review of *The Serpent Bride: Stories from Medieval Danish Ballads,* p. 25.

OTHER

Sybertooth, http://www.sybertooth.com/kvj/ (July 20, 2001).

Welcome to Pippin & Mabel's House, http://www.pippin.ca/ (August 7, 2001).

*　　　*　　　*

KELLEHER, Victor (Michael Kitchener) 1939-

Personal

Born July 19, 1939, in London, England; son of Joseph (a builder) and Matilda (a dressmaker; maiden name, Newman) Kelleher; married Alison Lyle (a potter and sculptor), January 2, 1962; children: Jason, Leila. *Education:* University of Natal, B.A., 1961; University of St. Andrews, Diploma in Education, 1963; University of the Witwatersrand, B.A. (with honors), 1969; University of South Africa, M.A., 1970, D.Litt. et Phil., 1973. *Religion:* Atheist. *Hobbies and other interests:* Films, politics, domestic architecture, travel.

Addresses

Home—P.O. Box 351, Bellingen, NSW, Australia 2454.

Career

University of the Witwatersrand, Johannesburg, South Africa, junior lecturer in English, 1969; University of South Africa, Pretoria, South Africa, lecturer, 1970-71, senior lecturer in English, 1972-73; Massey University, Palmerston North, New Zealand, lecturer in English, 1973-76; University of New England, Armidale, Australia, lecturer, 1976-79, senior lecturer, 1980-83, associate professor of English, 1984-87; writer. *Member:* Australian Society of Authors.

Awards, Honors

Patricia Hackett Prize, *Westerly* magazine, 1978, for story, "The Traveller"; Literature Board of the Australia Council senior writer's fellow, 1982; West Australian Library Association, West Australian Young Readers' Book Award, 1982, for *Forbidden Paths of Thual,* and West Australian Young Readers' Special Award, 1983, for *The Hunting of Shadroth;* Australian Children's Book of the Year Award, Children's Book Council of Australia, 1983, for *Master of the Grove;* Australian Science Fiction Achievement Award, National Science Fiction Association, 1984, for *The Beast of Heaven;* Honour Award, Children's Book Council of Australia, 1987, for *Taronga;* Australian Peace Prize, 1987, for *The Makers;* Koala Award, 1991, for *The Red King;* Honour Award, Children's Book Council of Australia, and West Australian Hoffmann Award, both 1992, both for *Brother Night; Del-Del* was shortlisted for the Carnegie Medal in Great Britain; Australian Children's Book of the Year Award shortlist, Children's Book Council of Australia, 1995, for *Parkland,* and 1997, for *Fire Dancer.*

Writings

Voices from the River (novel), Heinemann, 1979.

Africa and After (stories), University of Queensland Press (St. Lucia, Australia), 1983, published as *The Traveller: Stories of Two Continents* (also see below), 1987.

The Beast of Heaven (novel), University of Queensland Press (St. Lucia, Australia), 1984.

Em's Story: A Novel, University of Queensland Press (St. Lucia, Australia), 1988.

Wintering, University of Queensland Press (St. Lucia, Australia), 1990.

Micky Darlin' (also see below), University of Queensland Press (St. Lucia, Australia), 1992.

Double God, Mandarin, 1993.

The House that Jack Built, Mandarin, 1994.

Storyman, Random House (New York, NY), 1996.

Collected Stories (contains *The Traveller: Stories of Two Continents* and *Micky Darlin'*), University of Queensland Press (St. Lucia, Australia), 1999.

Into the Dark, Penguin (New York, NY), 1999.

The Other, Harper Collins (New York, NY), 2002.

FOR YOUNG ADULTS

Forbidden Paths of Thual, illustrated by Anthony Maitland, Penguin (Harmondsworth, England), 1979.

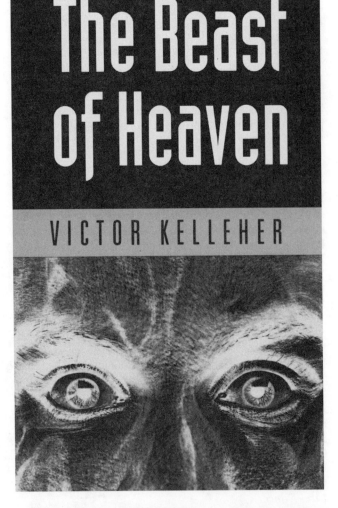

A beast roams a ruined earth destroyed by an atomic bomb in Victor Kelleher's The Beast of Heaven, *written by Victor Kelleher. (Photograph by Craig Voevodin.)*

The Hunting of Shadroth, Penguin (Harmondsworth, England), 1981.

Master of the Grove, Penguin (Harmondsworth, England), 1982.

Papio: A Novel of Adventure, Penguin (Ringwood, Australia), 1984, published as *Rescue!,* Dial (New York, NY), 1992.

The Green Piper, Penguin (Ringwood, Australia), 1984.

Taronga, Penguin (Ringwood, Australia), 1986.

The Makers, Penguin (Ringwood, Australia), 1987.

Baily's Bones, Penguin (Ringwood, Australia), 1988, Dial (New York, NY), 1989.

The Red King, Penguin (Ringwood, Australia), 1989, Dial (New York, NY), 1990.

Brother Night, illustrated by Peter Clarke, MacRae Books (New York, NY), 1990.

Del-Del, illustrated by Peter Clarke, MacRae Books/Random House (Milsons Point, Australia), 1991, Walker (New York, NY), 1992.

To the Dark Tower, MacRae Books/Random House (Milsons Point, Australia), 1992.

Parkland, Viking (Ringwood, Australia), 1994.

Where the Whales Sing, illustrated by Vivienne Goodman, Viking (Ringwood, Australia), 1995, published as *Riding the Whales,* Dial (New York, NY), 1995.

Fire Dancer, Viking (New York, NY), 1996.

Storyman, Random House (Milsons Point, Australia), 1996.

Johnny Wombat, Random House (Milsons Point, Australia), 1996.

Earth Song, Viking (Ringwood, Australia), 1997.

Slow Burn, Viking (Ringwood, Australia), 1997.

The Ivory Trail, Viking (Ringwood, Australia), 1999.

Beyond the Dusk, illustrated by Gregory Rogers, Red Fox (Milsons Point, Australia), 2000.

Red Heart, Viking (Ringwood, Australia), 2001.

The Other, Voyager (Pymble, Australia), 2001.

OTHER

Work represented in anthologies, including *Introduction 6,* Faber (London, England), 1977. Contributor of articles and stories to magazines.

Sidelights

Award-winning author Victor Kelleher writes for both juvenile and adult audiences. His younger readers delight in the fantasy and adventure found in such novels as *The Hunting of Shadroth* and *Taronga,* while his older readers are exposed to the darker thoughts of Kelleher's futuristic fantasy as found in *The Beast of Heaven.* Science fiction blends with futuristic fantasy in *Parkland, Earth Song,* and *Fire Dancer,* a trilogy exploring different scenarios for the future of humans on Earth. Kelleher began writing in 1973, after he left Africa, once commenting that it was a means of therapy. Soon his writing became an end in itself, and his first novels, *Voices from the River* and *Forbidden Paths of Thual,* were published in 1979. Since then, the author has described his adult fiction as falling into "the category of contemporary realism," as his work for young readers often deals with protagonists tackling important quests and searching for the answers to difficult moral questions.

Forbidden Paths of Thual is "an interesting, refreshing, worthwhile" young adult book according to Norman Culpan writing in the *School Librarian.* Quen, the protagonist, is the sole character capable, with the aid of a friendly fox, of freeing his land from the ruthless soldiers called grey Mollags. He is the only one who can overcome his own weaknesses and resist the temptations of cruelty and greed. Audrey Laski summed up Kelleher's story in the *Times Educational Supplement:* "It rests on one boy to dare everything that is necessary to defeat the conquerors."

Kelleher's next two books echo the single protagonist and animal companion of *Forbidden Paths of Thual. The Hunting of Shadroth* presents Tal, a boy with psychic talents who can see into the future, and his friendly cat-like aide, a creature called a Feln. Shadroth, the object of Tal's quest, is a physical beast representing the violent tendencies of Tal's people, a creature Tal must subdue, if not destroy. David Churchill, writing in *School*

Librarian, noted that *The Hunting of Shadroth* "is written with care and elegance." *Times Literary Supplement* contributor Edward Blishen commented in his conclusion: "The whole story is a morality, but without ever ceasing to be a story. There are satisfactory terrors ... and the final struggle rises to one climax only to reveal another beyond it."

In *Master of the Grove,* Kelleher turns to sorcery and a war-ravaged land as backdrops for a quest by Derin, who has lost his memory, yet must complete a journey he does not understand with a witch who dislikes him. Ultimately, he is charged with defeating an evil sorcerer who is at the root of all the strife in the land. "The story of a sorcerer's misuse of his knowledge may seem hackneyed, but it allows Kelleher to explore the theme of the responsibilities and temptations of power in a lively and well-fashioned narrative," declared Neil Philip in the *Times Educational Supplement.* Many critics offered mixed reviews of *Master of the Grove,* *School Librarian* contributor Dennis Hamley dubbing it a "worthy, well-crafted book," but noting that Kelleher's "style is ponderous." Dominic Hibberd also praised *Master of the Grove* in the *Times Literary Supplement* as "quite a good story," though he felt that because it contains so much material and grapples with such big ideas in its two hundred pages, the novel "becomes too ingenious because the book is too full."

Kelleher switches his writing focus from younger readers to an adult audience with his novel *The Beast of Heaven,* published in 1984. Set in a world laid waste by a nuclear holocaust, the book tells the tale of a group of gentle nomads who subsist on "mustools," a mushroom and toadstool combination, and milk from the animals they call Houdin, the beasts of heaven. Their peace-filled world turns violent as the Houdin's aggressiveness increases. The land is also slowly losing its ability to support life. *The Beast of Heaven* is "an engrossing fable," judged Paulette Minare in *Science Fiction Review,* while *Fantasy Review* contributor Michael J. Tolley declared the book a "poignant, readable novel, not without charm." And *Analog* reviewer Tom Easton proclaimed *The Beast of Heaven* "a fable for our times, a warning, a chastisement, well equipped with portentous symbolism."

Kelleher returned to children's fiction with the award-winning novel *Taronga.* Set in a post-"cataclysm" Australia, where cities are destroyed and people go hungry, *Taronga* is the story of telepathic, fourteen-year-old Ben and his experiences at the gang-controlled Taronga Park Zoo. His gift allows him to control the animals in the zoo, earning him a position, shared with an Aboriginal girl named Ellie, as keeper of the big cats. Released at night to frighten and repel the hungry, the cats must be put back into their cages each morning. As Ellie and Ben decide to fight the gangs by freeing all the zoo animals, *Taronga* becomes "a very violent story with complex strategies," according to Dorothy Atkinson in *School Librarian.* Reviewer Colin Greenland noted in the *Times Literary Supplement* that "once again

Victor Kelleher portrays the child's world as a miserable, shadowy place occupied by corrupt and violent adults."

In *Baily's Bones,* Kelleher takes a look at the supernatural, including ghosts, ghostly possession, and mystery. He also delves into the often violent relationship between the Aborigines and the early British settlers of Australia. When a vengeful spirit named Baily takes control of their mentally handicapped older brother, Kenny, Alex, and Dee must reconstruct the tragic events surrounding Baily's death in order to save Kenny's life and put Baily's ghost to rest. "Their efforts come to a climax in a stunning conclusion," determined a reviewer in *Horn Book.* Jeanette Larson, writing in *School Library Journal,* declared *Baily's Bones* to be a "haunting tale ... well told," while *Voice of Youth Advocates* contributor Deborah L. Dubois deemed the book "an exciting suspense novel ... that will appeal to most young adults."

Kelleher returns to fantasy worlds with his novel *The Red King.* The book's medieval overtones, and the battle staged between good and evil, invite comparisons with J. R. R. Tolkien's *The Hobbit.* The heroine, Timkin, is a talented acrobat. When the Red King spreads among the land a deadly disease that kills all her companions, Timkin is saved by a self-serving magician who wants to use Timkin's talent to help him steal the king's gold. *School Library Journal* contributor Bruce Anne Shook mentioned that "excitement and suspense are maintained throughout the story," and added: "Fantasy lovers will find this to be an intriguing tale that provides not only high adventure but also some challenging food for thought about the nature of good and evil." Laura Moss Gottlieb noted in a review for *Voice of Youth Advocates* the "thought-provoking questions" the novel raises, and adjudged Kelleher's writing to be "excellent."

Describing Kelleher's 1990 novel *Brother Night, Voice of Youth Advocates* reviewer Gladys Hardcastle found it to be "fantasy at its very best for young teens." Peter Clarke's illustrations add to the story, Hardcastle added, noting that they combine with the words "to bring a perilous quest through the shadowy realm of dark and light forces brilliantly to life." *Brother Night* is the story of twin boys, one handsome and one grotesque, who are separated at birth and who are rumored to be the children of Jenna the Moon Witch and Solmak the Sun Lord. Undertaking a dangerous journey, one boy seeks vengeance and the other wants only to bury their mother, Jenna; ultimately they both learn the truth about their heritage. *School Library Journal* reviewer JoAnn Rees found *Brother Night* "competently written, but no more," claiming the characters are like "cardboard cutouts"—either good or evil with no in-between. However, a critic for the *Bulletin of the Center for Children's Books* found the novel "Darker-toned than much juvenile fantasy," and praised it as "an adept and satisfying blend of action and atmosphere."

Kelleher moves into a modern setting with *Del-Del,* the story of a traumatized young genius. After the death of his eldest sister, seven-year-old Sam retreats behind an obnoxious, uncaring persona he calls Del-Del. For four years, the family tries everything they can think of, including exorcism, to rescue Sam. But it is his sister Beth, by risking her life, who restores Sam to himself and the family. A reviewer in *Publishers Weekly* noted that Kelleher "plots an unusual course for a sibling death theme, with confusing results" and a "pat resolution." The reader never gets "caught up in the horror, because it seems silly," claimed Caroline S. McKinney in the *Voice of Youth Advocates.* Viewing the novel more positively, *School Library Journal* contributor Sara Miller praised *Del-Del* as a "tense, involving story," and called it "a psychological thriller that's guaranteed to hold readers' attention."

The author turned to a late nineteenth-century setting with the publication of *To the Dark Tower.* With its title culled from a line in the famous French poem "Childe Roland," *To the Dark Tower* tells the story of Tom Roland, a poor climber's apprentice from a sea-side settlement threatened by the encroachment of modern industry. In his dreams, Tom is haunted by visions of the Sleeper, a supernatural creature some in his village wish to awaken. The young climber finds his abilities challenged when he is pressed to scale the daunting Tower Rock and reunite the Sleeper's soul with his resting body, thereby returning the village to an earlier prosperity. His task is made more difficult by his own questions whether progress should be halted, in a novel *School Librarian* reviewer Ann Darnton characterized as "a real cliff hanger," "not an easy read, but for a keen older pupil ... a rewarding one." Other critics also had praise for Kelleher's richly constructed and suspenseful fantasy. *Magpies* contributor Kevin Steinberger found the novel's "thrilling conclusion" brings relief to the reader. "And that, surely," continued Steinberger, "is the mark of a skillfully written quest."

Kelleher moves to a distant-future world for his 1994 work *Parkland,* a novel described by *Magpies* reviewer Carmel Ballinger as "typical Kelleher, challenging the reader to rethink some of our most basic beliefs." Cassie and her genetically engineered companions are prisoners in a zoo-like environment controlled by Cosmic "gardeners," alien visitors to Earth who decided that humans were an evolutionary mistake. After eliminating the dinosaurs millions of years earlier, the aliens return to Earth only to discover that the simian mammals they intended to prosper became too dominant, upsetting the desired balance of nature. Trying to correct the problem, the Cosmic gardeners attempt to breed a new type of creature—a mix of simian and human—to restore harmony to Earth's environment. One of these new creatures, Cassie, finds she has retained the human desire for freedom when she sees a feral boy outside the breeding compound gates. Wishing for the experience of life outside the compound, Cassie eventually seeks the lost knowledge of her human predecessors. A *Junior Bookshelf* contributor predicted that readers who en-joyed Kelleher's earlier works of science fiction would "be pleased to share the wonders of *Parkland* with Cassie and her adventurous friends."

The fate of humans on the Earth is also the center of Kelleher's *Earth Song,* a tale about two characters, Joe and Anna, who are chosen to help repopulate the previously abandoned planet. After deserting the polluted Earth centuries earlier, some humans took refuge on a planet at the other edge of the solar system. Arriving on Earth, Joe and Anna discover that those remaining on the planet transplanted human DNA into other creatures, hoping, in some way, that at least a few human genes would be preserved for future generations. The characters, separated from their supply ships during a miscalculated landing on Earth, must not only journey to find the equipment they so desperately need, but also adjust to the unexpected changes that have taken place on Earth. Writing in *Junior Bookshelf,* a critic concluded that *Earth Song* "reads well despite its complexity," while *School Librarian* reviewer Geoffrey Hammond found the novel "exciting and thought provoking."

Kelleher's fiction, especially for juveniles, generally tends to focus on the darker elements of literature and life. In his novels, many of the adult characters are forbidding or distant figures, and his young heroes and heroines are willing to risk all they have for what they believe. Futuristic, and at the same time moral in tone, Kelleher entertains while he imparts his lessons and views. As he once noted: "Regardless of the type of novel I'm writing, I always try to create a fast pace and strong story line. Equally important to me is the idea of a serious subtext which raises issues that are, I hope, both challenging and pertinent to all my readers, irrespective of their age."

Biographical and Critical Sources

BOOKS

Authors and Artists for Young Adults, Volume 31, Gale (Detroit, MI), 2000.
St. James Guide to Young Adult Writers, 2nd edition, St. James Press (Detroit, MI), 1999.

PERIODICALS

Analog, April, 1987, Tom Easton, review of *The Beast of Heaven.*
Books for Keeps, September, 1995, review of *Parkland,* p. 13.
Bulletin of the Center for Children's Books, June, 1991, review of *Brother Night,* p. 241.
Fantasy Review, September, 1984, Michael J. Tolley, review of *The Beast of Heaven,* p. 31.
Horn Book, March, 1990, review of *Baily's Bones,* p. 207.
Junior Bookshelf, August, 1995, review of *Parkland,* pp. 153-154; August, 1996, review of *Earth Song,* p. 165.
Locus, December, 1999, Jonathan Strahan, review of *The Ivory Trail,* pp. 29-30.
Magpies, May, 1993, Kevin Steinberger, review of *To the Dark Tower,* p. 32; November, 1994, Carmel

Ballinger, review of *Parkland*, p. 34; July, 1996, Jo Goodman, review of *Johnny Wombat*, pp. 25-26; November, 1998, Leonie Tyle, "Know the Author: Victor Kelleher."

Publishers Weekly, July 5, 1985, p. 58; June 15, 1992, review of *Del-Del.*

School Librarian, December, 1979, Norman Culpan, review of *Forbidden Paths of Thual*, p. 388, 391; June, 1981, David Churchill, review of *The Hunting of Shadroth*, p. 154; June, 1982, Dennis Hamley, review of *Master of the Grove*, p. 155; September, 1985, pp. 256, 259; May, 1988, Dorothy Atkinson, review of *Taronga;* February, 1993, Ann Darnton, review of *To the Dark Tower*, p. 30; August, 1996, Geoffrey Hammond, review of *Earth Song*, p. 120.

School Library Journal, November, 1989, Jeanette Larson, review of *Baily's Bones*, p. 111; July, 1990, Bruce Anne Shook, review of *The Red King*, p. 89; May, 1991, JoAnn Rees, review of *Brother Night*, p. 111; June, 1992, Sara Miller, review of *Del-Del*, p. 136.

Science Fiction Review, May, 1986, Paulette Minare, review of *The Beast of Heaven*, p. 7.

Times Educational Supplement, April 23, 1982, Neil Philip, "Action Men All"; November 11, 1983, Audrey Laski, review of *Forbidden Paths of Thual.*

Times Literary Supplement, March 27, 1981, Edward Blishen, "Moral Beasts;" March 26, 1982, Dominic Hibberd, "The Elements of Fantasy"; April 12, 1985; January 1, 1988, Colin Greenland, "Animal Liberation," p. 21.

Voice of Youth Advocates, April, 1990, Deborah L. Dubois, review of *Baily's Bones;* June, 1990, Laura Moss Gottlieb, review of *The Red King*, p. 116; October, 1991, Gladys Hardcastle, review of *Brother Night*, p. 244; June, 1992, Caroline S. McKinney, review of *Del-Del*, p. 110.

*   *   *

KELLEY, Patrick (G.) 1963-

Personal

Born November 11, 1963, in Kent County, MI; son of Peter (a telephone company employee) and Carol (a homemaker) Kelley. *Education:* Attended Grand Valley State University, 1981-84; attended Slade School of Art, London, 1983; Kendall College of Art and Design, B.F.A., 1987. *Politics:* "Pro-life supporter." *Religion:* Roman Catholic.

Addresses

Home and office—1040 Veto St. NW, Grand Rapids, MI 49504. *E-mail*—comartkelley@hotmail.com.

Career

Freelance artist, 1987—.

Awards, Honors

EPA Awards, 1993 and 1995.

Illustrator

Anne Sublett, *The Illustrated Rules of Softball*, Ideals Children's Books (Nashville, TN), 1996.

Nat Reed, *Thunderbird Gold*, Bob Jones University Press (Greenville, SC), 1997.

Elaine Murray Stone, *Maximilian Kolbe: Saint of Auschwitz*, Paulist Press (New York, NY), 1997.

Mary Emmanuel Alves, *Saint Francis of Assisi: Gentle Revolutionary*, Pauline Books and Media (Boston, MA), 1999.

Susan Heyboer O'Keefe, *It's Great to Be Catholic!*, Paulist Press (New York, NY), 2000.

Donna Giaimo and Patricia Edward Jablonski, *Saint Ignatius of Loyola: For the Greater Glory of God*, Pauline Books and Media (Boston, MA), 2001.

Peggy A. Sklar, *St. Ignatius of Loyola: In God's Service*, Paulist Press (New York, NY), 2001.

Chris Driscoll, *God's Little Flower: The Story of St. Therese of Lisieux*, Ambassador Books (Worcester, MA), 2001.

Patricia Edward Jablonski, *Saint Maximilian Kolbe*, Pauline Books and Media (Boston, MA), 2001.

Dennis Doyle and Patrick Doyle, *Rumors at School*, Paulist Press (New York, NY), 2001.

Elaine Murray Stone, *C. S. Lewis: Creator of Narnia*, Paulist Press (New York, NY), 2001.

Julie Walters, *Elizabeth Ann Seton: Saint for a New Nation*, Paulist Press (New York, NY), 2002.

Illustrator of *Mother Theresa*, by Elaine Murray Stone. Work included in *Spectrum*.

WRITTEN BY PATRICIA L. NEDERVELD

An Amazing Star: The Story of the Wise Men, CRC Publications (Grand Rapids, MI), 1998.

The Best Day Ever! The Story of Easter, CRC Publications (Grand Rapids, MI), 1998.

A Better Thing to Do: The Story of Jesus and Mary and Martha, CRC Publications (Grand Rapids, MI), 1998.

Come to Me! The Story of Jesus and the Children, CRC Publications (Grand Rapids, MI), 1998.

The Lost Sheep: The Story of the Good Shepherd, CRC Publications (Grand Rapids, MI), 1998.

Goodbye, for Now: The Story of Jesus' Return to Heaven, CRC Publications (Grand Rapids, MI), 1998.

Have a Great Day! The Story of Jesus and Zacchaeus, CRC Publications (Grand Rapids, MI), 1998.

Hosanna! The Story of Palm Sunday, CRC Publications (Grand Rapids, MI), 1998.

I Love You, Jesus! The Story of Mary's Gift to Jesus, CRC Publications (Grand Rapids, MI), 1998.

A Wonderful Sight! The Story of Jesus and a Man Who Couldn't See, CRC Publications (Grand Rapids, MI), 1998.

Work in Progress

Illustrating *Apostle's Creed* and *Stations of the Crib*, completion of both expected in 2003.

Sidelights

Patrick Kelley told *SATA:* "I enjoyed making animated movies as much as I did painting when I first began my artistic career some twenty years ago. Painting, like sculpting, was a wonder to watch unfold. I have kept this wonderment, continually refreshing my creativity. Now I am working more in the children's market, making fine art posters and prints, and enjoying it tremendously, much like I did all those years ago."

Biographical and Critical Sources

PERIODICALS

Booklist, October 1, 2001, Ilene Cooper, review of *God's Little Flower: The Story of St. Therese of Lisieux,* p. 334.

L

LANGTON, Jane (Gillson) 1922-

Personal

Born December 30, 1922, in Boston, MA; daughter of Joseph Lincoln (a geologist) and Grace (Brown) Gillson; married William Langton (a physicist), 1943; children: Christopher, David, Andrew. *Education:* Attended Wellesley College, 1940-42; University of Michigan, B.S., 1944, M.A., 1945; Radcliffe College, M.A., 1948; graduate study at Boston Museum School of Art, 1958-59. *Politics:* Democrat.

Addresses

Home—9 Baker Farm Rd., Lincoln, MA 01773.

Career

Writer. Teacher of writing for children at Graduate Center for the Study of Children's Literature, Simmons College, 1979-80, and at Eastern Writers' Conference, Salem State College. Prepared art work and visual material for educational program in the natural sciences entitled "Discovery," WGBH, Channel 2, Boston, MA, 1955-56. Volunteer worker for school and church. *Member:* Phi Beta Kappa.

Awards, Honors

Edgar Award nomination from Mystery Writers of America, 1962, for *The Diamond in the Window;* Newbery Honor Book award from Children's Services Division of American Library Association, 1980, for *The Fledgling;* Nero Wolfe Award, 1984, and Edgar Award nomination from Mystery Writers of America, 1985, both for *Emily Dickinson Is Dead.*

Writings

FOR CHILDREN

(And illustrator) *The Majesty of Grace,* Harper (New York, NY), 1961, published as *Her Majesty, Grace Jones,* pictures by Emily Arnold McCully, 1972.
The Diamond in the Window, illustrated by Erik Blegvad, Harper (New York, NY), 1962.
The Swing in the Summerhouse, pictures by Erik Blegvad, Harper (New York, NY), 1967.
The Astonishing Stereoscope, pictures by Erik Blegvad, Harper (New York, NY), 1971.
The Boyhood of Grace Jones, pictures by Emily Arnold McCully, Harper (New York, NY), 1972.
Paper Chains, Harper (New York, NY), 1977.
The Fledgling, Harper (New York, NY), 1980.
The Fragile Flag, Harper (New York, NY), 1984.
The Hedgehog Boy, illustrated by Ilse Plume, Harper (New York, NY), 1985.
Salt: From a Russian Folktale (picture book), illustrated by Ilse Plume, Hyperion Press (New York, NY), 1992.
The Queen's Necklace: A Swedish Folktale, illustrated by Ilse Plume, Hyperion Press (New York, NY), 1994.
The Time Bike, Harper Collins (New York, NY), 2000.

ADULT MYSTERY NOVELS

The Transcendental Murder, Harper (New York, NY), 1964, published as *The Minuteman Murder,* Dell (New York, NY), 1976.
(And illustrator) *Dark Nantucket Noon,* Harper (New York, NY), 1975.
(And illustrator) *The Memorial Hall Murder,* Harper (New York, NY), 1978.
(And illustrator) *Natural Enemy,* Ticknor & Fields (New York, NY), 1982.
(And illustrator) *Emily Dickinson Is Dead,* St. Martin's (New York, NY), 1984.
Good and Dead, St. Martin's (New York, NY), 1986.
(And illustrator) *Murder at the Gardner: A Novel of Suspense,* St. Martin's (New York, NY), 1988.
(And illustrator) *The Dante Game,* Viking (New York, NY), 1991.

(And illustrator) *God in Concord,* Viking (New York, NY), 1992.

(And illustrator) *Divine Inspiration: A Homer Kelly Mystery,* Viking (New York, NY), 1993.

The Shortest Day: Murder at the Revels, Viking (New York, NY), 1995.

(And illustrator) *Dead as a Dodo: A Homer Kelly Mystery,* Viking (New York, NY), 1996.

(And illustrator) *The Face on the Wall: A Homer Kelly Mystery,* Viking (New York, NY), 1998.

(And illustrator) *The Thief of Venice: A Homer Kelly Mystery,* Viking (New York, NY), 1999.

(And illustrator) *Murder at Monticello: A Homer Kelly Mystery,* Viking (New York, NY), 2001.

(Contributor of prose text) *Acts of Light* (includes poems by Emily Dickinson and paintings and drawings by Nancy Ekholm Burkert), New York Graphic Society, 1980. Manuscripts in the Kerlan Collection at University of Minnesota in Minneapolis and at Boston University.

Former children's book reviewer for the *New York Times Book Review.*

Sidelights

Jane Langton is the author of juvenile novels that focus on history, mystical adventures, and sometimes mystery, stories which "glow with a sense of history, place, and the value of the human individual spirit," according to a contributor for *St. James Guide to Young Adult Writers.* As an author for adults, Langston is known primarily as a mystery writer, particularly for her entertaining "Homer Kelly Mystery" series. "Without an inherited literary pattern, a writer could not even begin to write," said the award-winning author in an article for *Horn Book.* Langton once recalled that the children's fantasy novels of British authors Edith Nesbit and Arthur Ransome taught her "how sentences move along, how paragraphs wax and wane, how the action in a story rises and falls, how fictional characters talk to each other." "But if the memory of other books is his only source," she said in *Horn Book,* "his rehash will remain hash. In other words, if he doesn't use his own life experience in some way, if he makes no reference to reality as he has encountered it, his book will be inert, an exercise, a formula." Many of Langton's stories make use of her familiarity with the area around the town of Concord, Massachusetts, for their setting.

Langton once told of her father reading to his children the "Winnie the Pooh" stories and poetry of A. A. Milne. "We learned true things about human relations, about how to be a friend, about the many ways of being funny," Langton said of the stories. She also revealed that Milne's poetry was her introduction to that form of writing. "We understood, although we couldn't have explained it. It was a first grappling with tricky meanings, with unspoken things." Later, Langton started reading the poetry of British Romantic authors William Wordsworth, Samuel Taylor Coleridge, John Keats, and Percy Shelley. Commenting on Coleridge's "Kubla Khan," Langton declared that "The experience of

Jane Langton

delighted discovery was akin to the simpler pleasure of [Milne's] 'Halfway Down.'"

Langton said of one of her early attempts at writing, "One day I decided grandiosely to write a vast poem of my own. It would be about God and Heaven and Hell." But, she continued, "My tremendous poetic work on God and Heaven and Hell was never written, except for one amazing verse, which stunned me with its exalted splendor. I don't know how it came into my head. I could never think of other verses to equal it, and I gave up altogether."

Langton explored different fields of study at several schools. At the end of high school she became interested in art history because of a *Life* magazine series on art. After reading a biography of Marie Curie, Langton also thought of becoming a scientist. At Wellesley College, her freshman English teacher suggested majoring in English, but criticism from her next English teacher stifled the idea. In order to pursue a major in astronomy, Langton transferred to the University of Michigan, and she eventually married her physics laboratory partner, Bill. As a graduate student at Michigan, Langton changed her major to art history. Later, she transferred to Radcliffe College and Bill transferred to Harvard University, so that he could accept a job offer in Cambridge, Massachusetts. Uncertain about her dissertation work in art history, Langton decided to give up her studies in favor of becoming a mother.

Reading to her sons, Christopher and David, led Langton to think about writing children's books. Early in her career as an author, she wrote stories similar to those of Ransome and Nesbit. Langton remarked about her first attempts at writing books, "I began under the spell of those remembered English stories of gardens and kings and castles. Slowly over a period of several years I wrote three books. They all failed. But I'm glad I wrote them. Flops they were, but I was on the right path. Even as failures they were indispensable." Later, she said, the children's stories of Eleanor Estes showed her that "children's books didn't have to be about princesses in imaginary countries. They could be about ordinary people here and now."

In her article for *Horn Book,* Langton emphasized the value of writing stories that match the reader's experience: "And that is what is so important about getting down to the quick, down to this barely hidden level of daily reality. Whether he is a child or an adult, the reader recognizes it, he says, 'Yes that's right; that's the way it is. I couldn't have said it that beautifully, but it's true.' And then he feels a kind of relief at being found out, at being discovered. Bleak places in his own life are shown to be commonplace. His identical feelings are laid bare."

The first time one of her books was accepted for publication, the author felt that, in contrast to the many changes of direction when she was a student, she finally had a strong sense of her life's course. "It was a wonderful happiness. I've never forgotten how it felt, the understanding that from now on I was certain, that I knew what to do, I would go on the rest of my life from one book to another," she once recounted.

Georgie learns to fly with the help of a mysterious Canadian goose in this novel. (Cover illustration by Erik Blegvad.)

Langton once commented: "My books start with an interest in a place. This has been most often Concord, Massachusetts, with its several layers of history, both from revolutionary times and from nineteenth-century transcendental times. But it is the present time, littered about with the past, that I seem to want to write about. Putting real children (as real as I can make them) into a real setting (as real as I can copy it) and then pulling some sort of fantasy out of that litter of the past that lies around them—this is what particularly interests me.

"I am lucky in living in the town next to Concord. We go there very often for shopping, and walking or driving one is wading through air which to me seems thick with meaning."

The author further explained, "The town we had chosen to live in just happened to border on Walden Pond and the town of Concord. Slowly, almost unconsciously, I became aware of a man named Henry Thoreau, who had lived at the pond a century before our own time, and written a book called *Walden.*" Commenting on the impact of Thoreau upon her own work, Langton said, "For a writer it is essential, I think, to love the work of another writer. How can one care about one's own words, if one hasn't cared for the words of someone else? We all need high examples. I wasn't afraid that I would imitate Thoreau—how could anyone do that? But I could play with the ideas I so much loved." *The Diamond in the Window* quotes sections of Thoreau's writings. "The children in my story would live in Concord. Their adventures would spring from things that Thoreau had said, recited by a funny madman, their uncle Freddy."

In 1980, Langton received a Newbery Honor Book award for *The Fledgling,* a book about a girl whose dreams of flying come true when she rides on the back of a Canadian goose. "In lyrical nocturnal sequences, Georgie learns to fly, to sky-dive from the goose's back, twisting earthward in slow, diminishing spirals on the warm thermals over Walden Pond," noted Patricia Manning in a review for *School Library Journal.* Reviewing the audiocassette adaptation of that early story, Teresa Bateman, writing in *School Library Journal,* called the tale "gentle" and "exquisite."

The Fragile Flag, a sequel to *The Fledgling,* reflects Langton's involvement in protests against the war in Vietnam during the 1960s and early 1970s. "Eight years after the end of the war," the author once commented, "my recollection of the way we felt came rushing out in a book called *The Fragile Flag.* It's a story for young people about a children's march against nuclear weapons." "The portrayals of the children themselves are so effortless and true that it seems momentarily impossible that other writers could find it difficult to endow characters that young with distinctive personalities," said Nicholas Lemann in the *New York Times Book Review.* The author's children's books set in Concord, also including *The Astonishing Stereoscope* and *The Swing in the Summerhouse,* chronicle the Hall family as they learn about the world. In the sixth book in the series, *The*

Time Bike, eighth-grade Eddy gets a very mysterious bike which he discovers can take him through time. As he experiments traveling to different eras, a rotten banker in the present plots to evict the Halls from their house. Finally, the two plots "converge," according to a reviewer for *Book,* "in a coincidence that saves the house, ends the time travel, and leaves Eddy a bit wiser." A reviewer for *Publishers Weekly* felt that *The Time Bike* was a "whimsical and enthralling book, infused with a truly American flavor of magical realism."

In addition to children's books, Langton writes mystery novels for adults. Her children's book *The Diamond in the Window* and her adult mystery *Emily Dickinson Is Dead* both received Edgar Award nominations from the Mystery Writers of America. Langton also illustrates some of her adult crime novels. Commenting on *The Dante Game,* a writer for the *New York Times Book Review* asserted, "[Langton's] exuberant wit runs riot in the charming pen-and-ink drawings that have become her signature." The "Kelly" books, fourteen strong and growing, feature Homer and his wife Mary, both instructors at Harvard, who become sometimes unwilling sleuths in games of life and death. *Face on the Wall* deals with murder hitting close to the home of a children's book illustrator. Shelle Rosenfeld, writing in *Booklist,* found that book to be a "witty, sharp-edged mystery, while a contributor for *Publishers Weekly* called attention to "Langton's impish sense of humor" and a "wonderfully loathsome 10-year-old ... surely one of the most odious children created since *The Bad Seed.*" Reviewing 1999's *The Thief of Venice,* Bill Ott noted in *Booklist* that the book was an "ideal diversion for those who like to combine travel research with a little murder." A reviewer for *Publishers Weekly* also had high praise for *The Thief of Venice:* "With a master hand, Langton develops the various subplots into a sophisticated, elegantly constructed thriller...." Of *Murder at Monticello,* a contributor to *Publishers Weekly* felt that the "plot is as twisting and complex as the upper reaches of the Missouri River," while *Booklist*'s David Pitt found the same title to be a "clever mystery set against a fascinating historical backdrop" and a "surefire winner ... one of the high-water marks in a consistently outstanding series." The "Homer Kelly" series has also attracted a large young adult audience who enjoy Langton's pace and humor. In a review of *The Shortest Day,* a non-series mystery, *Booklist*'s Emily Melton summed up Langton's powers as a mystery writer, noting that, as always, the author "offers a charming story that's as cozy as a warm fire and a hot cup of tea on a cold day."

"As for things other than writing," Langton once commented, "I enjoy the confusion of domestic life; I especially like gardening, playing in a string group, and painting the house we live in, which is on the shore of what used to be known as Flint's Pond. Henry Thoreau first wanted to build his house here, but Mr. Flint wouldn't let him, and he had to make do with Walden, a mile or two away."

Biographical and Critical Sources

BOOKS

Carr, John C., *The Craft of Crime,* Houghton (Boston, MA), 1983.
Langton, Jane, *Something about the Author Autobiography Series,* Volume 5, Gale (Detroit, MI), 1988, pp. 203-221.
St. James Guide to Young Adult Writers, 5th edition, St. James Press (Detroit, MI), 1999.
Twentieth-Century Young Adult Writers, 1st edition, St. James Press (Detroit, MI), 1994.

PERIODICALS

Armchair Detective, winter, 1997.
Book, November, 2000, review of *The Time Bike,* p. 87.
Booklist, October 15, 1992, p. 434; November 1, 1993, p. 505; October 1, 1994, p. 327; November 1, 1995, Emily Melton, review of *The Shortest Day,* p. 457; October 15, 1996, p. 407; April 15, 1998, p. 1388; April 15, 1999, Bill Ott, review of *The Thief of Venice,* p. 1480; May 1, 2000, Shelle Rosenfeld, review of *The Face on the Wall,* p. 1609; January 1, 2001, David Pitt, review of *Murder at Monticello,* p. 924.
Christian Science Monitor, April 19, 1991, p. 13; August 6, 1992, p. 13; January 21, 1994, p. 17.
Horn Book, December, 1971; February, 1973, Jane Langton, "Down to the Quick: The Use of Daily Reality in Writing Fiction," pp. 24-30.
Library Journal, March 1, 1993, p. 124; October 1, 1995, p. 123; May 1, 1998, p. 143; February 1, 2001, p. 128.
Los Angeles Times Book Review, April 21, 1991.
New York Times, May 21, 1978.
New York Times Book Review, August 20, 1967; November 28, 1980; May 16, 1982; November 11, 1984, Nicholas Lemann, "Children's Crusade," p. 61; March 24, 1991, p. 37; June 21, 1992, p. 21; December 12, 1993, p. 29; December 10, 1995, p. 41; December 22, 1996, p. 21; February 18, 2001, p. 25.
New Yorker, August 13, 1984.
Newsweek, December 3, 1984.
Publishers Weekly, September 21, 1992, p. 94; August 23, 1993, p. 130; August 21, 1995, pp. 48-49; August 26, 1996, pp. 79-80; April 6, 1998, review of *The Face on the Wall,* p. 62; May 17, 1999, review of *The Thief of Venice,* p. 59; July 10, 2000, review of *The Time Bike,* p. 64; January 22, 2001, review of *Murder at Monticello,* p. 306.
School Library Journal, September, 1980, Patricia Manning, p. 73; December, 1992, p. 97; October, 1994, p. 110; September, 1998, p. 230; June, 2000, p. 148; April, 2001, Teresa Bateman, review of *The Fledgling,* p. 88.
Times Literary Supplement, December 4, 1969; April 16, 1970.
Tribune (Chicago), March 3, 1991.
Wall Street Journal, December 11, 1995, p. A13.
Washington Post Book World, May 11, 1980; December 21, 1980; June 17, 1984; January 13, 1985.
Wilson Library Bulletin, November, 1993, pp. 86-87.*

LAZARUS, Keo Felker 1913-1993

OBITUARY NOTICE—See index for *SATA* sketch: Born October 22, 1913, in Callaway, NE; died January 6, 1993, in Sunnyvale, CA. Physical education teacher and writer. Lazarus received her B.E. degree in 1938 from the University of California—Los Angeles. Her first book, *Rattlesnake Run,* was published in 1968. This work was followed by many additional titles for children, including *The Gismo, Tadpole Taylor, The Billy Goat in the Chili Patch, A Totem for Ti-Jacques* (1977), *The Gismonauts,* and *A Message from Monaal,* which was issued in 1980. In addition to writing books, she also contributed numerous stories and poems to the magazines *Jack and Jill, Cricket,* and *Highlights for Children.* She was a member of the Authors Guild, the Society of Children's Book Writers, the Chicago Children's Reading Round Table, Purdue University Writer's Group, and the Tippecanoe County Historical Association.

OBITUARIES AND OTHER SOURCES:

OTHER

Obituary research by Robert Reginald.

*   *   *

LEE, Huy Voun 1969-

Personal

Name is pronounced "Wei-wen Lee"; born April 2, 1969, in Cambodia; daughter of Ming Ching and Sung Chen (Chen) Lee; married Seiji Ikuta (a painter), November 9, 2000. *Education:* School of Visual Arts, B.F.A., 1992.

Addresses

Home—182 Bay 35th St., No. 2F, Brooklyn, NY 11214. *E-mail*—huylee-2000@yahoo.com.

Career

Writer and illustrator. Art work represented in exhibitions at Steinbaum Krauss Gallery, Barnes and Noble at Astor Place, and Society of Illustrators, all New York, NY. Authors Read Aloud, participant; art teacher to senior citizens at Caring Community and Greenwich House, New York, NY; gives readings of her works at public schools and other venues.

Writings

SELF-ILLUSTRATED CHILDREN'S BOOKS

At the Beach, Henry Holt (New York, NY), 1994.
In the Snow, Henry Holt (New York, NY), 1995.
In the Park, Henry Holt (New York, NY), 1998.
1, 2, 3, Go!, Henry Holt (New York, NY), 2000.
In the Autumn, Henry Holt (New York, NY), in press.

ILLUSTRATOR

Chang and the Tiger (reader), McGraw-Hill (New York, NY), 1997.
James Preller, *Cardinal and Sunflower,* HarperCollins (New York, NY), 1998.
Ray Crennan, *Hiroko Makes the Team* (reader), McGraw-Hill (New York, NY), 1999.

Contributor of illustrations to *America,* Lee & Low, 1997.

OTHER

Contributor to periodicals, including *Cricket, Spider, Let's Find Out,* and *BLL Teacher Planning Guide.*

Sidelights

Huy Voun Lee told *SATA,* "I cried a lot when I came to the United States from my war-torn country. In an effort to stop my persistent crying, my father recorded me and had me listen to myself over and over again. But every time the tape ended, I continued to cry. Then one day, he came home from Chinatown with a children's metal scissors and a glue stick, I was hooked. I spent countless hours cutting and glueing. When I was seven my brother and I broke my parent's bedroom door mirror while playing Tarzan. I decided to decorate the whole door with colorful construction papers. It was my largest collage ever. Unfortunately, my mother did not enjoy my creation. By the time I was in third grade, I spent the weekends making tiny blank books and illustrating the covers. Today, I am lucky to make a career of illustrating interiors of children's books, as well as the covers."

Biographical and Critical Sources

PERIODICALS

Booklist, June 1, 1994, Julie Corsaro, review of *At the Beach,* p. 1832; October 15, 1995, Susan Dove Lempke, review of *In the Snow,* p. 412; July, 1998, Susan Dove Lempke, review of *In the Park,* p. 1886; February 1, 2001, Ellen Mandel, review of *1, 2, 3, Go!,* p. 1054.
Publishers Weekly, April 11, 1994, review of *At the Beach,* p. 64; September 4, 1995, review of *In the Snow,* p. 69; April 13, 1998, review of *In the Park,* p. 74; November 27, 2000, review of *1, 2, 3, Go!,* p. 76.
School Library Journal, July, 1994, John Philbrook, review of *At the Beach,* pp. 95-96; December, 1995, Susan Middleton, review of *In the Snow,* p. 84; May, 1998, Margaret A. Chang, review of *In the Park,* p. 119; June, 1998, Carolyn Jenks, review of *Cardinal and Sunflower,* p. 118.

*   *   *

LESTER, Alison 1952-

Personal

Born November 17, 1952, in Foster, Australia; daughter of Donald Robert (a grazier) and Jean Rosalind (a nurse;

Alison Lester (sitting) with school children

maiden name, Billings) Lester; married Edwin Hume (a solicitor), January 22, 1977; children: Will, Clair, Lachlan. *Education:* Melbourne State College, Higher Diploma of Teaching, 1975. *Hobbies and other interests:* Horses, basketball, the beach, gardening, music, skiing, cooking, travel, photography, shopping for clothes.

Addresses

Home—Dore Rd., Nar Nar Goon North, Victoria 3812, Australia.

Career

Victorian Education Department, high school art teacher in Alexandra, Australia, 1976-77, high school art teacher at correspondence school in Melbourne, Australia, 1977-78; writer and illustrator, 1978—. *Exhibitions:* Post Office Gallery, Mornington, Victoria, Australia, 1984; Gallery Art Navie, Melbourne, Australia, 1985; Seasons Gallery, Sydney, Australia, 1985, 1986.

Awards, Honors

Picture Book of the Year Award, Children's Book Council of Australia, 1983, for illustrating *Thing;* Picture Book of the Year honour book/commendation/shortlist, Children's Book Council of Australia, 1986, for *Clive Eats Alligators,* 1988, for *Birk the Berserker,* 1990, for *The Journey Home,* and 1991, for *Magic Beach;* Australian Book Publishers Association design awards, 1989, for *Rosie Sips Spiders,* and 1990, for *Imagine.*

Writings

SELF-ILLUSTRATED

Clive Eats Alligators (also see below), Oxford University Press (Melbourne, Australia), 1985, Houghton (Boston, MA), 1986.

Ruby, Oxford University Press (Melbourne, Australia), 1987.

Rosie Sips Spiders (also see below), Oxford University Press (Melbourne, Australia), 1988, Houghton (Boston, MA), 1989.

Imagine, Allen & Unwin (Sydney, Australia), 1989, Houghton (Boston, MA), 1990.

The Journey Home, Oxford University Press (Melbourne, Australia), 1989, Houghton (Boston, MA), 1991.

Magic Beach, Allen & Unwin (Sydney, Australia), 1990, Little, Brown (Boston, MA), 1992.

Tessa Snaps Snakes (also see below), Oxford University Press (Melbourne, Australia), 1990, Houghton (Boston, MA), 1991.

Isabella's Bed, Oxford University Press (Melbourne, Australia), 1991, Houghton (Boston, MA), 1993.

My Farm, Allen & Unwin (St. Leonards, Australia), 1992, Houghton (Boston, MA), 1994.

I'm Green and I'm Grumpy, Dutton (New York, NY), 1993.

Monsters Are Knocking, Puffin (Ringwood, Australia), 1993.

Yikes!, Allen & Unwin (St. Leonards, Australia), 1993, Houghton (Boston, MA), 1995.

When Frank Was Four (also see below), Hodder Headline (Rydalmere, Australia), 1994, Houghton (Boston, MA), 1996.

Alice and Aldo, Allen & Unwin (St. Leonards, Australia), 1996.

Celeste Sails to Spain, Hodder Headline (Rydalmere, Australia), 1996, Houghton (Boston, MA), 1999.

Clive, Tessa, Rosie, and Frank (contains *Clive Eats Alligators, Tessa Snaps Snakes, Rosie Sips Spiders,* and *When Frank Was Four*), Hodder Headline (Sydney, Australia), 1997.

Ernie Dances to the Didgeridoo: For the Children of Gunbalanya, Houghton (Boston, MA), 2000.

SELF-ILLUSTRATED; "AUSTRALIAN BABY BOOKS" SERIES

Bibs and Boots, Viking Kestrel (Melbourne, Australia), 1989.

Happy and Sad, Viking Kestrel (Melbourne, Australia), 1989.

Crashing and Splashing, Viking Kestrel (Melbourne, Australia), 1989.

Bumping and Bouncing, Viking Kestrel (Melbourne, Australia), 1989.

JUVENILE NOVELS

The Quicksand Pony, Allen & Unwin (St. Leonards, Australia), 1996, Houghton (Boston, MA), 1998.

The Snow Pony, Allen & Unwin (Crows Nest, Australia), 2001.

ILLUSTRATOR

June Epstein, *Big Dipper,* Oxford University Press (Melbourne, Australia), 1980.

June Epstein, *Big Dipper Rides Again,* Oxford University Press (Melbourne, Australia), 1982.

Robin Klein, *Thing,* Oxford University Press (Melbourne, Australia), 1982.

Jumpety-Bumpety-Hop-and-Go-One: A Collection of Songs and Rhymes, Nelson (Melbourne, Australia), 1983.

Clanty Collective, *Taught Not Caught: Strategies for Sexuality Education,* Spiral (East Brunswick, Australia), 1983.

Robin Klein, *Thingnapped,* Oxford University Press (Melbourne, Australia), 1984.

Heather Fidge, *Kerplop!,* Oxford University Press (Melbourne, Australia), 1984.

Robin Klein, *Ratbags and Rascals,* Dent (Melbourne, Australia), 1985.

June Epstein, *Big Dipper Returns,* Oxford University Press (Melbourne, Australia), 1985.

June Epstein, *Big Dipper Songs,* Oxford University Press (Melbourne, Australia), 1985.

Maurice Saxby and Glenys Smith, compilers, *Just Imagine!,* Methuen (North Ryde, Australia), 1986.

Morris Lurie, *Night-Night! Seven Going-to-Bed Stories,* Oxford University Press (Melbourne, Australia), 1986.

June Epstein, *Noah's Ark Song,* Macmillan (South Melbourne, Australia), 1987.

June Factor, *Summer,* Puffin (Ringwood, Australia), 1987.

Robin Klein, *Birk the Berserker,* Omnibus Press (Adelaide, Australia), 1987.

Robin Klein, *Thinglets* (contains *Thingitis, Thing Gets a Job, Thing's Concert* and *Thing's Birthday*), Hodder Headline (Rydalmere, Australia), 1996.

ILLUSTRATOR; "AUGUSTUS" SERIES

June Epstein, *Augustus,* Nelson (Melbourne, Australia), 1984.

June Epstein, *Augustus Conducts the Band,* Nelson (Melbourne, Australia), 1984.

June Epstein, *Augustus Teaches the Children,* Nelson (Melbourne, Australia), 1984.

June Epstein, *Augustus Flies a Plane,* Nelson (Melbourne, Australia), 1984.

June Epstein, *Augustus Works in a Factory,* Nelson (Melbourne, Australia), 1984.

June Epstein, *Augustus Plays Football,* Nelson (Melbourne, Australia), 1984.

June Epstein, *Augustus the King,* Nelson (Melbourne, Australia), 1984.

June Epstein, *Augustus the Painter,* Nelson (Melbourne, Australia), 1984.

OTHER

S. O. S. (Speaking of Symbols), Nelson (Melbourne, Australia), 1984.

Sidelights

Since the publication of her first self-illustrated picture book in 1985, Australian artist Alison Lester has become internationally renowned for works that celebrate the creativity and energy of childhood. "Few writers and illustrators can match Alison Lester's ability to depict the rich imagination of children," Kevin Steinberger noted in *Magpies,* and in works such as *Imagine, The Journey Home, Magic Beach,* and *Isabella's Bed,* the author shows how a child's imagination can transform the ordinary into the fantastic. Lester has also created books that explore the everyday lives of children in all their individuality. The popular series beginning with *Clive Eats Alligators,* for instance, demonstrates that "Lester's insights into the world of young children are wonderfully perceptive," according to Joan Zahnleiter in another *Magpies* article. Additionally, the author has penned two novels for a younger audience that explore the lives of characters overcoming adversity to make the journey into adulthood.

"I grew up on a beef farm in Southern Victoria—an area of hot summers, but blasting cold wet winters," Lester once told *SATA*. "It is beautiful farming country, rolling from windswept hills down to great sandy beaches and sparkling sea. Life *was* the farm and as kids we were constantly riding after cattle (we loved it), or doing some other project on the farm." After spending four years at a boarding school, Lester finished secondary school; "like many of my contemporaries," she recalled, "[I] had no ambition other than to have a good time. Years of traveling, hiking, riding, and partying ensued. After I married Edwin, we traveled in South America for a year. I've also traveled in Australia and Southeast Asia."

Even after her marriage, Lester was not yet ready to develop her artistic interests into a career. "I'd always been fairly unambitious and lazy, I guess," she confessed to *SATA*, "until I was expecting my first child and saw a life as a housewife stretching out before me. I'd been illustrating class books at the correspondence school and loving it, so I took a folio to Oxford University Press and met Rosalind Price, then the children's editor at Oxford. My illustrating career took off from there." Lester illustrated several books by June Epstein and Robin Klein, including the latter's 1982 story *Thing*, which was named Picture Book of the Year by the Children's Book Council of Australia.

It was the publication of Lester's first self-penned and self-illustrated picture book, however, that really drew critical attention. *Clive Eats Alligators* follows a group of seven children as they participate in various everyday activities, such as playing or eating lunch, in their own unique style. The first six kids are featured in individual pictures over two pages; on the following double-page spread, the seventh is shown, usually acting in an unusual fashion; for instance, the daring Clive of the title actually eats alligator-shaped cereal for breakfast. Lester's watercolor illustrations are filled with detail but remain uncluttered; as a result, according to *Horn Book* contributor Ann A. Flowers, "the book is fun to look at, with lots to identify and lots to guess at." Lester uses the same format in *Rosie Sips Spiders,* which shows the children at home, gardening, and sleeping, among other activities. "The formula is brilliantly simple," Margery Fisher asserted in *Growing Point,* "and the wash and line pictures . . . invite long and delighted study by children." As Marcus Crouch remarked in *Junior Bookshelf, Rosie*

Having come out at the North Pole while digging a hole to China, two Australian children head home, meeting Santa Claus and Prince Charming, among other characters, on their fantastic journey. (From The Journey Home, *written and illustrated by Lester.)*

Sips Spiders shows "what the picturebook can achieve without benefit of story-line if word and picture proceed in perfect harmony."

Youngsters who enjoy search-and-find games will also enjoy *Imagine,* which shows a boy and girl using their imaginations to transport themselves into exotic landscapes filled with animals. In combining illustrations of children "playing pretend" with the "real" settings they have imagined, Lester "offers a lively—and lovely—exercise in using one's creativity," a *Publishers Weekly* reviewer noted. Another game of make-believe is the focus of *The Journey Home,* as two children voyage from the sandpit where they are digging to the North Pole and back. Along the way, Wild and Woolly meet Father Christmas, the Good Fairy, Prince Charming, and other characters from traditional tales. In *Horn Book,* Carolyn K. Jenks hailed Lester's "detailed, lighthearted watercolors," which are bordered with items corresponding to the characters, while a *Kirkus Reviews* critic commented that "the precise illustrations have an appealing blend of humor and charm." The combination of text and images in *The Journey Home,* a *Junior Bookshelf* reviewer concluded, "convey the movement of the journey and the possibilities that can be explored in dreams."

A summertime excursion is the inspiration for imaginary adventures in *Magic Beach,* as a sand castle is transformed into a palace rescue and beachcombing leads to buried treasure. The illustrations, featuring Lester's trademark border details, "both suit the mood and reinforce the verse," Nancy Menaldi-Scanlan remarked in *School Library Journal,* while the "rhymed text reads aloud beautifully," according to *Booklist* contributor Chris Sherman. Lester takes a more serious approach to *Isabella's Bed,* as the world of the imagination serves to heal a family. When Anna and Luis visit their grandmother, they love to sleep in "Isabella's" room, which is full of unusual objects from South America. Their grandmother will answer few questions about the items, instead telling the story of how Isabella left her home after her husband drowned. Described by a *Publishers Weekly* contributor as "fetching dreamscapes rendered in impressionistic brush strokes and intricate detailing," Lester's illustrations capture the children as they imagine how the mysterious objects fit into the story, and their discovery that "Isabella" is their grandmother allows them to help her with her grief. "The quiet, poetic text, exotic journey, and warm conclusion make a pleasant unusual tale," stated a *Kirkus Reviews* writer, adding praise for Lester's "serene, stylized illustrations." As a result, Steinberger concluded, *Isabella's Bed* is "a wonderful picture book to be savoured by readers of all ages."

Lester returned to the activities of seven friends Clive, Rosie, Frank, Ernie, Celeste, Tessa, and Nicky in *Tessa Snaps Snakes.* This time the children are portrayed keeping secrets, expressing dislikes, laughing at jokes, and sneaking midnight snacks. Praising the detailed illustrations and "cheerful zaniness" of Lester's prose, Lori A. Janick noted in *School Library Journal* that the author "proves adept at capturing the idiosyncrasies of

childhood." In *When Frank Was Four* Lester adds the dimension of a counting book to her account of the children's accomplishments. "Children will recognise themselves and their own prowess in the doings of the seven friends," *Magpies* contributor Joan Zahnleiter explained, especially as they are shown from ages one to seven. The critic praised the framed pictures and border details in *When Frank Was Four,* adding that the book's design "works as well and is as fresh and entertaining as is the book's predecessors."

The children's adventures continue in *Celeste Sails to Spain* and *Ernie Dances to the Didgeridoo: For the Children of Gunbalanya.* In the first title, the youngsters explore their favorite, but different, adventures in the same setting. For example, while visiting a museum, Clive searches out the dinosaurs while Tessa finds out how butter is made. This spotlight on the favorite activities "celebrate[s] individuality and stimulate[s] children to express their own likes and dislike," remarked *Booklist* contributor Lauren Peterson, who went on to recommend the book for educators looking "to discover their children's interests." *School Library Journal* critic Carol Ann Wilson claimed Lester's "crisp watercolor-and-pen artwork captures [the children's] adventuresome spirit." The characters' sixth adventure together, *Ernie Dances to the Didgeridoo,* follows Ernie as he spends a year with his family on an Australian aboriginal reserve. In letters to his six companions back home, the youngster talks about the new activities he does with his new friends, with Lester's illustrations providing a visual depiction of the events. Writing in *Booklist,* Peterson called *Ernie Dances to the Didgeridoo* an "entertaining picture book," while *School Library Journal* reviewer Grace Oliff found the book "a nicely designed, informative, and enjoyable addition, perfect for use with multicultural units."

Other characters are introduced in *Alice and Aldo,* an alphabet book that shares with young readers a day in the life of a young girl and her stuffed donkey, Aldo. After awaking, Alice begins her day by having "breakfast in bed" and continues through the day's alphabetically arranged events until she "yawns" in her yogurt and, eventually, falls asleep, "Zzzzz." According to *Horn Book* critic Lauren Adams, "with this combination of small, happy story and pictorial dictionary, Lester offers another child-appealing book." Other reviewers noticed the small, sometimes humorous, vignettes accompanying the larger illustrations, with a *Publishers Weekly* contributor remarking upon this "welcome splash of silliness" from author/illustrator Lester.

Lester journeyed back into her own childhood to create *My Farm,* an account of a typical year on an Australian farm. "In Lester's hands," Mary Lou Burket wrote in *Five Owls,* "the incidents of an unselfconscious childhood spent primarily out-of-doors, raising livestock and larking about, prove to have plenty of appeal." Illustrated with a combination of full-page paintings and miniature scenes, the book shows Lester's "particular knack" for inserting "lots of faithful, suggestive touches into the story," according to a *Kirkus Reviews* critic. *Bulletin of the Center for Children's Books* contributor

Betsy Hearne likewise praised the "vigorously varied" format and illustrations "that manage to include funny details without appearing crowded." Although the subject matter is ordinary, the critic concluded, in *My Farm* "it's the lively narrative action and rampant visual humor that energize everyday events for current listeners."

In her first children's novel, *The Quicksand Pony,* Lester offers "an intriguing, suspense-filled tale," according to *Horn Book* reviewer Kitty Flynn. The story focuses on two young characters who live quite different lives along the same rugged Australian coast. Thought to have drowned with his mother nine years earlier, Joe had been living alone with the mentally disturbed woman in an isolated valley. After she died when he was eight years old, Joe struggles to survive in the wild. Paralleling Joe's story is that of Biddy, another nine-year-old, who lives on her family's sheep and cattle ranch. While accompanying her family on a cattle drive, Biddy meets Joe after he saves her horse from a patch of quicksand. Torn between the need for human interaction and loyalty to the only home he has known, Joe follows Biddy and her family as they make their way across the headland, trying to decide if he should remain with them. Calling the book "an absorbing first novel with a strong sense of place," *Booklist* reviewer Carolyn Phelan predicted that "young readers will find plenty to like here." While noting that the shifting time periods and points of view might make for difficult reading, Flynn found Lester's "cliff-hanger chapter endings, well-developed characters, and vivid descriptions of both natural and emotional landscapes" attractive enough to encourage youngsters to keep turning the pages.

A companion volume, *The Snow Pony,* tells the story of another young girl living on a cattle farm in southeastern Australia. One day Dusty and her father find a wild pony in the mountains, a pony her father tames but who only allows Dusty as a rider. Drought conditions have made life rough for the farming family, and Dusty's winnings in the horse-jumping competitions she enters helps keep the family from losing their farm, but just barely. Tragedy strikes when a terrible accident occurs as the cattle are moved from their summer home in the mountains. With her father desperately needing medical attention, Dusty must quickly find a way down the snowy mountain in time to help her father. Reviewing the work in *Magpies,* Debbie Mulligan applauded *The Snow Pony*'s "emotionally intense plot describing all the hardships of living in the Australian bush."

"As my imagination increases, I can't think of any work I would rather be doing, unless it is driving cattle," Lester once told *SATA,* admitting that writing children's books is only one of several serious interests she plans to pursue. "I'm full of ideas about fabric design, toys, gardens, et cetera, and I may choose to follow one of these follies. It is hard to find time to work on all these creative things."

Her own memories of childhood memories, as well as her experiences with her own children provide much of Lester's inspiration. "I'm a country girl and still live in the bush," she added, "so the horses, dogs, cats, and garden also inspire me. I love to see the funny side of things. Kids are very funny and sharp, but it is difficult to communicate humor to them without being patronizing. I also love the exotic and strange."

Biographical and Critical Sources

BOOKS

Lester, Alison, *Alice and Aldo,* Allen & Unwin (St. Leonards, Australia), 1996.

PERIODICALS

Booklist, April 1, 1992, Chris Sherman, review of *Magic Beach,* p. 1457; March 1, 1998, Stephanie Zvirin, review of *Alice and Aldo,* p. 1140; December, 1998, Carolyn Phelan, review of *The Quicksand Pony,* p. 750; October 1, 1999, Lauren Peterson, review of *Celeste Sails to Spain,* p. 362; May 15, 2001, Lauren Peterson, review of *Ernie Dances to the Didgeridoo: For the Children of Gunbalanya,* p. 1759.

Bulletin of the Center for Children's Books, July-August, 1994, Betsy Hearne, review of *My Farm,* p. 365.

Five Owls, November-December, 1994, Mary Lou Burket, review of *My Farm,* pp. 35-36.

Growing Point, November, 1989, Margery Fisher, review of *Rosie Sips Spiders,* p. 5253.

Horn Book, July-August, 1986, Ann A. Flowers, review of *Clive Eats Alligators,* pp. 442-443; November-December, 1990, p. 729; Carolyn K. Jenks, review of *The Journey Home,* July-August, 1991, p. 449; July-August, 1998, Lauren Adams, review of *Alice and Aldo,* p. 476; January, 1999, Kitty Flynn, review of *The Quicksand Pony,* p. 66.

Junior Bookshelf, October, 1989, Marcus Crouch, review of *Rosie Sips Spiders,* pp. 216-217; April, 1990, p. 56; December, 1990, review of *The Journey Home,* p. 270.

Kirkus Reviews, April 15, 1991, review of *The Journey Home,* p. 545; March 15, 1992, p. 395; April 15, 1993, review of *Isabella's Bed,* p. 532; July 15, 1994, review of *My Farm,* p. 988.

Magpies, September, 1992, Kevin Steinberger, review of *Isabella's Bed,* p. 30; November, 1994, Joan Zahnleiter, review of *When Frank Was Four,* p. 14; May, 2001, Debbie Mulligan, review of *The Snow Pony,* p. 35.

Publishers Weekly, July 13, 1990, review of *Imagine,* p. 54; April 19, 1993, review of *Isabella's Bed,* p. 60; February 16, 1998, review of *Alice and Aldo,* p. 210; November 2, 1998, review of *The Quicksand Pony,* p. 83.

School Library Journal, May, 1990, p. 88; Lori A. Janick, review of *Tessa Snaps Snakes,* December, 1991, p. 96; June, 1992, Nancy Menaldi-Scanlan, review of *Magic Beach,* p. 97; August, 1988, Karen James, review of *Alice and Aldo,* p. 142; October, 1988, Connie Tyrrell Burns, review of *The Quicksand Pony,* p. 138; October, 1999, Carol Ann Wilson, review of *Celeste Sails to Spain,* p. 118; April, 2001, Grace Oliff, review of *Ernie Dances to the Didgeridoo,* p. 115.

OTHER

Allen & Unwin Web Site, http://www.allen-unwin.com.au/ (December 12, 2001).*

M

MAGUIRE, Gregory (Peter) 1954-

Personal

Born June 9, 1954, in Albany, NY; son of John (a journalist) and Helen (Gregory) Maguire; companion of Andy Newman (a painter); children: Luke, Alex, Helen. *Education:* State University of New York—Albany, B.A., 1976; Simmons College, M.A., 1978; Tufts University, Ph.D., 1990. *Politics:* Democrat. *Religion:* Roman Catholic. *Hobbies and other interests:* Painting in oils or watercolors, song writing, traveling.

Addresses

Agent—William Reiss, John Hawkins Associates, 71 West 23rd St., Ste. 1600, New York, NY 10010.

Career

Freelance writer, 1977—. Vincentian Grade School, Albany, NY, teacher of English, 1976-77; Simmons College Center for the Study of Children's Literature, Boston, MA, faculty member and associate director, 1979-87; Children's Literature New England, Cambridge, MA, codirector and consultant, 1987—. Residencies at Blue Mountain Center, 1986-90 and 1995-2001; artist-in-residence, Isabella Stewart Gardner Museum, 1994, Hambidge Center, 1998, and the Virginia Center for the Creative Arts, 1999.

Awards, Honors

Fellow at Bread Loaf Writers' Conference, 1978; 100 Best Books of the Year citation, New York Public Library, 1980, for *The Daughter of the Moon;* Children's Books of the Year citation, Child Study Children's Books Committee, 1983, and Teachers' Choice Award, National Council of Teachers of English, 1984, both for *The Dream Stealer;* Best Book for Young Adults citation, American Library Association (ALA), and Choices award, Cooperative Children's Book Center, 1989, both for *I Feel like the Morning Star;* Parents'

Gregory Maguire

Choice Award, and Children's Books of the Year citation, Child Study Committee, both 1994, both for *Missing Sisters;* Notable Children's Book citation, ALA, 1994, for *Seven Spiders Spinning;* Books for the Teen Age selection, New York Public Library, 1996, for *Oasis;* 100 Best Books citation, Young Book Trust (England), and Reading Association of Ireland Book Award finalist, both 1997, and Notable Social Studies Trade Book, National Council for the Social Studies/ Children's Book Council, all for *The Good Liar.*

Writings

FOR CHILDREN AND YOUNG ADULTS

The Lightning Time, Farrar, Straus (New York, NY), 1978.
The Daughter of the Moon, Farrar, Straus (New York, NY), 1980.

Lights on the Lake, Farrar, Straus (New York, NY), 1981.

The Dream Stealer, Harper (New York, NY), 1983.

The Peace and Quiet Diner (picture book), illustrated by David Perry, Parents' Magazine Press (New York, NY), 1988.

I Feel like the Morning Star, Harper (New York, NY), 1989.

Lucas Fishbone (picture book), illustrated by Frank Gargiulo, Harper (New York, NY), 1990.

Missing Sisters, M. K. McElderry Books (New York, NY), 1994.

Seven Spiders Spinning, Clarion (New York, NY), 1994.

The Good Liar, O'Brien Press (Dublin, Ireland), 1995, Clarion Books (New York, NY), 1999.

Oasis, Clarion Books (New York, NY), 1996.

Six Haunted Hairdos, illustrated by Elaine Clayton, Clarion Books (New York, NY), 1997.

Five Alien Elves, illustrated by Elaine Clayton, Clarion Books (New York, NY), 1998.

Crabby Cratchitt, illustrated by Andrew Glass, Clarion Books (New York, NY), 2000.

Four Stupid Cupids, illustrated by Elaine Clayton, Clarion Books (New York, NY), 2000.

Three Rotten Eggs, Clarion Books (New York, NY), 2002.

OTHER

(Editor, with Barbara Harrison) *Innocence and Experience: Essays and Conversations on Children's Literature,* Lothrop (Boston, MA), 1987.

Wicked: The Life and Times of the Wicked Witch of the West, Regan Books (New York, NY), 1995.

(Editor, with Barbara Harrison) *Origins of Story: On Writing for Children,* McElderry Books (New York, NY), 1999.

Confessions of an Ugly Stepsister, Regan Books (New York, NY), 1999.

Lost: A Novel, Regan Books (New York, NY), 2001.

Reviewer for *Horn Book, School Library Journal,* and *Christian Science Monitor;* contributor of story "The Honorary Shepherds" to collection *Am I Blue,* 1994.

Adaptations

Wicked: The Life and Times of the Wicked Witch is in develpment as a musical by composer Stephen Schwartz; *Confessions of an Ugly Stepsister* was filmed as a two-hour segment of ABC's Disney program, airing in March of 2002.

Sidelights

Gregory Maguire writes about people on the edge of crisis who manage to survive their ordeal and become stronger because of it. In forms as various as science fiction and fantasy, realistic problem novels, and rhyming picture books, Maguire explores the themes of loss, freedom, spirituality, the power of love, memory, and desire. Not one to shy away from complex plot development in his young-adult titles, Maguire also has a lighter side: his production might best be demonstrated by two 1994 titles: *Missing Sisters* and *Seven Spiders Spinning.* The former is a realistic portrait of growing up

Catholic and handicapped; the latter is a broad farce about seven Ice Age spiders that have some fun in a small Vermont town.

"Maguire's talents now look unpredictable," Jill Paton Walsh wrote in *Twentieth-Century Children's Writers* in 1989, and characterized such talents as "formidable and still developing." Walsh was a prescient critic: since the early 1990s Maguire has authored several more children's books as well as adult fiction and has edited writings on children's literature. While fantasy was his first inspiration, he has since expanded his genres to include realism and humor. However, through all his stories, both light and serious, one motif recurs: the loss of a mother.

In fact, Maguire's own mother was lost; she passed away while giving birth to him. With his writer father sick at the time of his birth, Maguire and his three older siblings were sent to stay with relatives for a time, although Maguire ended up in an orphanage until he was reunited with his newly remarried father. "It's right out of Dickens," Maguire conceded in an essay published in *Something about the Author Autobiographical Series* (*SAAS*). "But given the potential tragedy of those first couple of years, my childhood continued very warm and rewarding and free of any significant trauma." Three more children were born to his father and his stepmother, and Maguire finished his childhood years in a family of seven children, supported by his father's work as a humor columnist at the Albany *Times-Union* and science writer for the New York Health Department. "It wasn't exactly an affluent upbringing," Maguire explained. "There were library books, paper, and crayons, and that was it for the entertainment center. We did have a television, but that was really my father's hobby. We kids got to watch a few programs, but only ones we voted on and chose together. My parents were very strict about that. And it paid off. Talking with adult audiences now, I always tell them that one of the greatest stimulants to their kids' creativity is boredom. But children rarely have a chance to be bored anymore. We're always being entertained, by the T.V., the radio, computers."

Maguire grew up in a family that cared deeply about words. In addition to writing professionally, Maguire's father was also well known around Albany, New York, as a great storyteller, while his stepmother wrote poetry. A dictionary was kept with the cookbooks in the kitchen in case anybody needed to look up a word during dinner when the whole family was gathered together. "We were all very interested in word derivation, spurred on by my father and mother. Our favorite family story revolves around that passion. One night at dinner someone asked to have the butter passed, and my three-year-old brother, seated in his high chair, cocked his head. 'Butter,' he said reflectively. 'Is that from the Latin or the Greek?' So I guess we all had a love for words instilled in us from the beginning."

Maguire wrote his first story at age five and continued writing them—some as long as a hundred pages—

throughout high school and into college. In fact, he was only a junior in college when he wrote what would be his first published book, *The Lightning Time.* He began writing songs and painting at an early age, as well, two other creative outlets he has continued to develop. Life at the Irish-Catholic Maguire household was strict and regimented: "I had to pass the New York state drivers' test before I was allowed to ride a two-wheeled bicycle," Maguire recounted. "Now that's not just a Catholic upbringing; that's *strict.*"

Maguire attended Catholic school until he was eighteen. "In general," he recalled in *SAAS,* "I liked school. Although I was not at the top of the class, the nuns encouraged the creativity they saw in me. I have few of the horror stories that others do when they talk of their Catholic education. I thought that most of my teachers were intelligent and perceptive." A highlight of Maguire's early career in school was the authoring of a school play for Thanksgiving, a play with Catholic Pilgrims. "I didn't learn until I was in college that the Pilgrims weren't Catholic." But the play was a rousing success, so much so that when Maguire returned to the same school twelve years later as a teacher fresh out of college, he discovered the play was still being produced each Thanksgiving.

Maguire was also reading heavily in these years, and his interests tended toward fantasy writers such as Jane Langton, Madeleine L'Engle, and T. H. White. "I loved Langton's *The Diamond in the Window* when I read it at nine, and I even got the transcendental mysticism in it," Maguire recalled. "It was the first book I understood on several levels, and that was an eye-opener for me to see how powerful a book could be. White's *The Once and Future King* was another favorite. All of these book took you out of yourself and put you in another place and time. I thought that was wonderful magic and tried to do it with my own stories."

Maguire's stories led to the writing of *The Lightning Time* when he was twenty. "I went to SUNY in Albany," Maguire recalled, "an unmemorable experience. I was living at home and the courses were not demanding. It just wasn't what my idea of what college should be. When I was a junior majoring in English and art, I wrote a book for independent study, throwing in lots of the places and characters from my own youth. I went away to study in Dublin for a year, and when I came back I re-read the book and only then did I see it was probably a young adult title—the protagonist is twelve." Maguire typed one copy of the manuscript and sent it out four times over the next two years, choosing houses that published his favorite authors. The fourth bought it. "I was very lucky," Maguire explained.

The Lightning Time tells the story of young Daniel Rider, whose mother is away from home and in the hospital. The boy is staying with his grandmother in the Adirondacks. He meets a mysterious female cousin and together the two struggle to keep Saltbrook Mountain free from development. There is magic lightning that allows animals to talk, a villainous developer, and plenty

In Maguire's novel for teens, thirteen-year-old Hand overcomes guilt about his father's death and comes to forgive his mother for deserting them as she returns to revive her husband's Oasis Motel. (Cover illustration by Paul Hunt.)

of eerie effects. A contributor to *Publishers Weekly* thought that Maguire handled this first novel "with professional aplomb," and Ethel L. Heins concluded in *Horn Book* that Maguire "creates tension successfully, and writes with conviction and style."

Maguire followed up the success of his first fantasy with a related title, *The Daughter of the Moon,* which featured another cousin of Daniel Rider, twelve-year-old Erikka. Again the missing-mother theme is explored, this time because Erikka's real mother is dead and Erikka is being raised by a stepmother in Chicago. Searching for more refinement in her life, Erikka is drawn to a local bookshop as well as to a painting that an aunt has left with her. The painting is magic and Erikka can actually escape into the scene painted there, ultimately retrieving a long-lost lover of the Chicago bookshop owner. There are further sub-plots, resulting in a complexity that at least one critic felt bogged down the novel. A reviewer for *Horn Book,* while noting that some elements of the ambitious novel did not work, nevertheless concluded that Maguire "has created a fascinatingly complex heroine and a rich collection of adult and child characters."

As the third of Maguire's early fantasy novels, *Lights on the Lake* was meant to form a trilogy of sorts. Again the protagonist is Daniel Rider and he is once again in upstate New York, at Canaan Lake. This is Maguire country; a love for New York state's Lakes region developed during the author's youth. After the one friend Daniel makes, an Episcopalian priest, leaves on a vacation, the young man suddenly finds himself living in two different dimensions, influenced by the strange mists on the lake. A poet devastated by the death of a friend soon occupies Daniel's attention, and he sees a way to help the grieving man by bridging space and time and linking the living with the dead. "The provocative theme incorporates philosophical and spiritual concepts," noted Mary M. Burns in *Horn Book.* Although a reviewer for *Bulletin of the Center for Children's Books* thought that the elements of fantasy and realism did not work together, the reviewer did concede that Maguire "has a strong potential for polished and substantive writing."

"I basically look at those first three novels as novice work," Maguire recalled in his *SAAS* entry. "I was writing books as I thought books should be written. I wasn't really in touch with my own sense of what makes a book. They were imitative in form, but drew very heavily from my own past and preoccupations. When I look back at those three books, I see that I was working on the theme of accepting responsibility. But with my next book, I created my own form. I wasn't imitating anything else I'd read." That next book was *The Dream Stealer,* set in Russia and blending several age-old motifs from Russian folk tales: the Firebird, Vasilissa the Beautiful, and Baba Yaga. The story of how two children set out to save their village from the terrible wolf, the Blood Prince, *The Dream Stealer* blends magic and realism to create a "fantasy full of tension and narrative strength," according to Ethel L. Heins of *Horn Book.* "A first rate fantasy with blood chilling villainy countered with high humor and heroism," concluded Helen Gregory, reviewing the book in *School Library Journal.* And Walsh, writing in *Twentieth-Century Children's Writers,* called *The Dream Stealer* the work of "a writer finding his voice, and putting not a foot wrong."

"I'm still proud of that book," Maguire said. "I fictionalized a handful of different folk and fairy tales and blended them in a plot with its own trajectory and characterization. I was writing a book that connected more to my inner child—an inveterate reader of fantasy, that child—I wasn't simply developing a story inspired by others."

Meanwhile, Maguire had taken a position at Simmons College in their fledgling program in children's literature and was earning his doctorate in American and English literature. "I'm not sure there is a lot of carryover from being an academic in children's literature to the writing

of it," Maguire explained in *SAAS.* "You surely do not have to study literature or creative writing to be able to write. Reading helps, of course, and to that extent, a study of children's literature can help in the writing of it. You keep up with what is being published and you're exposed to many more books than you would be otherwise. But teaching children's literature doesn't automatically make somebody a children's book writer, just as all English literature professors are not necessarily fiction writers." Busy with studies and teaching as well as with the compilation of a book of essays in children's literature, Maguire did not publish his next fiction title for five years. 1989's *I Feel like the Morning Star* was a bit of a departure in that the fantasy element was played down. Set in a post-atomic underworld, the book has a science-fiction form, but is at heart an adventure novel about three rebellious teenagers who want to break out of their prison-like underworld colony. Roger Sutton, reviewing the novel in *Bulletin of the Center for Children's Books,* called attention to Maguire's penchant for figurative language and detail as a quality that "mired" an otherwise suspenseful escape novel. Other reviewers, such as Jane Beasley in *Voice of Youth Advocates,* thought the work compelling, with Beasley noting that the "suspense builds to a 'can't-put-it-down' threshold." And Pam Spencer, writing in *School Library Journal,* called the book a "top choice for young adults."

"Ultimately, *I Feel like the Morning Star* is about bucking authority," Maguire said. "It was during this time that I was involved with anti-nuclear demonstrations. The book grew out of those concerns." A for-hire picture book, *The Peace and Quiet Diner,* followed and then came *Lucas Fishbone,* an attempt at a sophisticated picture book for young adults. "Actually," Maguire once told *SATA,* "the writing in *Lucas* is some that I'm the most proud of. The story is a poetic meditation on death and the cycle of life, but somehow it never found its audience." Some critics were less than pleased, such as *School Library Journal* contributor Heide Piehler, who found the work "overwhelming and confusing," and a *Publishers Weekly* contributor who dubbed *Lucas Fishbone* "overwritten."

After the lukewarm reception accorded *Lucas Fishbone,* there followed another hiatus in Maguire's publishing career, although he continued to write his usual five pages a day. While living in London he did the writing on what would become *Missing Sisters.* While on a speaking tour in the U.S., "I saw something on television" Maguire explained. "It was the story of how two brothers who were separated at birth later rediscovered each other, and the story made a real impression on me." Maguire took that germ of an idea with him when he returned to England. Shorter than his other books, *Missing Sisters* is also Maguire's first realistic story, employing none of the fantasy and science fiction elements of his earlier books. It is set in the 1960s and tells the story of a hearing-and-speech-impaired girl who loses the one person close to her—a Catholic nun—but also finds her own missing sister. "The storytelling is sure and steady," wrote Roger

Sutton of *Bulletin of the Center for Children's Books,* while a *Horn Book* contributor found it "An unusual and compelling picture of life in a Catholic home." "What I wanted to accomplish with the book was pretty simple," Maguire explained in his interview. "To portray the positive effects of a religious childhood. I'm not trying to proselytize with this book, but I did have good experiences with the nuns when I was a kid, and I think it's important that people acknowledge the way religion can create a social context, can form community." When *Missing Sisters* won a Parents' Choice Award, Maguire felt his vision was redeemed.

Maguire's next title was inspired by reactions of the kids to his speaking engagements. "Over the years," Maguire explained to *SATA*, "I've developed a very funny presentation. The kids usually howl at my speech, but when they learn that I don't have any humorous books, they're disappointed." Maguire set out to cure that disappointment with *Seven Spiders Spinning,* which has been characterized as something on the order of Roald Dahl meets Mother Goose. Seven spiders from Siberia escape en route to a lab for study and make their way to Vermont, where they discover seven girls whom they focus on as their mothers. The problem is, the spiders literally have the kiss of death, and the girls dispatch several of them. There are humorous subplots galore in this "high-camp fantasy-mystery," according to *Publishers Weekly.* Hazel Rochman, writing in *Booklist,* commended Maguire on the "comic brew" and noted that the book would be "the stuff of many a grade-school skit." "A lighthearted fantasy," concluded a *Kirkus Reviews* critic, "that, while easily read, is as intricately structured as a spider's web."

The Good Liar, published in Ireland, was another stylistic departure for Maguire. Set in occupied France in 1942 and written in epistolary style, it tells the story of three brothers who have a fibbing contest that ultimately becomes a matter of life and death. *Oasis,* another young adult title, explores the effects of the loss of his father on thirteen-year-old boy Hand. "I was looking at the idea of crisis with the character Hand," Maguire explained. "At the idea that the rest of the world doesn't slow down when you're in crisis. You just have to keep functioning."

Maguire's largest shift in writing was the leap he made into adult fiction with *Wicked: The Life and Times of the Witch of the West.* "It was an amazing amount of fun working on that novel," Maguire said. "I could indulge myself in the complexity of an adult book. It spans thirty-eight years in a person's life and has over forty characters." He continued focusing on an adult readership with his next title, *Confessions of an Ugly Stepsister,* a combination of mystery, fairy tale, and fantasy set in seventeenth-century Holland. The story begins at a time when the country is engulfed in tulip trade, with thousands on the verge of losing fortunes invested in tulip bulbs. Among these are Margarethe and her two daughters, Iris and Ruth. Margarethe is a native of England, and following the murder of her husband, she is bringing her daughters back home to begin life in

the English village of Haarlem. Shunned by the locals, who believe she is a witch, Margarethe eventually finds work with an artist named Schoonmaker who lives on the outskirts of town. The family eventually moves to live with the van den Meers, a business family that has made its fortunes by luring people into making tulip investments. Iris, who is charged to serve as companion to Clara van den Meer, the daughter of the household, soon realizes that there is something amiss in the household and soon all their lives are in even greater turmoil as the three women learn to deal with this latest challenge in their lives.

Reviewing *Confessions of an Ugly Stepsister* for the *Tribune News Service,* Brenda Cronin praised this "arresting" novel, in particular for its "precise and inventive use of language." Cronin was especially impressed with Maguire's ability to "conjure familiar scenes with new descriptions" and his perceptive observations about human beings. Similarly, a reviewer for *Publishers Weekly* noted that Maguire is able to present "an astute balance of the ideal and sordid sides of human nature in a vision that fantasy lovers will find hard to resist." Maguire merged his interest in children's fairy tales and adult fantasy fiction in his next publication, *Lost.* A "deftly written, compulsively readable modern-day ghost story," said a reviewer for *Publishers Weekly, Lost* traces the adventures of American writer Winifred Rudge, as she visits London to research a novel about Jack the Ripper.

Of his future plans as a writer, Maguire explained that, "ideally, I'd like to continue writing for both children and adults. It's all writing. I still remember the writers I read as a child and the wonderful worlds they introduced me to. Children deserve the best that can be served up to them, and as a child I certainly profited from reading fantastic writers. I'd like someday to be a good enough writer to enrich a child's life as mine was enriched."

Biographical and Critical Sources

BOOKS

Something about the Author Autobiography Series, Volume 22, Gale (Detroit, MI), 1996.
Twentieth-Century Children's Writers, 3rd edition, St. James Press (New York, NY), 1989.

PERIODICALS

Booklist, March 15, 1994, p. 1342; June 1, 1994, p. 1798; September 15, 1994, Hazel Rochman, review of *Seven Spiders Spinning,* p. 136; September 15, 1996, p. 232; April 15, 1999, Carolyn Phelan, review of *The Good Liar,* p. 1530; December 1, 2000, GraceAnne A. DeCandido, review of *Four Stupid Cupids,* p. 706; October 15, 2001, Kristine Huntley, review of *Lost,* p. 383.
Bulletin of the Center for Children's Literature, July-August, 1980, p. 219; February, 1982, review of *Lights on the Lake;* May, 1989, Roger Sutton, review of *I Feel like the Morning Star,* p. 230; June, 1994, Roger Sutton, review of *Missing Sisters,* pp. 327-328.

Horn Book, October, 1978, Ethel L. Heins, review of *The Lightning Time,* pp. 517-518; June, 1980, Mary M. Burns, review of *The Daughter of the Moon;* April, 1982, Mary M. Burns, review of *Lights on the Lake,* pp. 167-168; October, 1983, Ethel L. Heins, review of *The Dream Stealer,* pp. 576-577; July-August, 1994, review of *Missing Sisters,* pp. 454-455; July, 1999, review of *The Good Liar,* p. 471; January, 2000, review of *Origins of Story: On Writing for Children,* p. 105.

Kirkus Reviews, July 15, 1978, p. 750; May 1, 1980, p. 585; February 1, 1982, p. 136; March 1, 1989, p. 380; February 15, 1994, p. 229; July 15, 1994, review of *Seven Spiders Spinning,* p. 989; August, 15, 2001, review of *Lost,* p. 1154.

Library Journal, September 1, 1999, Francisca Goldsmith, review of *Confessions of an Ugly Stepsister,* p. 234; October 1, 2001, Margee Smith, review of *Lost,* p. 141.

Los Angeles Times Book Review, October 29, 1995, p. 4.

New York Times, October 24, 1995, p. C17.

New York Times Book Review, November 26, 1995, p. 19; December 12, 1999, Gardner McFall, review of *Confessions of an Ugly Stepsister,* p. 28; December 26, 1999, Malachi Duffy, review of *Wicked: The Life and Times of the Wicked Witch of the West,* p. 19.

Publishers Weekly, June 5, 1978, review of *The Lightening Time,* p. 89; September, 1978, Pam Spencer, review of *I Feel like the Morning Star,* p. 143; September 28, 1990, review of *Lucas Fishbone,* pp. 101-102; August, 1994, review of *Seven Spiders Spinning* p. 80; March 22, 1999, review of *The Good Liar,* p. 93; August 16, 1999, review of *Confessions of an Ugly Stepsister,* p. 58; September 10, 2001, review of *Lost,* p. 60.

School Library Journal, September, 1978, p. 143; May, 1980, Marjorie Lewis, review of *The Daughter of the Moon,* p. 69; February, 1984, Helen Gregory, review of *The Dream Stealer,* p. 75; May, 1989, Pam Spencer, p. 127; December, 1990, Heide Piehler, review of *Lucas Fishbone,* p. 84; October, 2000, Eva Mitnick, review of *Four Stupid Cupids,* p.164.

Tribune News Service, December 22, 1999, Brenda Cronin, review of *Confessions of an Ugly Stepsister,* p. K2155.

Voice of Youth Advocates, June, 1989, Jane Beasley, review of *I Feel like the Morning Star,* p. 117; December, 1994, pp. 277-278; April, 1995, p. 24; February, 1997, p. 330.

Wilson Library Bulletin, December 1989, p. 113; September, 190, p. 12.

*   *   *

McCULLOCH, Sarah
See URE, Jean

McGIVERN, Justin 1985-

Personal

Born February 6, 1985, in Wausau, WI; son of Andrew (an exhibition curator) and Jeana (an art specialist; maiden name, Jaeger) McGivern. *Religion:* Unitarian-Universalist. *Hobbies and other interests:* Soccer.

Addresses

Agent—c/o Author Mail, Steck-Vaughn Publishing, P.O. Box 690789, Orlando, FL 32819-0789. *E-mail*—JAM10ZZ@aol.com.

Career

Student and writer. Guest on media programs. *Member:* Wisconsin Youth Soccer Association, Wausau Soccer Club.

Awards, Honors

Winner of "publish-a-book contest," Raintree Steck-Vaughn, 1998, for *Broccoli-Flavored Bubble Gum.*

Writings

Broccoli-Flavored Bubble Gum, illustrated by Patrick Girouard, Raintree Steck-Vaughn (Austin, TX), 1996.

"Kid editor," *Countdown,* 1996-97.

Work in Progress

Don't Talk with Food.

Biographical and Critical Sources

PERIODICALS

Countdown, summer, 1997, "Super Soccer."
Curiosity, January, 1996, "Justin McGivern: Kid Author."
Wisconsin Trails, summer, 1997.*

*   *   *

McGIVERN, Maureen Daly
See DALY, Maureen

*   *   *

McMILLAN, Bruce

Personal

Born in Boston, MA; son of Frank H., Jr. and Virginia M. W. McMillan; married V. Therese Loughran, 1969 (divorced, 1989); married Lori Beth Evans, 1997; children: (first marriage) Brett. *Education:* University of Maine—Orono, B.S., 1969.

Addresses

Home—176 County Rd., P.O. Box 85, Shapleigh, ME 04076-0085. *E-mail*—bruce@brucemcmillan.com.

Career

Maine Public Broadcasting Network, Orono, ME, director and photographer, 1969, producer and director, 1969-73; island caretaker, McGee Island, ME, 1973-75; photographic illustrator and writer, 1975—. University of Southern Maine, instructor in children's literature, 1985—; University of New Hampshire, instructor, 1988—. Book Adventures, Inc., puffin tour guide in Iceland, 1997—; public speaker, 1980—. Apple Island Books, publisher. *Member:* Authors Guild, Society of Children's Book Writers and Illustrators.

Awards, Honors

School Library Journal Best Book, American Booksellers Association (ABA) Pick of the List, and *Parents* magazine Best Kid's Book designations, all 1983, all for *Here a Chick, There a Chick;* ABA Pick of the List, and Library of Congress Children's Book of the Year, both 1984, both for *Kitten Can ...;* American Library Association (ALA) Notable Book, 1986, for *Counting Wildflowers;* Outstanding Science Trade Book for Children designation, National Science Teachers Association/Children's Book Council (NSTA/CBC), 1986, for

Bruce McMillan

Becca Backward, Becca Frontward; School Library Journal Best Book designation and *Parenting* certificate of excellence, both 1989, both for *Super, Super, Superwords; Time To ...* included among one hundred best books for reading and sharing, New York Public Library, 1989; *Parents* best kid's book, and Outstanding Science Trade Book for Children designation, NSTA/CBC, both 1990, and ALA Notable Book designation, 1991, all for *One Sun; Parenting* certificate of excellence, 1990, and Adkin Robinson Award, 1991, both for *Mary Had a Little Lamb;* Library of Congress children's book of the year, 1991, and *Scientific American* Young Reader's Book Award, 1996, both for *The Weather Sky; Parents* Best Kid's Book designation, 1991, for *Play Day;* ALA Notable Book, and *Parents* Best Kid's Book designations, both 1991, both for *Eating Fractions;* ABA Pick of the Lists, and Outstanding Science Trade Book for Children designation, NSTA/CBC, 1992, for *The Baby Zoo,* and 1995, for *Puffins Climb, Penguins Rhyme; Parenting* certificate of excellence, 1992, for *One, Two, One Pair!;* Outstanding Science Trade Book for Children designations, NSTA/CBC, 1992, for *Going on a Whale Watch,* 1993, for *Penguins at Home,* and 1995, for *Summer Ice;* John Burroughs Nature Book for Young Readers award, 1993, for *A Beach for the Birds;* ABA Pick of the Lists designations, 1994, for *Sense Suspense,* and 1997, for *Wild Flamingos;* Parents' Choice Honor Book, *School Library Journal* Best Book of the Year, and Outstanding Science Trade Book for Children designation, NSTA/CBC, all 1995, and ALA Notable Book, Maine Librarians Association Lupine Honor Book, and *Hungry Mind Review* Children's Book of Distinction, all 1996, all for *Nights of the Pufflings; Jelly Beans for Sale* cited among New York Public Library's one hundred best books for reading and sharing, 1996, and named an ALA Notable Book, 1997; Parent's Guide Children's Media Award for nonfiction, 1998, for *Salmon Summer.*

Writings

FOR CHILDREN; AUTHOR AND PHOTOGRAPHER

Finestkind o'Day: Lobstering in Maine, Lippincott (Philadelphia, PA), 1977.

The Alphabet Symphony, Greenwillow (New York, NY), 1977.

The Remarkable Riderless Runaway Tricycle, Houghton (Boston, MA), 1978.

Apples: How They Grow, Houghton (Boston, MA), 1979.

Making Sneakers, Houghton (Boston, MA), 1980.

(With son, Brett McMillan) *Puniddles,* Houghton (Boston, MA), 1982.

Here a Chick, There a Chick, Lothrop (New York, NY), 1983.

Ghost Doll, Houghton (Boston, MA), 1983, revised, Apple Island Books, 1997.

Kitten Can ..., Lothrop (New York, NY), 1984.

Counting Wildflowers, Lothrop (New York, NY), 1986.

Becca Backward, Becca Frontward: A Book of Concept Pairs, Lothrop (New York, NY), 1986.

Step by Step, Lothrop (New York, NY), 1987.

Dry or Wet?, Lothrop (New York, NY), 1988.

With the help of full-color photographs, young readers learn to count and identify twenty woodland flowers in **Counting Wildflowers,** *written and photo-illustrated by McMillan.*

Growing Colors, Lothrop (New York, NY), 1988.

Fire Engine Shapes, Lothrop (New York, NY), 1988.

Super, Super, Superwords, Lothrop (New York, NY), 1989.

Time To ..., Lothrop (New York, NY), 1989.

One, Two, One Pair!, Scholastic (New York, NY), 1990.

One Sun: A Book of Terse Verse, Holiday House (New York, NY), 1990.

The Weather Sky, Farrar, Straus (New York, NY), 1991.

Play Day: A Book of Terse Verse, Holiday House (New York, NY), 1991.

Eating Fractions, Scholastic (New York, NY), 1991.

The Baby Zoo, Scholastic (New York, NY), 1992.

Beach Ball—Left, Right, Holiday House (New York, NY), 1992.

Going on a Whale Watch, Scholastic (New York, NY), 1992.

Mouse Views: What the Class Pet Saw, Holiday House (New York, NY), 1993.

A Beach for the Birds, Houghton (Boston, MA), 1993.

Penguins at Home: Gentoos of Antarctica, Houghton (Boston, MA), 1993.

Sense Suspense: A Guessing Game for the Five Senses, Scholastic (New York, NY), 1994.

Nights of the Pufflings, Houghton (Boston, MA), 1995.

Puffins Climb, Penguins Rhyme, Harcourt (San Diego, CA), 1995.

Summer Ice: Life along the Antarctic Peninsula, Houghton (Boston, MA), 1995.

Grandfather's Trolley, Candlewick Press (Cambridge, MA), 1995.

Jelly Beans for Sale, Scholastic (New York, NY), 1996.

(With Kathy Mallat) *The Picture That Mom Drew,* Walker (New York, NY), 1997.

Wild Flamingos, Houghton (Boston, MA), 1997.

In the Wild, Wild North, Scholastic (New York, NY), 1997.

Salmon Summer, Houghton (Boston, MA), 1998.

Gletta the Foal, Marshall Cavendish (Freeport, NY), 1998.

Days of the Ducklings, Houghton (Boston, MA), 2001.

OTHER

(Photographer) *Punography* (adult), Penguin (New York, NY), 1978.

(Photographer) *Punography Too* (adult), Penguin (New York, NY), 1980.

(Photographer) Raffi, *Everything Grows* (children), Crown (New York, NY), 1989.

(Photographer) Sarah Josepha Hale, *Mary Had a Little Lamb* (children), Scholastic (New York, NY), 1990.

Contributor to *Natural History, New Advocate, Down East, Life, US,* and *Yankee.*

Adaptations

The Remarkable Riderless Runaway Tricycle was filmed by Evergreen Productions and Phoenix/BFA Films & Video.

Sidelights

Photographer and children's author Bruce McMillan specializes in "photo-illustration," which he describes as photographing ideas. "The ideas start in the mind of the illustrator," he once commented. "The ideas flow from the illustrator's mind to what he creates in front of him. He paints the scene with light. He sketches the scene with preliminary photos. Then the ideas flow back into the camera, the illustrator's tool." Many of McMillan's publications for children are concept books, which illustrate such things as money, geometry, growth, opposites, time, and counting, using a creative approach that invites readers to look at the world around them with fresh eyes. Praising his 1986 *Counting Wildflowers* as a "deftly constructed multipurpose concept book" in a review for *Horn Book,* Mary A. Burns added that McMillan here "excels in clarity of design and striking representation of an appealing subject." Catherine Wood made a similar assessment of McMillan's work in *School Library Journal,* noting that *Counting Wildflowers* "will be enjoyed by children and can be used in a number of ways by creative educators."

Raised in Maine, McMillan acquired his first camera when he was five, and by the time he reached high school he was proficient enough to be chief photographer for his school newspaper. A university degree in biology reflects his interest in science and wildlife that would provide the basis for many of his concept books. A love of the sea found him spending much of his time along the Maine coast, and assignments he received as a freelance photographer for magazines soon found him globe-hopping: from the Antarctic to Venezuela to the Caribbean to California. An interest in writing developed in his adult years, and meshed with his talent as a photographer to make him a successful artist-illustrator for children. Each of his books starts with a subject, which he researches. Then comes the photography—"I take many more bad pictures than people can imagine" before capturing the perfect image, he admitted to *Popular Nonfiction Authors for Children*—followed by the text. In addition to working on his own books, McMillan also teaches at several universities near his home in Maine.

McMillan's photos and two-word, rhyming sentences depict the daily life of puffins and penguins in **Puffins Climb, Penguins Rhyme.**

McMillan's 1983 picture book *Here a Chick, There a Chick* uses the life of a yellow chick from hatching through its discovery of the world as a way of illustrating the concept of opposites. According to a *New York Times Book Review* contributor, "The miracle of new life, almost palpable in these pages, lingers long after the lessons become rote." In *Kitten Can ...* McMillan uses the antics of a frisky kitten to demonstrate a variety of verbs, from "stare" to "crawl" and "dig." His work prompted *Horn Book* contributor Ann A. Flowers, to note that McMillan's "excellent colored photographs and the engaging calico kitten make an irresistible sequence." *Growing Colors* teaches children to recognize color by matching hues with fruits and vegetables. A *Bulletin of the Center for Children's Books* reviewer thought *Growing Colors* "consistently well designed," and maintained that "this is notably a treat for kids and an example of photography as an art form in picture books." *Dry or Wet?* introduces the concepts mentioned in its title, and photographs feature children in before-and-after poses. In *Super, Super, Superwords,* McMillan presents a colorful grammar lesson, as a group of children engage in activities kindergartners can relate to—measuring, sitting, carrying, playing—as a way to illustrate the concept of comparison. Another reviewer in *Bulletin of the Center for Children's Books* stated that McMillan "demonstrates the concept with clarity, humor, and occasional wit."

In addition to concept books, McMillan has been inspired by the beauty of the chillier parts of planet Earth. In *Summer Ice: Life along the Antarctic Peninsula,* he captures the wildlife and scenery of this southernmost region during the warm season, when humpback whales, penguins, and seals traverse the icy glaciers. In *Booklist,* Carolyn Phelan called *Summer Ice* a "handsome introduction to the wildlife of the Antarctic Peninsula," while *School Library Journal* contributor Melissa Hudak praised the fact that McMillan's photography—"brilliant in its beauty and attention to detail"—is augmented by information on plants and animals. Other books with a similar focus include *Penguins at Home: Gentoos of Antarctica* and *Going on a Whale Watch,* the last a documentary of a trip taken by a group of children off the coast of Maine. Praising McMillan's photographs as "bright, intense, and absolutely sparkling," *School Library Journal* contributor Valerie Lennox found *Going on a Whale Watch* "first-rate nonfiction" for young children. "Every choice McMillan makes here is informed by intelligence and an awareness of his audience," added a *Kirkus Reviews* critic.

Several trips to Iceland during the 1990s provided the opportunity for the photographer to produce *Night of the Pufflings, In the Wild, Wild North,* and *Gletta the Foal.* In *In the Wild, Wild North* McMillan introduces nine-year-old Margrét and follows her as she and her Icelandic pony Perla learn to herd sheep in preparation for *réttir*—the annual fall roundup that takes place in the island's rocky, mountainous interior. "The text flows smoothly," noted Carol Schene in *School Library Journal,* "capturing the young girl's activities and also

Icelandic children help baby puffins make their first flights in McMillan's unusual Night of the Pufflings.

providing informational insights into this way of life." *Gletta the Foal* is a gentle story about a young Icelandic foal—one of the smallest breeds of pony in the world—as it attempts to find the source of a sound it has never before encountered. Praising the "vivid blues and earth tones of the vast Icelandic landscape" captured by McMillan's camera lens, *School Library Journal* contributor Lee Bock called *Gletta the Foal* a "beautiful, quiet book for youngsters who enjoy solving a simple mystery."

McMillan once commented, "Three books into my career I realized that I made books with happy endings. It wasn't a conscious decision. It was a reflection of me. I'm a happy person and I love a happy ending. Since then, I've consciously followed this with all my books. My photo-illustrated concept books are a combination of teaching concepts and relating a story—with a happy ending.

"I feel my best work is yet to come. I consider myself fortunate to be producing children's photo-illustrated concept books. To date, I'm one of very few people who have produced a body of work in photo-illustrated concept books."

Biographical and Critical Sources

BOOKS

Popular Nonfiction Authors for Children: A Biographical and Thematic Guide, edited by Flora R. Wyatt and others, Libraries Unlimited (Englewood, CO), 1998.

PERIODICALS

Arithmetic Teacher, May, 1994, David J. Whitin, review of *Mouse Views,* p. 562.

Booklist, May 15, 1992, Deborah Abbott, review of *Beach Ball—Left, Right,* p. 1684; October 15, 1992, Carolyn Phelan, review of *Going on a Whale Watch,* p. 435; April 1, 1993, Kay Weisman, review of *A Beach for the Birds,* p. 1436; November 15, 1993, Elizabeth Bush, review of *Penguins at Home,* p. 620; December 1, 1994, Mary Harris Veeder, review of *Sense Suspense,* p. 675; March 15, 1995, Mary Harris Veeder, review of *Night of the Pufflings,* p. 1331; April 1, 1995, Mary Harris Veeder, review of *Puffins Climb, Penguins Rhyme,* p. 1421; October 15, 1995, Hazel Rochman, review of *Grandfather's Trolley,* p. 412; November 1, 1995, Carolyn Phelan, review of *Summer Ice,* p. 468; September 1, 1996, Lauren Peterson, review of *Jelly Beans for Sale,* p. 139; September 1, 1997, Carolyn Phelan, review of *In the Wild, Wild North,* p. 129; September 15, 1998, Lauren Peterson, review of *Gletta the Foal,* p. 248; September 15, 2001, Lauren Peterson, review of *Day of the Ducklings,* p. 228.

Bulletin of the Center for Children's Books, April, 1988; October 13, 1988; December, 1995, Roger Sutton, review of *Grandfather's Trolley,* p. 133; October, 1997, Deborah Stevenson, review of *In the Wild, Wild North,* pp. 58-59.

Christian Science Monitor, September 25, 1997, Karen Williams, review of *In the Wild, Wild North,* p. 211.

Horn Book, October, 1982, Richard Gaugert, review of *The Remarkable Riderless Runaway Tricycle,* pp. 541-542; June, 1983, Nancy Sheridan, review of *Here a Chick, There a Chick,* p. 293; September-October, 1984, Ann A. Flowers, review of *Kitten Can . . .,* p. 583; September-October, 1986, Margaret A. Bush, review of *Counting Wildflowers,* p. 610; November-December, 1987, Margaret A. Bush, review of *Step by Step,* p. 727; July-August, 1991, Maeve Visser Knoth, review of *The Weather Sky,* p. 486; March, 1992, Margaret A. Bush, review of *The Baby Zoo,* p. 217; July-August, 1995, Maeve Visser Knoth, review of *Night of the Pufflings,* p. 480; September, 1997, Margaret A. Bush, review of *Wild Flamingos,* p. 593; May-June, 1998, Ellen Fader, review of *Salmon Summer,* p. 362; January-February, 2002, Danielle J. Ford, review of *Day of the Ducklings,* p. 103.

Kirkus Reviews, January 1, 1992, review of *The Baby Zoo,* p. 54; July 15, 1992, review of *Going on a Whale Watch,* p. 922; March 15, 1993, review of *Mouse Views,* p. 375; April 1, 1993, review of *A Beach for the Birds,* p. 460; August 1, 1993, review of *Penguins at Home,* p. 1005.

Kliatt, July, 1996, Daniel J. Levinson, review of *The Weather Sky,* p. 35.

Language Arts, September, 1989, Janet Hickman, review of *Super, Super, Superwords,* p. 567; January, 1990, Susan Helper, review of *Time to . . .,* p. 79.

Los Angeles Times Book Review, September 26, 1982.

New York Times Book Review, November 9, 1980; March 27, 1983.

Providence Journal (Providence, RI), October 26, 1988.

Publishers Weekly, March 11, 1983, review of *Here a Chick, There a Chick,* p. 86; October 31, 1986, review of *Becca Backward, Becca Frontward,* p. 63; August 14, 1987, review of *Step by Step,* p. 101; January 15, 1988, review of *Dry or Wet?,* p. 93; May 12, 1989, review of *Super, Super, Superwords,* p. 290; September 29, 1989, review of *Time Two . . .,* p. 66; April 13, 1990, review of *One Sun,* p. 62; January 1, 1991, review of *One, Two, One Pair!,* p. 57; October 4, 1991, review of *Eating Fractions,* p. 87; October 25, 1991, review of *Play Day,* p. 67; January 30, 1995, review of *Puffins Climb, Penguins Rhyme,* p. 99.

School Library Journal, January, 1983, William Spangler, review of *The Remarkable Riderless Runaway Tricycle,* p. 44; January, 1984, Leslie Chamberlain, review of *Ghost Doll,* p. 66; December, 1984, Margaret L. Chatham, review of *Kitten Can . . .,* p. 73; August, 1986, Catherine Wood, review of *Counting Wildflowers,* p. 85; October, 1986, Constance A. Mellon, review of *Becca Backward, Becca Frontward,* p. 164; September, 1987, Anna Biagioni Hart, review of *Step by Step,* p. 167; May, 1988, Jennifer Smith, review of *Dry or Wet?,* p. 86; October, 1988, Patricia Dooley, review of *Fire Engine Shapes,* p. 125; April, 1989, Leda Schubert, review of *Super, Super, Superwords,* p. 86; September, 1989, Lori A. Janick, review of *Time Two . . .,* p. 241; July, 1990, Judith Gloyer, review of *One Sun,* p. 73; February, 1991, Louise L. Sherman, review of *One, Two, One Pair!,* pp. 72-73; May, 1991, Margaret M. Hegel, review of *The Weather Sky,* p. 104; May, 1992, Ellen Fader, review of *The Baby Zoo,* p. 106; June, 1992, Mary Lou Budd, review of *Beach Ball—Left, Right,* p. 110; April, 1993, Myra R. Oleynik, review of *Mouse Views,* p. 100, Valerie Lennox, review of *Going on a Whale Watch,* p. 112, and Diane Nunn, review of *A Beach for the Birds,* p. 137; December, 1993, Lisa Wu Stowe, review of *Penguins at Home,* pp. 128-129; March, 1995, Patricia Manning, review of *Nights of the Pufflings,* p. 198; May, 1995, Dot Minzer, review of *Puffins Climb, Penguins Rhyme,* pp. 100-101; September, 1995, Melissa Hudak, review of *Summer Ice,* p. 212; December, 1995, Virginia Opocensky, review of *Grandfather's Trolley,* p. 86; October, 1996, Beth Tegart, review of *Jelly Beans for Sale,* p. 115; April, 1997, review of *The Picture That Mom Drew,* p. 128; August, 1997, review of *Wild Flamingos,* pp. 148-149; September, 1997, Carol Schene, review of *In the Wild, Wild North,* pp. 204, 206; May, 1998, Susan Oliver, review of *Salmon Summer,* p. 134; December, 1998, Lee Bock, review of *Gletta the Foal,* p. 87.

OTHER

Bruce McMillan Web Site, http://www.brucemcmillan.com (March 3, 2002).*

MICKLOS, John J., Jr. 1956-

Personal

Born March 15, 1956, in Wilmington, DE; son of John J. (an engineer) and Shirley (a teacher; maiden name, Sipple) Micklos; married Deborah J. Amsden (an education consultant), June 1, 1985; children: Amy Lynn and John J. Micklos III. *Education:* Ohio University, B.A. (journalism), 1978. *Politics:* Democrat. *Religion:* Protestant. *Hobbies and other interests:* Golf, tennis.

Addresses

Home—14 Eileen Dr., Newark, DE 19711. *Office*—International Reading Association, 800 Barksdale Rd., Newark, DE 19711. *E-mail*—jmicklos@reading.org.

Career

International Reading Association, staff writer, 1978-1984, editor in chief, 1984—. Writer-in-residence, Thurgood Marshall Elementary School, Newark, DE, 2001. *Member:* Association of Educational Publishers (past president), Society of Children's Book Writers and Illustrators, National Writers Association.

Awards, Honors

Various journalistic awards from the Association of Educational Publishers, Association Trends, and the Society of National Association Publications.

Writings

Leonard Nimoy: A Star's Trek, Dillon Press (Minneapolis, MN,) 1988.
(Compiler and contributor) *Daddy Poems,* illustrated by Robert Casilla, Boyds Mills Press (Honesdale, PA), 2000.
(Compiler and contributor) *Mommy Poems,* illustrated by Lori McElrath-Eslick, Boyds Mills Press (Honesdale, PA), 2001.

Contributor to periodicals, including *Modern Bride, Cobblestone, Elks Magazine, Delaware Today, Reading Teacher, Education Digest, Journal of Adolescent & Adult Literacy, Real Estate Today,* and *Wilmington News Journal.*

Work in Progress

Grands Are Great: Poems About Grandparents, 2002. Research on bird rescue, the wild ponies of Assateaque, the search for Amelia Earhart, and children's poetry books about the beach and siblings.

Sidelights

Journalist John J. Micklos, Jr. has channeled his far-ranging interests to publish several books for children, including a biography of actor Leonard Nimoy and two collections of poems. *Leonard Nimoy: A Star's Trek,* written for the hi-lo audience, presents the life of Leonard Nimoy. Although perhaps best known for his role as Spock in the *Star Trek* television series and movies, Nimoy has acted in and directed a number of feature films and made-for-television movies and appeared in Broadway stage productions. According to a *Booklist* reviewer, Micklos gives readers an "easily read introduction" to Nimoy's life and work, and Deirdre R. Murray, writing in *School Library Journal,* complimented his "well-rounded . . . biography of a popular actor."

As a compiler and author of poetry for children, Micklos met with measured success with his *Daddy Poems* and *Mommy Poems,* picture book compilations of read-aloud poems. *Daddy Poems,* containing twenty-two poems, showcases the relationship between father and child, while *Mommy Poems,* containing eighteen poems, treats the mother-child bond in the same fashion. Each title includes works by contemporary children's poets as well as verse by Micklos, and styles range from free verse to rhymed and metered. These collections caught reviewers' attention. About *Daddy Poems, Booklist* reviewer Tim Arnold called the book a "welcome anthology," going on to write that in the poems, "dads will be reminded of the fundamental importance of their role." Linda DuVal called the work a "fine book to give dads to read to their own children" in her review for the *Knight-Ridder/Tribune News Service.* Despite remarking on the "uneven" quality of the works, Stephanie Zvirin of *Booklist* nonetheless found that some of the entries in *Mommy Poems* "are quite lovely, and all of the poems speak about moms in ways that sound familiar. Lauralyn Persson, writing in *School Library Journal,* judged some of the selections to be "memorable, like Gary Soto's 'Ode to Family Photographs.'"

Micklos told *SATA:* "As an author, parent, and long-time educational journalist for the International Reading Association, I believe strongly in the power of reading and in the critical role that parents can play in helping youngsters develop a love of books. I began writing and compiling *Daddy Poems* as a way to encourage fathers to read with their children. In doing so, I rediscovered my love of children's poetry, and I conceived the idea of a series of children's poetry books spotlighting the love that families share.

"I also enjoy writing nonfiction for children, and I enjoy the research that goes into learning about a topic and distilling the most interesting points."

Biographical and Critical Sources

PERIODICALS

Booklist, July, 1988, review of *Leonard Nimoy: A Star's Trek,* p. 1840; August, 2000, Tim Arnold, review of *Daddy Poems,* p. 2132; March 15, 2001, Stephanie Zvirin, review of *Mommy Poems,* p. 1395.

***John J. Micklos, Jr. compiled nearly twenty poems celebrating motherhood in his* Mommy Poems.** *(Illustrated by Lori McElrath-Eslick.)*

Childhood Education, winter, 2000, Jeanie Burnett, review of *Daddy Poems,* p. 107.

Knight-Ridder/Tribune News Service, June 15, 2000, Linda DuVal, review of *Daddy Poems,* p. K200.

School Library Journal, October, 1988, Deirdre R. Murray, review of *Leonard Nimoy,* p. 157; October, 2000, Nina Lindsay, review of *Daddy Poems,* p. 150; June, 2001, Lauralyn Persson, review of *Mommy Poems,* p. 139.*

MIKLOWITZ, Gloria D. 1927-

Personal

Surname is pronounced *Mick*-lo-witz; born May 18, 1927, in New York, NY; daughter of Simon (president of a steamship company) and Ella (a homemaker; maiden name, Goldberg) Dubov; married Julius Miklowitz (a college professor), August 28, 1948; children: Paul Stephen, David Jay. *Education:* Attended Hunter College (now Hunter College of the City University of New York), 1944-45; University of Michigan, B.A., 1948; New York University, graduate study, 1948. *Politics:* Democrat. *Religion:* Jewish.

Addresses

Home—5255 Vista Miguel Dr., La Canada, CA 91011. *Agent*—Curtis Brown Ltd., 10 Astor Place, New York, NY 10003. *E-mail*—glow7@aol.com.

Career

Writer, 1952—. U.S. Naval Ordnance Test Station, Pasadena, CA, scriptwriter, 1952-57; Pasadena City College, Pasadena, CA, instructor, 1971-80; instructor for Writers Digest School. *Member:* Society of Children's Book Writers and Illustrators, Southern California Council of Literature for Children and Young People.

Awards, Honors

Child Study Association of America's Children's Books of the Year selection, 1969, for *The Zoo Was My World,* and 1975, for *Harry Truman;* Outstanding Science Books for Children selection, National Council for Social Studies and the Children's Book Council, 1977, for *Earthquake!,* and 1978, for *Save That Raccoon!;* New York Public Library's Books for the Teen Age selection, 1980, for *Did You Hear What Happened to Andrea?,* 1981, for *The Love Bombers,* and 1982, for *The Young Tycoons;* Western Australia Young Reader Book Award, 1984, for *Did You Hear What Happened to Andrea?;* Iowa Books for Young Adults Poll, 1984, for *Close to the Edge,* 1986, for *The War between the Classes,* 1989, for *After the Bomb,* and 1989, for *Good-Bye Tomorrow;* Humanitas Prize for humanitarian values, 1985, for *CBS Schoolbreak Special* presentation of *The Day the Senior Class Got Married;* Emmy Award for Best Children's Special, 1986, for *CBS Schoolbreak Special* presentation of *The War between the Classes;* Recommended Books for Reluctant YA Readers selection, 1987, for *Good-Bye Tomorrow* and *Secrets Not Meant to Be Kept;* International Reading Association Young Adult Choices selection, 1989, for *Secrets Not Meant to Be Kept; Bucks Herald* (England) Top Teen Award, 1990; Sugarman Award, Washington Independent Writers Legal and Educational Fund, 1999, for excellence in children's literature; Notable book for

Gloria D. Miklowitz

older readers from Association of Jewish Libraries, 2002, for *Secrets in the House of Delgado.*

Writings

FICTION FOR CHILDREN

Barefoot Boy, Follett (Chicago, IL), 1964.

The Zoo That Moved, illustrated by Don Madden, Follett (Chicago, IL), 1968.

The Parade Starts at Noon, Putnam (New York, NY), 1969.

The Marshmallow Caper, illustrated by Cheryl Pelavin, Putnam (New York, NY), 1971.

Sad Song, Happy Song, illustrated by Earl Thollander, Putnam (New York, NY), 1973.

Ghastly Ghostly Riddles, Scholastic Book Services (New York, NY), 1977.

(With Peter Desberg) *Win, Lose, or Wear a Tie: Sports Riddles,* illustrated by Dave Ross, Random House (New York, NY), 1980.

FICTION FOR YOUNG ADULTS

Turning Off, Putnam (New York, NY), 1973.

A Time to Hurt, a Time to Heal, Tempo Books (New York, NY), 1974.

Runaway, Tempo Books (New York, NY), 1977.

Unwed Mother, Tempo Books (New York, NY), 1977.

Did You Hear What Happened to Andrea?, Delacorte (New York, NY), 1979.

The Love Bombers, Delacorte (New York, NY), 1980.

Before Love, Tempo Books (New York, NY), 1982.

Close to the Edge, Delacorte (New York, NY), 1983.

Carrie Loves Superman, Tempo Books (New York, NY), 1983.

The Day the Senior Class Got Married, Delacorte (New York, NY), 1983.

The War between the Classes, Delacorte (New York, NY), 1985.

After the Bomb (with teacher's guide), Scholastic (New York, NY), 1985.

Love Story, Take Three, Delacorte (New York, NY), 1986.

Good-Bye Tomorrow, Delacorte (New York, NY), 1987.

Secrets Not Meant to Be Kept, Delacorte (New York, NY), 1987.

After the Bomb: Week One, Scholastic (New York, NY), 1987.

The Emerson High Vigilantes, Delacorte (New York, NY), 1988.

Suddenly Super Rich, Bantam (New York, NY), 1989.

Anything to Win, Delacorte (New York, NY), 1989.

Standing Tall, Looking Good, Delacorte (New York, NY), 1991.

Desperate Pursuit, Bantam (New York, NY), 1992.

The Killing Boy, Bantam (New York, NY), 1993.

Past Forgiving, Simon & Schuster (New York, NY), 1995.

Camouflage, Harcourt (San Diego, CA), 1998.

Masada: The Last Fortress, Eerdmans (Grand Rapids, MI), 1998.

Secrets in the House of Delgado, Eerdmans (Grand Rapids, MI), 2001.

NONFICTION

(With Wesley A. Young) *The Zoo Was My World,* Dutton (New York, NY), 1969.

Harry Truman (biography), illustrated by Janet Scabrini, Putnam (New York, NY), 1975.

Paramedics, Scholastic Book Services (New York, NY), 1977.

Nadia Comaneci (biography), Tempo Books (New York, NY), 1977.

Earthquake!, illustrated by William Jaber, Messner (New York, NY), 1977.

Save That Raccoon!, illustrated by St. Tamara, Harcourt (New York, NY), 1978.

Tracy Austin (biography), Tempo Books (New York, NY), 1978.

Martin Luther King, Jr. (biography), Tempo Books (New York, NY), 1978.

Steve Cauthen (biography), Tempo Books (New York, NY), 1978.

Natalie Dunn, Roller Skating Champion (biography), Tempo Books (New York, NY), 1979.

Roller Skating, Tempo Books (New York, NY), 1979.

Movie Stunts and the People Who Do Them, Harcourt (New York, NY), 1980.

(With Madeleine Yates) *The Young Tycoons: Ten Success Stories,* Harcourt (New York, NY), 1981.

Contributor to anthologies of children's stories, and to periodicals, including *Sports Illustrated, American Girl,*

Seventeen, Hadassah, Writer, and *Publishers Weekly.* Miklowitz's writings may be found in the De Grummond Collection at the University of Southern Mississippi.

Adaptations

Andrea's Story: A Hitchhiking Tragedy (*After-School Special* television movie, based on *Did You Hear What Happened to Andrea?*), ABC-TV, September, 1983, video recording released as *Did You Hear What Happened to Andrea?,* New Kid Home Video (Santa Monica, CA), 1997; *The Day the Senior Class Got Married* (*Schoolbreak Special* television movie), CBS-TV, 1985; *The War between the Classes* (*Schoolbreak Special* television movie), CBS-TV, 1986.

Work in Progress

Enemy With a Face, 2003.

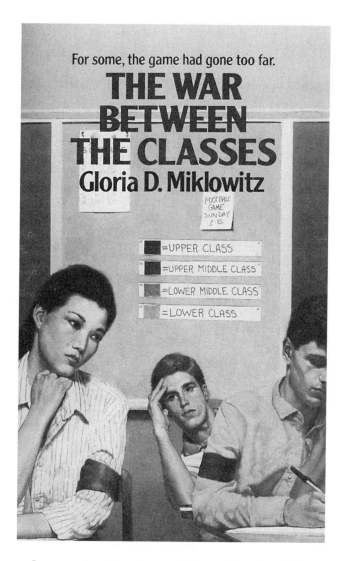

Japanese-American Amy rebels against the Color Game—designed to make students aware of class and racial prejudices—when it threatens her relationship with Adam.

Sidelights

Gloria D. Miklowitz's young adult books help teenagers confront serious contemporary problems such as nuclear war, religious cults, rape, teen suicide, and AIDS. "Teenage problems interest me," she once explained. "Young people are still malleable enough to be influenced to constructive change. I try to offer or suggest alternatives to destructive behavior in my books.... In each book, I enter lives I can never really live and try to bring to my readers compassion and understanding for those lives." "I want to be everyone's mom," she continued in a statement released by her publisher, Delacorte Press, "and smooth their way into adulthood in the only way I can—through my books."

"I was a middle child and a dreamer," Miklowitz once commented. "I was slow to read, but once I learned, I was always reading something, though I can't say anything of great consequence. I was stuck on the 'Nancy Drew' books for a while, and moved to reading adult literature by the age of twelve or thirteen. I wrote a composition in the third grade, 'My Brother Goo Goo,' which brought me instant family recognition. I received an 'A' for my effort and got to read it in the auditorium. My family made a big deal out of it, so I said I was going to be a writer. I didn't even really know what it meant, but that label was put on me at an early age.

"When I finished college, I moved to New York City to look for an editing job, which I thought was the only option for an English major. I worked at Bantam Books for about eight months as a secretary and did graduate work at New York University in education at night. I married and moved to Pasadena, California where my husband was hired to work as a researcher at the Naval Ordnance Test Station. The only job available to me was a secretarial position with the Navy. So I took it and persuaded them to train me as a writer when they opened a film branch. It was my job to research subjects, develop a script, and become involved in the shooting of the films. We were a small unit, only three people, but we won awards."

Miklowitz gave up her filmmaking job when her second son was born, preferring to devote her time to her family. "By the time the boys were two and three years old," she once commented, "I was reading picture books to them—about ten books a week. To satisfy my own need for intellectual stimulation, I took a class at a junior college called 'Writing for Publication,' where I learned about the Follett 'Beginning to Read' contest. I had already read most of the series to my own children, so I read the remaining books and wrote *Barefoot Boy,* which Follett bought and which became my first publication."

Many of Miklowitz's early books, such as *The Zoo That Moved* and *The Parade Starts at Noon,* were written for young children and focused on animals. "I write for children because the world of children interests me," she once related, "I am curious, as they are, about every-

Fifteen-year-old Alexandra's boyfriend becomes physically abusive in Miklowitz's honest portrayal of date violence and rape. (Cover illustration by John Clapp.)

thing: insects, animals, people, how things work and why, what it feels like to walk in the rain, or touch the snow. I ask a lot of questions, which most adults are reluctant to do—either because they know the answers, or they are embarrassed to reveal that they don't. But *I* want to know. When I meet strangers, I like to know what they do, how they do it, and what they think about. This curiosity, I think, is almost childlike, and maybe that's why I know what children might find interesting. If it interests me, it should interest them.

"When my children moved into the middle grades, I started reading middle-grade books. When they moved into high school, I realized that college was looming with its enormous costs. With two boys only thirteen months apart, I began thinking seriously about writing to sell.

"I stumbled into writing for young adults as a result of conversations I was having with a black cleaning lady who worked for me. We'd have lunch together and she would tell me about all the problems she had with one of her sons involved in drugs. That, combined with talks

I'd had with the director of the Los Angeles Zoo about young people involved in animal rescue operations, made me realize that when you reach your hand out to others, you usually don't get into trouble. And that resulted in *Turning Off,* my first novel for young adults."

From drugs Miklowitz moved on to explore such sensitive subjects as rape (in *Did You Hear What Happened to Andrea?*), racism (in *The War between the Classes*), nuclear holocaust (in *After the Bomb* and *After the Bomb: Week One*), AIDS (in *Good-Bye Tomorrow*), sexual abuse (in *Secrets Not Meant to Be Kept*), and steroid use (in *Anything to Win*). "I'm a very straightforward person and, as a rule, say what I think," Miklowitz once stated. "I don't know all the answers and in many of my books I'm searching for answers, too. I don't deliberately create characters to influence the reader's views. . . . Most of my female characters have a little of me in them, so something from my past will usually come out in every book. I think I'm honest and that it comes through in my writing. My readers say so. I truly

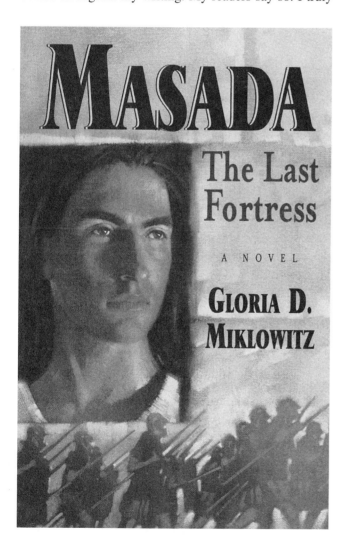

This powerful historical novel records the last stand of the Jewish Zealots at Masada through the eyes of seventeen-year-old Simon ben Eleazar. (Cover illustration by Greg Shed.)

like young people. I like to think that I guide them a little through my stories. Most times, I'll give both sides of an issue and let the reader decide."

Miklowitz thoroughly researches the subjects of her novels. For *Did You Hear What Happened to Andrea?,* for instance, she served on a rape hotline for a year, and talked extensively with victims, police, and doctors. For *The Love Bombers,* a book about religious cults, she spent several days with a Moonie group north of San Francisco. "Obtaining the information I need is always interesting," she once explained, "because it taxes my ingenuity in tracking down what I need to know. Sometimes I gather so much material it's hard to keep track of it all. I always fear I may have left some stone unturned and therefore keep digging for all sides to an issue.

"In summing up, it comes as a surprise to find I have written a large body of work on many important social issues, and to realize that what I have written has been enjoyed and has enriched many young people throughout the world."

Over the years, Miklowitz has earned praise not only for her sensitive portrayal of young adults dealing with personal and social problems, but also for her well-paced, tension-filled plots. While these continue to be the trademarks of her young adult books, her most recent novels, like *Masada: The Last Fortress* and *Secrets in the House of Delgado,* shift from contemporary issues and settings to the historical.

Secrets in the House of Delgado, for example, is set in Spain in 1492, when the infamous Spanish Inquisition is searching for religious heretics and Jews are being expelled from the country. With help from the Church, fourteen-year-old Maria, a Catholic orphan, becomes a servant in the home of the Delgados, a wealthy family of Jews who had converted to the Catholic faith. Forced to spy for the Church in exchange for her position, Maria must also confront questions of loyalty and betrayal, faith and bigotry. *Booklist*'s Ilene Cooper, who called the book "a page-turner," found that "the story shows depth and dimension." Cooper concluded, "Miklowitz does a fine job of making the Spanish Inquisition seem frighteningly real."

Biographical and Critical Sources

BOOKS

Authors and Artists for Young Adults, Volume 6, Gale (Detroit, MI), 1991.
Something about the Author Autobiography Series, Volume 17, Gale (Detroit, MI), 1994.
St. James Guide to Young Adult Writers, 2nd edition, St. James Press (Detroit, MI), 1999.

PERIODICALS

Booklist, May 1, 1995, review of *Past Forgiving,* p. 1563; October 1, 1998, review of *Masada: The Last Fortress,*

p. 338; October 1, 2001, Ilene Cooper, review of *Secrets in the House of Delgado,* p. 331.
Los Angeles Times, June 6, 1987.
Publishers Weekly, October 9, 1987; January 4, 1991, review of *Standing Tall, Looking Good,* p. 74; January 13, 1992, review of *Desperate Pursuit,* p. 58; June 26, 1995, review of *Past Forgiving,* p. 108; January 12, 1998, review of *Camouflage,* p. 60.
Writer, August, 1972; March, 1978; October, 1979.

* * *

MOGENSEN, Suzanne A(ncher) 1946-

Personal

Born December 6, 1946, in Copenhagen, Denmark; daughter of Jens Ancher (a chemist) and Fanny (a homemaker; maiden name, Nielsen) Mogensen; divorced; children: Oscar Macdonald. *Education:* Attended Central Technical School, 1964-67. *Politics:* "Left of center." *Religion:* "Baptized Lutheran."

Addresses

Home and office—223 Roncesvalles Ave., Apt. 5, Toronto, Ontario, Canada M6R 2L6. *Agent*—Irmeli Holmberg, 280 Madison Ave., New York, NY 10016.

Career

Sign writer and paste-up artist at a sign shop in Toronto, Canada, 1967-69; layout and paste-up artist for a magazine in Toronto, Canada, 1970-74; freelance illustrator and layout artist, 1974-78; illustrator and layout artist for a magazine in Copenhagen, Denmark, 1978-83; freelance illustrator in Copenhagen, Denmark, 1983-88, and Toronto, Canada, 1988—. Partisan Gallery, member of board of directors, 1995-99.

Awards, Honors

Achievement Award, Danish Ministry of Culture, 1988, for illustrating a series of nonsense stories by Peter Mouritzen.

Illustrator

Hans Christian Andersen, *Big Claus and Little Claus,* Gyldendal (Copenhagen, Denmark), 1989.
Jean Little, *Jenny and the Hanukkah Queen,* Penguin Canada (Toronto, Canada), 1995.
Pamela Hickman, *The Night Book,* Kids Can Press (Toronto, Canada), 1996.

Illustrator of a series of nonsense stories by Peter Mouritzen, Apostrof (Copenhagen, Denmark), eight volumes, 1986-89.

Work in Progress

Writing and illustrating revised nursery rhymes.

* * *

MORSE, Tony 1953-

Personal

Born March 15, 1953, in Willimantic, CT; son of James S. (a commercial filmmaker and watercolorist) and Patricia (a homemaker and artist; maiden name, Bennett) Morse; married Catherine Griffing (a teacher), November 29, 1980; children: Caitlin, Charles. *Education:* Attended Philadelphia College of Art, 1971-72; California College of Arts and Crafts, B.A., 1979. *Hobbies and other interests:* Musician.

Addresses

Home—Oakland, CA. *Agent*—c/o RDR Books, 4456 Piedmont Ave., Oakland, CA 94611. *E-mail*—aamorse@pacbell.net.

Career

Banana Republic (clothing company), San Francisco, CA, senior illustrator, 1986-92; freelance illustrator, Oakland, CA, 1992—. Academy of Art, San Francisco, teacher in advertising department, 1994-96; California College of Arts and Crafts, teacher of graphic design, 1995-96.

Illustrator

Discover Dinosaurs, Yes! Entertainment, 1994.
When Dinosaurs Roamed, Yes! Entertainment, 1994.
Peter J. Honigsberg, *Pillow of Dreams,* RDR Books (Oakland, CA), 1999.
Peter J. Honigsberg, *Armful of Memories,* RDR Books (Oakland, CA), 2001.

Sidelights

Tony Morse told *SATA:* "All my life I've had a fascination for illustrated books. I remember especially several books which belonged to my parents and grandparents—Scribner's *Mother Goose,* two wild picture books by Tony Sarg from the twenties, a wonderful library of children's literature called 'My Book House' from Random House, several books from the early editions of Frank Baum's 'Wizard of Oz' stories. I also had an artistic bent from early in life, which was nurtured by my parents, who were both artists themselves. They consistently drew my attention to things of beauty and visual interest in the world, and the habit definitely informed my ability to observe and imagine.

"In terms of influences on my current work, I have always loved natural history and landscape, so closely observed detail is always a strong element in my art. The books I have illustrated for Peter Honigsberg both feature anthropomorphized animals as their cast of characters, and I've had a lot of fun building a world which draws on both the traditional fairy tale illustration genre of Arthur Rackham and the whimsical animated 'bug-town' Warner Bros. cartoons of the thirties. The quirkiness of the stories has also inspired me to embed small visual puzzles, jokes, and puns in the illustrations, although they are always subsidiary to the overall composition and the story."

O–P

O'SHAUGHNESSY, Darren 1972-
(Darren Shan)

Personal

Born July 2, 1972, in London, England; son of Liam (a laborer) and Breda (a teacher; maiden name, Barry) O'Shaughnessy. *Education:* Roehampton Institute of Higher Education, B.Sc.

Addresses

Agent—Christopher Little, 10 Eel Brook Studios, 125 Moore Park Rd., London SW6 4PS, England. *E-mail*—post@darrenshan.com.

Career

Writer.

Writings

FOR ADULTS

Ayuamarca, Millennium Orion (London, England), 1999.
Hell's Horizon, Millennium Orion (London, England), 2000.

"THE SAGA OF DARREN SHAN" SERIES; NOVELS; UNDER PSEUDONYM DARREN SHAN

Cirque du Freak: A Living Nightmare, Little, Brown (New York, NY), 2001.
The Vampire's Assistant, Little, Brown (New York, NY), 2001.
Vampire Mountain, Collins (England), 2001.
Trials of Death, Collins (England), 2001.
The Vampire Prince, Collins (England), in press.
Tunnels of Blood, Little, Brown (New York, NY), in press.

Work in Progress

Additional titles in "The Saga of Darren Shan," a series of approximately twenty volumes.

Two boys meet a vampire and a deadly spider at an illegal freak show in Darren Shan's novel inspired by old Dracula movies. (Cover illustration by Jennifer Nelson.)

Sidelights

Darren O'Shaughnessy told *SATA:* "I've been writing all my life. I've always loved telling stories. I started out writing for adults (my 'grownup' books are published in the United Kingdom). *Cirque du Freak: A Living Nightmare* began as a side-project: I wanted to write a book which the ten-to-twelve-year-old within me thought was 'cool!!!' It's since pretty much taken over my life, with a series of a projected twenty or so books. Moral: beware of casual side-projects!

"I write to a page count: ten pages per day, five days a week. Sometimes I also edit other books while writing a new one. Occasionally I'll work on two books at the same time. My first aim is always to tell an exciting story which anyone with a good, basic grasp of the language can read.

"I also use my books to explore personal issues, or areas of interest to me; for example, loneliness, codes of honor, death, violence, friendship, fate, religion, et cetera. Childhood and coming of age revolve around such key issues, so I think children's books should, too. Most of my books are quite darkly themed—some are downright morbid—but I do work in humorous and warm moments. I like to mix genres. Thus, while the first three books of 'The Saga of Darren Shan' are primarily horror books, the next three will be fantasy. After that? Readers will just have to wait and see!

"Stephen King has been a huge influence on me. Other favorite writers and books include Roald Dahl, *The Secret Garden,* Alan Garner, Robert Cormier, Robert Westall, and *Rebecca's World.*

"My books have been and are being published in many countries, from Brazil to Japan to Israel—with more to come, hopefully. My aims for the future are to carry on writing and to improve. Writers should always be looking to go one better. On my deathbed, I want my last words to be, 'Hang on! I've just had a really good idea. . . .'"

Biographical and Critical Sources

PERIODICALS

Books for Keeps, May, 2000, review of *Cirque du Freak.*
Children's Books in Ireland, May, 2000, interview with Darren O'Shaughnessy.
Daily Telegraph, March 11, 2000, review of *Cirque du Freak.*
Independent, December 3, 1999, review of *Cirque du Freak.*
Manchester Evening News, February 24, 2001, review of *Cirque du Freak.*
Observer, October 22, 2000, review of *Cirque du Freak.*
Scotsman, February 5, 2000, review of *Cirque du Freak.*
Times (London, England), February 4, 2000, interview with Darren O'Shaughnessy; February 17, 2000, review of *Cirque du Freak.*

OTHER

Shanville, http://www.darrenshan.com/ (February 20, 2002).

PEARCE, Ann Philippa
See PEARCE, Philippa

*   *   *

PEARCE, Philippa 1920-
(Ann Philippa Pearce)

Personal

Born 1920 in Great Shelford, Cambridgeshire, England; daughter of Ernest Alexander (a flour miller and corn merchant) and Gertrude Alice (Ramsden) Pearce; married Martin Christie (a fruitgrower), May 9, 1963 (died, 1965); children: Sarah. *Education:* Girton College, Cambridge, B.A., M.A. (with honors), 1942.

Addresses

Home—Cambridge, England. *Agent*—c/o Kestrel Books, Penguin Books Ltd., 536 King's Rd., London SW10 0UH, England.

Career

Writer. Temporary civil servant, 1942-45; British Broadcasting Corp., London, England, script writer and producer in school broadcasting department, 1945-58; Clarendon Press, Oxford, England, editor in educational department, 1959-60; Andre Deutsch Ltd., London, England, editor of children's books, 1960-67. Part-time radio producer, British Broadcasting Corp., 1960-63. *Member:* Society of Authors.

Awards, Honors

Carnegie Commendation, Library Association (England), 1956, for *Minnow on the Say,* 1978, for *The Shadow-Cage and Other Tales of the Supernatural,* and 1979, for *The Battle of Bubble and Squeak;* International Board on Books for Young People honour list selection, 1956, for *Minnow on the Say,* 1960, for *Tom's Midnight Garden,* and 1974, for *What the Neighbours Did and Other Stories;* Lewis Carroll Shelf Award, 1959, for *The Minnow Leads to Treasure,* and 1963, for *Tom's Midnight Garden;* Carnegie Medal, Library Association, 1959, for *Tom's Midnight Garden; New York Herald Tribune* Children's Spring Book Festival Award, 1963, for *A Dog So Small;* Whitbread Award, 1978, for *The Battle of Bubble and Squeak;* Fellow of Royal Society of Literature, 1993.

Writings

UNDER NAME ANN PHILIPPA PEARCE

Minnow on the Say, Oxford University Press (Oxford, England), 1954, reprinted under name Philippa Pearce, Puffin (London, England), 1979, published as *The Minnow Leads to Treasure,* World Publishing (New York, NY), 1958.

Staying with his aunt and uncle while his brother recovers from measles, Tom discovers and makes friends with Hattie, a girl from the past. (From Tom's Midnight Garden, *written by Philippa Pearce and illustrated by Susan Einzig.)*

Tom's Midnight Garden, illustrated by Susan Einzig, Lippincott (Philadelphia, PA), 1958, reprinted under name Philippa Pearce, Dell (New York, NY), 1979.

UNDER NAME PHILIPPA PEARCE

Mrs. Cockle's Cat, Lippincott (Philadelphia, PA), 1961.

A Dog So Small, Constable (London, England), 1962, Lippincott (Philadelphia, PA), 1963.

(With Harold Scott) *From Inside Scotland Yard* (juvenile adaptation of Scott's *Scotland Yard*), Deutsch (London, England), 1963, Macmillan (New York, NY), 1965.

The Strange Sunflower, Thomas Nelson (London, England), 1966.

(With Brian Fairfax-Lucy) *The Children of the House,* Lippincott (Philadelphia, PA), 1968.

The Elm Street Lot, British Broadcasting Corp. (London, England), 1969, enlarged hardcover edition, Kestrel (London, England), 1979.

The Squirrel Wife, Longman (London, England), 1971, Crowell (New York, NY), 1972.

(Adapter) *Beauty and the Beast,* Crowell (New York, NY), 1972.

(Editor and author of preface) *Stories from Hans Christian Andersen,* Collins (New York, NY), 1972.

What the Neighbours Did and Other Stories, Longman (London, England), 1972, published as *What the Neighbors Did and Other Stories,* Crowell (New York, NY), 1973.

The Shadow-Cage and Other Tales of the Supernatural, Crowell (New York, NY), 1977.

The Battle of Bubble and Squeak, Deutsch (London, England), 1978.

(Translator) *Wings of Courage,* Kestrel (London, England), 1982.

A Picnic for Bunnykins, Viking (New York, NY), 1984.

Two Bunnykins Out to Tea, Viking (New York, NY), 1984.

Bunnykins in the Snow, Viking (New York, NY), 1985.

Lion at School and Other Stories, Greenwillow Books (New York, NY), 1985.

The Way to Sattin Shore, Viking (New York, NY), 1985.

The Tooth Ball, Deutsch (London, England), 1987.

Who's Afraid?, and Other Strange Stories, Greenwillow Books (New York, NY), 1987.

Emily's Own Elephant, Macrae Books, 1987.

Fresh, illustrated by Berta Zimdars, Creative Education (Mankato, MN), 1988.

Freddy, Deutsch (London, England), 1988.

Old Belle's Summer Holiday, Deutsch (London, England), 1989.

Children of Charlecote, Gollancz (London, England), 1989.

Here Comes Tod, Walker, 1992.

The Little White Hen, Deutsch/Shcolastic, 1996.

(Adaptor) *The Pedlar of Swoffham,* Scholastic, 2000

The Ghost in Annie's Room, Walker, 2000.

The Rope and Other Stories, Penguin Children's Books, 2000.

Editor of the first fourteen books in "People of the Past" social history series, 1961-64. Work is represented in anthologies, including *Another Six,* Basil Blackwell, 1959, *The Friday Miracle and Other Stories,* Puffin, 1969, and *Baker's Dozen,* Ward, Lock, 1974. Contributor of short stories to "Listening and Reading" radio series, BBC. Contributor of book reviews to periodicals.

Sidelights

Philippa Pearce enjoys a reputation as one of England's leading writers for children. John Rowe Townsend, speaking of *Tom's Midnight Garden* in his study *Written for Children: An Outline of English Children's Literature,* stated: "I have no reservations about it. If I were asked to name a single masterpiece of English children's literature since the last war ... it would be this

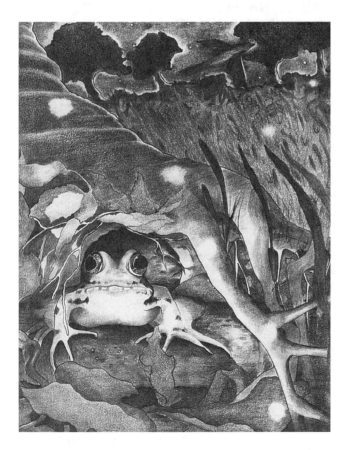

Two cousins decide to keep a mussel as a pet in Pearce's **Fresh.** *(Illustrated by Berta Zimdars.)*

outstandingly beautiful and absorbing book." Similarly, W. L. Webb of the *Manchester Guardian* called the novel "a rare, moving story, beautifully written, and true in every way that matters ... a modern classic."

Tom's Midnight Garden tells the story of a young boy who must spend the summer with his aunt and uncle in the country. At first bored with his surroundings, he soon learns that at midnight the backyard transforms into the Victorian garden that it was many years before. Every night in his dreams he explores the garden. One night he meets a little girl named Hatty and the two of them begin a series of explorations of the vast garden. Hatty begins to grow older while Tom remains the same age. At story's end, he discovers that the elderly woman who lives in the flat above his aunt and uncle is the Hatty he played with in the garden of her childhood.

The garden where Tom and Hatty meet is based on the garden Pearce played in as a girl. Her father was a miller and she lived in a mill house with a walled garden. "It is a beautiful early nineteenth-century house," Pearce told Roni Natov and Geraldine DeLuca in *The Lion and the Unicorn.* "You see houses like it everywhere in East Anglia, farm houses and mill houses that correspond to a period of great agricultural prosperity, probably during the Napoleonic wars. My father was born in that house because my grandfather was also a miller. We moved in when I was very small; my grandfather died and we took over. This is the house and the garden with its sundial on the wall in *Tom's Midnight Garden.* The garden was absolutely the image of that walled garden in the book." Pearce now lives in a cottage across the street from the mill house.

The idea that characters can meet each other across time came to Pearce from a book, *Experiment in Time,* written by J. W. Dunne. Dunne theorizes that there are many "times" co-existing and yet able to blend together. "I never really understood it properly," Pearce admitted in *Books for Keeps,* "but it was a sort of theoretical base for the book."

The story was meant to say something about the relationships between the young and the old too. Pearce told Natov and DeLuca: "*Tom's Midnight Garden* was an attempt to reconcile childhood and old age, to bring them together." Speaking in *Books for Keeps,* she said the real impulse behind the book was "the feeling of time passing, people becoming old. Even though I wasn't old I could see that if you were old you hadn't been old forever." Writing in *A Critical History of Children's Literature,* Ruth Hill Viguers claimed that in *Tom's Midnight Garden,* "the idea that time has no barriers was embodied in nearly perfect literary form."

Much of Pearce's other fiction is also based on her own childhood. She commented in *Cricket:* "I was the youngest of four children.... We lived in a big, shabby, beautiful mill house by the river. We swam, fished, boated, skated. We always had a dog, and sometimes a cat—the business cat from the mill, who would knock off from catching rats and mice to visit us. When I grew up and went to London to work, I took with me all the places that I had loved. They turned up in the stories I was beginning to write.... I think there is no story I have ever written that didn't start from something in my own life."

Pearce works out the plots of her stories in her head. "I never write things down," she explained to Natov and DeLuca. "I don't keep a folder. I have never in my life kept a note of anything. I let ideas mill around in my head. Things begin to settle out like muddy water. Perhaps if I had kept notes I would have written more, I don't know." She does write down the story as it comes to her, though: "I do believe it is very useful to write down the actual words you think of. When I wake up in the night with just the right words, I write them down so as not to lose them."

Biographical and Critical Sources

BOOKS

Blishen, Edward, editor, *The Thorny Paradise: Writers on Writing for Children*, Kestrel (London, England), 1975.

Butts, Dennis, editor, *Good Writers for Young Readers*, Hart-Davis, 1977.

Cameron, Eleanor, *The Green and Burning Tree: On the Writing and Enjoyment of Children's Books*, Little, Brown (Boston, MA), 1969.

Children's Literature Review, Volume 9, Gale (Detroit, MI), 1985.

Crouch, Marcus, *Treasure Seekers and Borrowers: Children's Books in Britain, 1900-1960*, Library Association, 1962.

Crouch, Marcus, *The Nesbit Tradition: The Children's Novel in England, 1945-1970*, Ernest Benn Limited, 1972.

Eyre, Frank, *British Children's Books in the Twentieth Century*, revised edition, Dutton (New York, NY), 1973.

Fisher, Margery, *Intent Upon Reading: A Critical Appraisal of Modern Fiction for Children*, Hodder & Stoughton (London, England), 1961.

Rees, David, *The Marble in the Water: Essays on Contemporary Writers of Fiction for Children and Young Adults*, Horn Book (Boston, MA), 1980.

Storr, Catherine, editor, *On Children's Literature*, Allen Lane, 1973.

Townsend, John Rowe, "The New Fantasy," *Written for Children: An Outline of English Children's Literature*, Lothrop (New York, NY), 1967.

Townsend, John Rowe, *A Sense of Story: Essays on Contemporary Writers for Children*, Lippincott (Philadelphia, PA), 1971.

Viguers, Ruth Hill, "Golden Years and Time of Tumult: 1920-1967," *A Critical History of Children's Literature*, revised edition, Macmillan (New York, NY), 1969.

PERIODICALS

Books for Keeps, November, 1983, pp. 14-15.
Book World, May 7, 1972.

Children's Literature in Education, March, 1971; autumn 1981.
Commonweal, May 23, 1958.
Cricket, August, 1976, p. 35.
Growing Point, November, 1983; March, 1986; July, 1987.
Horn Book, April, 1958; April, 1978; June, 1984; May-June, 1987.
Kirkus, July 15, 1959.
The Lion and the Unicorn, Volume 9, 1985, Roni Natov and Geraldine DeLuca, "An Interview with Philippa Pearce."
Manchester Guardian, December 5, 1958, Webb, W. L., review of *Tom's Midnight Garden*, p. 7.
New Statesman, November 15, 1958; May 18, 1962.
New York Herald Tribune Book Review, March 9, 1958; November 1, 1959.
New York Herald Tribune Books, May 12, 1963.
New York Times, May 4, 1958.
New York Times Book Review, November 1, 1959; March 12, 1972.
Saturday Review, August 23, 1958; May 11, 1963.
Signal, January, 1973; September, 1984.
Times Educational Supplement, September 30, 1983.
Times Literary Supplement, June 1, 1962; October 22, 1971; December 8, 1972; July 15, 1977; March 14, 1986.
Use of English, spring 1970.

*   *   *

PIERS, Robert
See ANTHONY, Piers

*   *   *

PORTER, Connie (Rose) 1959(?)-

Personal

Born c. 1959, in New York, NY. *Education:* Earned a degree from State University of New York—Albany; Louisiana State University, M.F.A. (creative writing).

Addresses

Home—Virginia Beach, VA. *Agent*—c/o Author Mail, Pleasant Company Publications, 8400 Fairway Pl., Middleton, WI 53562.

Career

Writer. Instructor of creative writing at Emerson College and Southern Illinois University—Carbondale.

Awards, Honors

Named a fellow to Bread Loaf Writers' Conference; regional winner, Granta's Best Young American Novelists Competition; *New York Times* Notable Book, for *All-Bright Court*.

Addy's teacher recommends her for the Institute for Colored Youth in 1860s Philadelphia in **High Hopes for Addy,** *a work from the "American Girls" series. (Written by Connie Porter and illustrated by John Thompson and Dahl Taylor.)*

Writings

All-Bright Court (novel), Houghton (Boston, MA), 1991.
Imani All Mine (novel), Houghton (Boston, MA), 1998.

"AMERICAN GIRLS" SERIES

Meet Addy: An American Girl (also see below), illustrated by Melodye Rosales, Pleasant Company (Middleton, WI), 1993.
Addy Learns a Lesson: A School Story (also see below), illustrated by Melodye Rosales, Pleasant Company (Middleton, WI), 1993.
Addy's Surprise: A Christmas Story (also see below), illustrated by Melodye Rosales, Pleasant Company (Middleton, WI), 1993.
Happy Birthday, Addy!: A Springtime Story (also see below), illustrated by Bradford Brown, Pleasant Company (Middleton, WI), 1993.
Changes for Addy: A Winter Story (also see below), illustrated by Bradford Brown, Pleasant Company (Middleton, WI), 1994.
Addy Saves the Day: A Summer Story (also see below), illustrated by Bradford Brown, Pleasant Company (Middleton, WI), 1994.
High Hopes for Addy, illustrated by John Thompson and Dahl Taylor, Pleasant Company (Middleton, WI), 1999.

Addy's Little Brother, illustrated by Gabriela Dellosso and Dahl Taylor, Pleasant Company (Middleton, WI), 2000.
Addy's Wedding Quilt, illustrated by Dahl Taylor, Pleasant Company (Middleton, WI), 2001.
Addy's Story Collection (contains *Meet Addy; Addy Learns a Lesson; Addy's Surprise; Happy Birthday, Addy!; Addy Saves the Day;* and *Changes for Addy*), illustrated by Dahl Taylor, Pleasant Company (Middleton, WI), 2001.
Addy Studies Freedom, illustrated by Dahl Taylor, Pleasant Company (Middleton, WI), 2002.

Adaptations

Addy Learns a Lesson was adapted into a play, *Friendship and Freedom,* by Valerie Tripp and published in *Addy's Theater Kit: A Play about Addy for You and Your Friends to Perform,* Pleasant Company (Middleton, WI), 1994.

Sidelights

Connie Porter is the author of two novels for adults as well as several books for children about the character Addy in the popular "American Girls" historical series. Her 1991 novel *All-Bright Court* garnered much positive critical response and was repeatedly praised as an exceptional debut novel. Following the publication of a half-dozen "Addy" titles, Porter released her second novel, *Imani All Mine,* in 1998. Both adult novels have in common central characters who are young, poor, and black. While the first book is set during the 1960s and 1970s, the second takes place during the 1990s.

All-Bright Court tells the story of a group of Southern blacks who move to a Northern steel town in search of higher-paying jobs, better living conditions, and a more egalitarian society. Faced with frequent layoffs and cruel and dangerous conditions in the mill in which they work, however, they find they have only traded one set of hardships for another. Yet a strong sense of community pervades the low-rent apartment complex where the novel is set, and, through vignettes centering on the Taylor family and their friends and neighbors, Porter depicts the many facets of poverty in an American ghetto. Adrian Oktenberg of *Women's Review of Books* called Porter's work "a novel of vision and integrity, wherein a community is seen whole, embedded in its economics and history, sparing nothing, and whose stories are told with great compassion."

After posting a high score on an intelligence test, one of the Taylors' sons, Mikey, is offered a scholarship to a private school and a possible way out of the cycle of poverty and degradation in which his family is trapped. His new friends expose him to a wealthy white world, and Mikey eventually takes on the speech and values of that other world and becomes ashamed of his family and the way they live. Jonathan Yardley commented in the *Washington Post Book World* that "Porter is sensitive to every nuance of the cultural encounter Mikey undergoes, and portrays each step of his journey with as much clarity as sympathy."

Porter earns praise for her depiction of both the desperation of the lives of her characters as well as the dignity inherent in their manner of coping. Gary Krist remarked in the *Hudson Review* that she "writes simply but powerfully, and with a command of detail that lends authority to the world she depicts." *New York Times* reviewer Michiko Kakutani noted that, "Though her prose is often lyrical, even poetic, [Porter] does not shirk from showing the reader the harsh reality of her characters' daily lives.... Indeed, the emotional power of *All-Bright Court* resides in her finely rendered characters, people "who come alive for the reader as individuals one has known firsthand."

All-Bright Court is based on a short story that Porter wrote as a student at Louisiana State University. The original piece was only twelve pages long and included descriptions of the place, family, and some of the events she later used in her novel. The expanded version fulfilled the author's hopes of writing about the steel industry and about the area in which she grew up.

In 1993, Porter released *Meet Addy: An American Girl,* the first book in a historical series that features a young black slave named Addy who escapes to freedom with

her mother during the American Civil War. In *Addy Learns a Lesson,* the title character faces the challenges of living in the urban North and finding friends at her school. Addy possesses "affability and pluck," noted a *Publishers Weekly* contributor, who found the series of novels "bright" and "poignant."

After producing five more books in the "American Girls" series, Porter addressed a more mature audience with her next publication, the 1998 novel *Imani All Mine.* While Tasha, her protagonist, is only fifteen years old, she has not experienced an average childhood. An honors student, Tasha plans to go to college and thereby escape the hardships of life in a poor inner-city neighborhood. But she becomes pregnant after being raped by a schoolmate and decides to keep her baby, whom she names Imani, meaning "faith." Tasha loves her child very deeply and tries to nurture her in a dangerous environment filled with drugs, gangs, poverty, and bigotry. She struggles to be a good mother while she deals with more common teen issues, including her emerging sexuality and her mother's new, white boyfriend.

Tasha serves as an effective narrator, speaking in the language of the street, noted reviewers. Critic Karen Anderson applauded the author's creation in a *Library Journal* review, saying "Porter ... gives Tasha great wisdom, grace, charm, and a moving poetic voice." *Booklist*'s Vanessa Bush called *Imani All Mine* a "deceptively simple novel" and, like Anderson, remarked that "through Tasha's stark voice, Porter offers well-drawn characters." A reviewer for *Publishers Weekly* found that sometimes the book has a "[young adult] simplicity" but nonetheless enjoys the way "Porter spins the tale in a series of flashbacks, telling Tasha's story in a nonlinear fashion and with a bold dialect, mirroring the survival strategies of indirection that Tasha employs."

In an interview furnished by her publisher, Porter named many authors who influenced her writing. As a child, she loved Lois Lenski and Beverly Cleary; later, she read Langston Hughes, Nella Larsen, Nikki Giovanni, Richard Wright, Louise Meriwether, Rosa Guy, and Maya Angelou, among others. When asked to describe herself as a writer, she said, "I would describe myself as a black female writer. I surely have been black and female all my life and now, because I'm a writer, I do not want to stop describing myself in that way. I do not fear that because there is some descriptive tag before the word 'writer' that I will be pigeonholed. Racism and sexism are what can pigeonhole you. They can limit, even stop you. Not describing myself as a black woman will not prevent that from happening."

Biographical and Critical Sources

BOOKS

Contemporary Literary Criticism, Volume 70, Gale (Detroit, MI), 1992, pp. 96-101.

PERIODICALS

American Libraries, February, 1992, p. 192.

Belles Lettres, winter, 1991, p. 7.

Booklist, August, 1993, p. 2063; January 1, 1999, Vanessa Bush, review of *Imani All Mine,* p. 834.

Chicago Tribune, August 25, 1991, p. 4.

Detroit Free Press, September 8, 1991, p. 8P.

Essence, September, 1991, p. 50; May, 1999, p. 90.

Hudson Review, spring, 1992, Gary Krist, review of *All-Bright Court,* p. 141-142.

Library Journal, February 1, 1999, Karen Anderson, review of *Imani All Mine,* p. 122.

Los Angeles Times Book Review, October 13, 1991, p. 9; September 6, 1992, p. 11.

New Yorker, September 9, 1991, p. 96.

New York Times, September 10, 1991, Michiko Kakutani, review of *All-Bright Court,* p. C14.

New York Times Book Review, October 27, 1991, p. 12; August 16, 1992, p. 32.

Publishers Weekly, July 5, 1993, review of *Addy Learns a Lesson,* p. 73; November 23, 1998, review of *Imani All Mine,* p. 58.

Tribune Books (Chicago, IL), August 25, 1991, p. 4.

Washington Post Book World, August 11, 1991, p. 3; December 1, 1991, p. 3; July 26, 1992, p. 12.

Women's Review of Books, April, 1992, Adrian Oktenberg, review of *All-Bright Court,* pp. 16-17.

OTHER

Canusius College, http://www2.canisius.edu/ (March 2, 2002), author profile of Connie Porter.

Houghton Mifflin, http://www.houghtonmifflinbooks.com/ (March 2, 2002), author profile of Connie Porter.*

*   *   *

PULVER, Harry, Jr. 1960-

Personal

Born July 31, 1960, in Hackensack, NJ; son of Harry (an engineer) and Thelma (a teacher; maiden name, Johnson) Pulver; married Tamera Menard (a teacher), March 13, 1988; children: Anna. *Education:* St. Olaf College, B.A., 1982; Minneapolis College of Art and Design, MCAD; attended Pratt Manhattan School of Design. *Politics:* Independent. *Religion:* Christian. *Hobbies and other interests:* Playing accordion and guitar in a polka rock bank.

Addresses

Home and office—105 Meadow Lane North, Minneapolis, MN 55422-5304. *E-mail*—hpulver@pclink.com.

Career

Freelance illustrator, animator, and designer. Composer of music for several animated cartoons, including *Pre Hysterical Daze* and *Good Wheel Hunting;* member of the Echo Boys, a band that creates music for commercials, in Minneapolis, MN. Volunteer for school and church. *Member:* Mr. Music Academy.

Awards, Honors

Best Polka Band, MMA, 2000, and 2001; Best Polka Recording, MMA, 2000.

Illustrator

James R. Delisle and Judy Galbraith, *The Gifted Kids Survival Guide II,* Free Spirit Publications (Minneapolis, MN), 1987.

Claire McInerney, *Find It!: The Inside Story at Your Library,* Lerner Publications (Minneapolis, MN), 1989.

Claire McInerney, *Tracking the Facts: How to Develop Research Skills,* Lerner Publications (Minneapolis, MN), 1990.

Scott Sheperd, *What Do You Think of You?: And Other Thoughts on Self-Esteem,* CompCare Publishers (Minneapolis, MN), 1990.

Alex J. Packer, *Bringing Up Parents: The Teenager's Handbook,* Free Spirit Publications (Minneapolis, MN), 1992.

Slam Dunk Trivia, Lerner Publications (Minneapolis, MN), 1998.

Bruce Adelson, *Touchdown Trivia: Secrets, Statistics, and Little-Known Facts about Football,* Lerner Publications (Minneapolis, MN), 1998.

Bruce Adelson, *Grand Slam Trivia: Secrets, Statistics, and Little-Known Facts about Pro Baseball,* Lerner Publications (Minneapolis, MN), 1999.

Bruce Adelson, *Hat Trick Trivia: Secrets, Statistics, and Little-Known Facts about Hockey,* Lerner Publications (Minneapolis, MN), 1999.

Harry Pulver, Jr.'s cartoons depict anecdotes, statistics, and little-known facts about pro baseball in **Grand Slam Trivia,** *written by Bruce Adelson.*

Work in Progress

Many freelance projects, including work for the Minnesota Safety Council and State of Health.

Sidelights

Harry Pulver, Jr. has provided humorous cartoons for several young adult nonfiction titles. In James Delisle and Judy Galbraith's *The Gifted Kids Survival Guide II,* the authors discuss topics such as social isolation, intelligence testing, boredom, and teen suicide in a manner that neither condescends to the audience nor over-intellectualizes the subjects. The book also contains interviews with a college student and a graduate student that Jerry D. Flack, writing in *School Library Journal,* found "especially revealing and fascinating." And Pulver's cartoon illustrations provide an "attractive" addition to a useful book, Flack concluded. Another useful book for adolescent students is Claire McInerney's *Tracking the Facts: How to Develop Research Skills.* Here the author provides detailed, clear instructions on how to pick a research topic, how to conduct interviews, how to use secondary sources and take notes, and how to create a bibliography. Pulver also provided the illustrations for *Bringing Up Parents,* by Alex J. Packer, "a serious, practical book that parents as well as teenagers should read," according to *Booklist* reviewer Stephanie Zvirin.

Biographical and Critical Sources

PERIODICALS

Back Stage, April 27, 1990, Jon Bream, "Echo Boys," p. 42B.
Booklist, May 1, 1993, Stephanie Zvirin, review of *Bringing up Parents,* p. 1596.
School Library Journal, December, 1987, Jerry D. Flack, review of *The Gifted Kids Survival Guide II,* p. 92; January, 1991, Anne Price, review of *Tracking the Facts,* pp. 102-103.

OTHER

Harry Pulver Web Site, http://www.pclink.com/hpulver/ (March 2, 2002).

R

RAAB, Evelyn 1951-

Personal

Born April 29, 1951; married George Raab (an artist-printmaker), September 4, 1977; children: Dustin, Jared. *Education:* Pratt Institute, B.F.A., 1972; University of Toronto, B.A.Ed., 1976.

Addresses

Agent—c/o Firefly Books, P.O. Box 1338, Ellicott Sta., Buffalo, NY 14205. *E-mail*—raabranch@nexicom.net.

Career

Writer.

Writings

Clueless in the Kitchen: A Cookbook for Teens, Firefly Books (Buffalo, NY), 1998.
The Clueless Vegetarian: A Cookbook for the Aspiring Vegetarian, Firefly Books (Buffalo, NY), 2000.
The Clueless Baker: Baking from Scratch, Firefly Books (Buffalo, NY), 2001.

For fifteen years, author of column "Cooking with Kids," in *Today's Parent Magazine* (Canada). Contributor of articles to magazines, including *Mr. Food's Easy Cooking, Toronto Parent,* and *Zellers Family Magazine.*

Work in Progress

Other cookbooks in the "Clueless" series; also a "Cooking with Kids" collection.

Sidelights

Evelyn Raab has combined her passion for cooking, love of writing, and talent for teaching into a career as a food writer. After earning a degree in fine arts from Pratt Institute and, later, a bachelor's degree in teaching from the University of Toronto, she worked for several years as a graphic artist and part time teacher. Yet, when she moved to a rural area northeast of Toronto, Ontario, where she lives with her artist husband and children, her employment options were limited. "While raising my two sons, I found myself writing a cooking column for a community newspaper," Raab told *Something about the Author.* "My column was quirky, weird, and fun to write. I discovered that you didn't have to be deadly serious to write about food. I explored the bizarre connection between men, basements, and liver; I ran a giant zucchini competition; I held a popcorn tasting in my kitchen. I didn't take it seriously. But, obviously, someone did." Her local column caught the attention of the editors of *Today's Parent,* a Canadian parenting magazine, who in 1987 asked Raab to write a "cooking with kids" column for their magazine. "The focus of this column was to be on parents cooking with their kids— simple, straightforward, and funny. I had two kids, I cooked with them, and I knew I could write about it." Fifteen years later, her children were grown, yet she was still writing the column.

The magazine column led Raab to write the "Clueless" series of cookbooks geared toward teenagers and novice cooks: *Clueless in the Kitchen: A Cookbook for Teens, The Clueless Vegetarian: A Cookbook for the Aspiring Vegetarian,* and *The Clueless Baker: Baking from Scratch.* Each cookbook deals with the fundamentals of cooking in a chatty tone. "What I see is that most people don't want to produce fancy, exotic dishes. They just want to make dinner," Raab told *SATA.* "It's the lack of confidence in their ability to cook from scratch that drives people to rely on frozen meals and packaged mixes. Cooking from scratch is just as easy, really; it just takes a little getting used to, and a few basic skills. It's my goal to teach people to cook well, using real ingredients, simple recipes, and a sense of humor." The original cookbook elicited praise from reviewers, such as Paula A. Kiely, of *School Library Journal,* who predicted that Raab's style would appeal to teenagers, and Paula Rohrlick, of *Kliatt,* who found that the work demystified the kitchen for new learners. *Booklist* critic

Anne O'Malley judged the "basic food message" to be "sensible and the recipes appealing." So too, Kim Childress, writing in *Girls' Life,* found some of Raab's vegetarian recipes in *The Clueless Vegetarian* to be "incredible," while a *Publishers Weekly* reviewer noted that Raab presented a few overlooked good ideas. Mark Knoblauch of *Booklist* predicted that teenagers "rebelling against the dominant 'burger culture,' will relish the irreverent tone of Evelyn Raab's delightfully illustrated *The Clueless Vegetarian.*"

Raab considered her lack of formal cooking training as an asset in writing for novices because she could empathize with them, and humor is another asset. According to Raab, cooking "isn't difficult or complicated or time-consuming—it just seems that way if you don't know what you're doing."

Biographical and Critical Sources

PERIODICALS

Booklist, July, 1998, Anne O'Malley, review of *Clueless in the Kitchen: A Cookbook for Teens,* p. 1872; September 15, 2000, Mark Knoblauch, review of *The Clueless Vegetarian: A Cookbook for the Aspiring Vegetarian,* p. 198.

Girls' Life, October, 2000, Kim Childress, "Out of this World," p. 40.

Kliatt, July, 1998, Paula Rohrlick, review of *Clueless in the Kitchen,* p. 36.

Publishers Weekly, July 3, 2000, review of *The Clueless Vegetarian,* p. 67.

School Library Journal, September, 1998, Paula A. Kiely, review of *Clueless in the Kitchen,* p. 224.

U.S. Catholic, April, 2001, Patrick McCormick, "McCormick's Quick Takes: Books to Stir the Cook in You," p. 40.

*   *   *

ROSENBERG, Liz 1958-

Personal

Born February 3, 1958, in Glen Cove, NY; daughter of Ross and Lucille Rosenberg; married John Gardner (a novelist), February 14, 1980 (died, 1982); married David Bosnick (a writer, teacher, and bookstore owner), 1983; children: (second marriage) Eli. *Education:* Bennington College, B.A.; Johns Hopkins University, M.A.; State University of New York, Ph.D. (comparative literature). *Politics:* "Bleeding heart liberal." *Religion:* Jewish Unitarian.

Addresses

Home—32 Highland Ave., Binghamton, NY 13905. *Office*—Department of English, State University of New York at Binghamton, Binghamton, NY 13902-6000.

Career

Poet, children's book author, and novelist. State University of New York at Binghamton, Binghamton, NY, professor of English, 1979—. Cofounder of the Indoor Playground of the City of Binghamton; member of the preschool school board, CHABAD, and the kindergarten task force. *Member:* Associated Writing Program, Poets and Writers, PEN.

Awards, Honors

Claudia Lewis Poetry Prize; Children's Choice Award; Chancellor's Award for Excellence in Teaching; National Kellogg fellow, 1982-85; Agnes Starrett Poetry Prize, 1986; Patterson Prize, and Books of Distinction Award, Hungry Mind Review, both for *Roots and Flowers: An Anthology of Poems about Family; The Carousel* was featured on the Public Broadcasting System (PBS) children's series *Reading Rainbow;* Lee Bennett Hopkins Poetry Prize, 2001, Books of Distinction Award, Hungry Mind Review, and Best Book selection, Bank Street College of Education, all for *Light-Gathering Poems.*

Writings

The Angel Poems, State Street Press Chapbooks (Pittsford, NY), 1984.

The Fire Music (poems), University of Pittsburgh Press (Pittsburgh, PA), 1986.

Adelaide and the Night Train, illustrated by Lisa Desimini, Harper (New York, NY), 1989.

Window, Mirror, Moon, illustrated by Ruth Richardson, Harper (New York, NY), 1990.

The Scrap Doll, illustrated by Robin Ballard, HarperCollins (New York, NY), 1992.

Monster Mama, illustrated by Stephen Gammell, Philomel (New York, NY), 1993.

Children of Paradise (poems), University of Pittsburgh Press (Pittsburgh, PA), 1993.

Mama Goose: A New Mother Goose, illustrated by Janet Street, Philomel (New York, NY), 1994.

The Carousel, illustrated by Jim LaMarche, Harcourt (San Diego, CA), 1995.

Grandmother and the Runaway Shadow, illustrated by Beth Peck, Harcourt (San Diego, CA), 1996.

Moonbathing, illustrated by Stephen Lambert, Harcourt (San Diego, CA), 1996.

(Consulting and contributing editor) *Total Immersion: A Mikvah Anthology,* J. Aronson (Northvale, NJ), 1996.

Heart and Soul, Harcourt (San Diego, CA), 1996.

(Editor and author of commentary) *The Invisible Ladder: An Anthology of Contemporary American Poems for Young Readers,* Holt (New York, NY), 1996.

Eli and Uncle Dawn, illustrated by Susan Gaber, Harcourt (San Diego, CA), 1997.

A Big and Little Alphabet, illustrated by Vera Rosenberg, Orchard Books (New York, NY), 1997.

I Did It Anyway, illustrated by Stephen Gammell, Harcourt (San Diego, CA), 1998.

(Editor) *Earth-Shattering Poems,* Holt (New York, NY), 1998.

Carousel horses come alive in the rain in Liz Rosenberg's **The Carousel,** *illustrated by Jim LaMarche.*

The Silence in the Mountains, illustrated by Chris Soent-piet, Orchard Books (New York, NY), 1999.

These Happy Eyes, Mammoth Press (DuBois, PA), 1999.

On Christmas Eve, illustrated by John Clapp, Dorling Kindersley (New York, NY), 2000.

(Editor) *Light-Gathering Poems,* Holt (New York, NY), 2000.

Eli's Night-Light, illustrated by Joanna Yardley, Orchard Books (New York, NY), 2001.

(Editor) *Roots and Flowers: An Anthology of Poems about Family,* Holt (New York, NY), 2001.

We Wanted You, illustrated by Peter Catalanotto, Roaring Brook Press (Brookfield, CT), 2002.

Contributor to periodicals, including *New York Times Book Review* and *Chicago Tribune.* Editor, *Manuscript* magazine, 1980-87; children's book review editor for *Parents* magazine.

Sidelights

Children's book author Liz Rosenberg "weaves empathetic storytelling with artfully placed details that set a comfortable rhythm," commented *New York Times Book Review* correspondent Eric Roston. Most of Rosenberg's work is for younger children—brightly-illustrated storybooks about walking on a moonlit beach, coming to

terms with grief or displacement by war, or purely whimsical takes on the alphabet and Mother Goose.

In *The Carousel,* for instance, two young sisters discover that the horses on an abandoned carousel have magically come alive. After riding them through the sky, the sisters realize that the horses are wild and destructive: they tame them with their deceased mother's tools and flute music. In a *Booklist* review of *The Carousel,* Stephanie Zvirin declared: "Fantasy blends beautifully with reality in a book that speaks to the emotions that stir in the wake of a parent's death."

Rosenberg eschews fantasy in *The Silence in the Mountains,* a tale in which a young boy's idyllic life is upended when a war forces him to flee to America with his family. *Booklist* correspondent John Peters noted of the work and its young character: "Iskander's feelings are certainly valid—and shared by refugees from violence the world over."

Rosenberg has also published several books for young adults, including the well-received *Earth-Shattering Poems, Light-Gathering Poems, Roots and Flowers: An Anthology of Poems about Family,* and *The Invisible Ladder: An Anthology of Contemporary American Poems for Young Readers.* A poet herself, Rosenberg has chosen poetry written by—and for—adults for her anthologies, feeling that younger readers can understand deep work. "These poems are not ones that usually make their way into anthologies for young people," observed Nancy Vasilakis in a *Horn Book* review of *Earth-Shattering Poems.* Vasilakis added that the mature poems, as well as Rosenberg's notes and commentary, "make this a particularly useful resource."

Heart and Soul, Rosenberg's first young adult novel, is a first-person tale narrated by a bewildered and depressed seventeen-year-old named Willie. Having returned home to Richmond after spending the school year in Philadelphia, Willie contemplates life with her needy mother and the increasing remoteness of her businessman father, who is gone on a trip. Rosenberg examines many issues in the work, including parent-child relationships, divorce, and self-esteem, concluding with a realistic, if optimistic, resolution. In the *New York Times Book Review,* Bruce Brooks wrote of *Heart and Soul:* "Rosenberg has put her novel together very carefully, and it is, in fact, strangely neat. The rightness of the deft, quick portraits—no one sticks around for long, but every

Seventeen-year-old Willie gains some relief from her depression by helping an eccentric fellow student in Rosenberg's first novel. (Cover illustration by Joseph Daniel Fiedler.)

single person is unforgettable—and the languid beauty of Willie's language are artfully constructed of very fine prose, matching a precise sensibility." In her *Horn Book* piece on the same work, Vasilakis stated: "Willie's adolescent angst can sometimes seem as thick as the heavy Richmond air, but the adolescent characters are compelling, and Willie's resolute search for her center grabs at your heart."

Rosenberg once commented: "Reading children's books was a large part of how I survived childhood. I read constantly, and never stopped reading books written for children. That mountain of books became a kind of leviathan—and I rode on its back through waves and storms. My childhood was happy, but seldom calm. In writing for children, I remember that past and repay that debt.

"The truly great books for children—*Charlotte's Web, A Wrinkle in Time,* among others—I still read them. Children love passionately; I think these first books stay with us, grow with us, for life. I believe there is nothing holier or higher than to write something fine for children. As A. A. Milne once said, 'It is impossible to take too much care when one is writing for children.'

"To me, writing children's books and writing poetry is two sides of the same activity. They are both visionary, illuminated art forms. They try to go directly to the heart of the matter, whatever is at stake—friendship, homesickness, immortality, love. In a way, both forms shortcut to the things that matter most, what C. G. Jung called 'the big dreams.' Poetry and children's books are big dreams written out in short-hand.

"I still have the original 'ugly old thing'—the doll I write about in *The Scrap Doll,* and sometimes my son likes to play with her. My belief in that book—as in life—is that the more you care for something, the more closely you look at it, the more you love it. Love and understanding go along hand in hand. I hope children will always find things in their lives to care for and to love, because from those activities come joy and peace of mind."

Biographical and Critical Sources

PERIODICALS

Booklist, November 15, 1994, p. 606; November 15, 1995, Stephanie Zvirin, review of *The Carousel,* p. 565; April 1, 1996, p. 1373; June 1, 1996, p. 1702; October 15, 1996, p. 422; May 15, 1997, p. 1581; November 1, 1997, p. 484; February 1, 1999, John Peters, review of *The Silence in the Mountains,* p. 982.

Horn Book, November-December, 1996, Nancy Vasilakis, review of *Heart and Soul,* p. 746; January-February, 1998, Nancy Vasilakis, review of *Earth-Shattering Poems,* p. 88.

Horn Book Guide, spring, 1995, Suzy Schmidt, review of *Mama Goose,* p. 112; spring, 1988, Maeve Visser Knoth, review of *A Big and Little Alphabet,* p. 18.

Los Angeles Times Book Review, January 28, 1990, p. 15.

New York Times Book Review, July 6, 1986, p. 23; April 1, 1990, p. 15; November 12, 1995, p. 26; September 22,

1996, Bruce Brooks, review of *Heart and Soul,* p. 28; July 18, 1999, Eric Roston, review of *The Silence in the Mountains,* p. 25.

Publishers Weekly, September 25, 1995, p. 56; October 23, 1995, p. 35; May 13, 1996, p. 76; February 3, 1997, p. 105; March 22, 1999, review of *The Silence in the Mountains,* p. 92.

School Library Journal, October, 1994, p. 114; January, 1996, Janet M. Bair, review of *The Carousel,* p. 94; March, 1996, p. 153; May, 1996, Leda Schubert, review of *Grandmother and the Runaway Shadow,* p. 98; October, 1996, p. 104; February, 1997, Kathleen Whalen, review of *The Invisible Ladder,* p. 124; June, 1997, Marianne Saccardi, review of *Eli and Uncle Dawn,* p. 100; October, 1997, p. 108; February, 1998, Sharon Korbeck, review of *Earth-Shattering Poems,* p. 124; July, 1999, Barbara Scotto, review of *The Silence in the Mountains,* p. 79.

S

SANTIAGO, Esmeralda 1948-

Personal

Born May 17, 1948, in San Juan, Puerto Rico; daughter of Pablo Santiago Díaz (a poet and carpenter) and Ramona Santiago (a factory worker); married Frank Cantor (a filmmaker), June 11, 1978; children: Lucas, Ila. *Education:* Harvard University, B.A. (magna cum laude), 1976; Sarah Lawrence College, M.F.A., 1992.

Addresses

Office—P.O. Box 679, Amawalk, NY 10501. *Agent*—Molly Friedrich, Priest Literary Agency, 708 Third Ave., New York, NY 10017.

Career

Journalist, memoirist, and novelist. ACCIION/AITEC, Cambridge, MA, bilingual secretary, 1974-76; H/M Multi Media Co., Boston, MA, producer, 1975-76; Cantomedia Corp., Boston, MA, cofounder and president, 1977—. Member of board of directors, Jacob Burns Film Center, Pleasantville, NY, and Alliance for Young Artists and Writers, New York, NY; founding member of DOVE-Domestic Violence Prevention Shelter, Quincy, MA, and Alianza Hispania Youth Unit, Dorchester, MA. Served as judge for National Endowment for the Arts (screenwriting), Massachusetts Arts and Humanities Council, and Scholastic Art and Writing Awards. *Member:* PEN (New York chapter), Writer's Guild of America (east region).

Awards, Honors

Silver Award, International Film and TV Festival, 1980; Gold Award, Houston International Film Festival, 1984; named New England Minority Businesswoman of the Year, and Minority Small Business of the Year, U.S. Department of Commerce, both 1988; Leadership Award, Massachusetts Latino Democratic Committee,

Esmeralda Santiago

1989; award from Coalition of Hispanic American Women, 1995; Best Book about Puerto Rico Life and Culture, Club Civico, for *When I Was Puerto Rican,* 1996; WomenRise! Award, Wider Opportunities for Women, 1998; American Library Association Alex Award, and Westchester Library System Best Books selection, both 1999, both for *Almost a Woman;* Literary Arts Award, Teatro Circulo, 1999; Orgullo Hispano, Univision Network, 2001; Radcliffe Association Alumnae Recognition Award, 2001; Women of Distinction Award, Girl Scouts of America, 2002. Honorary degrees from Trinity College, 1994, and Pace University, 2001.

Writings

When I Was Puerto Rican (memoir), Addison-Wesley (Reading, MA), 1993.
America's Dream (novel), HarperCollins (New York, NY), 1995.
Almost a Woman (memoir), Perseus (Reading, MA), 1998.
(Editor, with Joie Davidow) *Las Christmas: Favorite Latino Authors Share Their Holiday Memories,* illustrated by José Ortega, Knopf (New York, NY), 1998.
(Editor, with Joie Davidow) *Las Mamis: Favorite Latino Authors Remember Their Mothers,* Knopf (New York, NY), 1999.
Almost a Woman (screenplay; adapted from her memoir), ExxonMobil Masterpiece Theatre, 2001.

Also author of screenplays *Beverly Hills Supper Club,* 1980, and *Button, Button,* 1982. Contributor of articles and short stories to periodicals, including *Boston Globe, Christian Science Monitor, New York Times, Ploughshares,* and Spanish-language publications.

Santiago's books have been translated into seven different languages.

Work in Progress

A generational novel; a third memoir.

Sidelights

Esmeralda Santiago and her family, including ten other siblings moved to New York City from Puerto Rico when she was an adolescent. Part of a planned series of memoirs, *When I Was Puerto Rican* and *Almost a Woman* trace her experiences from her childhood home in Puerto Rico to her life in the United States from the age of thirteen and beyond. In addition to relating the events in Santiago's life as she adjusted to life in the United States and her growing need to achieve success in her new home, Santiago's memoirs also examine the tensions that her Americanization brought, both as she learned to live in New York and on her return trips to Puerto Rico.

Santiago's descriptions of her life in Puerto Rico are filled with memories of a loving family life, poverty, and ambition. As she relates the events of her childhood, punctuated each year with the arrival of a new sibling, fights between her parents, and the family's final move to Brooklyn to live with Santiago's grandmother, her "portraits are clear-sighted" and her "immigrant experience [is] ... artfully and movingly told" said a critic for *Publishers Weekly* about *When I Was Puerto Rican.* As Santiago moved between her life in the United States and visits to Puerto Rico, she found herself struggling with her inability to fit into either culture. She explained in interviews and essays that this struggle to define herself, the confusion that arose from not fitting into either culture drove her to write the book, and "in writing the book I wanted to get back to that feeling of Puertoricanness I had before I came [to the United States]." Critics applauded *When I Was Puerto Rican,*

praising it for both style and content. Yvonne V. Saphia, writing in the *Los Angeles Times,* characterized the work as "stylistically fluid and finely detailed" and "deserving a unique place in contemporary Latino storytelling." Similarly, a *Kirkus Reviews* contributor praised the memoir as "clear eyed, quietly powerful, and often lyrical: a story of true grit."

In her second memoir, *Almost a Woman,* Santiago continues her story, expanding on her experiences in New York as a young teenager struggling between helping her younger siblings adjust to their new life and trying to support her mother in ensuring the family's survival. The picture that emerges is of a young girl who has an independent spirit, and while this causes conflict with the traditions of her culture, "Santiago's good humor, zest for life and fighting spirit permeate her chronicle" enthused a reviewer for *Publishers Weekly.* Donna Seaman, writing for *Booklist,* noted that at the heart of this book is Santiago's relationship with her mother, the "fulcrum of [her] balancing act between life in their brimming barrio ... and life in the wider world."

Between the time she issued her two memoirs, Santiago also published a novel called *America's Dream.* This book tells the story of a Puerto Rican woman, as she struggles to break the cycle of early pregnancy and domestic violence in which she is caught and in which she fears her daughter will as well. America Gonzalez works at her job as a maid; trying to make a decent life for her family, she is dismayed when she learns that her fourteen-year-old daughter, Rosalinda, has run away with a boyfriend. America herself has been involved in an abusive relationship with Rosalinda's father, Correa, for over fifteen years and finds herself unable to break the cycle of violence and abuse. Yet, when the manager of the hotel where she works recommends her as a nanny for some wealthy American guests, America takes the chance and leaves. Reviewing the novel for *Publishers Weekly,* Paula Chin commented that Santiago has "written a timely and credible tale of a battered woman's struggle to break away."

In addition to her memoirs and novel, Santiago has also coedited two anthologies of Latino writings. *Las Mamis: Favorite Latino Authors Remember Their Mothers* is a collection of fourteen memoirs dedicated to the mothers who inspired the writers contributing to this anthology. While the immigrant experience is central to the stories included in this collection, Hazel Rochman noted that the "combination of family folklore and self-discovery ... makes these stories universal."

"As a child, I never imagined I'd be a writer," Santiago told *SATA.* "My dreams were to be an opera singer, but I can't carry a tune. Or to be a race-car driver, but I only learned to drive when I was thirty-three. Or to be a chemist, but I was never very good at memorizing the table of elements or at following formulas to the letter. I was a dancer for many years, and dreamed of being a dancer the rest of my life. But my joints and bones and other parts resist the movements I so painstakingly perfected in the dance studio, and right now I'd rather watch a dancer than be one. I decided to become a writer in early middle age, which coincided with my children's infancy. Watching them grow, teaching them what they needed at the moment, answering their questions, I became curious about my mother, who raised eleven children. It was the memories of her that led me to write, to explore what it was like to be her child, and to remember. Memory can be a terrible burden. So it was to release the tension of all those memories that I wrote, and to free myself to create more memories.

"It's taken me two memoirs to get through the first twenty years of my life!," Santiago added. "And it often feels as if everything I want people to know is contained in those books, and in the essays and op-ed pieces I've written. When I go to parties in which I'm expected to chit and chat, I often wish people would just read my books instead of asking me about myself. If I answer their questions, it feels as if I'm repeating what has already been said in a more coherent and considered way. That's the curse of the memoir writer. You end up boring yourself!"

Biographical and Critical Sources

BOOKS

Notable Hispanic American Women, Book 2, Gale (Detroit, MI), 1998.
Santiago, Esmeralda, *When I Was Puerto Rican*, Addison-Wesley (Reading, MA), 1993.

PERIODICALS

Booklist, May 15, 1996, Joanne Wilkinson, review of *America's Dream*, p. 1570; August, 1998, Donna Seaman, review of *Almost a Woman*, p. 1957; March 15, 2000, Hazel Rochman, review of *Las Mamis: Favorite Latino Authors Remember Their Mothers*, p. 1299.
Kirkus Reviews, August 15, 1993, p. 1058; March 1, 1996, p. 327.
Los Angeles Times, December 26, 1993, Yvonne V. Saphia, review of *When I Was Puerto Rican*, p. 9.
Publishers Weekly, September 13, 1993, review of *When I Was Puerto Rican*, p. 114; July 22, 1996, Paula Chin, review of *America's Dream;* June 15, 1998, review of *Almost a Woman*, p. 47.

*   *   *

SEFTON, Catherine
See WADDELL, Martin

*   *   *

SHAN, Darren
See O'SHAUGHNESSY, Darren

SHEFELMAN, Janice Jordan 1930-

Personal

Born April 12, 1930, in Baytown, TX; daughter of Gilbert John (a professor and writer) and Vera (Tiller) Jordan; married Thomas Whitehead Shefelman (an architect), September 18, 1954; children: Karl Jordan, Daniel Whitehead. *Ethnicity:* "German/English." *Education:* Southern Methodist University, B.A., 1951, M.Ed., 1952; University of Texas—Austin, Library Certificate, 1980.

Addresses

Home—1405 West 32nd St., Austin, TX 78703. *E-mail*—TJShef@aol.com and Shefelmanbooks.com.

Career

Teacher at public schools in Dallas, TX, 1952-54, and Episcopal schools in Austin, TX, 1955-57; volunteer worker, 1957-80; Lake Travis Independent School District, Austin, TX, librarian, 1980-84; full-time writer, 1980—. Storyteller and lecturer at public schools in Austin, TX. *Member:* Society of Children's Book Writers and Illustrators, Authors Guild, Austin Writers League.

Awards, Honors

Texas Library Association included *A Paradise Called Texas* in its Texas Bluebonnet Award Master List, 1985-86; "Pick of the Lists," *American Bookseller*, Notable Children's Trade Book in the Field of Social Studies, National Council for the Social Studies/Children's Book Council, and featured on the Public Broadcasting System's children's series *Reading Rainbow*, all 1992, all for *A Peddler's Dream*.

Writings

A Paradise Called Texas (children's novel), Eakin Press (Austin, TX), 1983.
Willow Creek Home (children's novel), Eakin Press (Austin, TX), 1985.
Spirit of Iron (children's novel), Eakin Press (Austin, TX), 1987.
Victoria House (picture book), illustrated by Tom Shefelman, Harcourt (San Diego, CA), 1988.
A Peddler's Dream (picture book), illustrated by Tom Shefelman, Houghton (Boston, MA), 1992.
A Mare for Young Wolf (easy-to-read book), illustrated by Tom Shefelman, Random House (New York, NY), 1993.
Young Wolf's First Hunt (easy-to-read book), illustrated by Tom Shefelman, Random House (New York, NY), 1995.
Young Wolf and Spirit Horse (easy-to-read book), illustrated by Tom Shefelman, Random House (New York, NY), 1997.
Comanche Song (young adult novel), Eakin Press (Austin, TX), 2000.

Contributor to periodicals.

Work in Progress

Sophie's War, a juvenile novel; *I, Antonio Vivaldi,* a picture book, with illustrations by Tom Shefelman.

Sidelights

Janice Jordan Shefelman once commented: "I have always thought of myself as a late bloomer, and I did not begin to write for children until I was forty-eight years old. Since my college days I have done freelance articles for magazines and newspapers, but it was not until I sat down at the proverbial dining room table and began to write *A Paradise Called Texas* that I found what it was I wanted to write: books for children.

"The idea for this first novel came from stories my father told me when I was a child, about how my great-grandfather left Germany in 1845 and brought his wife and young daughter with him to the Texas frontier. They had expected a paradise, but instead they found hardship, tragedy, and adventure. I wanted to make the daughter, Mina, come alive, and by writing her story, find out what she thought and felt. When I finished the book, the characters clamored for more adventures, so one book has grown into 'The Texas Trilogy.'

"Children's books have long been a favorite of mine ever since my father read *Winnie the Pooh* to me. As my two sons were growing up I read to them every night. At long last I decided that I too could write books like those I loved to read.

"A writer must read widely and live fully. One of my great pleasures is travel. When my husband and I married we sold all our possessions and traveled around the world for a year on freighters, living for several weeks in a Buddhist temple, all the while writing and illustrating our adventures for various newspapers. A dominant force in my life is the idea that one must dream and then go about making dreams come true. Perhaps this belief is the reason the story of my German ancestors' immigration to Texas was so appealing to me. The only way to realize a dream is to begin—to write the outline of a book, then the first paragraph. Then, as Goethe said, 'the mind grows heated.'"

Biographical and Critical Sources

PERIODICALS

Austin American-Statesman, November 1, 1983.
Booklist, October 15, 1988; February 15, 2001, Karen Hutt, review of *Comanche Song,* p. 1128.
Houston Post, April 8, 1984.
Kirkus Reviews, September 1, 1988; September 1, 1992.
New York Times Book Review, November 8, 1992.
School Library Journal, August, 1984; April, 1986; February, 1988; March, 1989; October, 1992; October, 2000, Coop Renner, review of *Comanche Song,* p. 171.

SHELTON, William Roy 1919-1995

OBITUARY NOTICE—See index for *SATA* sketch: Born April 9, 1919, in Rutherfordton, NC; died August 2, 1995, in Carbondale, IL. Journalist, writer, and film producer. Shelton began his career as an assistant professor of English at Rollins College, and later became bureau chief and correspondent for *Time* magazine, as well as a contributing editor to *Saturday Evening Post.* He wrote numerous books for younger readers, and also produced documentary and educational films. He authored a series of books (mostly about space exploration), including *Land of the Everglades* (1958), *Countdown: The Story of Cape Canaveral* (1960), *Flights of the Astronauts* (1963), *Man's Conquest of Space* (1968), and *Winning the Moon,* published in 1970. He also released a novel, *Stowaway to the Moon* (1973), and a collection of poems, *New Hope for the Dead,* which appeared in 1977. Shelton contributed short stories and articles to popular magazines, including *Atlantic, Fortune, Saturday Evening Post,* and *Life.* He received the *Atlantic Monthly* "First" Award in 1947 for his short story "The Snow Girl," and the O. Henry Prize Stories Award in 1948.

OBITUARIES AND OTHER SOURCES:

BOOKS

The Encyclopedia of Science Fiction, St. Martin's (New York, NY), 1993.

PERIODICALS

Locus, December, 1992, p. 68.
Orange County Register, October 1, 1992, p. F5.

*   *   *

SILLS, Leslie 1948-

Personal

Born January 26, 1948, in Brooklyn, NY; daughter of Louis (a stockbroker) and Sylvia (a proprietor of a women's clothing store; maiden name, Garland) Sills; married Robert Oresick (separated); children: Eric Sills Oresick. *Education:* Boston University, B.A., 1969; attended School of the Museum of Fine Arts (Boston, MA), 1970-73.

Addresses

Home and office—38 St. Paul St., Brookline, MA 02446. *Agent*—Elizabeth Harding, Curtis Brown Ltd., 10 Astor Pl., New York, NY 10003. *E-mail*—LESills@aol.com.

Career

Teacher in Brookline, MA, 1970—; artist and sculptor, 1971—; writer, 1985—. Work represented by Molina Gallery, Cambridge, MA, and also shown at exhibitions in the United States and in public and private collections, including one at Fidelity Management and Trust. Lecturer at colleges and universities, including School of

Leslie Sills with son, Eric

the Museum of Fine Arts, Massachusetts College of Art, Boston University, Wheelock College, Simmons College, Salem State College, and Regis College; workshop presenter; speaker on women artists at schools, libraries, and museums. *Member:* National Women's Caucus for Art, PEN New England (member of executive committee, Children's Book Caucus), Boston Women's Caucus for Art.

Awards, Honors

One Hundred Titles for Reading and Sharing citation, New York Public Library, Pick of the Lists selection, *American Bookseller,* Best Ten Books for Children selection, *Parenting* magazine, Editor's Choice selection, *Booklist,* and Notable Book selection, American Library Association, all 1989, and included in recommended list of biographies for children, *Boston Globe,* 1991, all for *Inspirations: Stories about Women Artists;* honored by National Women's Caucus for Art, 1989; Brookline Arts Lottery grant, 1989; grant from Barbara Deming Memorial Fund, 1991; One Hundred Titles for

Reading and Sharing selection, New York Public Library, Pick of the Lists selection, *American Bookseller,* Editor's Choice selection, *Booklist,* and Best Books for 1993 selection, *School Library Journal,* all 1993, and Notable Book selection, American Library Association, 1994, all for *Visions: Stories about Women Artists;* Mary B. Bishop/Francis S. Merritt scholar in woodworking, Haystack Mountain School of Crafts, 1994; fellow in crafts, New England Foundation for the Arts and National Endowment for the Arts, 1995; resident at Blue Mountain Center, 1999; Editor's Choice selection and One of the Best Ten Art Books for Children selection, *Booklist,* 2000, Best Books for the Teen Age selection and One Hundred Titles for Reading and Sharing selection, New York Public Library, and Best Books selection, Bank Street College of Education, both 2001, all for *In Real Life: Six Women Photographers.*

Writings

Inspirations: Stories about Women Artists, Albert Whitman (Morton Grove, IL), 1989.
Visions: Stories about Women Artists, Albert Whitman (Morton Grove, IL), 1993.
In Real Life: Six Women Photographers, Holiday House (New York, NY), 2000.
From Rags to Riches: A History of Girls Clothing in America, Holiday House (New York, NY), 2003.

Contributor to books, including *Pilgrims and Pioneers: New England Women in the Arts,* edited by Alicia Faxon and Sylvia Moore, Midmarch Arts Press (New York, NY), 1987. Contributor to periodicals, including *School Arts* and *Sojourner.*

Sidelights

Leslie Sills told *SATA:* "When I began to teach art in the 1970s, there were few books written for children on women artists. Because I was a professional artist (mixed-media sculptor) and struggled a great deal trying to exhibit and sell my work, I thought it important that future generations grow up knowing about women artists and accepting their work as an intrinsic part of our culture. I also wanted to encourage and support children's (particularly girls') creative efforts by providing role models.

"I had read many biographies of artists to help my artistic development. *Frida: A Biography of Frida Kahlo* by Hayden Herrera and *Alice Neel* by Patricia Hills made lasting impressions. I love the emotional power in the work of these artists and feel indebted to Herrera and Hills for introducing them. Kahlo's and Neel's life stories are inspiring as well, as they both had to overcome enormous obstacles to create their art and exhibit it. Moreover, my artwork is somewhat related to Kahlo's, which made her story especially meaningful.

"In the 1980s, when I wrote my first book, *Inspirations: Stories about Women Artists,* I began with Kahlo and Neel. I didn't think of myself as a writer then, but I was determined to change children's access to this information. I thought if I could write the same way I speak to children, perhaps I would be successful. I knew nothing of the children's book world, of journals, reviewers, or even many authors. Till then, I had spent most of my energies pursuing my art and art galleries.

"I was so surprised to find how many people liked what I wrote. People I didn't know from all over the country were supportive. One of my favorite reviews was from *School Library Journal,* in which Shirley Wilton said, 'This book should be put in the hands of as many young people as possible.' Eight-year-old Alexis Elmore, who reviewed *Inspirations* for the *San Francisco Review of Books,* wrote, 'And when you read this book you will be inspired too. The stories show how anyone can reach a goal if they try hard enough.'

"Since *Inspirations* I've written *Visions: Stories about Women Artists* and *In Real Life: Six Women Photographers.* I feel so fortunate that I've had opportunities to tell children about these exceptional women, to share art that I love, and to show what Alexis Elmore said, that one can reach their goal if they try. The artist and writer Faith Ringgold once said, 'Persistence is the key to success.'"

Biographical and Critical Sources

PERIODICALS

Booklist, January, 1989, review of *Inspirations: Stories about Women Artists;* April, 1993, review of *Visions: Stories about Women Artists;* December 1, 2000, Gillian Engberg, review of *In Real Life: Six Women Photographers,* p. 709.
Boston Globe, March 27, 1993, Nancy Stapen, "Inspiring Visions of Women Artists"; July 25, 1993, review of *Visions;* September 20, 1995, Christine Temin, "From Figurative to Fantastic, Women's Art That Keeps Symbols Alive."
Bulletin of the Center for Children's Books, February 3, 1993, review of *Visions.*
Chicago Tribune, April 9, 1989, review of *Inspirations.*
Childhood Education, winter, 1993-94, review of *Visions.*
Feminist Bookstore News, March-April, 1989, review of *Inspirations.*
Horn Book, September-October, 1991, review of *Inspirations;* July-August, 1993, review of *Visions;* January-February, 2001, review of *In Real Life.*
Kirkus Reviews, February, 1989, review of *Inspirations;* May, 1993, review of *Visions;* October 1, 2000, review of *In Real Life.*
Ms., May, 1989, review of *Inspirations.*
New York Times, December 16, 1993, review of *Visions.*
New York Times Book Review, February 12, 1989, review of *Inspirations.*
Publishers Weekly, November 25, 1988, review of *Inspirations;* May 10, 1993, review of *Visions;* October 9, 2000, review of *In Real Life.*
Reading Teacher, March, 1993, review of *Inspirations;* February, 1994, review of *Visions.*
San Francisco Review of Books, January-February, 1993, Alexis Elmore, review of *Inspirations.*

School Library Journal, January, 1989, Shirley Wilton, review of *Inspirations;* April, 1993, review of *Visions.*
Voice of Youth Advocates, February, 2001, Debbie Earl, review of *In Real Life.*

OTHER

Leslie Sills, http://www.lesliesills.com/ (August 7, 2001).

* * *

SIMON, Norma (Feldstein) 1927-

Personal

Born December 24, 1927, in New York, NY; daughter of Nathan Philip (a restaurant owner) and Winnie Bertha (Lepselter) Feldstein; married Edward Simon (in advertising and consumer research), June 7, 1951; children: Stephanie, Wendy (died, 1979), Jonathan. *Education:* Brooklyn College (now Brooklyn College of the City University of New York), B.A., 1947; Bank Street College of Education, certification in the education of young children, 1948, M.A., 1968; New School for Social Research, graduate study, 1948-50.

Addresses

Home—P.O. Box 428, South Wellfleet, MA 02663.

Career

Frances I. duPont & Co. (brokerage), New York City, clerical worker, 1943-46; teacher at Vassar Summer Institute, Poughkeepsie, NY, and for Department of Welfare, Brooklyn, NY, 1948-49, at Downtown Community School, New York City, 1949-52, and at Thomas School, Rowayton, CT, 1952-53; Norwalk Community Cooperative Nursery School, Rowayton, founder, director, and teacher, 1953-54; Norwalk Public Schools, teacher, 1962-63; Greater Bridgeport Child Guidance Center, Bridgeport, CT, group therapist, 1965-67; Mid-Fairfield Child Guidance center, Fairfield, CT, special teacher, 1967-69. Consultant, Stamford Pre-School Program, Stamford, CT, 1965-69; consultant to School Division, Macmillan Publishing Co., Inc., New York City, 1968-70; consultant, Davidson Films, Inc., 1969-74, and Aesop Films, 1975; consultant in children's advertising, Dancer-Fitzgerald-Sample, Inc., New York City, 1969-79. Bank Street College of Education, consultant to Publications Division, 1967-74, and to Follow-Through Program, 1971-72. Volunteer at Wellfleet Elementary School, MA, 1972-2000. *Member:* Authors Guild, Bank Street College Alumni Association, Friends of Wellfleet Library, Delta Kappa Gamma (honorary member).

Awards, Honors

Jeremiah Cahir Friend of Education award, Barnstable County Education Association, 1987, for outstanding and continuous service to education; Grand Marshall of parade in honor of children's literature, Wellfleet, MA, 2000.

Norma Simon shows that feelings of anger are normal in some situations in **I Was So Mad!** *(Illustrated by Dora Leder.)*

Writings

The Wet World, illustrated by Jane Miller, Lippincott, 1954, reprinted, Candlewick Press (Cambridge, MA), 1995.

Baby House, Lippincott, 1955, reprinted, Simon & Schuster Children's Books (New York, NY), 1995.

A Tree for Me, Lippincott, 1956.

Up and over the Hill, Lippincott, 1957.

My Beach House, Lippincott, 1958.

The Daddy Days, illustrated by Abner Graboff, Abelard, 1958.

A Day at the County Fair, Lippincott, 1959.

Happy Purim Night, illustrated by Ayala Gordon, United Synagogue of America, 1959.

The Purim Party, illustrated by A. Gordon, United Synagogue of America, 1959.

Rosh Hashanah, illustrated by A. Gordon, United Synagogue of America, 1959.

Yom Kippur, illustrated by A. Gordon, United Synagogue of America, 1959.

Our First Sukkah, illustrated by A. Gordon, United Synagogue of America, 1959.

My Simchat Torah Flag, illustrated by A. Gordon, United Synagogue of America, 1959.

Happy Hanukkah, United Synagogue of America, 1959.

Every Friday Night, illustrated by Harvey Weiss, United Synagogue of America, 1962.

My Family Seder, illustrated by H. Weiss, United Synagogue of America, 1962.

Tu Bishvat, illustrated by H. Weiss, United Synagogue of America, 1962.

Elly the Elephant, illustrated by Stanley Bleifeld, St. Martin's, 1962.

Passover, illustrated by Symeon Shimin, Crowell, 1965.

Benjy's Bird, Whitman (Morton Grove, IL), 1965.

Hanukkah, illustrated by S. Shimin, Crowell, 1966.

What Do I Say?, illustrated by Joe Lasker, Whitman (Morton Grove, IL), 1967, reprinted, Whitman (Morton Grove, IL), 1991.

Ruthie, Meredith Corp., 1968.

See the First Star, Whitman (Morton Grove, IL), 1968.

What Do I Do?, illustrated by J. Lasker, Whitman (Morton Grove, IL), 1969.

How Do I Feel?, illustrated by J. Lasker, Whitman (Morton Grove, IL), 1970.

I Know What I Like, illustrated by Dora Leder, Whitman (Morton Grove, IL), 1971.

I Was So Mad!, illustrated by D. Leder, Whitman (Morton Grove, IL), 1974.

All Kinds of Families, illustrated by J. Lasker, Whitman (Morton Grove, IL), 1976.

Why Am I Different?, illustrated by D. Leder, Whitman (Morton Grove, IL), 1976.

We Remember Philip, illustrated by Ruth Sanderson, Whitman (Morton Grove, IL), 1978.

I'm Busy, Too, illustrated by D. Leder, Whitman (Morton Grove, IL), 1980.

Go Away, Warts!, illustrated by Susan Lexa, Whitman (Morton Grove, IL), 1980.

Nobody's Perfect, Not Even My Mother, illustrated by D. Leder, Whitman (Morton Grove, IL), 1981.

Where Does My Cat Sleep?, illustrated by D. Leder, Whitman (Morton Grove, IL), 1982.

I Wish I Had My Father, Whitman (Morton Grove, IL), 1983.

Children express their emotions after the death of someone close in Simon's sensitively written **The Saddest Time.** *(Illustrated by Jacqueline Rogers.)*

Oh, That Cat!, illustrated by D. Leder, Whitman (Morton Grove, IL), 1986.

The Saddest Time, illustrated by Jacqueline Rogers, Whitman (Morton Grove, IL), 1986.

Cats Do, Dogs Don't, Whitman (Morton Grove, IL), 1986.

Children Do, Grownups Don't, illustrated by Helen Cogancherry, Whitman (Morton Grove, IL), 1987.

Wedding Days, illustrated by Christa Kieffer, Whitman (Morton Grove, IL), 1988.

I Am Not a Crybaby, illustrated by H. Cogancherry, Whitman (Morton Grove, IL), 1989.

Mama Cat's Year, illustrated by D. Leder, Whitman (Morton Grove, IL), 1991.

Story of Hanukkah, illustrated by Leonid Gore, HarperCollins (New York, NY), 1997.

Story of Passover, illustrated by Erica Weihs, HarperCollins (New York, NY), 1997.

Looking Back at Wellfleet: A Children's Historical Walking Tour, Wellfleet Historical Society and the Wellfleet Elementary School (Wellfleet, MA), 1997.

Fire Fighters, illustrated by Pamela Paparone, Simon & Schuster Children's Books (New York, NY), 1998.

All Kinds of Children, illustrated by Diane Paterson, Whitman (Morton Grove, IL), 1999.

Every Family Is Special, Whitman (Morton Grove, IL), 2003.

Contributor to *Dimensions of Language Experience,* edited by Charlotte Winsor, Agathon Press, 1975. Materials development and skills editor, Bank Street-Macmillan Early Childhood Discovery Materials, 1968; associate skills editor, "Discoveries," Houghton, 1972.

I Was So Mad!, What Do I Say? and *What Do I Do?* have been translated into Spanish. *All Kinds of Families* has been translated into Swedish, German, and Danish.

Simon's papers (1954-1991) are included in the de Grummond Collection at the University of Southern Mississippi and the Kerlan Collection at the University of Michigan.

Work in Progress

"Another Mama Cat book, a folk tale, two concept books, plus several other ideas I am developing for young children."

Dalmatian fire fighters depict the routine of gearing up, fighting, investigating, and cleaning up after a fire in **Fire Fighters.** *(Written by Simon and illustrated by Pamela Paparone.)*

Readers discover what they have in common with children around the world in Simon's **All Kinds of Children.** *(Illustrated by Diane Paterson.)*

Sidelights

Since the 1950s Norma Simon has been writing children's books that help young readers understand the world around them. Her books explore a range of sensitive topics, including parental separation in *I Wish I Had My Father,* developmental differences in *Why Am I Different?,* crying and its various causes in *I Am Not a Crybaby,* self-esteem in *Nobody's Perfect, Not Even My Mother,* and death in *We Remember Philip* and *The Saddest Time.* Simon has also written about the history and traditions surrounding various Jewish holidays in books such as *Passover, Hanukkah, Rosh Hashanah, Yom Kippur, Our First Sukkah,* and *Every Friday Night.* In 1999, *All Kinds of Children* was published. Ilene Cooper, in a review for *Booklist,* noted, "But this book, besides brimming with child appeal, may serve to get young children talking about how children are both the same and different the world over." Cooper concluded, "Depicted at work, at play, and with family and friends, the children exemplify both their uniqueness and their universality."

Orphaned at the age of 18, Simon went on to college to receive a Bachelor of Arts degree at Brooklyn College (which became Brooklyn College of the City University of New York) and certification in the education of young children at the Bank Street College of Education. She once commented that "the most important single influence on my work and my life has been my long and challenging association with the Bank Street College of Education." In 1951, she married Edward Simon, who worked in advertising and consumer research. Simon taught children in several schools in New York and Connecticut until the early 1960s and later worked as a group therapist and special teacher for two child guidance centers. She also served as a consultant to schools, publishers, and educational film companies.

Simon once commented: "I have thought of children as my life's work more than writing. Writing books for children is one of the ways in which I can touch the lives of children I will never see. Children themselves have provided the material and inspiration for most of my books, and children reading my books often nod their heads in agreement as they recognize my mirror for their very own feelings, experiences and expressions. I have tried to anchor for young children some of the certainties, joys and experiences they know and recognize in spite of the unstable, complex and confusing times of our lives.

"I love to read to children and watch their faces as they move into the feelings expressed in the story. As they are reminded of their own stories and discoveries, they are eager to share their memories with others, and to use language for communication, and this is what books are all about. I begin and end with children, and that explains most of my life."

Biographical and Critical Sources

PERIODICALS

Booklist, March 15, 1999, Ilene Cooper, review of *All Kinds of Children,* p. 1332.

School Library Journal, March 1997, Celia A. Huffman, review of *The Story of Passover,* p. 180; October 1997, Jane Marino, review of *The Story of Hannukkah,* p. 39; June 1999, Ann Welton, review of *All Kinds of Children,* p. 122.

*   *   *

STARKE, Ruth (Elaine) 1946-

Personal

Born May 15, 1946, in Adelaide, Australia; daughter of Jeffrey William and Edith (Mildenhall) Toolin; married Russell Stewart Starke, May, 1972 (marriage ended, 1985); children: Miranda Sheridan, Petra Meredith. *Education:* Flinders University of South Australia, B.A. (with honors), 1995, Ph.D., 2000.

Addresses

Home—P.O. Box 112, Goodwood, South Australia 5034. *Office*—Department of English, Flinders University of South Australia, G.P.O. Box 2100, Adelaide, South Australia 5001, Australia. *E-mail*—ruth.starke@flinders.edu.au.

Career

American Chamber of Commerce, Adelaide, Australia, manager, 1970-76; American Express, Adelaide, Australia, public relations executive, 1980-90; Flinders University of South Australia, Adelaide, Australia, part-time tutor and lecturer in English, 1996—; Adelaide Institute of Technical and Further Education, Adelaide, Australia, part-time lecturer in creative writing, 2000—. National Festival Awards for Literature, judge of children's books, 1996-2000. *Member:* Australian Society of Authors, Ekidnas South Australian Children's Bookwriters; South Australian Writers' Centre (chair, 1998-2001).

Awards, Honors

Southcorp Literary Award, 1997, for "Monkey Business"; Aurealis Award for Science Fiction (young adult short novel category), 1998, for *The Twist in the Tale;* Notable Book citation (older readers category), Children's Book Council of Australia, 1998, for *Coming Out;* Honour Book (younger readers category), Children's Book Council of Australia, 2000, for *NIPS XI.*

Writings

The Great Violin Fiddle, Reed Books, 1995.
The Psychic Dog, Reed Books, 1995.
Stalker, Omnibus (Norwood, Australia), 1995.
Coming Out, Omnibus (Norwood, Australia), 1996.
The Twist in the Tale, illustrated by Tom Jellett, Lothian (Port Melbourne, Australia), 1997.
(Editor, with Chris Tugwell) *Solo Spots: Senior Drama Monologues,* Oxford University Press (Melbourne, Australia), 1998.
Writers, Readers, and Rebels: Upfront and Backstage at Australia's Top Literary Festival (nonfiction for adults), Wakefield Press (Kent Town, Australia), 1998.
NIPS XI, Lothian (Port Melbourne, Australia), 2000.
Dead Red, Lothian (Port Melbourne, Australia), 2001.
Saving Saddler Street, Lothian (Port Melbourne, Australia), 2002.
Starstruck, Lothian (Port Melbourne, Australia), 2002.

Contributor of articles and reviews to periodicals, including *Viewpoint: On Books for Young Adults* and *Australian Review of Books.*

Sidelights

Ruth Starke told *SATA:* "I took a long time getting around to doing what I enjoy most: writing fiction. But it wasn't until I returned to university in 1992 to complete a long-abandoned degree that I worked out how to do it. Reading and studying the great books of English literature taught me how to write—and the reduced

Ruth Starke

income that goes with being a student gave me the motivation! All my books were written and published while I was also completing my degrees. I received my Ph.D. the day before my novel *NIPS XI* was shortlisted for the book of the year award of the Children's Book Council of Australia, and I don't know which thrilled me more.

"Although I have some regrets about my late start, I think all budding writers need to get some life experience under their belts first. I've lived and worked in the United Kingdom and Italy, and my years in travel marketing gave me numerous experiences to explore the world. I think the biggest and best change in Australia during my lifetime has been brought about by migration, and I wish that our multiculturalism was better reflected in our media and literature."

Biographical and Critical Sources

PERIODICALS

Adelaide Advertiser, December 9, 1995, Katharine England, review of *Stalker;* October 28, 2000, Katharine England, review of *NIPS XI.*
Age, September 9, 1995, Pam Macintyre, review of *Stalker.*
Australian Book Review, November, 2001, review of *Dead Red.*
Australian Review of Books, February, 2001, Pam Macintyre, review of *NIPS XI.*
Children's Book Council Newsletter, February, 2001, Katharine England, review of *NIPS XI.*
Lollipops, December-January, 2001, Cecile Ferguson, review of *NIPS XI.*
Magpies, November, 1995, Nola Allen, review of *The Great Violin Fiddle;* November, 1995, review of *Stalker;* November, 2000, Neville Barnard, review of *NIPS XI.*
Reading Time, February, 2001, Kevin Brophy, review of *NIPS XI.*
Viewpoint: On Books for Young Adults, Volume 4, number 4, 1996, Jenny Pausacker, review of *Coming Out;* spring, 1997, Jane Ponting, review of *The Twist in the Tale.*
Weekend Australian, October 14, 1995, Frances Kelly, review of *The Great Violin Fiddle.*

OTHER

Ruth Starke Web Site, http://www.ruthstarke.itgo.com/ (April 13, 2001).

*   *   *

STINE, Jovial Bob
See STINE, R(obert) L(awrence)

STINE, R(obert) L(awrence) 1943- (Eric Affabee, Zachary Blue, Jovial Bob Stine)

Personal

Born October 8, 1943 in Columbus, OH; son of Lewis (a shipping manager) and Anne (Feinstein) Stine; married Jane Waldhorn (owner/managing director of Parachute Press), June 22, 1969; children: Matthew Daniel. *Education:* Ohio State University, B.A. 1965; graduate study at New York University, 1966-67. *Religion:* Jewish. *Hobbies and other interests:* Swimming, watching old movie classics from the 1930s and 1940s, reading (especially P. G. Wodehouse novels).

Addresses

Office—c/o Parachute Press, 156 5th Avenue, New York, NY 10010.

Career

Author of books for children and adults, 1980—. Social studies teacher at a junior high school in Columbus, OH, 1965-66; writer for several magazines in New York City, 1966-68; assistant editor, *Junior Scholastic (New York, NY)* magazine, Scholastic (New York, NY), Inc., New York City, 1968-71; editor, *Search* magazine, Scholastic (New York, NY), Inc., New York City, 1972-75; editor/creator, *Bananas* magazine, Scholastic (New York, NY), Inc., New York City, 1975-84; editor/creator, *Maniac* magazine, Scholastic (New York, NY), Inc., New York City, 1984-85; head writer for *Eureeka's Castle,* Nickelodeon cable television network, 1986-87. *Member:* Writers Guild of America, Mystery Writers of America.

Awards, Honors

Children's Choice Award, American Library Association, for several novels; Lifetime Achievement Award, Ohioanna Library Association; *Guinness World Records* listing for best-selling children's series in history, 2000, for the "Goosebumps" series; three time winner of Nickelodeon Kid's Choice Award.

Writings

YOUNG ADULT NOVELS

Blind Date, Scholastic (New York, NY), 1986.
Twisted, Scholastic (New York, NY), 1987.
Broken Date ("Crosswinds" Series), Simon & Schuster (New York, NY), 1988.
The Baby-Sitter, Scholastic (New York, NY), 1989.
Phone Calls, Archway (New York, NY), 1990.
How I Broke Up with Ernie, Archway (New York, NY), 1990.
Curtains, Archway (New York, NY), 1990.
The Boyfriend, Scholastic (New York, NY), 1990.
Beach Party, Scholastic (New York, NY), 1990.
Snowman, Scholastic (New York, NY), 1991.

The Girlfriend, Scholastic (New York, NY), 1991.
Baby-Sitter II, Scholastic (New York, NY), 1991.
Beach House, Scholastic (New York, NY), 1992.
Hit and Run, Scholastic (New York, NY), 1992.
Hitchhiker, Scholastic (New York, NY), 1993.
Baby-Sitter III, Scholastic (New York, NY), 1993.
The Dead Girl Friend, Scholastic (New York, NY), 1993.
Halloween Night, Scholastic (New York, NY), 1993.
Call Waiting, Scholastic (New York, NY), 1994.
Halloween Night 2, Scholastic (New York, NY), 1994.

"FEAR STREET" SERIES

The New Girl, Archway (New York, NY), 1989.
The Surprise Party, Archway (New York, NY), 1990.
The Stepsister, Archway (New York, NY), 1990.
Missing, Archway (New York, NY), 1990.
Halloween Party, Archway (New York, NY), 1990.
The Wrong Number, Archway (New York, NY), 1990.
The Sleepwalker, Archway (New York, NY) 1991.
Ski Weekend, Archway (New York, NY), 1991.
The Secret Bedroom, Archway (New York, NY), 1991.
The Overnight, Archway (New York, NY), 1991.
Lights Out, Archway (New York, NY), 1991.
Haunted, Archway (New York, NY), 1991.
The Fire Game, Archway (New York, NY), 1991.
The Knife, Archway (New York, NY), 1992.
Prom Queen, Archway (New York, NY), 1992.
First Date, Archway (New York, NY), 1992.
The Best Friend, Archway (New York, NY), 1992.
Sunburn, Archway (New York, NY), 1993.
The Cheater, Archway (New York, NY), 1993.
The New Boy, Archway (New York, NY), 1994.
Bad Dreams, Archway (New York, NY), 1994.
The Dare, Archway (New York, NY), 1994.
Double Date, Archway (New York, NY), 1994.
The First Horror, Archway (New York, NY), 1994.
The Mind Reader, Archway (New York, NY), 1994.
One Evil Summer, Archway (New York, NY), 1994.
The Second Horror, Archway (New York, NY), 1994.
The Third Horror, Archway (New York, NY), 1994.
The Thrill Club, Archway (New York, NY), 1994.
College Weekend, Archway (New York, NY), 1995.
Final Grade, Archway (New York, NY), 1995.
The Stepsister 2, Archway (New York, NY), 1995.
Switched, Archway (New York, NY), 1995.
Truth or Dare, Archway (New York, NY), 1995.
Wrong Number 2, Archway (New York, NY), 1995.
What Holly Heard, Pocket Books (New York, NY), 1996.
The Face, Pocket Books (New York, NY), 1996.
Secret Admirer, Pocket Books (New York, NY), 1996.
The Perfect Date, Pocket Books (New York, NY), 1996.
The Boy Next Door, Simon & Schuster (New York, NY), 1996.
Night Games, Pocket Books (New York, NY), 1996.
Runaway, Archway (New York, NY), 1997.
Killer's Kiss, Archway (New York, NY), 1997.
All-Night Party, Archway (New York, NY), 1997.
The Rich Girl, Archway (New York, NY), 1997.
Cat, Archway (New York, NY), 1997.
Fear Hall: The Beginning, Archway (New York, NY), 1997.
Fear Hall: The Conclusion, Archway (New York, NY), 1997.

R. L. Stine

"FEAR STREET SUPER CHILLER" SERIES

Party Summer, Archway (New York, NY), 1991.
Goodnight Kiss, Archway (New York, NY), 1992.
Silent Night, Archway (New York, NY), 1992.
Broken Hearts, Archway (New York, NY), 1993.
Silent Night II, Archway (New York, NY), 1993.
The Dead Lifeguard, Archway (New York, NY), 1994.
Bad Moonlight, Archway (New York, NY), 1995.
Dead End, Archway (New York, NY), 1995.
High Tide, Archway (New York, NY), 1997.

"FEAR STREET CHEERLEADERS" SERIES

The First Evil, Archway (New York, NY), 1992.
The Second Evil, Archway (New York, NY), 1992.
The Third Evil, Archway (New York, NY), 1992.
The New Evil, Archway (New York, NY), 1994.

"FEAR STREET SAGA" SERIES

The Betrayal, Archway (New York, NY), 1993.
The Secret, Archway (New York, NY), 1993.
The Burning, Archway (New York, NY), 1993.
A New Fear, Pocket Books (New York, NY), 1996.
House of Whispers, Simon & Schuster (New York, NY), 1996.
The Hidden Evil, Archway (New York, NY), 1997.
Daughters of Silence, Archway (New York, NY), 1997.
Children of Fear, Archway (New York, NY), 1997.

"GHOSTS OF FEAR STREET" SERIES

Nightmare in 3-D, Pocket Books (New York, NY), 1996.
Stay Away from the Treehouse, Pocket Books (New York, NY), 1996.
Eye of the Fortuneteller, Pocket Books (New York, NY), 1996.
Fright Knight, Pocket Books (New York, NY), 1996.
Revenge of the Shadow People, Pocket Books (New York, NY), 1996.
The Bugman Lives, Pocket Books (New York, NY), 1996.
The Boy Who Ate Fear Street, Pocket Books (New York, NY), 1996.
Night of the Werecat, Pocket Books (New York, NY), 1996.
Body Switchers from Outer Space, Pocket Books (New York, NY), 1996.
Fright Christmas, Pocket Books (New York, NY), 1996.
Don't Ever Get Sick at Granny's, Pocket Books (New York, NY), 1997.

"GOOSEBUMPS" SERIES

Welcome to Dead House, Scholastic (New York, NY), 1992.
Stay out of the Basement, Scholastic (New York, NY), 1992.
Monster Blood, Scholastic (New York, NY), 1992.
Say Cheese and Die, Scholastic (New York, NY), 1992.
The Curse of the Mummy's Tomb, Scholastic (New York, NY), 1993.
Let's Get Invisible, Scholastic (New York, NY), 1993.
Night of the Living Dummy, Scholastic (New York, NY), 1993.
The Girl Who Cried Monster, Scholastic (New York, NY), 1993.
Welcome to Camp Nightmare, Scholastic (New York, NY), 1993.
The Ghost Next Door, Scholastic (New York, NY), 1993.
The Haunted Mask, Scholastic (New York, NY), 1993.
Be Careful What You Wish For, Scholastic (New York, NY), 1993.
Piano Lessons Can Be Murder, Scholastic (New York, NY), 1993.
The Werewolf of Fever Swamp, Scholastic (New York, NY), 1993.
You Can't Scare Me, Scholastic (New York, NY), 1993.
One Day at Horrorland, Scholastic (New York, NY), 1994.
Why I'm Afraid of Bees, Scholastic (New York, NY), 1994.
Monster Blood 2, Scholastic (New York, NY), 1994.
Deep Trouble, Scholastic (New York, NY), 1994.
The Scarecrow Walks at Midnight, Scholastic (New York, NY), 1994.
Go Eat Worms!, Scholastic (New York, NY), 1994.
Ghost Beach, Scholastic (New York, NY), 1994.
Return of the Mummy, Scholastic (New York, NY), 1994.
Phantom of the Auditorium, Scholastic (New York, NY), 1994.
Attack of the Mutant, Scholastic (New York, NY), 1994.
My Hairiest Adventure, Scholastic (New York, NY), 1994.
A Night in Terror Tower, Scholastic (New York, NY), 1995.
The Cuckoo Clock of Doom, Scholastic (New York, NY), 1995.

Monster Blood 3, Scholastic (New York, NY), 1995.
It Came from Beneath the Sink, Scholastic (New York, NY), 1995.
The Night of the Living Dummy 2, Scholastic (New York, NY), 1995.
The Barking Ghost, Scholastic (New York, NY), 1995.
The Horror at Camp Jellyjam, Scholastic (New York, NY), 1995.
Revenge of the Lawn Gnomes, Scholastic (New York, NY), 1995.
A Shocker on Shock Street, Scholastic (New York, NY), 1995.
The Haunted Mask 2, Scholastic (New York, NY), 1995.
The Headless Ghost, Scholastic (New York, NY), 1995.
The Abominable Snowman of Pasadena, Scholastic (New York, NY), 1995.
How I Got My Shrunken Head, Scholastic (New York, NY), 1996.
Night of the Living Dummy 3, Scholastic (New York, NY), 1996.
Bad Hare Day, Scholastic (New York, NY), 1996.
Egg Monsters from Mars, Scholastic (New York, NY), 1996.
The Beast from the East, Scholastic (New York, NY), 1996.
Say Cheese and Die—Again!, Scholastic (New York, NY), 1996.
Ghost Camp, Scholastic (New York, NY), 1996.
How to Kill a Monster, Scholastic (New York, NY), 1996.
Legend of the Lost Legend, Scholastic (New York, NY), 1996.
Attack of the Jack-o'-Lanterns, Scholastic (New York, NY), 1996.
Vampire Breath, Scholastic (New York, NY), 1996.
Calling All Creeps!, Scholastic (New York, NY), 1996.
Beware the Snowman, Scholastic (New York, NY), 1997.
How I Learned to Fly, Scholastic (New York, NY), 1997.
Chicken, Chicken, Scholastic (New York, NY), 1997.
Don't Go to Sleep!, Scholastic (New York, NY), 1997.
The Blob That Ate Everyone, Scholastic (New York, NY), 1997.
The Curse of Camp Cold Lake, Scholastic (New York, NY), 1997.
My Best Friend Is Invisible, Scholastic (New York, NY), 1997.
Deep Trouble II, Scholastic (New York, NY), 1997.
The Haunted School, Scholastic (New York, NY), 1997.
Werewolf Skin, Scholastic (New York, NY), 1997.
I Live in Your Basement!, Scholastic (New York, NY), 1997.
Monster Blood IV, Scholastic (New York, NY), 1997.

Also author of "Goosebumps Presents" books based on the television series, including *The Girl Who Cried Monster,* 1996, and *Welcome to Camp Nightmare,* 1996.

"GIVE YOURSELF GOOSEBUMPS" SERIES

Escape from the Carnival of Horrors, Scholastic (New York, NY), 1995.
Tick Tock, You're Dead, Scholastic (New York, NY), 1995.
Trapped in Bat Wing Hall, Scholastic (New York, NY), 1995.

The Deadly Experiments of Dr. Eeek, Scholastic (New York, NY), 1996.

Night in Werewolf Woods, Scholastic (New York, NY), 1996.

Beware of the Purple Peanut Butter, Scholastic (New York, NY), 1996.

Under the Magician's Spell, Scholastic (New York, NY), 1996.

The Curse of the Creeping Coffin, Scholastic (New York, NY), 1996.

The Knight in Screaming Armor, Scholastic (New York, NY), 1996.

Diary of a Mad Mummy, Scholastic (New York, NY), 1996.

Deep in the Jungle of Doom, Scholastic (New York, NY), 1996.

Welcome to the Wicked Wax Museum, Scholastic (New York, NY), 1996.

Scream of the Evil Genie, Scholastic (New York, NY), 1997.

The Creepy Creations of Professor Shock, Scholastic (New York, NY), 1997.

Please Don't Feed the Vampire, Scholastic (New York, NY), 1997.

Secret Agent Grandma, Scholastic (New York, NY), 1997.

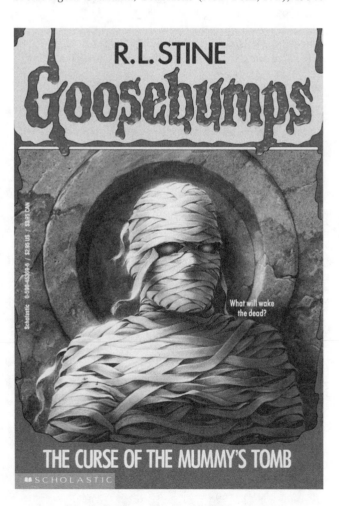

Gabe discovers the meaning of a legendary curse while lost in a pyramid in Egypt. (Cover illustration by Tim Jacobus.)

The Little Comic Shop of Horrors, Scholastic (New York, NY), 1997.

Attack of the Beastly-Babysitter, Scholastic (New York, NY), 1997.

Escape From Camp Run For Your Life, Scholastic (New York, NY), 1997.

Toy Terror: Batteries Included, Scholastic (New York, NY), 1997.

The Twisted Tale of Tiki Island, Scholastic (New York, NY), 1997.

Return to the Carnival of Horrors, Scholastic (New York, NY), 1998.

Zapped in Space, Scholastic (New York, NY), 1998.

Lost In Stinkeye Swamp, Scholastic (New York, NY), 1998.

Shop Till You Drop . . . Dead, Scholastic (New York, NY), 1998.

Alone in Snakebite Canyon, Scholastic (New York, NY), 1998.

Checkout Time at the Dead-End Hotel, Scholastic (New York, NY), 1998.

Night of a Thousand Claws, Scholastic (New York, NY), 1998.

You're Plant Food!, Scholastic (New York, NY), 1998.

Werewolf of Twisted Tree Lodge, Scholastic (New York, NY), 1998.

It's Only a Nightmare!, Scholastic (New York, NY), 1998.

It Came from the Internet, Scholastic (New York, NY), 1999.

Elevator to Nowhere, Scholastic (New York, NY), 1999.

Hocus-Pocus Horror, Scholastic (New York, NY), 1999.

Ship of Ghouls, Scholastic (New York, NY), 1999.

Escape from Horror House, Scholastic (New York, NY), 1999.

Into the Twister of Terror, Scholastic (New York, NY), 1999.

Scary Birthday to You!, Scholastic (New York, NY), 1999.

Zombie School, Scholastic (New York, NY), 1999.

Danger Time, Scholastic (New York, NY), 2000.

All-Day Nightmare, Scholastic (New York, NY), 2000.

"GIVE YOURSELF GOOSEBUMPS SPECIAL EDITION" SERIES

Into the Jaws of Doom, Scholastic (New York, NY), 1998.

Return to Terror Tower, Scholastic (New York, NY), 1998.

Trapped in the Circus of Fear, Scholastic (New York, NY), 1998.

One Night in Payne House, Scholastic (New York, NY), 1998.

The Curse of the Cave Creatures, Scholastic (New York, NY), 1999.

Revenge of the Body Squeezers, Scholastic (New York, NY), 1999.

Trick or . . . Trapped, Scholastic (New York, NY), 1999.

Weekend at Poison Lake, Scholastic (New York, NY), 1999.

"GOOSEBUMPS 2000" SERIES

Cry of the Cat, Scholastic (New York, NY), 1998.

Bride of the Living Dummy, Scholastic (New York, NY), 1998.

Creature Teacher, Scholastic (New York, NY), 1998.

Invasion of the Body Squeezers Part 1, Scholastic (New York, NY), 1998.

Invasion of the Body Squeezers Part 2, Scholastic (New York, NY), 1998.
I Am Your Evil Twin, Scholastic (New York, NY), 1998.
Revenge R Us, Scholastic (New York, NY), 1998.
Fright Camp, Scholastic (New York, NY), 1998.
Are You Terrified Yet?, Scholastic (New York, NY), 1998.
Headless Halloween, Scholastic (New York, NY), 1999.
Attack of the Graveyard Ghouls, Scholastic (New York, NY), 1999.
Brain Juice, Scholastic (New York, NY), 1999.
Return to Horrorland, Scholastic (New York, NY), 1999.
Jekyll and Heidi, Scholastic (New York, NY), 1999.
Scream School, Scholastic (New York, NY), 1999.
The Mummy Walks, Scholastic (New York, NY), 1999.
The Werewolf in the Living Room, Scholastic (New York, NY), 1999.
Horrors of the Black Ring, Scholastic (New York, NY), 1999.
Return to Ghost Camp, Scholastic (New York, NY), 1999.
Be Afraid—Be Very Afraid!, Scholastic (New York, NY), 1999.
The Haunted Car!, Scholastic (New York, NY), 1999.
Full Moon Fever, Scholastic (New York, NY), 1999.
Slappy's Nightmare, Scholastic (New York, NY), 1999.
Earth Geeks Must Go!, Scholastic (New York, NY), 1999.
Ghost in the Mirror, Scholastic (New York, NY), 2000.

Also author of *Tales to Give You Goosebumps,* and *More Tales to Give You Goosebumps.*

"NIGHTMARE ROOM" SERIES

Liar, Liar, HarperCollins (New York, NY), 2000.
Locker 13, Avon (New York, NY), 2000.
Don't Forget Me!, Avon (New York, NY), 2000.
Dear Diary, I'm Dead, HarperCollins (New York, NY), 2000.
Shadow Girl, Avon (New York, NY), 2001.
The Howler, Avon (New York, NY), 2001.
Camp Nowhere, HarperCollins (New York, NY), 2001.
They Call Me Creature, HarperCollins (New York, NY), 2001.

JUVENILE

The Time Raider, illustrations by David Febland, Scholastic (New York, NY), 1982.
The Golden Sword of Dragonwalk, illustrations by Febland, Scholastic (New York, NY), 1983.
Horrors of the Haunted Museum, Scholastic (New York, NY), 1984.
Instant Millionaire, illustrations by Jowill Woodman, Scholastic (New York, NY), 1984.
Through the Forest of Twisted Dreams, Avon (New York, NY), 1984.
The Badlands of Hark, illustrations by Bob Roper, Scholastic (New York, NY), 1985.
The Invaders of Hark, Scholastic (New York, NY), 1985.
Demons of the Deep, illustrations by Fred Carrillo, Golden Books (New York, NY), 1985.
Challenge of the Wolf Knight ("Wizards, Warriors and You" series), Avon (New York, NY), 1985.
James Bond in Win, Place, or Die, Ballantine (New York, NY), 1985.

Lost in his new school, Tommy hears voices of kids calling for help.

Conquest of the Time Master, Avon (New York, NY), 1985.
Cavern of the Phantoms, Avon (New York, NY), 1986.
Mystery of the Imposter, Avon (New York, NY), 1986.
Golden Girl and the Vanishing Unicorn ("Golden Girl" series), Ballantine (New York, NY), 1986.
The Beast, Minstrel (New York, NY), 1994.
I Saw You That Night!, Scholastic (New York, NY), 1994.
The Beast 2, Minstrel (New York, NY), 1995.
When Good Ghouls Go Bad, Avon (New York, NY), 2001.

JUVENILE: "INDIANA JONES" SERIES

Indiana Jones and the Curse of Horror Island, Ballantine (New York, NY), 1984.
Indiana Jones and the Giants of the Silver Tower, Ballantine (New York, NY), 1984.
Indiana Jones and the Cult of the Mummy's Crypt, Ballantine (New York, NY), 1985.
Indiana Jones and the Ape Slaves of Howling Island, Ballantine (New York, NY), 1987.

JUVENILE: "G. I. JOE" SERIES

Operation: Deadly Decoy, Ballantine (New York, NY), 1986.
Operation: Mindbender, Ballantine (New York, NY), 1986.
Serpentor and the Mummy Warrior, 1987.
Jungle Raid, Ballantine (New York, NY), 1988.

Siege of Serpentor ("G.I. Joe" series), Ballantine (New York, NY), 1988.

JUVENILE; UNDER NAME JOVIAL BOB STINE

The Absurdly Silly Encyclopedia and Flyswatter, illustrations by Bob Taylor, Scholastic (New York, NY), 1978.

How to Be Funny: An Extremely Silly Guidebook, illustrations by Carol Nicklaus, Dutton (New York, NY), 1978.

The Complete Book of Nerds, illustrations by Sam Viviano, Scholastic (New York, NY), 1979.

The Dynamite Do-It-Yourself Pen Pal Kit, illustrations by Jared Lee, Scholastic (New York, NY), 1980.

Dynamite's Funny Book of the Sad Facts of Life, illustrations by Lee, Scholastic (New York, NY), 1980.

Going Out! Going Steady! Going Bananas!, photographs by Dan Nelken, Scholastic (New York, NY), 1980.

The Pig's Book of World Records, illustrations by Peter Lippman, Random House (New York, NY), 1980.

(With wife, Jane Stine) *The Sick of Being Sick Book,* edited by Ann Durrell, illustrations by Nicklaus, Dutton (New York, NY), 1980.

Bananas Looks at TV, Scholastic (New York, NY), 1981.

The Beast Handbook, illustrations by Taylor, Scholastic (New York, NY), 1981.

(With J. Stine) *The Cool Kids' Guide to Summer Camp,* illustrations by Jerry Zimmerman, Scholastic (New York, NY), 1981.

Gnasty Gnomes, illustrations by Lippman, Random House (New York, NY), 1981.

Don't Stand in the Soup, illustrations by Nicklaus, Bantam (New York, NY), 1982.

(With J. Stine) *Bored with Being Bored!: How to Beat the Boredom Blahs,* illustrations by Zimmerman, Four Winds (New York, NY), 1982.

Blips!: The First Book of Video Game Funnies, illustrations by Bryan Hendrix, Scholastic (New York, NY), 1983.

(With J. Stine) *Everything You Need to Survive: Brothers and Sisters,* illustrated by Sal Murdocca, Random House (New York, NY), 1983.

(With J. Stine) *Everything You Need to Survive: First Dates,* illustrated by Murdocca, Random House (New York, NY), 1983.

(With J. Stine) *Everything You Need to Survive: Homework,* illustrated by Murdocca, Random House (New York, NY), 1983.

(With J. Stine) *Everything You Need to Survive: Money Problems,* illustrated by Murdocca, Random House (New York, NY), 1983.

Jovial Bob's Computer Joke Book, Scholastic (New York, NY), 1985

Miami Mice, illustrations by Eric Gurney, Scholastic (New York, NY), 1986.

One Hundred and One Silly Monster Jokes, Scholastic (New York, NY), 1986.

The Doggone Dog Joke Book, Parachute Press, 1986.

Pork & Beans: Play Date, illustrations by Jose Aruego and Ariane Dewey, Scholastic (New York, NY), 1989.

Ghostbusters II Storybook, Scholastic (New York, NY), 1989.

One Hundred and One Vacation Jokes, illustrated by Rick Majica, Scholastic (New York, NY), 1990.

The Amazing Adventures of Me, Myself and I, Bantam (New York, NY), 1991.

OTHER

Superstitious (adult horror), Warner Books (New York, NY), 1995.

It Came from Ohio: My Life as a Writer, (autobiography), Scholastic (New York, NY), 1997.

Nightmare Hour (short stories), HarperCollins (New York, NY), 1999.

The Haunting Hour (short stories), HarperCollins (New York, NY), 2001.

Beware! R. L. Stine Picks His Favorite Scary Stories, HarperCollins (New York, NY), 2002.

Also author of several "Twistaplot" books for Scholastic and "You Choose the Storyline" books for Ballantine and Avon.

Adaptations

The "Goosebumps" series was produced by Scholastic Inc. as a live-action television series for the Fox Television Network beginning in 1995; *When Good Ghouls Go Bad* was adapted for video by Fox, 2001; *The Nightmare Room* series was adapted for a television show by Kids WB (Warner Brothers) network, 2001.

Sidelights

"As she gazed at the plate, the eggs shimmered, then transformed themselves. Corky's mouth dropped open as she now stared at two enormous wet eyeballs. 'No!' The eyeballs stared back at her. Their color darkened to gray. Then the gray became a sickening green, the green of decay, and a foul odor rose up from the plate." Where does R. L. Stine, the author of over two hundred books for children and teenagers, get ideas for scenes like this one? "That's the question people ask me most often, but to this date I don't really have a good answer," Stine once commented. "I get ideas from all kinds of places. People know how desperate I am for ideas, because I'm doing so many books, so they try to help me. Just recently I was on vacation, lying on the beach, talking to a guy I'd just met. I told him I wrote horror books, and he said, 'You should do one on earwigs. Earwigs are really scary.' Everybody has an idea ... sometimes people send me things like newspaper clippings of stories they found. I actually did a 'Fear Street' based on a true story, about a girl who planned to murder her teacher. I've never dreamed an idea—kids always ask me if I have—and I've never woken up in the morning with one. It's a shame ... I'm still waiting for that. Mostly, I spend a lot of time just thinking about it. My son always asks me, 'Dad, how do you get an idea?' And I have to say, 'You sit down and think until you have one.' He hates that answer, but I have no choice—I have to have the ideas."

With several best-selling series going full speed, Stine *really* didn't have a choice. For his popular "Fear Street" series and his "Goosebumps" series, Stine wrote twenty-four horror novels a year. His newest series, "Nightmare

Room," required an equally gargantuan effort of word-smithing. As if that weren't enough to keep him almost perpetually chained to his computer, Stine also does the occasional "special" title.

Stine claims he never planned to write horror novels in the first place. For many years, R. L. Stine was known as "Jovial Bob Stine," and his specialty was making younger kids laugh, not giving teens the shivers. He began his career in children's publishing at Scholastic (New York, NY), where he spent sixteen years working on four different magazines, two of which he created. These two periodicals, *Bananas* and *Maniac,* focused on humor, and eventually led Stine to his career as an author of children's books. Ellen Rudin, an editor at Dutton, was impressed with *Bananas,* and asked Stine to consider writing a humorous book for younger readers. Since starting his magazine career, Stine hadn't thought seriously about writing a book, but he readily agreed to work up an idea anyway. The result was *How to Be Funny* by Jovial Bob Stine, published in 1978. Many more funny books followed during the late seventies and well into the eighties. Most of these titles were published by several different publishing houses, and some were co-authored by Stine's wife, Jane (who at that time was the editor of *Dynamite,* another children's magazine published by Scholastic).

During the eighties, Stine also began writing "Twista-plot" books for Scholastic (New York, NY), as well as other "You Choose the Storyline" books for Ballantine (New York, NY) and Avon (New York, NY), some under the pseudonyms Eric Affabee and Zachary Blue. These books, which featured as many as thirty endings and many plot twists, proved to be great training for future novel writing.

When Scholastic began having financial trouble in the mid-1980s, Stine was let go in a reorganization. Far from a personal disaster, however, being fired provided Stine with the opportunity to devote more time to writing books. It was around this time that Jean Feiwel, editorial director of Scholastic Books, suggested that the author try his hand at a horror novel. The result was *Blind Date,* which features a teenage boy with a memory lapse, the mysterious teenage girl who wants to date him, and plenty of twists and turns in the plot.

Like several of Stine's horror novels that have been written in the interim, *Blind Date* had a title long before it had characters or a storyline. Feiwel suggested the title, and Stine went home to build a novel around it. Since then, titles often come to him before the stories themselves. "If I can get a title first, then I start getting ideas for it. Like *The Baby-Sitter.* You start to think, what's scary about being a baby-sitter? Or *The Stepsister* . . . what would be scary about getting a new stepsister? Usually the title will lead me to ideas about what the book should be," Stine once commented.

This same process worked for Stine's "Fear Street" series. With the success of *Blind Date* and two Scholastic (New York, NY) novels that followed, *Twisted* and

The Baby-Sitter, it occurred to the author and his wife that a series of novels that came out on a regular basis might sell well. By this time, Jane had also left Scholastic to open her own book packaging company, Parachute Press. Jane suggested that Stine come up with a concept for a series that she could sell through Parachute Press. "So I sat down and thought," Stine once remarked. "When the words 'Fear Street' sort of magically appeared, I wrote them down, and then came up with the concept."

The "Fear Street" series, which now has one hundred titles and millions of copies in print, is a collection of novels connected primarily by their setting. The main characters usually reside on Fear Street, a place "where your worst nightmares live," according to the cover copy on early titles. All the series' characters attend Shady-side High, a school where the death rate must be horrific, since nearly every book features at least one murder.

As Paul Gray noted in *Time* magazine, "Fear Street" stories, like other "teen tinglers," subscribe to "a fairly consistent set of formulas." The teenage heroes or heroines are normal (although not always nice) kids who suddenly find their lives fraught with danger. Sometimes the menace comes from supernatural forces, as in the "Cheerleaders" series. The first book of this series introduces Bobbi and Corky Corcoran, sisters who join the cheerleading squad at their new school, Shadyside High. After Bobbi dies in a bizarre "accident," Corky realizes there may have been some truth to her sister's ravings about the strange things she had seen and experienced recently. Investigating her sister's death, Corky discovers the "evil," a century-old force that has risen from the grave. Although she seemingly outwits the evil by the end of the book, it returns to terrorize the cheerleading squad through two more books, until Corky is finally able to permanently destroy it.

Sometimes the villains in the "Fear Street" novels are mere mortals with murderous tendencies, as in *Silent Night* and *Broken Hearts. Silent Night* is the story of Reva Dalby, a beautiful but cold rich girl who finds herself on the receiving end of some cruel practical jokes. When two people are murdered, it appears that Reva may be the killer's next target. *Broken Hearts* features another entirely human killer. This murderer announces his intentions by sending future victims valentines with nasty messages inside ("Who's sending these cards?/ Don't bother to wonder/ On Valentine's Day/ You'll be six feet under.") Whatever the source of the menace, these kids don't turn to adults for salvation. They consult friends and do their best to find their own way out of their predicaments. Or sometimes, like Bobbi in *The First Evil* and Josie in *Broken Hearts,* they never find a way out, but simply die trying.

Other important components of the "Fear Street" formula are an emphasis on plot over characterization, and a hair-raising pace. One way Stine keeps his stories moving is to end every chapter with a cliff-hanger, a feature the author says his readers find particularly appealing. It doesn't seem to matter that the suspense sometimes dissolves instantly when the reader turns the page, such as when the "hideous, bloated head of a corpse" in Corky's bed turns out to be a Halloween mask, or when the man who tries to accost Reva in a dimly lit department store turns out to be a mannequin she's brushed against. As Stine once commented, his fans "like the fact that there is some kind of jolt at the end of every chapter. They know that if they read to the end of the chapter they're going to have some kind of funny surprise, something scary, something that's going to happen ... and force them to keep reading."

While Stine's fans don't seem to mind the formulaic nature of his books, the critics are sometimes less generous. In a review of *Twisted,* a *Publishers Weekly* reviewer said that "For shock value, this book adds up to a lot of cheap tricks." A *Publishers Weekly* review of *Ski Weekend* was similarly critical, noting that "the contrived plot barely manages to hold together a series of bland cliffhangers." In a review of *The Second Evil* for *Voice of Youth Advocates,* Caroline S. McKinney declared that "these formula stories are very predictable and require very little thought on the part of the reader." Nevertheless, many reviewers have recognized—sometimes begrudgingly—Stine's talent for hooking his readers and keeping them entertained. Alice Cronin, in a review of *The Sleepwalker* for *School Library Journal,* stated that "Stine writes a good story. Teens will love the action." In a review of *Curtains,* a *Publishers Weekly* columnist noted that although "the book ... will never be mistaken for serious literature, it is sure to engross Stine's considerable following." And in a review of *Silent Night* in *Voice of Youth Advocates,* Sylvia C. Mitchell declared that "If all series books were this good, I'd begin to drop my ... prejudices against them."

Stine agrees that the merit of his work lies in the books' entertainment value, not their literary significance, but he sees nothing wrong with that. "I believe that kids as well as adults are entitled to books of no socially redeeming value," he once noted. And although his books may be frightening, the scares are "safe scares," as he told Gray. "You're home in your room and reading. The books are not half as scary as the real world."

In fact, Stine makes a point of ensuring that the horror in his books retains an element of the unreal. "I don't put in anything that would be too close to their lives," he once commented, when asked what would be going too far for his readers. "I wouldn't do child abuse, or AIDS, or suicide, or anything that could really touch someone's life like that. The books are supposed to be just entertainment, that's all they are."

To work, though, the teens in his books must seem real, even if the horror elements stay in the realm of the fantastic. Stine works hard at making his characters talk like real kids, dress like real kids, and have the concerns of real kids. Though they may be worried about some unseen evil or a mysterious killer, they still care about whether or not they have a date for Saturday night.

When it comes to the way his characters look, sound and behave, "I don't want to sound like some middle-aged guy who doesn't know what he's doing," Stine commented.

Luckily, Stine has a son, Matt, who provided him with plenty of first-hand experience with teens. "He had lots of friends," Stine said in his interview, "and I listened to them." Stine does his homework, too, by reading teen magazines and watching MTV. "It's very important in these books," he says, "that the kids sound and look like real kids, suddenly trapped in something horrible."

One thing Stine does not do, however, is try to keep up with the latest in teen slang. "I don't have them saying things like 'gnarly,' and other stuff people accuse me of putting in," Stine once remarked. "I'd like these books to be read five years from now, and that kind of slang really dates them fast. Besides," he added, "most kids talk normal."

An indication of the degree of admiration Stine engenders in his readers is the amount of fan mail he receives. Stine commented that the letters are the "best part" of his success, and he reads every one. Most of the kids

Readers wake up from a nightmare in a strange place and with an unknown identity, and follow the instructions at the bottom of the pages to choose their own adventure.

who write tell Stine how much they enjoy his books, and some say that his novels are the only ones they read. Stine gets letters from teachers and librarians too, sometimes telling about students who would never read a book before, but now can't wait for the next Stine thriller.

On one occasion, though, the mail brought a strange letter that baffled and disturbed Stine. A girl from Florida wrote, "I loved your book *The Baby-Sitter*. You made it all seem so real. The same thing happened to me, only it was my uncle who tried to kill me. Keep up the good work. Thanks a lot." Stine didn't quite know what to make of it. "I didn't know if she was putting me on, or if it was a plea for help, or what," he says. Fortunately, the letter came in a group from a class, and Stine had the teacher's name and address: "I wrote to her and said, 'Maybe you should look into this.'" Stine never got a response from the teacher, though, and he still wonders what the real story behind that letter was.

At times, teen writer-wannabes ask Stine for his advice on becoming successful. He tells them not to do what he did, which was spend a good portion of his teen years sending his work to publishers, hoping to make a sale. All he accomplished, Stine once commented, was to waste people's time and collect a lot of rejection letters, which was "horrible." Instead, Stine tells them to read, read—and read some more. That way "you pick up all these different styles, almost by osmosis," he said, "and you'll be a better writer for it."

Aspiring writers might also want to take a tip from Stine's method of crafting his horror stories. These days he always begins with a chapter-by-chapter outline that details the action. This wasn't the case with his first novels. "I started doing it this way kicking and screaming," Stine once recalled. "I didn't want any part of these outlines, because sometimes you end up revising the outline, and revising it again until (the editor) approves it, and it's an arduous process. But that's the whole work. An outline helps me see whether or not the books make sense. I always start with the ending—that's the first thing I know. Then I can go back and figure out how to fool the reader, how to keep them from guessing the ending. By the time I sit down to write the book, I really know everything that's going to happen. I can just have fun and write it."

With over 300 million copies of his books in print, Stine has become a household word in children's books, enshrined in the *Guinness World Records 2000: Millennium Edition* as author of the world's top-selling children's stories. The success of the "Fear Street" and "Goosebumps" series did not slow him down; in 2000 he began the "Nightmare Room" series with a new publisher, HarperCollins, aimed at the eight-to twelve-year-olds market. Stine told Andrea Sachs in *Time* magazine that he saw the new series "more like a fun house" than the "roller coaster ride" which "Goosebumps" was intended to be. "You step inside this place, and everything seems normal at first. And then you look and see, ah, the floor is tilted. And then it looks like the walls are closing in on

you .... You're not in your old reality." Sachs felt that two early titles in the series, *Don't Forget Me!* and *Locker 13*, "read like slightly more sophisticated installments of 'Goosebumps.'" Stine's prose is, according to Sachs, "as usual, simple, his dialogue attuned to the speech of the young.... The plots of both involve Stine's trademark: teenagers being frightened witless in a context assuring readers that nothing truly dangerous will occur." This safety in the midst of terror is Stine's signature. As he admitted to Sachs, "There's more teasing than horror in my books." The "Nightmare Room" quickly became Stine's second TV series. He told *SATA* that he promises lots more scares are on the way.

Biographical and Critical Sources

BOOKS

Authors and Artists for Young Adults, Volume 13, Gale (Detroit, MI), 1994.
Children's Literature Review, Volume 37, Gale (Detroit, MI), 1996, pp. 101-23.
Guinness World Records 2000: Millennium Edition, Mint (New York, NY), 2000.
Jones, Patrick, *What's So Scary about R. L. Stine?,* Scarecrow Press (Metuchen, NJ), 1998.
Roginski, Jim, *Behind the Covers,* Libraries Unlimited, 1985, pp. 206-13.
Stine, R. L., *The Third Evil,* Archway (New York, NY), 1992.
Stine, R. L., *Broken Hearts,* Archway (New York, NY), 1993.
St. James Guide to Young Adult Writers, 2nd edition, St. James Press, 1999.

PERIODICALS

Booklist, October 15, 1999, p. 446.
Language Arts, November, 1998, pp. 115-122.
Los Angeles Times, June 29, 1997, p. 1.
Newsweek, January 24, 2001, p. 8.
New York Times, April 2, 1997, p. A16.
Publishers Weekly, July 10, 1987, review of *Twisted,* p. 87; September 28, 1990, review of *Curtains,* p. 104; December 7, 1990, review of *Fear Street: Ski Weekend,* p. 830; May 11, 1998, p. 20; August 30, 1999, p. 85; September 25, 2000, p. 118; September 10, 2001, p. 29; September 24, 2001, p. 94.
School Library Journal, September, 1990, Alice Cronin, review of *The Sleepwalker;* December, 1997, p. 70; December, 1999, p. 142; April, 2001, p. 149.
Storyworks, January, 2001, p. 7.
Time, August 2, 1992, Paul Gray, "Carnage: An Open Book," p. 54; August 28, 2000, Andrea Sachs, "Another Stab at Chills," pp. 56-57.
Voice of Youth Advocates, April, 1992, Sylvia C. Mitchell, review of *Silent Night,* pp. 36-37; February, 1993, Caroline S. McKinney, review of *Cheerleaders: The Second Evil,* p. 360.
Washington Post, May 5, 1996, p. X13; January 19, 1997, p. C7.

STRINGER, Lauren 1957-

Personal

Born March 29, 1957, in Great Falls, MT; daughter of Albert Maine (an engineer) and Marla Josephine (a social worker; maiden name, Stanford) Stringer; married Matthew Sawyer Smith (an artist-composer), May 7, 1988; children: Ruby Smith, Cooper Smith. *Education:* University of California—Santa Cruz, B.A. (with honors in art and art history), 1980; Whitney Museum of American Art, Independent Study Program, 1981-82. *Politics:* Democrat.

Addresses

Home—432 Newton Avenue South, Minneapolis, MN 55405.

Career

Painter and sculptor. Has worked as an exhibitions preparator (art handler, designer, framer, etc.), in museums in Minneapolis, MN, New York, NY, Boston, MA, and Washington, DC; and a visiting artist in the schools, Minnesota State Arts Board and COMPAS Writers and Artists Program, 1990-97. Set designer and painter for theater, dance, and performance art, in Minneapolis, MN, St. Paul, MN, and New York, NY. Millay Colony for the Arts, Inc., artist-in-residence, and Edward Albee Foundation, art-in-residence, both 1984; Altos de Chavon, artist-in-residence, 1986. *Member:* Society of Children Book Writers and Illustrators, Kerlan Friends.

Awards, Honors

McKnight Foundation fellowship, 1991; Minnesota Book Award for illustration, 1996, International Reading Association/Children's Book Council Children's Choice Award, and Crayola Kids Best Book of the Year, all for *Mud; Scarecrow* was a Minnesota Book Awards finalist, and participated in the Society of Illustrators 1998 exhibition; *Castles, Caves, and Honeycombs* was a selection of the Children's Book-of-the-Month Club, Nest Literary Classics, and the Junior Literary Guild, and an Editor's Choice, *Booklist.*

Illustrator

Mary Lyn Ray, *Mud,* Harcourt Brace (San Diego, CA), 1996.

Cynthia Rylant, *Scarecrow,* Harcourt Brace (San Diego, CA), 1998.

Mary Lyn Ray, *Red Rubber Boot Day,* Harcourt (San Diego, CA), 2000.

Linda Ashman, *Castles, Caves, and Honeycombs,* Harcourt (San Diego, CA), 2001.

Lisa Westberg Peters, *Our Family Tree,* Harcourt (San Diego, CA), 2003.

Contributor to exhibition catalogues, including *Curator's choice,* Bronx Museum of the Arts, New York, NY, 1985; *Artista de Residencia,* Altos de Chavon,

Lauren Stringer

Dominican Republic, 1986; *Western Places,* Missoula Museum of Fine Arts, Missoula, MT, 1987; and *8 McKnight Artists,* MCAD Gallery, Minneapolis, MN, 1992; contributor of illustrations to Lee Galda and Bernice E. Cullinan, *Literature and the Child,* Wadsworth-Thomson Learning, 2002.

Sidelights

Lauren Stringer told *SATA:* "When I was six and in the first grade I began to see the disadvantages of learning to read. I loved looking at pictures in books more than reading the words. I felt sorry for my older sister as she advanced to lengthy chapter books containing no pictures at all. I remember peeking at her Christmas wish list and becoming very excited when I read, 'any Nancy Drew books.' I imagined books filled with pictures which Nancy *drew!* Since I loved to draw, I could not wait to see these 'picture books.' When my sister unwrapped two thick pictureless books Christmas morning I saw my future with books slipping into a dismal world of black-and-white type.

"However, I did learn to read and I read a lot, though I never lost my hunger for pictures. To satisfy this hunger, I discovered the wonder of art books. My family had a huge album of *The History of the World's Great Paintings,* which lay heavily on a shelf beneath the TV. Each month a new section of great paintings came in the mail and was added to its three-ring binder. I spent hours studying the paintings of battles and love scenes between gods and goddesses, landscapes of hunters on snowy days, the curly wind of starry nights, still-lives of apples, flowers and books. It was my early love for looking at pictures in books that led me to pursue my life as an artist.

"After graduating from college with degrees in art and art history, I spent fourteen years working as a painter and sculptor before I even began work on my first picture book. Painting children's picture books was a surprise turn in my career as an artist. In 1994, my friend, Debra Frasier, took slides of my artwork to her editor at Harcourt who reacted immediately to the images and soon work was begun on my first book, *Mud.* Now making children's books is one of my passions, along with painting and sculpting, reading books, playing the violin, gardening, walking, and being a mother.

"Since I was not trained in illustration I have developed my own process for painting a book. Upon accepting a story I copy it out in large letters on a huge sheet of paper and hang it on the wall of my studio so that I always have the words available to me. Then I go through a hunting and gathering phase which may last several months. I visit museums and libraries, look through my own library of art books and picture books, file through my collection of postcards of my favorite paintings and photographs, and leaf through magazines and catalogues, searching for anything that might inspire me in creating the pictures for the book. I hang the found images, and my sketches and notes all over the wall until my studio is transformed into a kind of shrine to the

A scarecrow appreciates his life and the wonder of nature in Cynthia Rylant's **Scarecrow,** *illustrated by Stringer.*

story on which I am working. By the time I am ready to begin painting the final illustrations, I have made hundreds of thumbnail sketches and color studies, numerous storyboards to organize page flow and text placement, and several small mock-ups of the book to help me see my paintings as a book.

"As an artist I have always tried to make my paintings and sculptures a kind of visual poetry that can add to or alter the way we perceive the world around us. As a book illustrator I am trying to do the same thing. Since it takes me one to three years to complete a book, I am careful to choose stories that enhance the growth of my artistic vision. The stories I illustrate become a part of my life, weaving in and out of my memories and experiences. *Red Rubber Boot Day* allowed me to capture in paint the activities of my four-year-old son before he grew beyond his first toys and games. I was also able to add visual elements from my own childhood in each of the illustrations, such as the wallpaper from my grandmother's house and my favorite rag doll. *Scarecrow* became a portrait not only of the scarecrow, but of the artist; the artist who observes the world, day and night, season to season, experiencing the wonders of the natural world, and understanding the brief moment of life we each have here on earth. The books I paint must capture the imagination and experiences of childhood and at the same time satisfy the adult artist in me. How lucky I am to be able to paint for children and myself; I can stay young and enjoy growing old at the same time!"

Ray's picture book *Mud* is considered Lauren Stringer's debut as a children's book illustrator, and an auspicious debut it was. While Ray's poem celebrates the joys of early spring days, when the frozen earth comes alive with mud, Stringer's "bold acrylic paintings burst from the full-bleed spreads like tulips," according to a reviewer in *Publishers Weekly.* Stringer's illustrations depict a gloriously messy child first in boots, then in bare feet, dancing through puddles of mud with glee. "The artist makes a pair of grimy feet jump for joy and feel good to be alive," proclaimed Ruth Semrau in *School Library Journal.* Likewise, Trish Wesley, reviewing *Mud* for the adult readers of *Horticulture: The Art of American Gardening,* recommended the book for its ability to evoke pleasant childhood memories of making mud pies in the garden. "*Mud* is just the book for reveling in your gloppy memories while encouraging keen observation of one of the main elements of a child's and a gardener's outdoor fun," Wesley remarked. Stringer teamed up with Ray for another celebration of what some might call bad weather in *Red Rubber Boot Day.* In this picture book, a young child enumerates the fun things there are to do both indoors and out on a rainy day. And Stringer's illustrations provide "a magnified view of the child's world," according to Tina Hudak in *School Library Journal.* For this critic, *Red Rubber Boot Day* joins a long list of successful picture books about rainy days.

Stringer's richly colored illustrations grace another well-regarded picture book, *Castles, Caves, and Honeycombs.*

Written by Linda Ashman, the text of this book is a lilting rhyme about animal (including human) homes, their comforts and pleasures, and Stringer's illustrations reinforce those feelings, according to reviewers. The artist created a series of single-page and double-page spreads, each relying on "the repetition of rounded forms and subtly graded shades of color," according to Carolyn Phelan in *Booklist,* and "the result is a warm, comforting vision of home." Likewise, a reviewer in *Horn Book* concluded that "together, the concise text and the womb-like illustrations convey the feelings of love, safety, and security that a home should have." "'There's no place like home' has been said many times and in many ways, but rarely so convincingly," concluded a reviewer for *Publishers Weekly.*

Biographical and Critical Sources

PERIODICALS

Booklist, April, 1998, Helen Rosenberg, review of *Scarecrow,* p. 1333; March 15, 2001, Carolyn Phelan, review of *Castles, Caves, and Honeycombs,* p. 1400.

Horn Book, July, 2001, review of *Castles, Caves, and Honeycombs,* p. 438.

Horticulture: The Art of American Gardening, April, 1999, Trish Wesley, review of *Mud,* p. 98.

Publishers Weekly, May 6, 1996, review of *Mud,* p. 79; July 1, 1996, Julie Yates Walton, "Flying Starts," p. 34; March 9, 1998, review of *Scarecrow,* p. 68; February 19, 2001, review of *Castles, Caves, and Honeycombs,* p. 89.

School Library Journal, June, 1996, Ruth Semrau, review of *Mud,* p. 108; April, 1998, Lauralyn Persson, review of *Scarecrow,* p. 109; April, 2000, Tina Hudak, review of *Red Rubber Boot Day,* p. 112; April, 2001, Maura Bresnahan, review of *Castles, Caves, and Honeycombs,* p. 98.

SUHR, Joanne
(Annie-Jo, a joint pseudonym)

Personal

Married Harold Suhr; children: Jacqueline, Joseph. *Education:* Attended University of Rochester; Rochester Institute of Technology, B.S.; State University of New York College at Brockport, M.Ed.

Addresses

Agent—c/o Richard C. Owen Publishers, Inc., P.O. Box 585, Katonah, NY 10536. *E-mail*—wbgc@lakeplains.net.

Career

Lyndonville Central School, Lyndonville, NY, elementary teacher.

Writings

WITH PATRICIA BLANCHARD

There Was a Mouse, illustrated by Valeri Gorbachev, Richard C. Owen Publishers (Katonah, NY), 1997.

My Bug Box, Richard C. Owen Publishers (Katonah, NY), 1999.

Old Bumpy Alligator, Richard C. Owen Publishers (Katonah, NY), 2000.

WITH PATRICIA BLANCHARD; UNDER JOINT PSEUDONYM ANNIE-JO

In the Woods, Mondo Publishing, 1998.

Itch, Itch, Mondo Publishing, 1998.*

T–U

THARP, Louise (Marshall) Hall 1898-1992

OBITUARY NOTICE—See index for *SATA* sketch: Born June 19, 1898, in Oneonta, NY; died May 2, 1992, in Darien, CT. Writer. Tharp was the author of numerous works for children and adults. Her first book was *Tory Hole* (1940), the initial volume in a series of eight fictionalized accounts of historical personages written for young readers. She is best remembered for *The Peabody Sisters of Salem,* which was first published in 1950. Tharp's other titles include *Until Victory* (1953), *Three Saints and a Sinner* (1956), *Adventurous Alliance* (1959), *The Baroness and the General* (1962), *Mrs. Jack* (1965), *Saint-Gaudens and the Gilded Era* (1969), and *The Appletons of Beacon Hill,* which was published in 1973. She received honorary degrees from several institutions, including Mount Holyoke College, and also received the Connecticut Bicentennial Award in 1976 for *Tory Hole.*

OBITUARIES AND OTHER SOURCES:

OTHER

Obituary research by Robert Reginald.

*　　*　　*

UHLIG, Susan 1955-
(S. M. Ford)

Personal

Surname is pronounced *You*-lig; born November 10, 1955, in Klamath Falls, OR; daughter of Charles (an electrician and television repairer) and Violette (Pearson) Uhlig; married Don Ford (an engineer), July 19, 1975; children: Angela Ford Base, Rachel. *Education:* Oregon Institute of Technology, A.S., 1975. *Religion:* Christian.

Addresses

Home—14816 205th Ave. SE, Renton, WA 98059-8926. *E-mail*—dnsford@oz.net.

Career

Writer. *Member:* Society of Children's Book Writers and Illustrators (regional adviser, Washington/Northern Idaho region, 2000—), Northwest Christian Writers Association.

Susan Uhlig

Awards, Honors

"Read America!" collection selection, 2000, for *Things Little Kids Need to Know*.

Writings

Lindsey Hits the Club (novel), New Canaan Publishing (New Canaan, CT), 1999.
Things Little Kids Need to Know, Our Child Press (Wayne, PA), 2000.
Lindsey and the Tree House Gang, New Canaan Publishing (New Canaan, CT), 2000.

Contributor to books, including (under name S. M. Ford) *Life's Little Rule Book: Simple Rules to Bring Joy and Happiness to Your Life,* Starburst Publishers, 1999. Contributor of more than 100 short stories and articles to periodicals for children and adults, including *Nature Friend, Cricket, Real People, Northwest Baby and Child, Parents' Monthly, Visions, Ladybug, My Friend, Real Time,* and *Jack and Jill.* Writings for adults appear under the name S. M. Ford.

Work in Progress

Notes on the Porch, a middle-grade novel about an eleven-year-old who is the prey of a stalker; *Maid of Saragossa,* a book for a reading intervention program, for Waterford Institute.

Sidelights

Susan Uhlig told *SATA:* "When I was a child, I told myself stories to go to sleep. Though I never told anyone about that or my desire to be an 'author,' I was an avid reader dreaming of 'someday' being a writer. After high school, I attended Oregon Institute of Technology and graduated with an associates' degree in computer systems engineering technology. I'd never met a writer, so I thought writing wasn't a 'real' occupation.

"Marriage, children, and cross-country relocations followed. During this time my dream of writing blossomed and, due to the support and encouragement of my husband, I took some classes. (Later he bought me a computer, too!) But it wasn't until my youngest child entered first grade that I began to work seriously at writing. Not long after that I met other writers and realized it was okay to say 'I am a writer.'

"Three years later and with lots of rejection slips to my credit, I made my first sale. That was in 1992. Yippee!

"Since that time I have sold a children's middle grade novel (for ages seven to ten), a picture book, and over 100 short stories and articles, mainly for children's magazines. Along the way I also learned to do storytelling—absolutely astounding, considering I always hated to get up in front of people. Now I enjoy being on stage, especially when talking about writing.

"Writing continues to be a lot of fun. Usually, I have a number of projects in various stages going on at once. I like the quick reward of finishing a magazine piece and the challenge and complexity of longer works. I keep learning more and more and continue to work on improving my skills. One of the most valuable helps to me has been my critique groups, where we share our projects, get advice, correction, and inspiration.

"On the home front, I am happily married. My husband and I have two daughters—one still living at home and one married, expecting our first grandchild. Our family also includes an American Eskimo puppy and two cats. My favorite thing to do? Read a good book! And I still tell myself stories to go to sleep."

Biographical and Critical Sources

OTHER

Susan Uhlig Web Site, http://www.oz.net/~dnsford (February 23, 2002).*

*   *   *

UNCLE CARTER
See BOUCHER, (Clarence) Carter

*   *   *

URE, Jean 1943-
(Ann Colin, Jean Gregory, Sarah McCulloch)

Personal

Surname sounds like "Ewer"; born January 1, 1943, in Surrey, England; daughter of William (an insurance officer) and Vera (Belsen) Ure; married Leonard Gregory (an actor and writer), 1967. *Education:* Attended Webber-Douglas Academy of Dramatic Art, 1965-67. *Hobbies and other interests:* Reading, writing letters, walking dogs, playing with cats, music, working for animal rights.

Addresses

Home—88 Southbridge Rd., Croydon, Surrey CR0 1AF, England. *Agent*—Maggie Noach, 21 Redan St., London W14 0AB, England.

Career

Writer. Worked variously as a waitress, cook, washer-up, nursing assistant, newspaper seller, shop assistant, theater usherette, temporary shorthand-typist, translator, secretary with NATO and UNESCO, and television production assistant. *Member:* Society of Authors.

Jean Ure

Awards, Honors

American Library Association Best Book for Young Adults citation, 1983, for *See You Thursday; See You Thursday* and *Supermouse* were Junior Literary Guild selections.

Writings

FOR YOUNG ADULTS

A Proper Little Nooryeff, Bodley Head (London, England), 1982, published in the United States as *What If They Saw Me Now?,* Delacorte (New York, NY), 1984.

If It Weren't for Sebastian, Bodley Head (London, England), 1982, Delacorte (New York, NY), 1985.

You Win Some, You Lose Some, Bodley Head (London, England), 1984, Delacorte (New York, NY), 1987.

The Other Side of the Fence, Bodley Head (London, England), 1986, Delacorte (New York, NY), 1988.

One Green Leaf, Bodley Head (London, England), 1987, Delacorte (New York, NY), 1989.

Play Nimrod for Him, Bodley Head (London, England), 1990.

Dreaming of Larry, Doubleday (New York, NY), 1991.

Always Sebastian, Bodley Head (London, England), 1993.

A Place to Scream, Doubleday (New York, NY), 1993.

Has Anyone Seen This Girl?, Bodley Head (London, England), 1996.

Dance with Death, Scholastic (New York, NY), 1996.

Just Sixteen, Orchard, 1999.

Family Fan Club, Harper Collins (New York, NY), 2000.

Secret Life of Sally Tomato, Harper Collins (New York, NY), 2000.

Skinny Melon and Me, Holt (New York, NY), 2001.

Boys on the Brain, Harper Collins (New York, NY), 2002.

"PLAGUE" TRILOGY

Plague 99, Methuen (London, England), 1990, published as *Plague,* Harcourt (New York, NY), 1991.

Come Lucky April, Methuen (London, England), 1992.

Watchers at the Shrine, Methuen (London, England), 1992

FOR CHILDREN

Ballet Dance for Two, F. Watts (New York, NY), 1960, published as *Dance for Two,* illustrated by Richard Kennedy, Harrap (London, England), 1960.

Hi There, Supermouse!, illustrated by Martin White, Hutchinson (London, England), 1983, published as *Supermouse,* illustrated by Ellen Eagle, Morrow (New York, NY), 1984.

You Two, illustrated by Ellen Eagle, Morrow (New York, NY), 1984, published in England as *The You-Two,* illustrated by Martin White, Hutchinson (London, England), 1984.

Nicola Mimosa, illustrated by Martin White, Hutchinson (London, England), 1985, published as *The Most Important Thing,* illustrated by Ellen Eagle, Morrow (New York, NY), 1986.

Megastar, Blackie (Glasgow, Scotland), 1985.

Swings and Roundabouts, Blackie (Glasgow, Scotland), 1986.

A Bottled Cherry Angel, Hutchinson (London, England), 1986.

Brenda the Bold, illustrated by Glenys Ambrus, Heinemann (London, England), 1986.

Tea-Leaf on the Roof, illustrated by Val Sassoon, Blackie (Glasgow, Scotland), 1987.

War with Old Mouldy!, illustrated by Alice Englander, Methuen (London, England), 1987.

Who's Talking?, Orchard (New York, NY), 1987.

Frankie's Dad, Hutchinson (London, England), 1988.

(With Michael Lewis) *A Muddy Kind of Magic,* Blackie (Glasgow, Scotland), 1988.

(With Michael Lewis) *Two Men in a Boat,* Blackie (Glasgow, Scotland), 1988.

Cool Simon, Orchard (New York, NY), 1990.

Jo in the Middle, Hutchinson (London, England), 1990.

The Wizard in the Woods, illustrated by David Anstley, Walker (London, England), 1990, Candlewick Press (New York, NY), 1992.

Fat Lollipop, Hutchinson (London, England), 1991.

William in Love, Blackie (Glasgow, Scotland), 1991.

Wizard in Wonderland, illustrated by David Anstley, Walker (London, England), 1991, Candlewick Press (Cambridge, MA), 1993.

Spooky Cottage, Heinemann (London, England), 1992.

The Unknown Planet, Walker (London, England), 1992.

Wizard in the Woods, Walker (London, England), 1992.

The Ghost That Lives on the Hill, Methuen (London, England), 1992.

Bossyboots, Hutchinson (London, England), 1993.

Captain Cranko and the Crybaby, Walker (London, England), 1993.

Phantom Knicker Nicker, Blackie (Glasgow, Scotland), 1993.

Star Turn, Hutchinson (London, England), 1994.

The Children Next Door, Scholastic (New York, NY), 1996.

Becky Bananas, Harper Collins (New York, NY), 1997.

Whistle and I'll Come, Scholastic (New York, NY), 1997.

Danny Dynamite, Transworld, 1998.

Fruit and Nutcase, Harper Collins (New York, NY), 1998.

Girl in the Blue Tunic, Scholastic (New York, NY), 1998.

Big Tom, Harper Collins (New York, NY), 2000.

Monster in the Mirror, Harper Collins (New York, NY), 2000.

Puppy Present, Harper Collins (New York, NY), 2000.

A Twist in Time, Walker, 1999.

Shrinking Violet, Harper Collins (New York, NY), 2002.

"CHUMS" SERIES

Buster, Harper Collins (New York, NY), 2000.

Bella, Harper Collins (New York, NY), 2000.

Bouncer, Harper Collins (New York, NY), 2000.

Bonnie, Harper Collins (New York, NY), 2000.

"WOODSIDE SCHOOL" SERIES

The Fright, Orchard Books (New York, NY), 1987.

Loud Mouth, Orchard Books (New York, NY), 1988.

Soppy Birthday, Orchard Books (New York, NY), 1988.

Jilly and Clara rescue a wounded fox and protest against fox hunting.

King of Spuds, Orchard Books (New York, NY), 1989.

Who's for the Zoo?, Orchard Books (New York, NY), 1989.

"THURSDAY" TRILOGY

See You Thursday, Kestrel (London, England), 1981, Delacorte (New York, NY), 1983.

After Thursday, Kestrel (London, England), 1985, Delacorte (New York, NY), 1987.

Tomorrow Is Also a Day, Methuen (London, England), 1989.

"VANESSA" TRILOGY

Trouble with Vanessa, Transworld (London, England), 1988.

There's Always Danny, Transworld (London, England), 1989.

Say Goodbye, Transworld (London, England), 1989.

"WE LOVE ANIMALS" SERIES

Foxglove, Barron's Educational Series (Happauge, NY), 1999.

Snow Kittens, Barron's Educational Series (Happauge, NY), 1999.

Daffy down Donkey, Barron's Educational Series (Happauge, NY), 1999.

Muddy Four Paws, Barron's Educational Series (Happauge, NY), 1999.

FOR ADULTS

The Other Theater, Transworld (London, England), 1966.

The Test of Love, Corgi (London, England), 1968.

If You Speak Love, Corgi (London, England), 1972.

Had We but World Enough and Time, Corgi (London, England), 1972.

The Farther off from England, White Lion, 1973.

Daybreak, Corgi (London, England), 1974.

All Thy Love, Corgi (London, England), 1975.

Marriage of True Minds, Corgi (London, England), 1975.

No Precious Time, Corgi (London, England), 1976.

Hear No Evil, Corgi (London, England), 1976.

Curtain Fall, Corgi (London, England), 1978.

Masquerade, Corgi (London, England), 1979.

A Girl like That, Corgi (London, England), 1979.

(Under pseudonym Ann Colin) *A Different Class of Doctor,* Corgi (London, England), 1980.

(Under pseudonym Ann Colin) *Doctor Jamie,* Corgi (London, England), 1980.

(Under name Jean Gregory) *Love beyond Telling,* Corgi (London, England), 1986.

"RIVERSIDE THEATER ROMANCE" SERIES

Early Stages, Corgi (London, England), 1977.

Dress Rehearsal, Corgi (London, England), 1977.

All in a Summer Season, Corgi (London, England), 1977.

Bid Time Return, Corgi (London, England), 1978.

GEORGIAN ROMANCES; UNDER PSEUDONYM SARAH McCULLOCH

Not Quite a Lady, Corgi (London, England), 1980, Fawcett (New York, NY), 1981.

A Most Insistent Lady, Corgi (London, England), 1981.

A Lady for Ludovic, Corgi (London, England), 1981.

Merely a Gentleman, Corgi (London, England), 1982.
A Perfect Gentleman, Corgi (London, England), 1982.

TRANSLATOR

Henri Vernes, *City of a Thousand Drums,* Corgi (London, England), 1966.
Henri Vernes, *The Dinosaur Hunters,* Corgi (London, England), 1966.
Henri Vernes, *The Yellow Shadow,* Corgi (London, England), 1966.
Jean Bruce, *Cold Spell,* Corgi (London, England), 1967.
Bruce, *Top Secret,* Corgi (London, England), 1967.
Henri Vernes, *Treasure of the Golcondas,* Corgi (London, England), 1967.
Henri Vernes, *The White Gorilla,* Corgi (London, England), 1967.
Henri Vernes, *Operation Parrot,* Corgi (London, England), 1968.
Jean Bruce, *Strip Tease,* Corgi (London, England), 1968.
Noel Calef, *The Snare,* Souvenir Press, 1969.
Sven Hassel, *March Battalion,* Corgi (London, England), 1970.
Sven Hassel, *Assignment Gestapo,* Corgi (London, England), 1971.
Laszlo Havas, *Hitler's Plot to Kill the Big Three,* Corgi (London, England), 1971.
Sven Hassel, *SS General,* Corgi (London, England), 1972.
Sven Hassel, *Reign of Hell,* Corgi (London, England), 1973.

OTHER

Contributor of articles to periodicals, including *Vegan, Writers' Monthly, Books for Keeps,* and *School Librarian.*

Sidelights

Jean Ure's young adult books combine her lively sense of humor with unique stories that often contain off-beat situations and characters. Ure is a vegetarian who is avid about animal rights, and while her books make references to these tendencies among her characters, they are never considered preachy by reviewers. Class struggles, homosexuality, sexual awakenings, and feminism are also among her Ure's topics, all of which she discusses with freshness and immediacy.

Ure does not remember a time when she did not want to be a writer. Born in Surrey, England, as a young girl she would steal notebooks from her school to fill them with imaginative stories. "I was brought up in a tradition of writing, inasmuch as my father's family were inveterate ode writers, sending one another long screeds of poetry on every possible occasion," Ure recalled in an essay for *Something about the Author Autobiography Series* (*SAAS*). She was also happy to read poetry or dance in front of a room of adoring relatives.

Going to school, however, was painful for Ure. She constantly felt that she did not fit in. Ure humorously speculated in *SAAS* on the reasons why she never felt a part of the crowd. "The more I think about it, the more it seems to me that hair was the root cause of all my

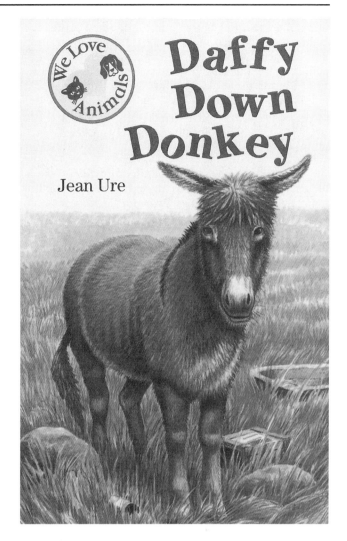

Eleven-year-old Jilly and Clara try to save a sick, neglected donkey.

problems," she said, citing limp and unmanageable locks. "I am almost seriously persuaded that had it not been for hair, I would have gone to the party along with everyone else."

Being outside of the popular crowd caused Ure to fantasize about many things, including being in love and dancing. Being a compulsive writer, Ure wrote down these fantasies. She sent the manuscript off to a publisher, and at the age of seventeen she became a published writer. "Writing *Dance for Two* was a very cathartic exercise and brought me great solace," she told *SAAS.* "I almost managed to believe that . . . I really *did* have a sweetheart called Noel, that I really *was* a ballet dancer."

Ambition and not wanting to continue with the pain of school-life were reasons why Ure chose to try writing as a profession rather than go to college. She spent a long time doing menial jobs while trying to get her work published. Discouraged by her lack of success, Ure enrolled in a drama class and found she had a talent for entertaining. While attending drama school, she met her husband, Leonard Gregory, at one of the few parties she attended, and he became a major influence in her life. Shortly afterward, her writing career suddenly took off, and she started writing romantic novels and translating books. While these did not stimulate her intellectually, they helped her learn her craft and earn a living at the same time. After a few years, however, she began to feel like she was compromising herself by writing these books.

The year 1980 was a turning point for Ure. She wrote in *SAAS,* "I really emerged as myself, with a book for young adults called *See You Thursday.*" It focuses on a blind pianist named Abe and a sixteen-year-old rebel named Marianne. Although Abe is eight years older, wiser, and from a different background than Marianne, the pair become attracted to each other, and the relationship blossoms as Marianne sheds her shyness and finds a new maturity. In *After Thursday,* the sequel that followed this popular book, the romance of Abe and Marianne is further tested by their differing perspectives on independence. Ure was extremely happy to have found this fresh audience for her writing. "The reason I turned to writing for young adults was, basically, that it offered a freedom which 'genre' writing does not allow," she related to *SAAS.* Ure used her instinctive talent for writing to create these books. She commented, "When I created Abe, my blind pianist, I did the very minimum of research into blindness, but was able to gain direct knowledge, albeit to a severely limited extent, of how it would be to be blind by tying a scarf about my eyes and blundering around the house." *See You Thursday* won the American Library Association's Best Book for Young Adults citation in 1983.

Ure returned to the themes of autonomy and awakening sexuality in the "Vanessa" trilogy, which includes *Trouble with Vanessa, There's Always Danny,* and *Say Goodbye,* as well as in *The Other Side of the Fence.* Describing the first two books of the "Vanessa" trilogy as more than a romantic tale, Stephanie Nettell in the *Times Literary Supplement* labeled Ure's novels "intelligent, spiky and imaginative." Similarly enthusiastic about *The Other Side of the Fence,* reviewers such as *Bulletin of the Center for Children's Books* contributor Zena Sutherland praised the novel as "mature and sensitive. . . . [It is] told with both momentum and nuance." This romance is unusual, however, because it concerns a young homosexual, Richard, who meets and finds friendship with Bonny, a girl who is attracted to him but cannot understand, until the end, why her sexual interest is not returned. Although one critic, *School Library Journal* writer Karen K. Radtke, questioned Bonny's "naivete" regarding Richard (when she is otherwise street-smart), Radtke admitted that the story may be satisfying to teenagers who "harbor secret fantasies about . . . flaunting parental authority."

Ure's sensitive treatment of relationships is often the focus of critical reviews. The special rivalry among sisters is explored in *Supermouse* when a shy but talented girl, Nicola, is offered a dancing role over her more favored younger sister, Rose. Mary M. Burns wrote in *Horn Book* that even though the story is told from the point of view of an eleven-year-old, "the author has managed to suggest subtle emotions which underlie the family's values and actions." The story is continued in *The Most Important Thing* when Nicola, now fourteen, must decide whether her future career will include ballet, or whether she should concentrate instead on science and maybe become a doctor. Cynthia K. Leibold concluded in the *School Library Journal* that "Ure is skillful at creating colorful characters . . . and her characters execute their roles perfectly."

Using insight and sometimes humor, Ure's novels often question values and touch upon subjects such as social standards. In one such book, *What If They Saw Me Now?,* an athletic young man is caught in an amusing dilemma when he is asked to dance the male lead in a ballet. Described by Zena Sutherland in the *Bulletin of the Center for Children's Books* as "a funny and liberating" novel, Ure's treatment of the subject may appeal to both boys and girls as they appreciate Jamie's predicament—to overcome his own and others' "macho" stereotypes.

Coping with illness is the theme of two of Ure's contemporary works, *If It Weren't for Sebastian* and *One Green Leaf,* the first focusing on mental illness, and the latter on a fatal physical sickness. In *If It Weren't for Sebastian* the title character is an intense, but peace-loving, young man whose "strangeness" is an object of scorn and misunderstanding to others. Maggie becomes his friend and soon discovers that Sebastian is being treated as an outpatient at a mental health clinic. Ure "explores the borderline psychotic and his relationships with great sensitivity and understanding," declared Zena Sutherland in a *Bulletin of the Center for Children's Books* review. Fatal illness is treated with similar sympathy and skill in *One Green Leaf.* After an unsuccessful surgery, it becomes obvious that David's cancer is terminal. Ure's emphasis, however, is on how David copes, and on the affection of his friends during his illness. According to Tess McKellen in the *School Library Journal,* the author "dramatizes successfully the effect of unexpected tragedy on young minds and emotions" in the novel.

Other topics for Ure's creative energy often center around her current passions: music, vegetarianism, animal rights, books, and theater. Her main motive is not to convert people, but to stimulate them. She told *SAAS* that, when writing, she sets out "to make people think: to make them examine their motives and question their assumptions." She concluded by summing up her reasons for writing, explaining that "it will always be my characters who interest me the most; and my aim, if conscious aim I have . . . will still be to stimulate and entertain."

The 1993 novel *Always Sebastian* brought back the unique title character of Ure's previous novel. Its plot follows the relationship between Sebastian, now deeply involved in the animal-rights movement, and Maggie, a single parent with two daughters. That same year, Ure also authored a science-fiction thriller for teens, *A Place to Scream.* The work is set in the year 2015, and it is a future in which social problems caused by incautious economic policies have worsened immensely. Its protagonist is the teenage Gillian, who has been fortunate enough to grow up in an affluent household, but feels overwhelmed by the world outside. Her involvement with a maverick new friend brings both romance and a sense of purpose to her life.

Ure won critical plaudits for her next series, "Plague," which includes the post-apocalyptic tales *Plague 99* (published in the United States as *Plague), Come Lucky April,* and *Watchers at the Shrine.* All were published between 1990 and 1992, and set in Ure's native England. *Plague 99* opens in the twentieth century in a world where biological warfare germs have triggered a contagious and deadly illness. Returning from camp, Fran Latimer finds both of her parents dead and her best friend looking to her for help. The two girls team up with Shahid, a schoolmate, and as the plague worsens in their hometown, with death seemingly everywhere, they journey across London in search of Shhid's brother, only to find the family there decimated as well. When Shahid becomes sick, Fran nurses him as they hide out in an old bookstore, and he recovers enough for them to once more begin their journey to safety. As *Plague 99* concludes, they are on their way to distant Cornwall, where Fran's grandmother lives.

Plague 99 proved such a popular book with teens that Ure decided to continue the story. *After the Plague* follows the story of Fran and Shahid's great-grandson, Daniel. A hundred years after the fateful flight to Cornwall, Daniel learns of the existence of Fran's fascinating journal, which she wrote during the plague. He travels to Croydon where it was left behind, but the London suburb is now an entirely feminist-governed community in which new births are the result of artificial insemination. Male offspring in Croydon are routinely castrated, though Ure only hints the practice is part of their legal system. A virtual outlaw in this community by reason of his gender, Daniel falls in love with one of its members, April, and she must choose between remaining in her progressive, nonviolent society or leaving with him and entering a harshly ordered, retrogressive outside world.

Watchers at the Shrine, Ure's third installment in the "Plague" series, reveals that in the year 2099 April did not leave Croydon, but remained behind and gave birth to a son, Hal. When the boy nears puberty, he is sent to Cornwall to escape castration, but he has trouble adjusting to the vastly different patriarchal community. A large number of birth defects occur in Cornwall since an abandoned nuclear power plant nearby is still emitting radiation. Hal is shocked to discover that both people in the greater Cornwall community and inside the odd religious sect known as the Watchers, with whom he is sent to live, display an ignorance of history and science, and, in contrast to Croydon, women are treated quite brutally. He falls in love with a Watchers' daughter, who was born with a birth defect, and as a result, will soon be relegated to the community's brigade of officially sanctioned prostitutes. Instead, the pair escape to Croydon where a crisis has brought some positive changes to the feminist community's system of social order. In a review of *Watchers at the Shrine,* a *Junior Bookshelf* critic commended Ure's powers of description in creating a desolate, post-plague Britain, termed here "intriguing as well as shocking and forbidding, and she contrives associations for Hal which increase the horror of societies which have lost their way."

Ure is also the author of the 1996 teen novel *Has Anyone Seen This Girl?* Told in diary form, the book begins with fourteen-year-old Caroline riding in a train to her new boarding school. Aboard the train, she meets Rachel, and the two become fast friends. At school, however, the quirky Rachel is an outcast, and Caroline is torn between peer pressure to reject her and a sense of loyalty to her first friend. Rachel makes friendship difficult, however, as she proves to be a demanding, asocial friend, and Caroline suffers tremendous guilt when Rachel runs away from the school. "Jean Ure once again writes with a sympathetic understanding of young people," said Maggie Bignell in *Quill & Quire.*

Biographical and Critical Sources

BOOKS

Authors and Artists for Young Adults, Volume 33, Gale (Detroit, MI), 2000.
Children's Literature Review, Volume 34, Gale (Detroit, MI), 1994.
St. James Guide to Young Adult Writers, 2nd edition, St. James (Detroit, MI), 1999.
Something about the Author Autobiography Series, Volume 14, Gale (Detroit, MI), 1992.

PERIODICALS

Booklist, January 1, 2001, Ilene Cooper, review of *Skinny Melon and Me,* p. 961.
Books for Keeps, July, 1993, p. 28; November, 1993, p. 29; October, 1994, p. 28; May, 1996, p. 16.
British Book News, March, 1985.
Bulletin of the Center for Children's Books, December, 1983, p. 79; May, 1984, p. 176; June, 1984, Zena Sutherland, review of *What If They Saw Me Now?,* p. 195; October, 1984, p. 36; June, 1985, p. 197; April, 1986, p. 160; June, 1986, Zena Sutherland, review of *If It Weren't for Sebastian,* p. 198; May, 1987, p. 180; February, 1988, Zena Sutherland, review of *The Other Side of the Fence,* p. 127; May, 1989, p. 238; October, 1991, p. 52.
Horn Book, December, 1983, p. 720; June, 1984, Mary M. Burns, review of *Supermouse,* p. 334; August, 1984, p. 479; March, 1988, p. 212.
Junior Bookshelf, August, 1993, pp. 163-164; October, 1994, review of *Watchers at the Shrine,* p. 191; June, 1996, p. 127.
Publishers Weekly, November 25, 1983, p. 64; April 13, 1984, p. 72; February 8, 1985, p. 77; May 30, 1986, p. 68; June 12, 1987, p. 86; November 27, 2000, review of *Skinny Melon and Me,* p. 77.

Quill & Quire, February, 1996, p. 33; August, 1996, Maggie Bignell, review of *Has Anyone Seen This Girl?*, p. 121.

School Librarian, November, 1993, p. 168; November, 1994; February 1, 1995, p. 6.

School Library Journal, August, 1984, p. 87; October, 1984, p. 163; August, 1985, p. 82; May, 1986, Cynthia K. Leibold, review of *The Most Important Thing*, p. 110; August, 1986, p. 108; April, 1988, Karen K. Radtke, review of *The Other Side of the Fence*, p. 114; May, 1989, Tess McKellen, review of *One Green Leaf*, p. 128; October, 1991, p. 150; October, 1992, pp. 122-123; July, 1993, p. 87; January, 2001, Ashley Larsen, review of *Skinny Melon and Me*, p. 134.

Times Literary Supplement, July 16, 1985, p. 910; November 28, 1986, p. 1347; June 9, 1989, Stephanie Nettell, review of *Trouble with Vanessa* and *There's Always Danny*, p. 648; September 1, 1989, p. 957.

Voice of Youth Advocates, August-October, 1986, p. 152; October, 1989, p. 218.

* * *

USCHAN, Michael V. 1948-

Personal

Born August 10, 1948, in Milwaukee, WI; son of Vincent (a master machinist) and Rose Marie (a homemaker; maiden name, Friedrich) Uschan; married Barbara Ann Bates (a teacher), July 18, 1973. *Education:* University of Wisconsin—Milwaukee, B.A., 1970. *Politics:* Democrat. *Religion:* Roman Catholic. *Hobbies and other interests:* Golf, Tai Chi Chuan.

Michael V. Uschan

Addresses

Home and office—10149 West Friar Lane, Franklin, WI 53132. *E-mail*—scribe@execpc.com.

Career

Freelance author. United Press International, reporter and editor, 1970-90; Associated Press, stringer, 1991—; Franklin Public Library Foundation, vice president, 1999—; affiliated with Lucent Books, San Diego, CA. *Member:* Council for Wisconsin Writers.

Writings

CHILDREN'S NONFICTION

A Multicultural Portrait of World War I, Benchmark Books (Tarrytown, NY), 1996.

A Cultural History of the United States: The 1940s, Lucent Books (San Diego, CA), 1999.

A Cultural History of the United States: The 1910s, Lucent Books (San Diego, CA), 1999.

The Importance of John F. Kennedy, Lucent Books (San Diego, CA), 1999.

Tiger Woods ("People in the News" series), Lucent Books (San Diego, CA), 1999.

Male Olympic Champions ("History Makers" series), Lucent Books (San Diego, CA), 2000.

America's Founders ("History Makers" series), Lucent Books (San Diego, CA), 2000.

Westward Expansion ("World History" series), Lucent Books (San Diego, CA), 2000.

Home Run Kings ("History Makers" series), Lucent Books (San Diego, CA), 2000.

Jesse Ventura ("People in the News" series), Lucent Books (San Diego, CA), 2000.

Golf (History of Sports" series), Lucent Books (San Diego, CA), 2001.

The Korean War, Lucent Books (San Diego, CA), 2001.

The Kennedys ("History Makers" series), Lucent Books (San Diego, CA), 2001.

North Carolina, Lucent Books (San Diego, CA), 2001.

The Drug Library, Lucent Books (San Diego, CA), 2001.

The Fall of Saigon: The End of the Vietnam War ("Point of Impact" series), Heinemann Library (Chicago, IL), 2001.

Alcohol, Lucent Books (San Diego, CA), 2002.

Franklin D. Roosevelt, Lucent Books (San Diego, CA), 2002.

Abraham Lincoln ("Beginning Biographies" series), Raintree Steck-Vaughn (Austin, TX), 2002.

Thomas Jefferson ("Beginning Biographies" series), Raintree Steck-Vaughn (Austin, TX), 2002.

Politicians and Military Strategists ("Cold War" series), Lucent Books (San Diego, CA), 2003.

Sidelights

Author Michael V. Uschan writes mostly nonfiction books for younger readers, and has focused on subjects as varied as the history of the United States and baseball. His first book, *A Multicultural Portrait of World War I*, relates the story of U.S. involvement in World War I through the eyes of the country's ethnic minorities, including the changes that occurred after the armistice that brought the "Great War" to a close. In a review for *School Library Journal,* David A. Lindsey noted that this well-written work helps "fill large gaps in the story of our nation." Similarly, Uschan's volume *A Cultural History of the United States: The 1910s*—part of a series of books focusing on the cultural history of the United States—is a helpful guide to readers seeking information on the "growth and development of America," noted a critic for *Children's Book Review Service.* As part of the same series, Uschan also issued *A Cultural History of the United States: The 1940s,* a similar history of the United States, this time focusing largely on the effects of World War II.

In addition to writing books on historical events, Uschan has also penned several biographies of significant people, including two books on the Kennedy family. In his *The Importance of John F. Kennedy,* Uschan provides an overview of President Kennedy's life and his legacy, mining some "well-chosen primary source material" in the process, according to Phyllis Graves in *School Library Journal.* And in his *Male Olympic Champions,* Uschan profiles seven athletes who achieved Olympic success, including track star Jesse Owens, skier Jean-Claude Killy, and swimmer Mark Spitz. Also included in the narrative is a brief history of the Olympic games, as well as a chronology, bibliography, and recommended reading list. Praised by critics for his focus on both the successes and challenges that these seven athletes faced, Randy Meyer of *Booklist* was particularly appreciative of Uschan's efforts to "look beyond the record books to the spirit, drama, and tragedy of the Olympic Games."

According to Uschan, "Journalism is sometimes called 'history in a hurry.'" As he told *SATA,* "for two decades as a reporter and editor for United Press International, I recorded the events unfolding before my eyes as fast as possible, whether it was yet another home run by the legendary Hank Aaron or the crash of a passenger airplane that took the lives of nearly forty people. In the helter-skelter world of wire service news there was a 'deadline every minute,' and the overriding requirement of my job was to transmit stories I was working on to our newspaper and broadcast clients—and thus to the entire world—as fast as humanly possible.

"When I began writing books, however, I was able to slow down. This downshift in writing gears made it possible for me to consider not just the *what* of an important event but the *why* and *how,* whether it was *why* John F. Kennedy was a key figure in American history to *how* Hank Aaron became the most prolific home-run hitter of all time. At first, the transition from journalist to author was difficult. Once accustomed to having only minutes to gather facts, write a story, and disseminate it to the world, I now enjoyed the luxury of being able to labor for many weeks to research, write,

and rewrite a manuscript. I would then have to wait several months before I could *finally* hold the finished product in my hand. The instant when I first open that book and gaze at what I have created—with the help, of course, of a host of talented editors, graphic artists, and printers—is the real reward for my efforts. Because the reason I write is that I love to read.

"When I was growing up, nothing filled me with more pleasure—nor does it now—than opening a book and becoming lost in the words it contained. I learned to love not only books but also their authors, who by writing them gave me so much pleasure. They became my heroes, and my great dream was to one day go to the library in my hometown of West Allis, walk up to the wooden chests of drawers that contained a card for every book in the library, and be able to riffle through them and find a card with my name printed on it.

"However, by the time I wrote my first book in 1996 (*A Multicultural Portrait of World War I*), the library I had haunted for so many hours while growing up had been closed. Gone as well were the tall card catalogs that had once towered over my head. They had been replaced by modern technology, computers that could search the library's entire database in a matter of seconds to find any book I wanted. When I typed in my name under *AUTHOR,* the title of my first book appeared almost instantly on the computer screen. It was one of the most satisfying experiences of my life. On my next visit there was another great moment; I looked up my book again, just for the sheer joy of it, and discovered that it was *OUT*! Somebody was reading a book I had written! The circle was complete—the little boy who once read books was now an author whose work was providing a pleasurable reading experience for someone else."

Biographical and Critical Sources

PERIODICALS

Booklist, January 1, 2000, Randy Meyer, review of *Male Olympic Champions,* p. 901.

Children's Book Review Service, February, 1999, review of *A Cultural History of the United States: The 1910s,* p. 80.

Horn Book Guide, fall, 1996, Peter D. Sieruta, review of *A Multicultural Portrait of World War I,* p. 381.

School Library Journal, June, 1996, David A. Lindsey, review of *A Multicultural Portrait of World War I,* p. 166; January, 1999, Starr E. Smith, review of *A Cultural History of the United States: The 1940s,* pp. 156-157; April, 1999, Phyllis Graves, review of *The Importance of John F. Kennedy,* pp. 159-160.

Voice of Youth Advocates, August, 1999, Jamie S. Hansen, review of *The Importance of John F. Kennedy,* p. 208; May, 2000, Jeffrey A. French, review of *Male Olympic Champions,* p. 188; January, 2001, Janice C. Hayes, review of *Golf,* p. 133; January, 2001, Dona H. Helmer, review of *Westward Expansion,* p. 142.

WADDELL, Martin 1941-
(Catherine Sefton)

Personal

Born April 10, 1941, in Belfast, Northern Ireland; son of Mayne (a linen manufacturer) and Alice (a homemaker; maiden name, Duffell) Waddell; married Rosaleen Carragher (a teacher), December 27, 1969; children: Thomas Mayne, David Martin, Peter Matthew. *Education:* "Almost nil." *Religion:* "Troubled agnostic." *Hobbies and other interests:* Chess.

Addresses

Home and office—139 Central Promenade, Newcastle, County Down, Northern Ireland. *Agent*—Gina Pollinger, 222 Old Brompton Rd. London SW5 OB2, England.

Career

Writer, 1966—. Has worked in several other occupations, including book-selling and junk-stalling. *Member:* Society of Authors, Children's Literature Association of Ireland, Irish Writers Union.

Awards, Honors

Federation of Children's Book Club Award runner-up, 1982, for *The Ghost and Bertie Boggin;* Carnegie Award nomination, 1984, for *Island of the Strangers;* Guardian Award runner-up, 1984, and Other Award, 1986, both for *Starry Night;* Smarties Grand Prize, 1988, and Le Prix des Critiques de Livres pour Enfants, Belgium, 1989, both for *Can't You Sleep, Little Bear?; Can't You Sleep, Little Bear?,* illustrated by Barbara Firth, received the Kate Greenaway Medal, Library Association, 1988; Kurt Maschler/Emil Award, 1989, for *The Park in the Dark;* Best Book for Babies Award, 1990, for *Rosie's Babies;* Smarties Prize, 1991, and shortlist for Smarties Prize, 1992.

Writings

FOR CHILDREN

Ernie's Chemistry Set, illustrated by Ronnie Baird, Blackstaff (Belfast, Northern Ireland), 1978.
Ernie's Flying Trousers, illustrated by Ronnie Baird, Blackstaff (Belfast, Northern Ireland), 1978.
The Great Green Mouse Disaster, illustrated by Philippe Dupasquier, Andersen (London, England), 1981.
The House under the Stairs, Methuen (London, England), 1983.
(Editor) *A Tale to Tell,* Northern Ireland Arts Council, 1983.
Going West, illustrated by Philippe Dupasquier, Andersen (London, England), 1983, Harper (New York, NY), 1984.
Big Bad Bertie, illustrated by Glynis Ambrus, Methuen (London, England), 1984.
The Budgie Said GRRRR, illustrated by Glynis Ambrus, Methuen (London, England), 1985.
The School Reporter's Notebook, Beaver, 1985.
The Day It Rained Elephants, illustrated by Glynis Ambrus, Methuen (London, England), 1986.
Our Wild Weekend, Methuen (London, England), 1986.
Owl and Billy, Methuen (London, England), 1986.
The Tough Princess, illustrated by Patrick Benson, Walker Books (London, England), 1986, Putnam (New York, NY), 1987.
The Tall Story of Wilbur Small, Blackie & Son (London, England), 1987.
Alice the Artist, illustrated by Jonathan Langley, Methuen (London, England), 1988, Dutton (New York, NY), 1988.
Can't You Sleep, Little Bear?, illustrated by Barbara Firth, Walker Books (London, England), 1988, Candlewick (Cambridge, MA), 1992.
Class Three and the Beanstalk, illustrated by Toni Goffe, Blackie & Son (London, England), 1988.
Great Gran Gorilla and the Robbers, illustrated by Dom Mansell, Walker Books (London, England), 1988.
Great Gran Gorilla to the Rescue, illustrated by Dom Mansell, Walker Books (London, England), 1988.
Our Sleepysaurus, Walker Books (London, England), 1988.

Owl and Billy and the Space Days, Methuen (London, England), 1988.

Tales from the Shop That Never Shuts, illustrated by Maureen Bradley, Viking Kestrel (London, England), 1988.

Fred the Angel, Walker Books (London, England), 1989.

Judy the Bad Fairy, Walker Books (London, England), 1989.

Once There Were Giants, illustrated by Penny Dale, Walker Books (London, England), 1989, Delacorte (New York, NY), 1989.

The Park in the Dark, illustrated by Barbara Firth, edited by D. Briley, Walker Books (London, England), 1989, Lothrop (New York, NY), 1989.

Amy Said, illustrated by Charlotte Voake, Walker Books (London, England), 1990, Little Brown (Boston, MA), 1990.

Daisy's Christmas, illustrated by Jonathan Langley, Methuen (London, England), 1990, Ideals, 1990.

The Ghost Family Robinson, illustrated by Jacqui Thomas, Viking Kestrel (London, England), 1990.

The Hidden House, illustrated by Angela Barrett, Walker Books (London, England), 1990, Putnam (New York, NY), 1990.

My Great Grandpa, illustrated by Dom Mansell, Walker Books (London, England), 1990, Putnam (New York, NY), 1990.

Rosie's Babies, illustrated by Penny Dale, Walker Books (London, England), 1990, Candlewick (Cambridge, MA), 1999.

We Love Them, illustrated by Barbara Firth, Walker Books (London, England), 1990, Lothrop (New York, NY), 1990.

Grandma's Bill, illustrated by Jane Johnson, Simon & Schuster, 1990, Orchard Books (New York, NY), 1991.

Coming Home, illustrated by Neil Reed, Simon & Schuster (New York, NY), 1991.

Farmer Duck, illustrated by Helen Oxenbury, Walker Books (London, England), 1991, Candlewick (Cambridge, MA), 1992.

The Happy Hedgehog Band, illustrated by Jill Barton, Walker Books (London, England), 1991, Candlewick (Cambridge, MA), 1992.

Herbie Whistle, illustrated by Anthony Ian Lewis, Viking Kestrel (London, England), 1991.

Let's Go Home, Little Bear, Walker Books (London, England), 1991, Candlewick (Cambridge, MA), 1991.

Little Obie and the Kidnap, illustrated by Elsie Lennox, Walker Books (London, England), 1991, Candlewick (Cambridge, MA), 1994.

Man Mountain, illustrated by Claudio Munoz, Viking Kestrel (London, England), 1991.

Squeak-a-Lot, illustrated by Virginia Miller, Walker Books (London, England), 1991, Greenwillow (New York, NY), 1991.

The Ghost Family Robinson at the Seaside, illustrated by Jacqui Thomas, Viking Kestrel (London, England), 1992.

Little Obie and the Flood, illustrated by Elsi Lennox, Candlewick (Cambridge, MA), 1992.

Owl Babies, illustrated by Patrick Benson, Walker Books (London, England), 1992, Candlewick (Cambridge, MA), 1992.

The Pig in the Pond, illustrated by Jill Barton, Walker Books (London, England), 1992, Candlewick (Cambridge, MA), 1992.

Sailor Bear, illustrated by Virginia Miller, Walker Books (London, England), 1992, Candlewick (Cambridge, MA), 1992.

Sam Vole and His Brothers, illustrated by Barbara Firth, Walker Books (London, England), 1992, Candlewick (Cambridge, MA), 1992.

The Toymaker: A Story in Two Parts, illustrated by Terry Milne, Walker Books (London, England), 1992, Candlewick (Cambridge, MA), 1992.

Baby's Hammer, illustrated by John Watson, Walker Books (London, England), 1993.

The Big Bad Mole's Coming!, illustrated by John Bendall-Brunello, Walker Books (London, England), 1993.

The Fishface Feud, illustrated by Arthur Robins, Walker Books (London, England), 1993.

Little Mo, illustrated by Jill Barton, Walker Books (London, England), 1993, Candlewick (Cambridge, MA), 1993.

The Lucky Duck Song, illustrated by Judy Brown, Puffin (London, England), 1993.

Rubberneck's Revenge, illustrated by Arthur Robins, O'Brien Press (Dublin, Ireland), 1993.

The School That Went to Sea, illustrated by Leo Hartas, O'Brien Press (Dublin, Ireland), 1993.

Stories from the Bible: Old Testament Stories, illustrated by Geoffrey Patterson, Frances Lincoln (London, England), 1993, Ticknor & Fields (New York, NY), 1993.

Shipwreck at Old Jelly's Farm, Ginn (Aylesbury, England), 1994.

Upside Down Harry Brown, Ginn (Aylesbury, England), 1994.

The Big, Big Sea, illustrated by Jennifer Eachas, Candlewick (Cambridge, MA), 1994.

The Kidnapping of Suzie Q, Hamish Hamilton (London, England), 1994, Candlewick Press (Cambridge, MA), 1996.

When the Teddy Bears Came, illustrated by Penny Dale, Candlewick (Cambridge, MA), 1995.

John Joe and the Big Hen, illustrated by Paul Howard, Candlewick (Cambridge, MA), 1995.

Tango's Baby, Candlewick (Cambridge, MA), 1995.

Mimi and the Dream House, Candlewick (Cambridge, MA), 1995.

Mimi and the Picnic, Candlewick (Cambridge, MA), 1996.

Cup Final Kid, illustrated by Jeff Cummins, Walker (London, England), 1996.

Bears Everywhere, Candlewick (Cambridge, MA), 1996.

You and Me, Little Bear, illustrated by Barbara Firth, Candlewick (Cambridge, MA), 1996.

What Use Is a Moose?, illustrated by Arthur Robins, Candlewick (Cambridge, MA), 1996.

Small Bear Lost, illustrated by Virginia Austin, Candlewick (Cambridge, MA), 1996.

Mimi's Christmas, Candlewick (Cambridge, MA), 1997.

Little Frog and the Dog, illustrated by Trevor Dunton, Sundance (Littleton, MA), 1997.

Little Frog and the Frog Olympics, illustrated by Trevor Dunton, Sundance (Littleton, MA), 1997.

Little Frog and the Tadpoles, illustrated by Trevor Dunton, Sundance (Littleton, MA), 1997.

Little Frog in the Throat, illustrated by Trevor Dunton, Sundance (Littleton, MA), 1997.

The Adventures of Pete and Mary Kate, illustrated by Terry Milne, Walker (London, England), 1997.

We Love Them, illustrated by Barbara Firth, Candlewick (Cambridge, MA), 1997.

The Life and Loves of Zoe T. Curley, Walker (London, England), 1997.

Yum, Yum, Yummy, illustrated by John Bendall-Brunello, Candlewick (Cambridge, MA), 1998.

Who Do You Love?, illustrated by Camilla Ashforth, Candlewick (Cambridge, MA), 1999.

Good Job, Little Bear!, illustrated by Barbara Firth, Candlewick (Cambridge, MA), 1999.

The Hollyhock Wall, illustrated by Salley Mavor, Candlewick (Cambridge, MA), 1999.

Night, Night Cuddly Bear, illustrated by Penny Dale, Candlewick (Cambridge, MA), 2000.

Webster J. Duck, illustrated by David Parkins, Candlewick (Cambridge, MA), 2001.

Tom Rabbit, illustrated by Barbara Firth, Candlewick (Cambridge, MA), 2001.

A Kitten Called Moonlight, illustrated by Christian Birmingham, Candlewick (Cambridge, MA), 2001.

Hi, Harry!, illustrated by Barbara Firth, Candlewick (Cambridge, MA), in press.

"NAPPER" SERIES

Napper Goes for Goal, illustrated by Barrie Mitchell, Puffin (London, England), 1981.

Napper Strikes Again, illustrated by Barrie Mitchell, Puffin (London, England), 1981.

Napper's Golden Goals, illustrated by Barrie Mitchell, Puffin (London, England), 1984.

Napper's Luck, illustrated by Richard Berridge, Puffin (London, England), 1993.

Napper's Big Match, illustrated by Richard Berridge, Puffin (London, England), 1993.

Napper Super-Sub, illustrated by Richard Berridge, Puffin (London, England), 1993.

"THE MYSTERY SQUAD" SERIES

The Mystery Squad and the Dead Man's Message, illustrated by Terry McKenna, Blackie & Son (London, England), 1984.

The Mystery Squad and the Whistling Teeth, illustrated by Terry McKenna, Blackie & Son (London, England), 1984.

The Mystery Squad and Mr. Midnight, illustrated by Terry McKenna, Blackie & Son (London, England), 1984.

The Mystery Squad and the Artful Dodger, illustrated by Terry McKenna, Blackie & Son (London, England), 1984.

The Mystery Squad and the Creeping Castle, illustrated by Terry McKenna, Blackie & Son (London, England), 1985.

The Mystery Squad and the Gemini Job, illustrated by Terry McKenna, Blackie & Son (London, England), 1985.

The Mystery Squad and the Candid Camera, illustrated by Terry McKenna, Blackie & Son (London, England), 1985.

The Mystery Squad and Cannonball Kid, illustrated by Terry McKenna, Blackie & Son (London, England), 1986.

The Mystery Squad and the Robot's Revenge, illustrated by Terry McKenna, Blackie & Son (London, England), 1986.

"HARRIET" SERIES

Harriet and the Crocodiles, illustrated by Mark Burgess, Abelard (London, England), 1982, Little, Brown (Boston, MA), 1984.

Harriet and the Haunted School, illustrated by Mark Burgess, Abelard (London, England), 1984, Little, Brown (Boston, MA), 1986.

Harriet and the Robot, illustrated by Mark Burgess, Abelard (London, England), 1985, Little, Brown (Boston, MA), 1987.

Harriet and the Flying Teachers, illustrated by Mark Burgess, Blackie & Son (London, England), 1987.

"LITTLE DRACULA" SERIES

Little Dracula's Christmas, illustrated by Joseph Wright, Viking Penguin (London, England), 1986.

Little Dracula's First Bite, illustrated by Joseph Wright, Viking Penguin (London, England), 1986.

Little Dracula at the Seaside, illustrated by Joseph Wright, Walker Books (London, England), 1987, Candlewick (Cambridge, MA), 1992.

Little Dracula Goes to School, illustrated by Joseph Wright, Walker Books (London, England), 1987, Candlewick (Cambridge, MA), 1992.

Little Dracula at the Seashore, illustrated by Joseph Wright, Candlewick (Cambridge, MA), 1992.

FOR YOUNG ADULTS; UNDER PSEUDONYM CATHERINE SEFTON

In a Blue Velvet Dress: Almost a Ghost Story, illustrated by Gareth Floyd, Faber (London, England), 1972, published as *In a Blue Velvet Dress*, illustrated by Eros Keith, Harper (New York, NY), 1973.

The Sleepers on the Hill, Faber (London, England), 1973.

The Back House Ghosts, Faber (London, England), 1974, published as *The Haunting of Ellen: A Story of Suspense*, Harper (New York, NY), 1975.

The Ghost and Bertie Boggin, illustrated by Jill Bennett, Faber (London, England), 1980.

Emer's Ghost, Hamish Hamilton (London, England), 1981.

The Finn Gang, illustrated by Sally Holmes, Hamish Hamilton (London, England), 1981.

The Emma Dilemma, illustrated by Jill Bennett, Faber (London, England), 1982.

A Puff of Smoke, illustrated by Thelma Lambert, Hamish Hamilton (London, England), 1982.

Island of the Strangers, Hamish Hamilton (London, England), 1983, Harcourt (San Diego, CA), 1985.

It's My Gang, illustrated by Catherine Bradbury, Hamish Hamilton (London, England), 1984.

The Blue Misty Monsters, illustrated by Elaine McGregor Turney, Faber (London, England), 1985.

The Ghost Girl, Hamish Hamilton (London, England), 1985.

The Ghost Ship, illustrated by Martin Ursell, Hamish Hamilton (London, England), 1985.

Flying Sam, illustrated by Margaret Chamberlain, Hamish Hamilton (London, England), 1986.

Shadows on the Lake, Hamish Hamilton (London, England), 1987.

Bertie Boggin and the Ghost Again!, Faber (London, England), 1988.

The Day the Smells Went Wrong, illustrated by John Rogan, Hamish Hamilton (London, England), 1988.

The Haunted Schoolbag, illustrated by Caroline Crossland, Hamish Hamilton (London, England), 1989.

The Boggart in the Barrel, illustrated by Maureen Bradley, Hamish Hamilton (London, England), 1991.

Horace the Ghost, illustrated by Caroline Crossland, Hamish Hamilton (London, England), 1991.

Along a Lonely Road, Puffin (London, England), 1993.

The Ghosts of the Cobweb and the Skully Bones Mystery, Hamish Hamilton (London, England), 1993.

The Ghosts of the Cobweb Street and the Circus Star, illustrated by Jean Baylis, Hamish Hamilton (London, England), 1993.

The Cast-Off, Hamish Hamilton (London, England), 1993.

The Ghosts of Cobweb and the TV Battle, Hamish Hamilton (London, England), 1994.

The Ghosts of Cobweb, Puffin (London, England), 1994.

"IRISH POLITICAL" TRILOGY; UNDER PSEUDONYM CATHERINE SEFTON

Starry Night, Hamish Hamilton (London, England), 1986.

Frankie's Story, Hamish Hamilton (London, England), 1988.

The Beat of the Drum, Hamish Hamilton (London, England), 1989.

FICTION; FOR ADULTS

Otley, Hodder & Stoughton (London, England), 1966, Stein & Day (Briarcliff Manor, NY), 1966.

Otley Pursued, Hodder & Stoughton (London, England), 1967, Stein & Day (Briarcliff Manor, NY), 1967.

Otley Forever, Hodder & Stoughton (London, England), 1968, Stein & Day (Briarcliff Manor, NY), 1968.

Come Back When I'm Sober, Hodder & Stoughton (London, England), 1969.

Otley Victorious, Hodder & Stoughton (London, England), 1969, Stein & Day (Briarcliff Manor, NY), 1969.

A Little Bit British: Being the Diary of an Ulsterman, August, 1969, Tom Stacey, 1970.

OTHER

Author of radio play *The Fleas and Mr. Morgan,* 1969; contributor of sketches to "Bazaar" series, 1974, and "One Potato, Two Potato" series, 1975. *Owl Babies* has been translated into Spanish by Andrea B. Bermudez as *Las lechucitas,* Compton, 1994.

Adaptations

Otley was adapted for a motion picture starring Romy Schneider and Tom Courtenay, Columbia, 1969; *In a Blue Velvet Dress* was adapted for "Jackanory" reading, BBC-TV, 1974; *The Sleepers on the Hill* was adapted as a television serial by BBC-TV, 1976; *Fred the Angel* was broadcast on BBC-TV; *Island of the Strangers* was broadcast on Thames TV.

Sidelights

The author of over 150 books, Belfast-born Martin Waddell is many writers in one. There is the Martin Waddell who writes children's mysteries, picture books, slapstick comedies, football stories, and ghost stories under his own name; that prolific Martin Waddell has over a hundred books to his credit and the number is growing. Waddell, wearing a different hat, has penned books for adults, as well, including the popular spy series featuring Otley. Then there is the Martin Waddell who writes more emotionally charged young adult titles under the pseudonym Catherine Sefton. Under both names, Waddell provides stories with a "hook," so that children and adults read on to discover the "what-happened-then" of the story; his themes range from the consequences of prejudice to individual rights to inter-generational relations.

The same dichotomy found in Waddell's books is also apparent in the strife-ridden land where he resides. A citizen of Northern Ireland, he has experienced daily the duality of Ireland: Protestant against Catholic, Ulster Loyalist against Irish Nationalist. With many of his books, Waddell has attempted to "counter the 'Them' and 'Us' mentality which has cost so many lives and caused so much heartbreak to the people I live amongst," as he remarked in his *Something about the Author Autobiography Series (SAAS)* essay.

Born in 1941, Waddell came into a family with a long ancestry in County Down. Part of this ancestry includes the writers the Waddell clan has produced, four of whom were authors of note. Waddell, like other small children, was evacuated to rural safety from Belfast during the bombings of World War II. With the end of the war, he and the family returned to Belfast, but his parents soon divorced, and from the age of eleven young Waddell was raised in County Down by his single mother. Leaving school at fifteen, he worked for a time for a local newspaper; then tried his hand—or foot—at professional soccer. When that came to nothing, he found himself living in England and needing to make a living. He turned to the tradition of his ancestors and took up writing.

"Why writing?" he asked himself in *SAAS.* "I suppose the answer is that writing had always come easily to me. I had never had to work at it at school; it was something I knew I could do. That goes back to story, and reading. My love of story, of being told stories and being read to, had transferred to a love of books."

After six years of working at the craft, Waddell had a stack of unpublished novels. But he also had an agent, Jonathan Clowes, who believed in his abilities. It was Clowes who introduced Waddell to the work of Len Deighton, the spy novelist. Shortly thereafter, in 1966,

Waddell produced *Otley,* a satirical spy-thriller. A movie adaptation, plus subsequent adult novels about Otley, provided the financial security for Waddell to return to Ireland and buy a house in Donaghadee, a quiet seaside town. In 1969 Waddell married, and his career took an entirely different course. It was then that he wrote his first book for children, *In a Blue Velvet Dress,* a Victorian ghost story that M. Hobbs, writing in *Junior Bookshelf,* felt was narrated with "most endearing and effective humor." Waddell had come to a decision about his writing. "The lyrical novels weren't even publishable," he wrote in *SAAS.* "The thrillers were hopelessly padded to make the length, but *Blue Velvet* at 25,000 words was full of fun and adventure and emotion. I had got it right, at last!"

Waddell published the book under a pen name because his own was associated with comedies and thrillers. He came up with Catherine Sefton, taken from his grandmother's maiden name and the Christian name of Catherine, which he had always liked. *In a Blue Velvet Dress* was dramatized by the BBC, and a second Catherine Sefton book, *The Sleepers on the Hill,* an Irish mystery, was also dramatized by the BBC.

Waddell and his wife had their first two children and his career seemed to be in high gear by mid-1972. Then Waddell was nearly killed in a bomb blast in a local church, and for the next six years he was unable to write, suffering a mental and emotional block. *The Back House Ghosts* by Catherine Sefton, a combination of ghost story and daily adventures of a group of young people, was the only work to emerge from this time. It is a "story that is full of excitement and humor," remarked Sylvia Mogg in *Children's Book Review.* Waddell moved back to his original village of Newcastle; his wife went back to teaching to help with finances, and their third son was born during this time, too.

In 1978 the ability to tell stories suddenly came back to Waddell. In a flurry he wrote children's books of all genres. There were two Catherine Sefton books for young adults, *The Ghost and Bertie Boggin* and *Emer's Ghost,* the latter set in Northern Ireland and praised by many critics. For example, *Times Literary Supplement* contributor Ann Evans called it "a beautifully wrought story" and described Waddell as "a writer of rare order." Under his own name, Waddell also began his "Napper" series—soccer books in which he uses his own history as a goalkeeper to tell stories that bring the game and the characters to life. In this same period he wrote his first picture book, *The Great Green Mouse Disaster,* a "magnificent wordless saga," according to George Hunt in *Books for Keeps,* in which a group of mice invade a hotel, wreaking havoc from floor to floor.

Catherine Sefton kept "her" ghost stories and more emotionally charged books for young adults flowing, but Martin Waddell began producing more fun-oriented books in the "Napper" series, the "Mystery Squad" series, the "Harriet" stories (which relate the comic adventures of an accident-prone child), and the "Little Dracula" books about a young vampire and his family.

Additionally, there are the picture books for which Waddell has become increasingly known and which he takes quite seriously despite their light themes. "Books for beginners should be clearly and brightly written with vivid characterization and exciting or amusing situations piling one on top of the other," Waddell commented in *SAAS.* "Add to this the need to use words and images which are freshly minted, not recycled, and the [very short text] becomes a daunting challenge."

It is a challenge Waddell has met, according to critics, in such notable picture books as *Going West, The Park in the Dark, Farmer Duck, Sam Vole and His Brothers,* and *Can't You Sleep, Little Bear? Going West* is an unsentimental depiction of a family's move west by wagon train. "It is a story of high adventure . . . ," wrote Colin Greenland in the *Times Literary Supplement,* "but also elemental, bare, summoning the reader's own emotional responses." With *Can't You Sleep, Little Bear?,* Waddell and illustrator Barbara Firth "created a classic picture book," according to Keith Barker in *School Library Journal.* Another of Waddell's nighttime books also drew critical acclaim. "Here is a picture of childhood which is beautiful and true and is also accessible," Marcus Crouch noted in a *Junior Bookshelf* review of *The Park in the Dark.* In *Farmer Duck* Waddell fashioned a picture book resonant of George Orwell's *Animal Farm,* "with a sharp edge to its wit," according to Crouch in another *Junior Bookshelf* review. About the same title, a critic in *Publishers Weekly* observed, "Waddell's uncomplicated story gently encourages readers to recognize and fight injustice." And in *Sam Vole and His Brothers,* Waddell "pleasantly presents the subtle shades of emotions among siblings," in the words of Judith Gloyer, writing in *School Library Journal.*

Writing as Catherine Sefton, Waddell has also earned critical praise, particularly for his examination of Northern Ireland's problems. In *Island of the Strangers,* for example, a busload of Belfast children enter a remote village, causing prejudice and violence to erupt. "A strong, sure-handed effort," Ilene Cooper noted in *Booklist.* Pauline Thomas, writing in *School Librarian,* stated that it "is done in powerful prose . . . simple, spare, and sinewy." Sefton's Irish trilogy, *Starry Night, Frankie's Story,* and *The Beat of the Drum,* has also explored the "troubles," as the strife in Northern Ireland is referred to, and its effect on the youth of the country. "These have been called a trilogy," Waddell wrote in *SAAS,* "but they aren't really, each being a separate story. What they have in common is a set of ideas, laid out in *Starry Night* and observed in action in the other two. *Frankie's Story* and *The Beat of the Drum* are basically the same story: one about a Catholic girl resisting the forces of extremism in her world, and the other about a Protestant boy doing the same in his." Robert Leeson, writing in the *Times Educational Supplement,* had this to say of the three books: "The author has resolutely completed his aim, to help the teenage reader grasp the reality of Northern Ireland's tragedy. The trilogy is a real contribution to the understanding which must one day bring that suffering to an end." Sefton's

Along a Lonely Road once again explores the "troubles," but in a much edgier format, creating a "masterpiece of suspense," observed D. A. Young in *Junior Bookshelf*.

During the 1990s Waddell concentrated almost wholly on picture books, expanding his ever-popular "Little Bear" books, illustrated by Barbara Firth, and adding other endearing titles such as *Sailor Bear* and *Small Bear Lost,* as well as a jumble of other books featuring animals from frogs to mice to ducks to rabbits and kittens. In *Let's Go Home, Little Bear,* the wee one is frightened on the way home, fearful of the scary noises he hears in the woods. "They're back!" declared a reviewer for *Publishers Weekly.* "Little Bear and Big Bear, arguably the most winning ursine specimens since Paddington and Pooh, return to print in a thoroughly delectable sequel." The same reviewer noted that this yarn contains "minimal plot but a great deal of heart." *You and Me, Little Bear,* continues the adventures in a "warm tale of togetherness," according to a contributor for *Publishers Weekly,* who went on to note that Waddell and Firth "are a match made in heaven." *Booklist* contributor April Judge called the same book a "charming combination of words and pictures" that will "captivate old and new bear friends." And with *Good Job, Little Bear!,* Waddell presents a "paean to familial love and security," according to *Horn Book* reviewer Ellen Fader.

Working with illustrators Virginia Miller and Virginia Austin, respectively, Waddell has created other bear books, including *Sailor Bear* and *Small Bear Lost,* which relate the adventures of a very plucky stuffed bear. A contributor for *Publishers Weekly* dubbed *Sailor Bear* a "classic, comforting bedtime story," while *Booklist*'s Carolyn Phelan called *Small Bear Lost* a "simple, satisfying story for preschoolers." More bears are served up in *Night Night, Cuddly Bear.*

With *What Use Is a Moose?* Waddell moves away from ursine matters, introducing a character that "is arguably the goofiest and most endearing moose to come down the pike since Bullwinkle," according to a reviewer for *Publishers Weekly.* A feline family is presented in *Who Do You Love?* in a "story that almost melts with geniality," according to a contributor for *Kirkus Reviews,* while a mouse takes center stage in the "Mimi" books. Reviewing *Mimi and the Picnic* in *Booklist,* Phelan felt that "Waddell's use of repetition and internal rhyme give his writing a lilting quality that storytellers will appreciate and young children will savor."

Tom Rabbit is set on an English farm and tells of a little boy and his wonderful stuffed rabbit. Phelan dubbed this picture book "winsome" in a *Booklist* review, and a "beguiling little adventure, written with simplicity, brevity, and a fine-tuned sensitivity to the emotional lives of small children." *A Kitten Called Moonlight,* a rescue adventure tale, is a "glowing picture book," according to *Booklist*'s Hazel Rochman, while *Webster J. Duck* is a "heartwarming tale," according to a *Publishers Weekly* contributor, of a plucky duck who sets off to search for the mother he never saw.

Turning from four-legged critters to humans, Waddell also has created picture books featuring child protagonists. In *Rosie's Babies* four-year-old Rosie continues to ask her mother questions, vying for attention, as the mother takes care of her infant sibling. A reviewer for *Publishers Weekly* felt that Waddell "perfectly captures the nuances of a child's conversation with her mother in this disarming story." *The Hollyhock Wall* features a girl named Mary whose rock garden comes alive, and she is suddenly playing in it with her friend Tom. Then, the next day, the garden is once again inanimate. Mary is puzzled until she discovers that her grandmother has a garden similar to hers, with the real Tom in it waiting to play. A critic for *Kirkus Reviews* noted that Waddell "toys with the boundaries between real life and imaginary realms in this convoluted fantasy," while *Booklist*'s Ilene Cooper called this picture book "eminently appealing." In *The Adventures of Pete and Mary Kate* a grandmother tries to get a little boy to play with a doll, a request met largely with disgust on the part of the boy, until the doll starts to talk to him. Michael Kirby, reviewing the title in *School Librarian,* felt it was a "gem of a book" and "warm and cuddly." Also, Waddell presents the adventures of a toddler on a farm in *John Joe and the Big Hen,* a "beautiful and accessible book," as a reviewer for *Books for Keeps* described it.

Waddell has also published works for older readers, including *Tango's Baby, The Life and Loves of Zoe T. Curley,* and *The Kidnapping of Suzie Q.* In the first novel, Brian Tangello does all he can to keep his girlfriend and their baby. A British teenager often on the wrong side of the law, Brian is not really a bad youth. A friend of Tango's narrates this "funky story with wry humor and wonderful sketches," according to *Booklist* writer Anne O'Malley. A novel written in the form of diary entries, *The Life and Loves of Zoe T. Curley* "offers the fantasies of a young teenager about the possibility of falling in love with a boy," according to Michael Glover in the *New Statesman.* This "funny and precocious" autobiography, as Glover described it, deals with Zoe's family as well as her feelings of insecurity about herself. Included in the family menagerie are her very unsuccessful father and his attempts at writing and cartooning, and her two oafish brothers, whom she dubs Creep and Ob-Noxious. Reviewing the title in *School Librarian,* Cecilia J. Hynes-Higman called it a "most enjoyable lively book." Hynes-Higman went on to note that though the book was created by a man, "the character of Zoe is utterly 'female adolescent.'" *The Kidnapping of Suzie Q* is a thriller, dealing with a teen who is taken hostage during a grocery store robbery. A reviewer for *Publishers Weekly* thought that the "smart, breezy writing, jaunty heroine and tense setting should keep readers on the hook."

"I believe in writing very carefully for children, because they become much more involved in the small details of character than the average reader," Waddell once commented. "I do not suggest that children should be written down to, but that they should be written *for;* and this means rewards, ghosts, football, fantasy, treats, adventures, relationships. . . . I believe that children's stories should be directed first and foremost to their interests, and that they should be quick, clear, emotionally strong, and verbally bright." Waddell's wide variety of writing, under his own name and that of Catherine Sefton, attests to the fact that he has put his philosophy into practice.

Biographical and Critical Sources

BOOKS

Children's Literature Review, Volume 31, Gale (Detroit, MI), 1993.

St. James Guide to Children's Writers, 5th edition, St. James (Detroit, MI), 1999.

Something about the Author Autobiography Series, Volume 15, Gale (Detroit, MI), 1993.

PERIODICALS

Booklist, January 1, 1986, Ilene Cooper, review of *Island of the Strangers,* p. 687; December 15, 1995, Anne O'Malley, review of *Tango's Baby,* p. 698; May 1, 1996, p. 1499; September 15, 1996, Carolyn Phelan, *Small Bear Lost,* p. 251; October 1, 1996, April Judge, review of *You and Me, Little Bear,* p. 360; April 15, 1998, Carolyn Phelan, review of *Mimi and the Picnic,* pp. 1454-1455; June 1, 1999, p. 1845; August, 1999, Ilene Cooper, review of *The Hollyhock Wall,* p. 2067; November 15, 2000, p. 651; March 1, 2001, Carolyn Phelan, review of *Tom Rabbit,* p. 1289; April 1, 2001, Hazel Rochman, review of *A Kitten Called Moonlight,* p. 1480.

Books for Keeps, September, 1989, George Hunt, review of *The Great Green Mouse Disaster,* p. 9; September, 1997, review of *John Joe and the Big Hen,* p. 21.

Children's Book Review, spring, 1975, Sylvia Mogg, review of *The Back House Ghosts,* pp. 22-23.

Horn Book, March-April, 1999, Ellen Fader, review of *Good Job, Little Bear!,* p. 203.

Junior Bookshelf, November, 1972, M. Hobbs, review of *In a Blue Velvet Dress,* p. 2036; April, 1989, Marcus Crouch, review of *The Park in the Dark,* pp. 64-65; December, 1991, Marcus Crouch, review of *Farmer Duck,* p. 246; April, 1992, D. A. Young, review of *Along the Lonely Road,* p. 79.

Kirkus Reviews, March 15, 1999, review of *Who Do You Love?,* p. 458; June 1, 1999, review of *The Hollyhock Wall,* p. 890.

New Statesman, December 5, 1997, Michael Glover, review of *The Life and Loves of Zoe T. Curley,* p. 66.

New York Times Book Review, May 21, 1967; July 28, 1968; February 1, 1970; May 4, 1975; March 25, 1984; May 6, 1990.

Publishers Weekly, January 20, 1992, review of *Farmer Duck,* p. 64; March 22, 1993, review of *Let's Go Home, Little Bear,* p. 78; October 24, 1994, p. 32; January 22, 1996, review of *Sailor Bear,* p. 74; June 10, 1996, review of *The Kidnapping of Suzie Q,* p. 101; July 1, 1996, review of *What Use Is a Moose?,* p. 60; July 8, 1996, review of *You and Me, Little Bear,* p. 83; February 22, 1999, review of *Rosie's Babies,* p. 93; April 26, 1999, p. 80; August 7, 2000, p. 93; February 5, 2001, p. 88; June 18, 2001, review of *Webster J. Duck,* p. 80.

Saturday Review, June 24, 1967.

School Librarian, September, 1983, Pauline Thomas, review of *Island of the Strangers,* pp. 272-275; August, 1997, Cecilia J. Hynes-Higman, review of *The Life and Loves of Zoe T. Curley,* pp. 161-162; summer, 1998, Michael Kirby, review of *The Adventures of Pete and Mary Kate,* p. 90.

School Library Journal, May, 1989, Keith Barker, review of *Can't You Sleep, Little Bear?,* p. 56; January, 1993, Judith Gloyer, review of *Sam Vole and His Brothers,* p. 86; September, 1994, p. 200; October, 1994, p. 128; November, 1995, p. 124; April, 1996, p. 158; September, 1996, p. 193; October, 1997, p. 44; August, 1998, p. 146; March, 1999, pp. 187-188; June, 1999, p. 108; November, 2000, p. 136; April, 2001, p. 124; July, 2001, Gay Lynn Van Vleck, review of *Webster J. Duck,* p. 90.

Times (London, England), June 24, 1989; March 17, 1990.

Times Educational Supplement, May 5, 1989, Robert Leeson, review of *The Beat of the Drum,* p. B7.

Times Literary Supplement, March 16, 1967; November 6, 1969; November 23, 1973; December 6, 1974; November 20, 1981, Ann Evans, review of *Emer's Ghost,* p. 1359; February 10, 1984, Colin Greenland, review of *Going West,* p. 150; October 17, 1986; April 17, 1987; May 20, 1988.*

—Sketch by J. Sydney Jones

*   *   *

Autobiography Feature

Martin Waddell

I am writing this in my workroom, looking out through the window at the apple tree in the garden, rich with red apples, and the green of the woods on the slopes of the Mountains of Mourne, which rise sharply above the small town of Newcastle, in County Down, Northern Ireland. Two hundred yards from here there is another house, a cottage called Rock Cottage. Fifty years ago I was brought to it, as a baby. My childhood in Newcastle and the later time spent bringing up my children here has shaped me and made me what I am.

Well, what am I?

I am a writer, halfway through my writing life. The page in front of me is filling up with words at this minute, these words. For most of my life I have been filling pages with words, the words that make the stories that grow in my head.

There have been a lot of stories, most of them written at this table, looking out at the mountains. The stories are on the bookshelves beside me. They are my *other* children . . . not to be confused with my real children, my sons Tom and David and Peter. My stories are my mind-children, if you like. They are on my shelves, and growing in my head

Martin Waddell in Italy, 2001

Martin Waddell at nine months

are others, waiting to attract my attention, fighting with each other about who-comes-first. It is a magic thing about stories that they come before the words ... you can feel them stirring, but you don't know what form they will take. The good ones won't wait their turn to be written and thought about. The best ones, the really strong ones, pour themselves out on the page. They know what comes next, long before the poor writer does.

RULE ONE for being-a-writer: When a story wants to be written is when it gets written, not after-the-next-one, or when I've got-some-free-time, or maybe-next-year if I can fit it in.

NOW.

The important-looking Professional Writer's Schedule on the wall says that I'm about to write a beautiful picture book I've been planning for some time, called "Dear Eliza." When I came to my workroom and sat down in my red, thinking chair by the window (there's a picture of that chair in *Can't You Sleep, Little Bear?*), I thought I was ready for "Dear Eliza" ... but "Dear Eliza" didn't think so ... and this one did.

This one is different from my other stories. It is supposed to be about who I am and what I do and how I do it and why I do it and what it feels like to do it ... all about being Martin Waddell, the name that is on the back of most of my books. (There is another name on some of them, "Catherine Sefton," but I'll come to the how and why of her later on in the story.)

I am a writer, a storyteller, so I'll tell you a story, about Martin Waddell.

It begins in Scotland, in 1679, with a battle between the Scots and the English. The battle was at a place called Bothwell Brig and eight of my ancestors had turned up to fight on the Scottish side. They were Presbyterian Covenanters, and they were fighting to defend their Presbyterianism against the English government's desire to impose Anglicanism on Scotland. To cut short a long, sad story, they lost. Six of the eight Waddells were hanged, and the remaining two were put on a ship to be transported. The ship was wrecked in a storm off the Orkneys, and the two Waddells escaped. No one quite knows what happened next, but the two brothers turned up in Ireland, in a townland called Ouley, which is about twenty miles from where I'm sitting writing this.

They started to farm there. It is in the nature of Irish history that the family has been at Ouley ever since. There are Waddells there to this day, in the shadow of the Mournes, just the other side of the mountains from my town, Newcastle.

That is how the Waddells came to Ireland, and therefore how I come to be Irish, though some Irishmen would call me a Scot, even yet. The English used the Scots in Ireland to suppress the native Irish, and so my forefathers had the good land, and my wife's forefathers, native Irish, were driven up into the rocky ground, on the hills. My Protestant family is still on the good ground, her Catholic family is still on the bad ground, and that puts a lot of Irish history into a personal perspective.

I was brought up in this divided community, though without the bitterness that often goes with the division, for my branch of the family had a liberal streak. I am neither Protestant nor Catholic, Ulster Loyalist nor Irish Nationalist, and so it is difficult for me to identify with any of these groups. This difficulty is explored in many of my books: *Island of the Strangers; The Ghost Girl; Starry Night; Frankie's Story, The Beat of the Drum.* They are my attempt (actually Catherine Sefton's, for they are written under my pen name) to counter the "Them" and "Us" mentality which has cost so many lives and caused so much heartbreak to the people I live amongst.

The blood and the bitterness of Northern Ireland are a part of me, as a writer, as are the speech patterns and phrases I hear each day, and the gentle grey mountains sweeping down outside my window, and the waves that wash my doorstep in winter.

Writing is in my bones. A host of devout Waddells have written on religion almost since anyone thought of doing it, and there have been others with a wider range of subject matter. My great-aunt was Helen Waddell, still in print all over the world, and my great-uncle, under the name Rutherford Mayne, wrote many plays that were famous in their day. Even that name echoes another writer in the family, Captain Mayne Reid, a famous Victorian writer of adventure stories, whose sister was my great-great-great-grandmother.

Where do I come in? Better get on with my story.

I began with a bang! I was born on a night when the Luftwaffe were bombing Belfast. Mother and child spent the night under a steel-topped table in a Belfast nursing home and the next day my father, Mayne, a linen handkerchief manufacturer, whipped us out of the blitzed city and away to the village of Bryansford, three miles from where I am today. Very shortly after that we moved again, to Rock Cottage, on Newcastle's Main Street.

The cottage was named after a local landmark, the Black Rock, where the parish church looks out over Dundrum Bay. It was an old ramshackle cottage, which had once been a tollhouse. In its walls, though we didn't know it then, was a secret staircase hidden behind a bulbous lump of plaster, which looked like one of the rough stones the cottage was made from. The lump was removed during later renovations, and a spiral staircase was revealed, heading to a hidden space in the roof where old rifle stocks and clothing were discovered . . . but that was later. Lots of secret places creep into my books, so perhaps a seed was planted by this discovery.

The war came to Newcastle, with the buildup to D Day (the invasion of Europe) in June 1944. American soldiers moved into Nissen huts in the demesne of the local lord's dower house, a mansion called Donard Lodge, set in the woods at the foot of the mountains. The American soldiers brought money, and music, and candy, what we call "sweeties."

I know about the sweeties, because they were my own personal dividend from the war. The garden in front of the cottage was on one of the "escape" routes from the camp, which the soldiers came down on their way into town. There, in the garden, was a little fat baby in a pram. My pram, according to my mother, used to fill up with sweeties, until she had to tell the soldiers to stop it.

I have the vaguest of memories of a bonfire that was built on the beach behind the then council offices to celebrate V-E Day (Victory in Europe . . . May 1945) and all the local people gathering on the beach around it, but perhaps that was some other day, some other celebration?

That is the sum total of my war memories.

The aftermath of war brought a continuation of the austerity that had gone with it, confused in Northern Ireland by the closeness of the border with the then Free State, now the Republic of Ireland. The Free State was not in the war (although their fire engines broke the rules and came to help when Belfast was blitzed), and the rationing and food restrictions which existed in the North did not apply down there, twenty miles away. I remember once smuggling butter and eggs with my father and mother in a boat across Carlingford Lough, and another time in a car travelling along a little-used mountain road, when a fog descended and we almost drove into a gully below. I remember . . . maybe I do, or maybe I have just been told the stories, for surely I must have been too young to remember anything.

I know I remember the woods and the waterfalls on the mountainside behind Rock Cottage, and the hours and hours I spent there in the company of a wonderful storyteller. He was a man called Terence Pym, a small-time actor with a haunted face and red hair, steeped in story and legend, and he placed the stories of Andersen and Grimm and the Norse sagas in my woods, behind my house, so that they became real and personal for me. Terence read to me from books, but he also told the stories as he walked, with dark eyes and an actor's intonation. He was part of the stories, he was the characters, and I am sure that some of my love of story comes from those long days living stories in the woods around the burned-out ruin of the dower house, Donard Lodge. (I forgot to mention that bit. The

American soldiers had a big party and somehow set it on fire. It burned out completely, but still stood as a granite shell in the woods until 1969, when it had to be blown up for safety reasons. It, and the woods, play a large part in my first book for children, *In a Blue Velvet Dress.*)

I spent my summers in the woods behind Newcastle, and on the four miles of beach in front of it, but my postwar winters, up to the age of seven or eight, were spent in Greenwood Park, Belfast, where my parents had bought a house, once Belfast was safe to return to.

Greenwood Park had detached houses stretching up a slight slope. The slope was wonderful for tricycle racing, because there was no traffic, for the very good reason that Greenwood Park was a cul-de-sac. I had friends: I remember Frankie Bean, who was my Best Friend (very important), and a redheaded girl called Rosemary Menzies, and her sister, and a boy called Alan Knight, I think. There were eleven or twelve of us, and we had rival gangs. The membership changed from time to time. We played in a disused air-raid shelter, and once we built an underground hide by excavating a deep hole on some waste ground and roofing it over with tree branches and foliage. My uncle Peter came home from being a pilot in the war. He arrived on a roaring motorbike and brought me a model plane that flew, but it was a totally illegal ride on the back of the

"My parents, Ali and Mayne Waddell," 1947

Martin (left) with Terence Pym and a friend, Hubert Baily, 1949

motorbike that really impressed me. Then I was given a pedal-powered tin jeep, and I rode it on the pavement up and down to the shops at Ballyhackamore.

My father was a very busy and often absent father, who still found time when he did appear (which wasn't every night) for my story. It was a continuous story involving Dick Turpin the Highwayman, which went on and on and on for years. The point of it for me as a child was that when my father came to me at bedtime he always brought my story. I had his full attention for as long as it took to tell the next instalment. I believe that a regular period in the day when a child has the undivided attention of an otherwise busy-with-living parent is very important, for the child and the parent.

When I write books for the very small, books such as *Can't You Sleep, Little Bear?* and *Farmer Duck,* I have this period in mind. A good book acts as a "script" the parent can vary according to his or her understanding of the child, so that the book becomes a very personal shared thing. It comes before "reading" because the child is being read to, but the good ones, using rhyme, rhythm, and repetition with the words closely interlinked with the pictures, lead to a kind of reading, where children know what words come next and can anticipate them. The "words" are just blobs on the page to a small child, but with the right book the child will soon "read" them. Is this reading, or just memorizing? I believe it is the beginning of reading, and it certainly goes a long way to creating confidence in reading, and also in

associating the idea of reading a book with the idea of pleasure.

For me, that idea came early, with Terence Pym's stories, and my father's long, long, long story, and the books my mother read to me: *Babar,* and *Little Grey Rabbit,* and one special book that is still on my shelf, *Elizabeth the Cow Ghost* by I-don't-know-who because it is isn't printed in the book! It is a little black-and-yellow book, and it is the one I carried around with me and chewed and tore and played with as a child. My own drawings are all over the white spaces. Books are books, and I can make the case for beautiful books not being abused, but I still believe that children need books to play with as well. They can be made into forts or houses or mazes, and you can hit people over the head with them, and you can do what you want with them because they belong to you, and so does the story inside. "I want *my* story *now*" is very important, and the "my" is as important as the "story." I don't know who wrote *Elizabeth the Cow Ghost,* but I do know that it "belongs" to me in a very real sense, because it is part of my childhood. Everyone who loves books has a few that are specially important. For older people it is what the book has to say to them about their lives . . . the story . . . but for the very young it *can* be the book itself, as an object.

I was lucky. I grew up with books, so the transition from being a reader to being a writer was always a possibility.

Cinema and theatre played a part too. My auntie Bee was an actress, and so, briefly, was my mother. I am told that I was "onstage" in the Group Theatre, Belfast, whilst I was still in the womb! Certainly I have memories of being a toddler-in-the-wings, waiting for Auntie Bee to come off. But the best thing about Bee was that she took me to the Children's Cinema Club in the old Gaumont Cinema in Belfast (it is British Home Stores now). There I saw Roy Rogers, and Gene Autry, and a selection of films specially made for British children by a unit set up for the purpose. It was the Big Event of the week, and afterwards we went to Woolworths and I got something-for-a-penny. They had a lot of penny-somethings in those days, and the ride home in a Belfast blue tram afterwards was always a ride of triumph.

It all sounds like happy days, and I thought it was, but it seems I was wrong. I didn't know it then, but my parents were growing apart, and the seeds of many later problems were being sown.

In about 1948, I think, the Belfast house was given up, and my mother and I moved down to Newcastle, to Rock Cottage, to live there permanently. Newcastle is about thirty miles from Belfast, where my father's firm was, and at first he commuted daily, but then he didn't. Sometimes he came home, and sometimes he stayed away. My parents' personal life continued to deteriorate, and in 1952, when I was eleven, they planned a new start. My father's work often took him to London, and the idea was that the family should move there and take a flat, and he would see more of us.

The move to London was not a happy one. I was sent to a posh school, in Eaton Square, where children were prepared for entry to "public schools." Why this was done, with the family and my father's business in a state of terminal collapse, is quite beyond me, but it was. Then the money ran out, and I had to be withdrawn from school halfway through a term because the bills hadn't been paid.

Then it was home to Ireland and, after a brief sojourn in my grandfather's house, back to the cottage in Newcastle. Miraculously, the cottage itself had not been sold, merely mortgaged several times over, and my step-grandmother stepped in and paid what was owing, so we had a roof over our heads.

I went to the local grammar school, Down High, which had a wonderful new attraction . . . girls! I didn't know how to cope with girls, but I had great fun finding out!

Down High was a good school with an excellent headmaster, Arthur Fowweather, and a mix of country and small-town children who retained a kind of innocence. There was a kindness about the place, in the way we were treated by the staff, and the way we treated each other.

I made some progress there but not enough. At age fifteen, just after my birthday, I left to join the local paper as a printer's apprentice/cub reporter, for the princely wage of £1.25p per week.

It was a mistake for which I paid very dearly over the next ten years!

The cub-reporter bit was all right, because stringing words together to make sense was never a problem, but the more practical end of printing was quite beyond me. The space bands I cleaned stuck in the machine. Never was more ink strewn around a print shop than when I inked the ducts. The climax was probably when I caused the heating system to spray hot water all over Derek, the linotype operator. The job on the local paper lasted nine months due, in part at least, to the patience of the newspaper owner, Mr. Hawthorne.

The big Get-Away-From-School idea of being a whizz-kid cub reporter was replaced by an even more ambitious idea, based on my footballing skill. I was, I announced to my mother, giving up the job and going to

Playing soccer, 1961

Martin and Rosaleen's wedding, 1969

England to play professional football. Somebody else's mother might have pointed out that this wasn't very likely to happen, based on a season as the boy-wonder goalkeeper of the Newcastle soccer team, but mine didn't! My mother had a blind faith in my ability to do anything. My school records and my disasters in the printing works certainly suggested otherwise to me, but I was coming up sixteen and if I was going to be a footballer something had to happen soon, so I went and . . . it *almost* worked!

I wrote to Fulham Football Club, a London club, then in the English First Division, giving them my football pedigree and asking for a trial. The trial took place, followed by another, and another, and they signed me on amateur forms!

Eight months later, they told me I could go.

End of a dream . . . 1958.

Beginning of . . . what?

I was almost eighteen, with no qualifications of any kind, and stuck in a job which didn't interest me at all. The job hadn't been important, because it wasn't going to be my career: football was. But now football wasn't. I suppose it is to my credit that I recognized the fact. My brief sojourn at Fulham had shown me enough of the life of a professional footballer to indicate that it was beyond me.

That is when I started to write.

Why does someone start to write?

In my case, it was because I had to do something.

Why writing, why not something else?

I suppose the answer is that writing had always come easily to me. I had never had to work at it at school, it was just something I knew I could do. That goes back to story,

and reading. My love of story, of being told stories and being read to, had transferred to a love of books and reading at a very early stage. My father and mother both read, and books were all about our house. One of the things grown-ups did was to read, and so I read. I read everything: Enid Blyton, Freud, Jung, E. Nesbit, G. K. Chesterton, Frank Richards, George Orwell. . . . I didn't read to learn, as my more earnest friends did. I read for fun. I still do. This might not seem to square with the footballing ambition but really it was all of a piece. I never minded doing things I liked doing, and football and reading both fitted that bill.

How did I start writing?

Well, I wrote. There isn't really any other way to learn the craft. In my case, I bought an ancient Underwood typewriter and a pile of Gestetner paper, and started page one, Chapter One, in a bed-sit in Carlyle Square, Chelsea.

I was lucky. I had something to write about that mattered more than anything else in the world at that time. A girl. There was a real girl with whom I was passionately in love, although it wasn't the real girl I wrote about. I hadn't got very far with the real girl, because I wasn't much of a catch as a boyfriend, let alone anything else. I'd left the real girl behind, on the beach in Newcastle. I felt sad, lovelorn, and homesick, and it hurt. Because it hurt so much, it wasn't difficult to find things to say about it. Quite simply, I wrote a book about being at home, in Newcastle, with the girl I loved. The book was true to life in one sense: the hero didn't get the girl. In fact he never got within miles of her, but he dreamed that one day he might, and I wrote about how that felt, about being shy and ineffectual and watching your girlfriend go off with someone else, and the pages came alive under my fingertips, which is a wonderful, exhilarating feeling. It is the reason for writing. When you have had that feeling once, you never forget it. The need to feel it again is what keeps me writing.

That feeling, the pure excitement of a story coming alive as you work on it, is the real reward of being a writer. Being a writer, however, is one thing, and being a writer who is published and paid for it is quite another. Some writers find their voices and say what they want to say with full and honest commitment . . . but no one wants to listen. That is hurtful, but it does not mean that the writer can't write. It simply means that, there and then, no one wants to read what has been written. The book has a prospective audience of one: the person who wrote it. This is difficult to face up to, but true. There are and always will be writers who write for that audience of one, some by choice, and a great many others by misfortune, writing a book whose time has not come or, in a way more sadly, writing a book whose time has passed. These concepts, "a book whose time has not come" or "a book whose time has passed," are commercial concepts and, in the ultimate analysis, have very little to do with real writing.

My first book was like that. It was called "The Lonely Children." It wasn't a bad book, but it wasn't publishable. It led me into contact with a publisher, Hutchinson, where I got a job, and through them onto the books of a literary agent, Jonathan Clowes. I got the chance to read the manuscripts of other aspiring authors at Hutchinson, which taught me a lot about what not to do, and I spent many hours at Jonathan's flat in Camden Town where he wheedled, bullied, and encouraged me, but all to no avail.

After six years of trying, all I had to show for my writing was a set of half a dozen not-very-slick formula short stories which were published but shouldn't have been (I regret them to this day!), and a pile of something like thirty books, most of them completed, but all of them pale imitations of "The Lonely Children."

It was Jonathan who pointed out that I wasn't writing from real experiences anymore. I was simply copying what I had written before.

In desperation, he threw me a copy of Len Deighton's then about to be published spy-thriller, *The Ipcress File,* and said: "Why don't you write something like that?"

"Because I don't write like that!" I said. "This is fast and funny and full of detail about something he knows about!"

The author (far right) with (from left) director Dick Clement, producer Bruce Cohn Curtis, and actors Tom Courtenay and Romy Schneider during the filming of Otley, *1968*

Waddell with his three sons David (far left), Peter, and Tom (and their dog, Fred), 1987

Long pause and then Jonathan said: "You are funny, sometimes. In between the bits you write from memory about being a sad teenager, there are *some* funny bits. And you've got a junk stall in Camden Passage Antique Market, so you must know something about that! Go away and try it."

So Otley was born. Gerald Arthur Otley was the hero of my first published book. Like me, he knew nothing about spies, but then, I reasoned, that didn't matter. Len Deighton's world of spies had everybody knowing everything … What if a complete innocent got caught up in it? What if everybody else thought his apparent innocence was a disguise, that he was the Masterspy of Masterspies? I had a background to write against, London of the sixties, and the street markets, so I planted him firmly in it, and off he went.

It worked.

In April 1966, on publication day, Martin Waddell, unpublishable lyrical novelist of Irish teenage life, was transformed at a stroke into Britain's Youngest Satirist. That is what my publicity said anyway. There was a lot of publicity, because *Otley* was made into a film starring Tom Courtenay and Romy Schneider and a lot of rights were snatched up. Suddenly I was a success!

I think, on the whole, I deserved it. I had been working at it for nearly eight years! *Otley* is not a brilliant book, it is little more than a string of jokes, but it has a believable central character and an atmosphere of dingy Earl's Court bed-sits and the so-called "Swinging London" of the mid-sixties that is spot on.

The point about "Swinging London" is that it wasn't swinging for someone like me. At the time I wrote *Otley* I had a job in a library supply company on the Gloucester Road, where I worked very hard, but not very efficiently, for a wonderfully understanding employer called Harry Karnac. I had just said goodbye to a not-very-keen-on-me girlfriend called Linque Leung (if she reads this I hope she gets in touch). I had no money, no prospects, and the only swinging I did was from the job to the typewriter. Those who swung, swung, and those who watched, watched. I was a watcher, very serious-minded and lonely, a misfit on the edge of the crowd.

Otley wasn't! He was me-if-I-hadn't-been-me, a live-for-the-moment desperate chancer who hadn't a serious thought in his head, bar whom he could beg, steal, or borrow the price of the next fake antique from. It was great. I really enjoyed writing him because the element of anarchy in my makeup which had been suppressed by my own inhibitions broke loose and ran all over the book.

The follow-up books to *Otley* gave me enough money to return home to Ireland, buy two small houses, one for me and one for my mother, and the time to write what I wanted to.

There is simply no substitute for having time to write. Different people solve that problem in different ways. I solved it with one genuine book that turned into an almost best-seller, and some lesser books that bought my freedom for several years.

In those years, home again in Ireland, I learned to write and I began to live as well.

I got married in 1969, and my wife, Rosaleen, and I settled in a small seaside town called Donaghadee, where I wrote my first book for children: *In a Blue Velvet Dress.*

There comes a moment when you find out what you can do, and *Blue Velvet* was it! The lyrical novels weren't even publishable, the thrillers were hopelessly padded to make the length, but *Blue Velvet* at 25,000 words was full of fun and adventure and emotion. I had got it right, at last!

The emotion was something I knew how to handle, from the failed lyrical novels; the sense of fun and adventure came from the thrillers. The big breakthrough was in learning to condense what I was writing to the 25,000 word-frame, instead of expanding it to meet the 80,000 to 100,000 words then demanded for an adult book. I knew I could write up to about 40,000 words well, I have always been able to do that, but now I handled the 40,000 by trimming it to 25,000, using only the words and scenes I absolutely wanted to use, instead of doubling it to 80,000!

My reputation at this point was as a comedy-thriller writer and this seemed to be at odds with *Blue Velvet,* which I see as a kind of pastiche of a Victorian children's book. I was advised to publish it under a pen name. Hence "Catherine Sefton."

Why a woman's name? I have been badgered with this question ever since. It was a decision made without much thought, in the middle of a telephone conversation. "What shall we call you?" my agent asked. Pause: "Catherine Sefton." It just came into my head. Catherine was a name I liked, Sefton was my grandmother's maiden name and, as the idea was to adopt a hidden identity for a different style of writing, using a woman's name seemed a good idea.

I thought then that the thrillers would continue, and the two careers, "Catherine's" and mine, would coexist. It didn't work out that way.

I have tried, once or twice, but I've never been able to write a thriller since. In my time, with *Otley,* I have made a lot of money from thrillers, but I know they are not right for me. I am not really interested in the stories.

Writing for children is first and foremost about story. If the story doesn't work, the book doesn't work. That brings me straight back to Terence Pym's stories in the woods, my father's long story, and the many, many stories my mother read to me when I was a very small child. Story is what I am about. It just took me a very long time to realize it.

We were content. Our first child, Tom, was born in November 1970, followed very soon afterwards by our second, David, and we were all living happily together (in the house which is described in *Blue Velvet).* The second

Catherine Sefton book, *Sleepers on the Hill,* was written and accepted. I was just about making a living as a writer by mid-1972 and everything was looking great and . . .

I went for a walk with my dog.

There was a small Catholic church in the main street of Donaghadee, a largely Protestant town. I saw some young boys running away from it. There had been attempts to vandalize it before, and an unofficial "Keep an eye on the place" request had gone out. I went into the church to see what the boys had been up to.

There was something like a wasps' nest on the floor of the vestry. It was fizzing.

I woke up in hospital, convinced that my house had been blown up, and my wife and children were dead.

Well, they weren't, and I wasn't either. The wasps' nest was a bomb, and it blew up within about five or six feet of me. I don't understand why I wasn't killed, but apparently if you are in exactly the right position when a bomb goes up you don't get blown to pieces. I was thrown up in the air, and dropped back down again, with most of the church on top of me. I was lucky; someone had seen me go in, they knew I was under the rubble somewhere, and people started digging like mad.

I should have been dead, but I wasn't.

It was the luckiest thing that ever happened to me!

Because of that explosion, we moved back to Newcastle and bought the house we live in today, a then forgotten-about and rapidly disintegrating ex-guest house on the seafront, with trillions of rooms and virtually no electricity and a roof that leaked and nothing-to-put-on-the-floor.

We bought it, but it swallowed most of our money, and the after-effects of the explosion left me unable to sustain the effort of writing.

That was 1972.

Six years followed, in which I wrote a lot but published only one real book, *The Back House Ghosts* by Catherine Sefton, which is set in this house, written in the room upstairs, now Peter's bedroom. It is an odd book, packed with every Enid Blyton device, and has been happily in print almost ever since. I wrote it in 1973 while still suffering from the immediate effects of the explosion,

Visiting a public school in Ballymena, County Antrim, 1990

At the Children's Book Award ceremony with illustrator Barbara Firth, 1989

and fighting against the feeling that I would never be able to write again. A contract for it arrived almost at once, followed some weeks later by a lengthy letter from my then editor, Phyllis Hunt of Faber, full of suggestions. The version that was eventually published owes a great deal to her advice and persistence. Publishers are not noted for their charity, but the way Phyllis and Faber handled this book is a very good example of publishing with a human face. Another editor, a different publisher, and the original manuscript might well have been turned down flat, which would have crushed me at the time.

I got used to being crushed, but I still kept trying. I had to take a job to support my family, but I never stopped writing, although without success. Yes, it was unpleasant, and yes, it hurt. I was back to square one, trying to prove I could write, and failing. My wife watched, and in 1976 she acted. Rosaleen went back to teaching, and I came home to look after the children and write. It wasn't a totally mad idea, for I still had some writing income from short radio pieces and the royalties on the existing books.

The big plus during this time was the birth of our youngest son, Peter, in 1975. Otherwise it is not a period I remember with any great pleasure except that ... well, I became very close to my children, something that is denied many fathers, and the actual day-to-day business of coping

with them stored up all sorts of material I would later use to great advantage. I know it now, but I didn't know it then. Then, I was getting pretty desperate, writing more and more without ever seeming to quite get it right, in between pram-pushing and knee-bandaging and cooking meals, propped up by a worried wife.

I don't understand what happened next but suddenly, in early 1978, the ability to tell stories came back. It happened all in a rush, and stories just flowed out. I wrote two Catherine Sefton books, *The Ghost and Bertie Boggin,* based on my radio pieces, and *Emer's Ghost,* based on a place where I played as a child, and the first two of my football stories in the "Napper" series and my first picture book, with Philippe Dupasquier, *The Great Green Mouse Disaster* ... I *wrote* them, and they were all taken up by publishers, one after the other, in a headlong rush.

It was a wonderful feeling. The books were coming right, and I was earning money again. I keep on about earning money, because it really matters if you want to write what you *want* to write, and not what people tell you to. Money equals time to write, and there is no simple way round that equation.

Over the years we acquired curtains and carpets and central heating and a car and a big dog called Bonnie and a cat! With the coming of carpets to the upstairs bedrooms, the children moved and the nursery became my writing room, but in a way they have always stayed there. Their lives, their friends, their conversations have never gone directly into my books, but they have provided a window of understanding for me into the world I left when I grew up.

Being "Daddy," changing nappies and wheeling prams and setting up football matches in the garden and dealing with the hundred and one difficulties children get into, gave me what seems like an inexhaustible store of material to work from. As I said at the beginning of this piece, the experiences of my own childhood have been important to me as a writer, but the later experiences I shared with my children in the same setting are just as crucial. Now Tom, David, and Peter are almost fully grown, and I am losing that "window." ... It will be interesting to see what happens next.

Perhaps my most important move in 1978, at the beginning of my comeback as a writer, was acquiring an agent who specialized in books for children, Gina Pollinger. The writing comeback was already under way when I first met Gina, but she *sold* the books. A new writer is a big commitment for an agent, who can only handle so many writers at a time. Agents live on a percentage of what the writer makes, and finding an agent to take you on is almost as difficult as finding a publisher. When I first went to her office, with one book published in six years, I can't have looked like much of a prospect, but Gina had no hesitation. She believed in me at a time when no one else but my wife did, and that meant a lot.

People often don't really understand what an agent does, and why some writers ... not all ... need them. A good agent encourages and cajoles all the time, pushing a writer to better work and helping to nurture ideas. There is a lot more to it than just doing the deals and vetting the contracts, not least the need to restrain authors who are apt to rush off into projects that are going nowhere. Gina Pollinger has been, and is, very important to me, especially on the creative side, and also through the business ability she shares with her husband, Murray. She doesn't intervene very often, but when she does she is trenchant and to the point, and I don't think I can remember her ever getting it wrong!

Under Gina's guidance, Martin Waddell (as opposed to Catherine Sefton) began to develop what you could call "fun" books: the "Napper" football stories, the "Mystery Squad" series of books, and the mad "Harriet" stories. These were not books with literary pretensions, they were written directly for child interest ... mainly biff-bang-wallop stories.

Catherine Sefton, we decided, was going to be different, more thoughtful. The Catherine Sefton titles post-1978 began to grow with my real children, as their interests expanded and I became more aware of teenage interests. Inevitably, because I live in the middle of it, these books came to reflect on the effects of the Northern Ireland Troubles on teenagers. *The Island of the Strangers* and *The Ghost Girl* both fall into this category and, by the time they were published, the children were older again and facing different problems, which required more explicit answers. Hence the three books for older teenagers: *Starry Night, Frankie's Story,* and *The Beat of the Drum.*

These have been called a trilogy, but they aren't really, each being a separate story. What they have in common is a set of ideas, laid out in *Starry Night* and observed in action in the other two. *Frankie's Story* and *The Beat of the Drum* are basically the same story: one about a Catholic girl resisting the forces of extremism in her world, and the other about a Protestant boy doing the same thing in his. I wrote the story twice ... something I would otherwise never do ... because I wanted both sides to read it and understand something about themselves, if possible drawing the parallels between the two books.

I am also very interested in small "beginner" books, an area quite separate from both the Catherine Sefton novels and the Martin Waddell "fun" books. I have written in various series under both names at this level, and I find these stories extremely challenging and satisfying to work on. Hardly any critical attention is paid to these books, but they take a lot of work. The brief is to compress a proper story, with a beginning, a middle, and an end, with properly realized characters and a convincing setting into somewhere between 1000 and 3000 words, depending on the series.

To the outsider, 3000 words may seem substantial, compared with the essays people do at school, but any writer will tell you that it is an extremely difficult length. An adult short story of this length is often very slight, but children will not put up with that. They demand a "proper" story. They also lack the frame of reference which comes with reading experience and age, the ability to infer a great deal from nuances of speech or character. In books for early readers the main points of the story have to be plainly and directly put over. In poorly written books of this kind, stereotype creeps in very easily ... or, what is almost worse, books are written deliberately *against* stereotype. This kind of inversion delights adults with political points to make to small children, but rarely leads to a successful story.

At best, books for beginners should be clearly and brightly written, with vivid characterization and exciting or

Martin and Rosaleen Waddell in Australia, July 1991

Martin and Rosaleen in Oregon, 1997

amusing situations piling one on top of the other, whilst at the same time moving to a conclusion which will satisfy a child ... not merely the traditional "happy ending," but something that makes sense in terms of the story. Add to this the need to use words and images which are freshly minted, not recycled, and the 3000-word book becomes a daunting challenge. The best writers can do it and make it look simple and instinctive and direct ... but it takes a lot of doing.

My stories have developed in a number of different forms, some written for the biff-bang-wallopers, some for beginners to lead them to more sophisticated stories, and some written for children who are adult in all but years.

There were one hundred and eight "Martin Waddell" or "Catherine Sefton" books in 1991, about ninety published, the rest on their way, and they are translated into different languages all over the world. I have won my share of awards and prizes and flown on jet planes to strange places to speak to children ... Malaysia, America, Australia, and other places that I had never dreamed of visiting.

A lot of my recent work has been with yet another type of story, stories written as texts for picture books, and the best of my work in this area comes from my association with one particular publisher, the late Sebastian Walker of Walker Books.

By 1985 I had done two good picture books with Philippe Dupasquier for Andersen Press, *Going West* and *The Great Green Mouse Disaster,* and three or four others which made no impact at all, but picture books were very much a sideline to the main Catherine Sefton work for Hamish Hamilton and Faber, and the "fun" books I wrote as Martin Waddell.

It had been a bad day.

I walked into Sebastian Walker's office, just after a fight with another publisher over £5 expenses incurred on a 400-mile promotional trip. I walked out of Sebastian's office clutching a contract for five books.

It was *Otley* all over again!

Freedom! Freedom to learn how to write a different way, without having to worry about how long it might take.

I can still remember the glow of that journey home!

My wife met me in Ireland at the airport. We waltzed round the arrivals lounge! Bills could be paid, at last, and there would be time to stop and think, and think again, and get the books just right.

You need time to get a book just right and, in the case of a picture book, you need more than that. You need a whole team of people who care deeply about it, and are prepared to work on and on and on, hammering at the idea to get it into shape. A picture book is more than the text, more than the pictures, it is the combination of the right writer with the right artist and the right design and production team.

Sebastian Walker gave me that freedom to write ... which means more than merely the money to stay alive, although he provided that too. "Freedom" means the possibility of working on books that don't seem to work, but do, when they are fought over and fought over, shaped and reshaped and turned inside out with the belief that somewhere-in-this-there-is-something. A number of my books have come that way, in long meandering walks along the beach or through the woods with my Walker editor, David Lloyd. He calls it "fishing" for a story, and that is what it is. As a method it might not work for another writer, or even for me with another editor, and it may not work in the future, but it works now, and that is what counts.

In a conventional publishing arrangement, long walks on the beach don't happen. Neither editor nor writer expects them to. That is what I mean by "Freedom." Freedom to think, talk, rethink, rethink-the-rethink, talk, rethink again, and write. In the end, I have to retreat to my room and write them all by myself like Sam Vole in *Sam Vole and His Brothers* because I have to find the words as well as the story, but it isn't done all in a flash. I suppose I am talking about the fact that for me, Sebastian Walker created the atmosphere in which my stories could grow without financial pressure, and be turned into beautiful picture books by a sheer love-of-what-we're-doing group of people. I use the word "love" with due thought and if it sounds an overromantic thing to say about a professional publisher and his business operations, then I'm sorry, but it is what I feel.

It shows in the books. The idea for *Can't You Sleep, Little Bear?* came from the firm's trademark, Helen Oxenbury's lovely bear with a lamp. I looked at the bear on a postcard I'd been sent and followed my usual hunt-the-story routine: What-where-when-why? What is that bear doing? He is carrying a lamp. Where is he carrying it? In a bear cave. When is he doing it? It must be night. Why is he doing it? To bring the light to a little bear. The little bear can't sleep. The little bear is afraid of the dark. That gave me the story outline, all I needed was the words. A breakthrough came with the phrase "The dark all around us," which gave the story wider meaning. That was the first breakthrough. The second came when the book was given to Barbara Firth, who brought to it her wonderful humpy-backed bears and the cave full of the furniture of their lives. Barbara's bears are *real* bears with claws, but the emotional force of her pictures is the love between child and parent. The love is there in the shapes of their bodies, the big and the small.

I wrote the text in a very short time, but the text is just a small part of the total achievement. It was worked and reworked ... *that* took a long time ... just as the pictures were worked and reworked by Barbara. Time and care and professionalism were lavished on every aspect of the book ... I think it shows. It isn't perfect, no book ever can be, but it is probably as near to perfect as any book I will ever do.

Maybe not.

Maybe tomorrow there will be another story better than *Bear,* or *Farmer Duck,* my other big favourite, with Helen Oxenbury's incredibly credible hard-working, hard-done-by duck, or *The Hidden House,* surely the strangest of my books, hauntingly illustrated by Angela Barrett, or Joe Wright's fiendish *Little Dracula.*

Or maybe tomorrow I will be working on a different story altogether, one I don't know anything about yet ... or at least I don't know that I know. Stories surprise you sometimes, the best ones do anyway.

But if I keep to the schedule, I'll finish this "story" first.

There is so much that I haven't said about important things ... like having cancer and getting over it, and writing *Little Obie and the Flood* in my mind while I was lying in intensive care ... like the stories that lie behind the three "Irish Political" books, *Starry Night, Beat of the Drum,* and *Frankie's Story* ... like how Harriet came to be, or the Mystery Squad, or why the Napper books are written the way they are, so that no adult likes them but kids do. Lots of important-to-me things like that, but there isn't enough room to write them here.

I'm only fifty years old. That means I am halfway through my professional writing life, if I manage to keep going to seventy-five, which is what I hope to do. It is altogether too soon to be writing the story of Martin Waddell 1941—? I am more interested in what will happen next than in what has already happened to me, and so I won't finish this story with my usual words:

THE END

Instead, I'll just put:

TO BE CONTINUED ...

UPDATE (2001)

What happened next?
I went on writing.
I'm still writing ... but not in the old house on the sea-front, two hundred yards from Rock Cottage. I'm writing this second instalment of my life story in the loft above an old stable, which is tucked in at one side of my new old house, Rockmore, which is two doors away from Rock Cottage where I lived as a child.

I've come home.

Home is a rambling, low-fronted Regency house on top of the Rock. At night, when there is a service in St. John's Church of Ireland next door, the light streams out over our stone-walled garden, as it has for over a hundred and sixty years since the Church was built in 1836. Rockmore was there well before the Church was built, and my stable then opened onto a lane. They filled up the lane and closed up the doors and windows on the Church side ... but they left one window, complete with glass, with the soil and rubble pressed up against it. That's in the downstairs bit of the stable, where the horses were kept. I work upstairs, in a long room where the stable boys slept, with a window looking out over the sea, and a skylight through which I can see my mountains . . . the Mountains of Mourne.

The house is a warren of passages with many rooms added-on higgeldy-piggedly over the centuries, as times changed and social habits changed with them. The basement, which once contained a house-keeper's sitting room, we use as a space to store the bric-a-brac of thirty years of marriage, from the boys' old wooden playpen to the boxes and boxes and boxes of manuscripts . . . most of them unpublishable . . . which are part of a writer's life. We have a sea-room that looks out over the sea, a beautiful sunlit garden room, a big dining-room and a bedroom that is ten times the size of the bed-sit in London in which I wrote my first book, *Otley*. We haven't got any servants, but the two servants' rooms at the back of the house have been knocked together to make an office for Rosaleen, where she looks after all the business bits of a writer's life, while I'm in the loft over the stables, trying to think of something to write.

So what else has changed?

My writing has changed, but then so has my life. Our three sons are grown men, living their own lives, two of them with their own wives. No grandchildren have yet appeared.

It is big change, the boys being grown-up, because my experiences with Tom, David and Peter were the mainspring of all my best work. I drew many of my stories from their lives, and now their lives have moved on, away from the kind of things I want to write about. I don't hear the day-to-day small-talk of children anymore. The moments of inspiration that gave me *Can't You Sleep, Little Bear?* and *Farmer Duck* and *Owl Babies* and dozens of other stories just don't happen naturally while-making-the-dinner as they once did.

I have to find stories now, where once I lived among them. The problem is . . . they have to be good stories, stories I need to write, because they are strong and mean something to me.

When I wrote the ending of this autobiography in 1991 I said, "maybe tomorrow there will be another story, better than *Bear* or *Farmer Duck*." 'Better' wasn't a good word to use. All stories are different, and on different days and in different moods one may seem better than another to the person who wrote them, but that is all it is, a 'seeming', not an objective reality. Children always ask, "Which is your best book?" and I can't answer them. I don't believe writers can or should be the judges of their own stories, and whether a book is well received or not has very little to do

On a school visit in 1999

with how I feel about it, deep down inside my working head. Some books sell hundreds of thousands of copies all over the world like *Owl Babies* ... some sell only a few thousand copies like *Tango's Baby* ... but each book is written for a reason. When I start a book, I believe in it and want to do it ... and then it goes wrong. It never, ever, ever comes out as I've dreamed it to be; when I've talked about it to my dog Ben, on those long lonely walks on the beach where my best thinking is done. It doesn't matter ... you do what you can each time, again and again and again ... and it's lovely doing it.

I write for fun.... I enjoy doing it. The bad days are when I'm not writing, because I have nothing to write about or a story just won't work. That is a horrible feeling, desolate, lost ... nothing to do but sit and look at the books I've already written and think about them.

As my children grew, so my stories grew with them, from the comforting *Owl Babies* at one end of the age scale, to the harsh and bitter distress of *Tango's Baby* at the other. Those two, very different, books matter a great deal to me and they explain a lot about what goes on in my head ... and is still going on.

Owl Babies came from an incident in a supermarket. A child had become separated from his mother and would not be comforted by anybody. All he would cry was, "I want my mummy." Thankfully she found him quickly but his cry stayed in my mind, "I want my mummy!" and I wrote the story. But why is *Owl Babies* so special to me?

Because children love it. Because it works, that's why. It W-O-R-K-S! It works because children can identify completely with the baby owls. Sarah, the eldest, is trying to be reassuring, Percy, in the middle, tries hard to be optimistic but panics rapidly and Bill, from the start, simply repeats, "I want my mummy!" I have read the book time and time again, with audiences varying in size from one child at bedtime, to five hundred small faces packed into the Everyman Threatre at Cheltenham Festival.... It worked! It once worked with a thousand adults in San Antonio at eight o'clock in the morning.

What seems to adults to be the very small drama of three little Owls, Sarah and Percy and Bill whose mother is missing, is huge to very small readers. It grabs them, and holds them until ... what a relief ... their owl-mother comes swooping back in the "*AND SHE CAME*" page which resolves the story. So powerful is Patrick Benson's picture of the Owl Mother that it forced the words, "soft and silent, she swooped through the trees, to Sarah and Percy and Bill," off the spread where I had envisaged them going. Onto the next page they had to go.

This is a very clear example of how important design is in a picture book. Often the illustration and design involve the omission of words or alteration of their placing. A picture book is a *picture* book ... it is about the perfect interaction of words and picture, where illustration and text and design come together to form something greater than the sum of each of the parts. A failure or partial failure of one of these three elements can ruin what seemed to be the most perfect story when it simply existed as text.

Are the words not all that important then?

Of course they are!

Initally, it is the pictures that attract someone to a picture book, but if the words are wrong, often the book is read only once, because children soon feel that it isn't right.

A picture book that works, either in the classroom or one-to-one at home (or preferably both), will be read repeatedly. My job is to give the artist and the designer the material to work on.

This is where the words are very important. The book has to be about something that matters to very small children, what I call the "Wuthering Heights" element. (When a book really works it often says something that matters to grown-ups too.)

I use the phrase "Wuthering Heights" as shorthand to describe an emotional punch that a very small child will understand instantly, without having to be told what the book is about. In *Can't You Sleep, Little Bear?* it was, "I don't like the dark." In my forthcoming book with Barbara Firth, *Hi, Harry!*, it is, "Can I play with you?" (All children know the importance of that question.) In *Farmer Duck* the words, "It isn't fair!" don't appear in the text at all; they are expressed visually in the big spread of Helen Oxenbury's fat, lazy Farmer lying back in bed while the Duck does the work. In the *Owl Babies* the most powerful emotion of them all comes into play with, "I want my Mummy."

With *Owl Babies,* I got it almost right ... not completely right, because no-one can ever do that, but as as near as possible to it.

That's why *Owl Babies* is special to me.

How about *Tango's Baby*?

It is special to me too ... and it works, not in the way *Owl Babies* has worked, for hundreds of thousands of people ... but for me, inside, and (I hope) for the young adult audience it was written for.

Someone said to me that *Tango's Baby* is an adult story, and should never have been written for a youth audience, that it offers only despair ... not hope.

I do not believe this is so.

Hope is a key word for me, in writing for children. I have no right to present despair to those whose minds are still unformed. The younger the audience the greater the emphasis on hope. As children grow older and learn more of the world, so the stories they read can contain more darkness. I have no right to wilfully mislead, to impose a happy ending that is unreal in the setting of a particular story. My aim is to present the world, and to offer some of the whys and wherefores that make life what it is. The dark is dark ... but not all dark, there is always some light within it. *Tango's Baby* hovers just on the child-side of the cut-off point between literature for children and adult literature.

Tango is a hapless, ambling teenager who can't bring anything off. He is hopeless at school, he can't hold down a job, he has only one asset going for him ... a huge capacity for love. Tango loves Crystal, a much smarter, tougher girl. She and her friends mock Tango but he is there for her in a dark moment, and she turns to him for support. Briefly he wins her over, and she becomes pregnant. Tango is delighted, entranced, "Me a daddy! Me ... .!" But Crystal soon learns that Tango is all words; when it comes to action he is hopeless. He loves her, he loves the baby desperately, but he cannot provide for either of them. Fiercely protective of her child, Crystal breaks with Tango. She takes Tango's baby from him, which is Tango's tragedy.

The story is told through the reactions of their various friends, trying to sift through the half truths that they learn

The author with dog, Ben, in Newcastle, 2001

from the couple, trying to help Tango and Crystal when they can.

Tango's capacity for love is the 'Wuthering Heights' in the story ... an emotion teenagers can connect to directly. He inhabits a dysfunctional world kids will recognise, and his failures are not glossed over.

The story explores deep emotions in the young, which is its strength. I don't believe in telling teenagers lies about life, just to present a positive story. My approach is exactly the same as that employed in my picture books for the very young. I believe in Big Bear's "Look at the dark, Little Bear." There is a chink of light in Tango's darkness ... but only just.

The hope lies in the repeated and desperate efforts of the deeply flawed minor characters, most in their own chaotic ways trying to help. Tango's story could not legitimately have a happy ending, for he is cursed with an infinite capacity to muck things up ... but the others care, and show their caring. That is the message of the book ... or at least the message I was trying to convey. However dark the day, people care for each other as best they can, and somehow survive.

It may be that there is some magical Never-Never Land somewhere, where teenagers see and hear nothing that could disturb them ... but it isn't the world I live in, and it isn't the world my readers live in either. Day and daily the confusions of the real world are simplified and trivialised in T.V. soap operas and banal films where the emotional consequences of the situations they depict are

not played out. They can't be ... there is a pressing need to move on swiftly to the next sensation. Thin characters bounce from one dramatic interlude to the next. Violent death, drugs, abortion, divorce, separation, love, hate, are played out at an hysterical pace.

For too many teenagers this is their window on the world ... a world they feel a desperate need to come to terms with, and understand. The message is re-inforced each time they sit down in front of their T.V. or go out to the movies. It is heady stuff, exciting, entertaining stuff for adults ... when well done, it looks real, a picture of the world they live in ... but it isn't.

What people say and do, how they treat each other ... these things have their consequences. What you do, you do, and it lives with you. It is part of becoming what you are. In the no-consequence world presented in these stories, one huge emotional storm gives way to another and another and another. No one grieves for long ... for the play must go on. These stories betray children, and cheat them of their innocence.

That is why I, and many others like me, sometimes write the difficult books we do. It took me a long time to write Tango, because every turn in a story like that requires balance and reflection. It is a serious attempt to present very difficult issues in a thoughtful way, not simply an entertainment.

Tango's Baby is the sort of book that not many people will read and fewer still will understand. It is the sort of difficult book authors write because we feel they should be written, in the setting of our world-as-it-is for some people, not as we might like it to be.

That is why *Tango's Baby* is important to me.

I feel the same way about *Starry Night* and *Beat of the Drum* and *Frankie's Story* which deal with the terrible truths of living where I do, in present day Northern Ireland. The reality of the lives teenagers live, in areas which are effectively ruled by local gunmen who make their own law, has been distorted in innumerable books and films by simplification of the issues ... goodies versus baddies, bring on the guns. Ireland's troubles are a mix of bitter sectarianism and, on both sides, an addiction to hymns of patriotic death ... on both sides. The hymns of hate are sung on every street corner, and so the next generation of heroes is recruited. I see that. I write against that. I try to show that there is no simple right, no simple wrong on either side. It isn't my job to make choices for young readers, to tell them what is right and wrong in a given situation. I want to persuade them to try to seek the truth out for themselves ... to learn to think things out. That can't be done by ignoring the issues, or simplifying them.

These books are difficult ... they are meant to be. The world is a difficult place. Telling writers to go away and write about something pleasant just isn't helpful. I have written many books for fun, to brighten up the world ... but not all books can be like that, nor should they be. The job is there to be done ... so I do it.

That is ... I did. As I said at the outset of this piece, my writing has changed yet again.

I have more beautiful picture books on the way. I'm very pleased with one called, *Hi, Harry!* and another called, *Room for a Little One*. Those two fill me with the same sort of excitement as *Owl Babies,* because they are beautiful, and different, and marvellously unlike what I've tried to do before. There will be more pictures books ... but it's a good while now since I've written a book like *Tango's Baby* or *Beat of the Drum.* Tango and the three Northern Ireland books seem to have burned out the part of me that did the serious thing ... but I have used the word "seem" very deliberately, for I never really know what I will write next. It may well be that another Tango is growing in my mind, who will take-over and demand to be written when I least expect him, her, or it.

It may be ... but I don't think there is ... well, not this week anyway, for something else is growing, from seed set in my past ... those long years ago, when I was a child in the woods above Newcastle, with Terence Pym and all his stories. I am back on the Rock, almost beside the house where I lived as a child, and now those stories have come back to me.

It began with a book called *Ghostly Stories* I wrote five years ago. They were all my own original stories, but as a game ... most writers love writing games.... I used the form and shape and approach of traditional Irish stories to flavour them. They read and sound like the stories I was told by Terence and others. I love that book. It was terrific fun to do.

Next thing I knew, I had done another. *The Storyteller* has yet to be published, but it is a collection of thirty old folktales, reshaped and re-written. They are not my own original stories and yet in a very definite way they are my own. The breakthrough for me has been the discovery that folk and fairy tales have the capacity to be retold ... differently. They are not written in stone. They change when each generation of storytellers finds them and retells them.

Right now I'm exploring some very old stories ... and my writing brain is ticking over, very much alive! I know the stories can take different forms ... some very short, some long ... perhaps some novel length ... I don't know if there are novels in them ... but there could be. There must be, somewhere ... I think.

For me, this afternoon, at my working table in the stable loft, it seems a whole new world of writing is beginning.

Yesterday it was (of all things!) the story of Macbeth in 6000 simple words, for children who have only just learned to read. Last week, I re-wrote "The Prince and the Tortoise" from the the Arabian Nights. Next on the list will be a Silkie story ... and after that. back again, to "The Butterfly Girl", a new version of a version of a story of my own.

There are so many stories there to re-work, re-shape, re-tell and enjoy.

What happens next?

I'll go on writing. That's what writers do.

So I'll end this piece just as before ...

I'll put ...

       ... TO BE CONTINUED.

Cumulative Indexes

Illustrations Index

(In the following index, the number of the *volume* in which an illustrator's work appears is given *before* the colon, and the *page number* on which it appears is given *after* the colon. For example, a drawing by Adams, Adrienne appears in Volume 2 on page 6, another drawing by her appears in Volume 3 on page 80, another drawing in Volume 8 on page 1, and so on and so on....)

YABC

Index references to *YABC* refer to listings appearing in the two-volume *Yesterday's Authors of Books for Children,* also published by The Gale Group. *YABC* covers prominent authors and illustrators who died prior to 1960.

A

Illustrations Index

Author Index

The following index gives the number of the volume in which an author's biographical sketch, Autobiography Feature, Brief Entry, or Obituary appears.

This index includes references to all entries in the following series, which are also published by The Gale Group.

YABC—*Yesterday's Authors of Books for Children: Facts and Pictures about Authors and Illustrators of Books for Young People from Early Times to 1960*

CLR—*Children's Literature Review: Excerpts from Reviews, Criticism, and Commentary on Books for Children*

SAAS—*Something about the Author Autobiography Series*

/ /

Offenbacher, Ami 1958- *91*
Offit, Sidney 1928- *10*
Ofosu-Appiah, L(awrence) H(enry)
 1920- *13*
Ogan, George F. 1912-1983 ....*13*
Ogan, M. G.
 See Ogan, George F.
 and Ogan, Margaret E. (Nettles)
Ogan, Margaret E. (Nettles)
 1923-1979 ....*13*
Ogburn, Charlton (Jr.) 1911-1998 ....*3*
 Obituary *109*
Ogilvie, Elisabeth May 1917- *40*
 Brief entry *29*
Ogilvy, Gavin
 See Barrie, J(ames) M(atthew)
O'Green, Jennifer
 See Roberson, Jennifer
O'Green, Jennifer Roberson
 See Roberson, Jennifer
O'Hagan, Caroline 1946- *38*
O'Hanlon, Jacklyn
 See Meek, Jacklyn O'Hanlon
O'Hara, Elizabeth
 See Ni Dhuibhne, Eilis
O'Hara, Kenneth
 See Morris, (Margaret) Jean
O'Hara, Mary
 See Alsop, Mary O'Hara
O'Hara (Alsop), Mary
 See Alsop, Mary O'Hara
O'Hare, Jeff(rey A.) 1958- *105*
Ohi, Ruth 1964- *95*
Ohiyesa 1858-1939
 See Eastman, Charles A(lexander)
Ohlsson, Ib 1935- *7*
Ohmi, Ayano 1959- *115*
Ohtomo, Yasuo 1946- *37*
o huigin, sean 1942-
 See CLR 75
Oke, Janette 1935- *97*
O'Keeffe, Frank 1938- *99*
O'Kelley, Mattie Lou 1908-1997 ....*97*
 Earlier sketch in SATA 36
Okimoto, Jean Davies 1942- *103*
 Earlier sketch in SATA 34
Okomfo, Amasewa
 See Cousins, Linda
Olaleye, Isaac O. 1941- *96*
 See also SAAS 23
Olcott, Frances Jenkins 1872(?)-1963 ......*19*
Old Boy
 See Hughes, Thomas
Oldenburg, E(gbert) William
 1936-1974 ....*35*
Older, Effin 1942- *114*
Older, Jules 1940- *114*
Oldfield, Margaret J(ean) 1932- *56*
Oldfield, Pamela 1931- *86*
Oldham, June *70*
Oldham, Mary 1944- *65*
Olds, Elizabeth 1896-1991 ....*3*
 Obituary *66*
Olds, Helen Diehl 1895-1981 ....*9*
 Obituary *25*
Oldstyle, Jonathan
 See Irving, Washington
O'Leary, Brian (Todd) 1940- *6*
O'Leary, Patsy B(aker) 1937- *97*
Oliphant, B. J.
 See Tepper, Sheri S.
Oliver, Burton
 See Burt, Olive Woolley
Oliver, Chad
 See Oliver, Symmes C(hadwick)
Oliver, John Edward 1933- *21*
Oliver, Marilyn Tower 1935- *89*
Oliver, Shirley (Louise Dawkins)
 1958- *74*
Oliver, Symmes C(hadwick)
 1928-1993 ....*101*
 See Oliver, Chad

Oliviero, Jamie 1950- *84*
Olmsted, Lorena Ann 1890-1989 ....*13*
Olney, Ross R. 1929- *13*
Olschewski, Alfred (Erich) 1920- *7*
Olsen, Carol 1945- *89*
Olsen, Ib Spang 1921- *81*
 Earlier sketch in SATA 6
Olsen, Violet (Mae) 1922-1991 ....*58*
Olson, Arielle North 1932- *67*
Olson, Gene 1922- *32*
Olson, Helen Kronberg *48*
Olugebefola, Ademole 1941- *15*
Oluonye, Mary N(kechi) 1955- *111*
Oman, Carola (Mary Anima)
 1897-1978 ....*35*
O'Meara, Walter (Andrew)
 1897-1989 ....*65*
Ommanney, F(rancis) D(ownes)
 1903-1980 ....*23*
O Mude
 See Gorey, Edward (St. John)
Oneal, Elizabeth 1934- *82*
 Earlier sketch in SATA 30
 See Oneal, Zibby
O'Neal, Reagan
 See Rigney, James Oliver, Jr.
Oneal, Zibby
 See CLR 13
 See Oneal, Elizabeth
O'Neill, Amanda 1951- *111*
O'Neill, Gerard K(itchen) 1927-1992 ......*65*
O'Neill, Judith (Beatrice) 1930- *34*
O'Neill, Mary L(e Duc) 1908(?)-1990 ......*2*
 Obituary *64*
Onslow, Annette Rosemary MacArthur
 See MacArthur-Onslow, Annette Rosemary
Onyefulu, Ifeoma 1959- *115*
 Earlier sketch in SATA 81
Opie, Iona (Margaret Balfour)
 1923- *118*
 Earlier sketches in SATA 3, 63
 See also SAAS 6
Opie, Peter (Mason) 1918-1982 ....*118*
 Obituary *28*
 Earlier sketches in SATA 3, 63
Oppel, Kenneth 1967- *99*
Oppenheim, Joanne 1934- *82*
 Earlier sketch in SATA 5
Oppenheimer, Joan L(etson) 1925- *28*
Optic, Oliver
 See Adams, William Taylor
 and Stratemeyer, Edward L.
Oram, Hiawyn 1946- *101*
 Earlier sketch in SATA 56
Orbach, Ruth Gary 1941- *21*
Orczy, Emma
 See Orczy, Baroness Emmuska
Orczy, Emma Magdalena Rosalia Maria
 Josefa
 See Orczy, Baroness Emmuska
Orczy, Emmuska
 See Orczy, Baroness Emmuska
Orczy, Baroness Emmuska
 1865-1947 ....*40*
 See Orczy, Emma
Orde, A. J.
 See Tepper, Sheri S.
O'Reilly, Jackson
 See Rigney, James Oliver, Jr.
Orgel, Doris 1929- *85*
 Earlier sketch in SATA 7
 See also CLR 48
 See also SAAS 19
Orleans, Ilo 1897-1962 ....*10*
Orlev, Uri 1931- *58*
 See also CLR 30
 See also SAAS 19
Ormai, Stella *57*
 Brief entry *48*

Ormerod, Jan(ette Louise) 1946- *70*
 Brief entry *44*
 Earlier sketch in SATA 55
 See also CLR 20
Ormondroyd, Edward 1925- *14*
Ormsby, Virginia H(aire) 1906-1990 ......*11*
Orr, Katherine S(helley) 1950- *72*
Orr, Wendy 1953- *90*
Orris
 See Ingelow, Jean
Orth, Richard
 See Gardner, Richard (M.)
Orwell, George
 See CLR 68
 See Blair, Eric (Arthur)
Osborn, Lois D(orothy) 1915- *61*
Osborne, Charles 1927- *59*
Osborne, Chester G(orham)
 1915-1987 ....*11*
Osborne, David
 See Silverberg, Robert
Osborne, George
 See Silverberg, Robert
Osborne, Leone Neal 1914- *2*
Osborne, Mary Pope 1949- *98*
 Earlier sketches in SATA 41, 55
Osceola
 See Blixen, Karen (Christentze Dinesen)
Osgood, William E(dward) 1926- *37*
O'Shaughnessy, Darren 1972- *129*
O'Shaughnessy, Ellen Cassels 1937- *78*
O'Shea, (Catherine) Pat(ricia Shiels)
 1931- *87*
 See also CLR 18
Osmond, Edward 1900- *10*
Ossoli, Sarah Margaret (Fuller)
 1810-1850 ....*25*
 See Fuller, Margaret
 and Fuller, Sarah Margaret
Ostendorf, (Arthur) Lloyd, (Jr.)
 1921-2000 ....*65*
 Obituary *125*
Otfinoski, Steven 1949- *116*
 Earlier sketch in SATA 56
Otis, James
 See Kaler, James Otis
O'Toole, Thomas 1941- *71*
O'Trigger, Sir Lucius
 See Horne, Richard Henry
Otten, Charlotte F(ennema) 1926- *98*
Ottley, Matt 1962- *102*
Ottley, Reginald Leslie 1909-1985 ....*26*
 See also CLR 16
Otto, Svend
 See Soerensen, Svend Otto
Oughton, Jerrie 1937- *76*
Oughton, (William) Taylor 1925- *104*
Ouida
 See De La Ramee, (Marie) Louise
Ousley, Odille 1896-1976 ....*10*
Outcalt, Todd 1960- *123*
Overmyer, James E. 1946- *88*
Overton, Jenny (Margaret Mary)
 1942- *52*
 Brief entry *36*
Owen, Annie 1949- *75*
Owen, Caroline Dale
 See Snedeker, Caroline Dale (Parke)
Owen, Clifford
 See Hamilton, Charles (Harold St. John)
Owen, Dilys
 See Gater, Dilys
Owen, (Benjamin) Evan 1918-1984 ....*38*
Owen, Gareth 1936- *83*
 See also CLR 31
 See also SAAS 14
Owens, Bryant 1968- *116*
Owens, Gail 1939- *54*
Owens, Thomas S(heldon) 1960- *86*
Owens, Tom
 See Owens, Thomas S(heldon)

Q

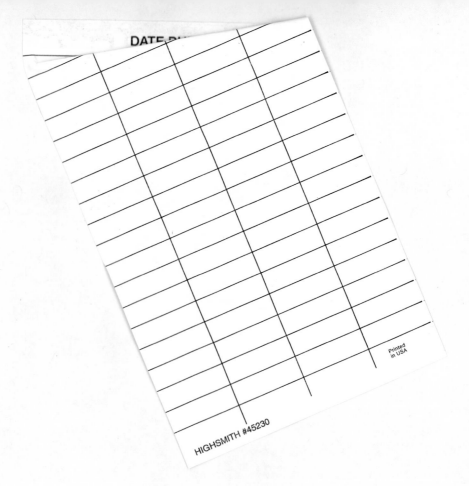

DATE DU

HIGHSMITH #45230

Printed
in USA